MORAL RECONSTRUCTION

MORAL

RECONSTRUCTION

CHRISTIAN LOBBYISTS AND THE

FEDERAL LEGISLATION OF MORALITY,

1865–1920

Gaines M. Foster

The University of North Carolina Press

Chapel Hill and London

© 2002 The University of North Carolina Press
Manufactured in the United States of America

Designed by April Leidig-Higgins
Set in Minion by Copperline Book Services, Inc.

The paper in this book meets the guidelines for permanence and
durability of the Committee on Production Guidelines for Book
Longevity of the Council on Library Resources.

Library of Congress Cataloging-in-Publication Data
Foster, Gaines M.   Moral reconstruction: Christian lobbyists and the
Federal legislation of morality, 1865–1920 / Gaines M. Foster.
p. cm. Includes bibliographical references and index.
ISBN 0-8078-2697-9 (cloth: alk. paper)
ISBN 0-8078-5366-6 (pbk.: alk. paper)
1. Christianity and politics—United States—History—19th century.
2. Christian ethics—United States—History—19th century. 3. Law and
ethics—History—19th century. 4. Christianity and politics—United
States—History—20th century. 5. Christian ethics—United States—
History—20th century. 6. Law and ethics—History—20th century.
I. Title.
BR517 .F59 2002   322.4'4'097309034—dc21   2001059764

cloth 06 05 04 03 02   5 4 3 2 1
paper 06 05 04 03 02   5 4 3 2 1

To Mary

CONTENTS

ACKNOWLEDGMENTS

Of the making of many books, the writer of Ecclesiastes says, there is no end. Of the making of just this one, there often seemed no end. In the far too long that I took to complete it, I have amassed an inordinate number of debts that I happily, if insufficiently, acknowledge here.

I could not have completed this project without the microfilm collection of the Temperance and Prohibition Papers, and I could not have read of it what I did without the help of the Louisiana State University and Florida State University interlibrary loan offices. Another group in the LSU library, Smittie Bolner and the staff of the Government Documents division, were unfailingly gracious and helpful as I worked through the *Congressional Record*, serial sets, and related documents.

Countless other librarians and archivists helped me during visits to their collections, and a few saved me from having to go to theirs. Rather than single out individuals, especially since I stayed at this so long that some personnel changed, I want to thank the staffs of the following collections or libraries: the Alabama Department of Archives and History, the Manuscripts Division of the University of Alabama Library, the Bentley Historical Library at the University of Michigan, the Rare and Manuscripts Collections of the Cornell University Library, the Rare Book, Manuscript, and Special Collections Library at Duke University, Special Collections of the Goddard Library at Clarke University, the Davis Papers at Rice University, the library of Geneva College, Hill Memorial Library at Louisiana State University, the Houghton Library at Harvard University, the Manuscripts Division of the Library of Congress, the Massachusetts Historical Society, the Mississippi Department of Archives and History, the Center for Legislative Archives at the National Archives, the New Hampshire Historical Society, the Manuscripts and Archives Section of the New York Public Library, the Ohio Historical Society, the Department of History of the Presbyterian Church USA, the Richard Russell Library at the University of Georgia, the Southern Historical Collection at the University of North Carolina at Chapel Hill, the Center for American History at the University of Texas, the Ticonderoga Historical Society, the Vermont Historical Society, Special Collections at the Bailey/Howe Library of the University of Vermont, the Manuscripts Division of Alderman Library at the University of Virginia, the Manuscripts and Rare Books Department of the Swem Library at the College of William and Mary, the Westerville, Ohio, Public Library, and the Frances E. Willard Memorial Library at the Woman's Christian Temperance Union Headquarters.

Several individuals must be mentioned by name. Most of the student workers I tried to get to help me count and code petitions quit—I hope daunted by the *Congressional Record* rather than appalled by their supervisor—but a few stuck it out, and I am very much indebted to them: Tracey Gates, Sherri Franks, Gabrielle Matese, Keoka Grayson, Becky Daigle, and especially Audrey Johnson. Will Lampton helped enormously by checking all the citations the LSU library allowed.

James Garand, of LSU's Political Science Department, guided, nay directed, my efforts to use both the ICPSR computer tapes on congressional roll call votes and logistical regression. Harry McKowen answered a frantic call for help on pictures. Several friends read chapters of the manuscript and offered their insights: Timothy Gilfoyle, Richard John, Anastatia Sims, and Ian Tyrrell. William Cooper, Ken Murchison, and John Rodrigue, friends and colleagues at LSU, read an early, much longer version of the entire manuscript and made many useful suggestions. As they have with almost everything I have ever written, Charles Eagles and Anne Loveland each provided an incredibly detailed and astute critique of that same version. Paul Paskoff not only read the longer version but also furnished much advice and support along the way. Charles Royster read both an early and a later version, an uncommon kindness. As I completed a final draft, Ronald Walters offered especially helpful suggestions.

Although such criticism is priceless, financial support helps as well. A grant from the Institute for the Study of American Evangelicals allowed me to microfilm much of the *Christian Statesman*. LSU provided that most valuable of commodities for historians, time for research and writing, with two sabbaticals and a Manship Research leave. Garnett Foster and Frances Grimes subsidized my stays in Washington with gracious hospitality and a willingness to ignore Ben Franklin's warning about when company begins to smell.

The dedication of the book is paltry payment toward my greatest debt, one that I can never repay—although all my washing and cooking should count for something. I debated whether it would be more moving if the dedication page read "For" or "To," but at times considered "Despite." My wife, Mary

Mikell, works hard to make a more just society and often tried to get her husband out of the library and into the world. But she also read three drafts of the manuscript and fiercely urged brevity and clarity. The reader can only hope that she had more success at making this a better book than she did in making its author a better person. I thank her for both.

Righteousness, righteousness, righteousness exalteth the nation.

—Alfred H. Colquitt, senator from Georgia, 12 July 1892

In the late 1970s, Christian conservatives became a powerful force in American politics. They believed that the government had become hostile to religion and that Americans had lost their way in a secular society that denigrated religious belief and promoted sinful personal behavior — drug abuse, pornography, unrestrained sexuality, abortion. In response, organizations such as the Moral Majority and, later, the Christian Coalition, mobilized individual Christians and many churches in an attempt to establish a Christian nation and a moral social order, in part through legislating personal morality. Opponents condemned their calls for the government to promote morality as a violation of the separation of church and state and as an abridgment of individual freedom. The resulting debate prompted partisans as well as scholars to search for historical precedents. They found them in the opponents of Sunday mail and Indian removal, the abolitionists, the prohibitionists, the anti-Semitic right of the 1930s, and perhaps most often, the civil rights movement. Except for brief references to the Woman's Christian Temperance Union or the Anti-Saloon League, neither partisans nor scholars explored the most intriguing parallel to the current campaign to legislate morality, a Christian lobby active in Washington between the Civil War and the adoption of Prohibition.[1]

The Christian lobby that formed in the late nineteenth century campaigned to expand the moral powers of the federal government and to establish the religious authority of the state. Some of the lobbyists believed the power of the government rested in God, but most sought only to force government to respect God's law and thereby prove itself worthy to exercise its powers. During the Civil War, the National Association to Amend the Constitution first lobbied to have an acknowledgment of God, Christ, and the authority of the Bible incorporated into the preamble to the Constitution. That crusade for what came to be called the Christian amendment continued after the war, because its proponents believed the nation owed allegiance to God. But they also thought the amendment would demonstrate the religious authority of the state and provide an unassailable constitutional basis for the federal legislation of morality.[2]

The legislation of personal morality remained the primary goal of the reformers who made up the Christian lobby. Anthony Comstock lobbied for tougher federal laws against obscenity, birth control, and abortion in the early 1870s. Soon thereafter, his friend Joseph Cook, a Boston-based minister who earned his living on the lecture circuit, campaigned for laws against polygamy, Sabbath breaking, and other behavior he considered sinful. Henry Blair, a Republican senator from New Hampshire, first introduced a prohibition amendment in Congress in the 1870s and worked for a broad array of moral legislation, even after he left Congress. Blair became an ally and friend of Frances Willard, who, along with Comstock, was perhaps the best known of the Christian lobbyists. Far less well-known but important nonetheless was Wilbur J. Crafts, who founded the International Reform Bureau, proclaimed himself a Christian lobbyist, and opened an office on Capitol Hill in 1895.

By that time, Comstock, Cook, Willard, Crafts, and others had helped form a loose alliance, a Christian lobby, that operated in Washington but whose power rested in a group of organizations that mobilized Christians and churches across the nation. The National Association to Amend the Constitution changed its name to the National Reform Association and promoted not just the Christian amendment but a broad array of moral legislation. Crafts's Reform Bureau advocated a similar agenda. The National Temperance Society, as its name indicated, sought only to restrict the sale of alcohol. By far the largest and most influential of the early organizations within the Christian lobby was the Woman's Christian Temperance Union, which generated much of the public pressure on Congress to pass not just prohibition but other types of moral legislation. Several of the WCTU's leaders, including Willard, Ada Bittenbender, and Margaret Dye Ellis, lobbied on Capitol Hill. In the early twentieth century, even as the Reform Bureau and the WCTU continued their efforts, a new single-issue organization, the American Anti-Saloon League, and its chief lobbyists, Edwin Dinwiddie and James Cannon Jr., became very influential in congressional debates leading to the adoption of prohibition.

Like members of the Anti-Saloon League, most of the Christian lobbyists defined morality primarily in terms of righteousness or virtue, not justice. The laws they advocated did not seek to create a more equal society, to reorganize the economic order, or to foster similar types of societal change, although a few individuals within the Christian lobby at times advocated such reforms. Most of them and the alliance as a whole sought only to use the law to create a social environment that promoted biblical standards of personal behavior. In effect, they preached a social gospel centered on shaping individual behavior. Working at the local, state, and federal level, they sought laws to control drinking, obscenity, polygamy, divorce, Sabbath observance, gambling, smoking, prizefighting, prostitution, and sex with underage girls.[3]

Historians have not ignored post–Civil War moral reform. Every cause that the Christian lobby championed has been studied, in some cases by several scholars. The first of these studies dismissed the temperance and similar movements as backward-looking, sometimes irrational attempts to maintain an older way of life or the reformers' own status. Aspects of such an interpretation persist, but recent accounts more often acknowledge that reformers sought to solve real problems and adopted very modern methods in attacking them. *Moral Reconstruction* does not seek to confront these many, able studies of postbellum reform. Rather it seeks to build upon them by establishing the personal and organizational connections among postbellum moral reformers, by explicating their shared beliefs and concerns, by recounting their combined lobbying efforts in Congress, and finally by analyzing the resulting debates there in order to understand the national government's changing role in imposing morality.[4]

The Civil War helped spur a new interest in using the federal government to regulate morality. The Christian lobbyists, many of whom came of age in the crucible of the war and Reconstruction, believed, probably correctly, that the disruptions of the war and the freedom that soldiers had enjoyed in the army had led to an increase in drinking and other behaviors thought to be immoral. At the same time, the lobbyists, like the northern intellectuals and clergy historian George Fredrickson has written about, developed a strong sense of nationalism and a new faith in coercion and federal power to restrain immorality. The lobbyists thought that in the Thirteenth Amendment they had found a powerful precedent. If the federal government could abolish the sin of slavery, they claimed, it could also outlaw other forms of immorality. Although historians have pointed to a continuity between abolition and postwar moral reform, the Christian lobbyists' ties to abolition were hardly so direct. Few of these lobbyists actually embraced the abolitionists' goal of expanding human freedom; instead they exploited what might best be called an antislavery precedent to outlaw sin, not to promote justice or equality.[5]

Although efforts to secure federal legislation began almost as soon as the Civil War ended, the lobbyists consolidated and expanded their efforts in the

1880s and then achieved their greatest success after the turn of the century. During those years, the United States experienced the expansion of industrialization, the emergence of a national business system, the beginnings of a commercial culture, a growth in the number and size of cities, and an influx of immigrants with new customs. The Christian lobbyists believed these changes contributed to a dramatic rise in drinking, gambling, prostitution, divorce, and other sins. Demonstrating whether or not their fears were real is beyond the scope of this study. Several scholars, though, have contended that various forms of public immorality did increase. More important to understanding the efforts of the Christian lobby is the distinctive way in which the Christian lobbyists conceived of the problem, an understanding that shaped the legislation they advocated and Congress eventually passed. The Christian lobbyists attributed increasing immorality not directly to social changes but to individual failings. They blamed appetite, by which they meant the individual's desire for various forms of sensual pleasure, exacerbated by avarice, the greed for gold that drove commercial vice.[6]

The Christian lobbyists sometimes singled out immigrants and workers for special concern, which suggests that class interests helped fuel their fears, a factor historians have frequently cited in explaining postbellum moral reform. Several scholars portray reformers as members of the middle class who used standards of moral behavior to define themselves in opposition to both the upper and the working classes. Others add that middle-class activists sought social control, envisioning their reforms as a means to make the lower orders behave as the middle class thought they should. Most of the Christian lobbyists were middle class, and they certainly thought workers, immigrants, and the newly freed slaves were especially susceptible to the temptations that the new society brought and sought to save them from themselves. But too much stress on class bias obscures the fact that the lobbyists also condemned the behavior of the elite and worried endlessly about the fate of "our boys," young middle-class males whom they also felt faced new, powerful forms of temptation in postwar society. To protect them as well as to reform the lower orders and the elite, the Christian lobby advocated laws to control everyone's behavior.[7]

Rather than class, other historians have emphasized gender in explaining postbellum moral reform. Women, several scholars have argued, sought empowerment through reform activities. The efforts of women in lobbying Congress and mobilizing the churches were even more important to the passage of moral legislation than most scholars have acknowledged. Their gender obviously influenced their reform activities; the female culture of the WCTU, for example, helped inspire and sustain many of them. In addition, as Paula C. Baker has argued, their subordinate status encouraged women to perceive government as a potential source of protection from dangerous males; females therefore more readily advocated an expansion of government's functions. However, like class, gender does not fully explain the motives of the Christian lobbyists. Women in the Christian lobby always worked easily with men, and the men sought women's help, because both shared a moral reform agenda and a deep Christian faith. In the final analysis, their Christian faith and its proscriptions about personal behavior proved more important in leading many women to support moral legislation than did the goal of expanding their role, just as the promotion of Christian values proved more vital than the preservation of class privilege.[8]

Although the Christian lobbyists acted from traditional Christian values and feared the society emerging about them, they still adopted modern methods of reform. As some scholars have pointed out, they created bureaucratic organizations with broad national grassroots support. The Christian lobbyists also pioneered the development of a new form of political activity, interest-group politics, in which popularly based organizations exerted pressure on Congress outside of the party structure. Even the WCTU, which endorsed the Prohibition Party, adopted a nonpartisan approach when lobbying Congress for moral legislation.[9]

Because of its modern organization, its use of interest-group politics, and its attacks on big business, K. Austin Kerr treats the American Anti-Saloon League as part of the Progressive movement. Paul Boyer, as well, includes Prohibition and other plans to regulate morality among Progressive reforms, terming them the coercive environmental approach within the larger movement. The lobbyists did have much in common with the Progressives. Evangelical Protestantism influenced both, and both sought to impose morality. Many Progressives supported Prohibition and other of the Christian lobbyists' legislation. Nevertheless, the lobbyists should not be subsumed under the rubric of Progressive reform. Their efforts began long before the emergence of Progressivism in the 1890s. The lobbyists first embraced national legislative solutions as early as the 1860s and 1870s and formed their alliance in the late 1880s. More important, they never shared the Progressives' interest in expanding democracy, increasing efficiency, or limiting the power of monopolies. When the Christian lobbyists attacked business, they articulated their criticism in the language of individual sin—avarice—and never campaigned for structural economic changes.[10]

The Christian lobby, however, did seek fundamental changes in the nation's moral polity, the system through which American society sought to maintain a virtuous population. The founders of the United States deemed moral citizens essential to the perpetuation of the republic, yet they created a secular national government that lacked any power to regulate morality. Ensuring a virtuous population became primarily the responsibility of the churches and reform groups that relied not on coercion but on moral suasion. Some states did regulate various forms of personal morality, but only on very rare occasions before the Civil War did Congress pass moral legislation.[11]

That changed after the war because the Christian lobby convinced the federal government to accept a far greater role in regulating moral behavior. The story of the lobby's campaigns in Congress and the subsequent debates over the bills they presented thus forms part of a larger story, that of the reconstruction of the American state in the years between the Civil War and World War I. Thomas R. Pegram makes the case that Prohibition was part of the expansion of the state, and Morton Keller shows how various campaigns to regulate moral behavior helped expand governmental power. Keller's important work, in fact, describes the old polity much as it is here. Most scholars, however, have focused on the role of liberals and economic regulation in expanding the size and functions of government, not moral reform. Giving appropriate attention to the role played by conservative Christians adds complexity to the historical narrative of the creation of the twentieth-century state.[12]

In the case of the moral polity, it is not a story of a total transformation. Older traditions of personal liberty, moral suasion, and states' rights persisted, and Congress rejected much of the Christian lobbyists' agenda. Members of Congress had no intention of creating a "Christian government"; they steadfastly refused to acknowledge Christ in the Constitution or even enact substantial Sunday laws, which involved a tacit acknowledgment of the government's responsibility to God. Congress also blocked the lobbyists' repeated attempts to pass constitutional amendments granting the federal government power over marriage and divorce, gambling, and other forms of behavior. Yet, often at the behest of the Christian lobbyists, Congress did substantially expand the moral powers of the federal government. It forced an end to polygamy in Utah. It banned obscenity, information on birth control and abortion, lottery materials, and prizefight films from the mails and interstate commerce. It enacted less sweeping laws to restrict divorce, prostitution, and underage sex. And, in the crowning achievement of moral reconstruction, Congress passed and sent to the states for ratification a constitutional amendment that banned the manufacture and sale of alcohol throughout the nation.

The adoption of Prohibition, like many of the lobbyists' victories, rested in part on the votes of southern congressmen. Elizabeth Sanders has made a strong case for the important role southerners played in the expansion of the national government after the Civil War, but most historians have emphasized instead the region's continued advocacy of states' rights. Before the Civil War, white southerners had opposed federal moral legislation, fearing it would establish a precedent that could be turned against slavery. When emancipation eliminated their need to defend slavery, and when the politics of race replaced those of slavery, southern attitudes began to change. By the early twentieth century, secure in the racial repression they had imposed on the region, white southerners provided crucial votes and leadership in national legislative campaigns to impose morality. The white South's support for moral laws helped earn it a reputation as the Bible Belt, an appellation nineteenth-century northerners would hardly have applied to a region they believed tainted by the sin of slavery. Many late-twentieth-century southerners assume that the South had supported moral legislation all along but would be surprised to learn that it advocated the use of federal power.[13]

Moral Reconstruction, then, is in part the story of the Reconstruction that followed the Civil War. Emancipation began the process that led to the white South's support for federal moral legislation and provided a powerful precedent for outlawing immoral behavior. But it is more the story of the reconstruction of the antebellum moral polity and, in the process, the reconstruction of the American state.[14]

CHAPTER ONE

The Antebellum Moral Polity

T he founders of the American Republic built into its polity a fundamental tension. The nation state would have no responsibility to
promote religion even though, most of the founders believed, the
survival of the new nation depended in part upon its citizens'
morality, which most saw as deriving from religion. In the Northwest Ordinance, Congress proclaimed unequivocally that "Religion, Morality and knowledge" were "necessary to good government and the happiness of mankind." Yet
in it Congress provided financial support for schools but not churches.[1]

The Constitution, written the same year, contained no appeal to God for
sanction or guidance, not even to the vague "Nature's God" or "Creator" of the
Declaration of Independence. It did include "in the Year of our Lord" in the
date and prohibited counting Sunday in the ten days allowed the president to
veto a bill, but neither provision undermined the inescapable conclusion that
the writers of the Constitution purposefully left God out, that they intended to
create a secular national government, one with no responsibility for religion or
morality. The Constitution left both religion and morality to the states. The
First Amendment, with its troubling tension between a ban on establishing religion and "prohibiting" its "free exercise" (a confusion that has kept courts oc-
cupied into a third century) did nothing to undermine the secular nature of
the new federal government. Rather, the Bill of Rights, of which it was a part,
affirmed and codified the Revolution's emphasis on individual liberty. The
First Amendment did not apply to the states, of course. Most provided some
acknowledgment of God's guidance in their constitutions, and in all, regulating public morality remained, as one historian has concluded, a "crucial obligation." Even the states, though, disestablished religion. Starting in Virginia in
1785 and ending in Massachusetts in 1833, all of the states that had once had established churches separated church and state.[2]

The founders, in sum, created a thoroughly secular national government, which left the regulation of morals to the states and the promotion of morality among its citizens primarily to the churches. What came to be called a voluntary system of religion emerged; even though churches received no aid from the government, they tacitly assumed responsibility for ensuring the moral population most Americans still thought necessary to a republic's survival. After the Civil War, Christian lobbyists would challenge the system created by the founders, and even before the war, not all Americans favored the new voluntary system. Some—especially among New England Federalists—sought an acknowledgment by the state of God's authority as well as a role for the national government in enforcing morality. The first major controversy over the emerging moral polity erupted over the government's transportation and delivery of the mail on Sunday.

The post office had transported mail on Sunday since the beginning of the Republic, but in 1810, Congress passed a law requiring postmasters to open their offices every day on which mail arrived and to deliver any item requested by a patron on any day of the week. Even though the postmaster general interpreted the law to minimize the time post offices would open and to avoid conflicts with worship services, ministers and churches protested the new law. Much of the agitation arose among Presbyterians and Congregationalists, denominations within a Reformed tradition that taught that the state was an institution of God and that people were called not only to salvation but to shape their society. Over the next five years, Presbyterians, Congregationalists, and other church people sent Congress over one hundred petitions against Sunday mail service. Lawmakers took no action, however, and the post office continued to operate on Sunday.[3]

In 1828, protests over Sunday mail service revived, led by the newly formed General Union for Promoting the Observance of the Christian Sabbath. Some of its leaders opposed lobbying the government, but others favored it. One of them, Jeremiah Evarts, a Boston lawyer, spent two years in Washington lobbying for a change in the law. His efforts were buttressed by over 900 petitions, a little over half from the mid-Atlantic states and New England, demanding an end to Sunday mail.[4]

The petitions offered various arguments against transporting the mail and operating post offices on Sunday. They contended that Christians had a right to undisturbed worship, or proclaimed the temporal and spiritual benefits of a day of rest, or pointed to the hardships faced by postal workers who had to work on Sunday. Some of the petitions also maintained that the government itself had a responsibility to follow God's law and warned that if the nation did not, it was doomed. Other petitions claimed that the government had a responsibility to stop "the iniquities prevailing in private life." The transportation and delivery of the mail on Sunday are "*injurious to the morals* and to the civil and religious institutions of our country," proclaimed a Maryland group. Sabbath desecration threatened to undermine morality and, in the words of a pamphlet that compiled the petitions, "leave our beloved land a moral desolation."[5]

Despite all the petitions, Evarts found little support in Congress for changing the law. Few legislators even attended church regularly, he complained, and most greatly feared "that religion is likely to gain too much influence." Congress's official response came in two reports by Richard M. Johnson, a Jacksonian Democrat from Kentucky. One was presented in 1829, when Johnson served in the Senate, the other the following year, after he had been elected to the House.[6]

The "proper object of government," Johnson's first report stated, "is to protect all persons in the enjoyment of their religious, as well as civil rights," and therefore, he added in the second report, the "principles of our Government do not recognize in the majority, any authority over, the minority, except in matters which regard the conduct of man to his fellow man." The reports also implicitly defended the American system of separation of church and state, explicitly extolled the religious freedom it promised Christians, Jews, and even pagans, and warned that past religious persecution would recur if these principles were violated even in so small a way as stopping the mail on Sunday. The diversity of moral opinion among "the good citizens of this nation," Johnson implied, made such restraint especially necessary. Jews and others did not observe the same Sabbath as Christians, and the government had no right to declare the practice of one faith right and the other wrong. The Constitution gave Congress no authority "to inquire and determine what part of time, or whether any, has been set apart by the Almighty for religious exercises." Determining God's law, in other words, was not a federal responsibility. If any "arm of Government be necessary to compel men to respect and obey the laws of God," Johnson argued, the states should. But in the final analysis, he questioned whether compelling men to be moral was the job of any level of government. Ensuring public morality, he concluded, rested with Christians themselves. When they succeeded in instructing "the public mind" and awakening "the consciences of individuals to make them believe that it is a violation of God's law to carry the mail, open post offices, or receive letters, on Sunday, the evil of which they complain will cease of itself, without any exertion of the strong arm of the civil power."[7]

A few legislators challenged Johnson's reports. One senator tried again to stop Sunday mails, but the Senate tabled his motion to instruct the Post Office Committee to report such a bill. Congress steadfastly refused to legislate an end to post office activities on Sunday. The Sabbatarian movement did help secure administrative changes that later restricted Sunday mail shipments. By that time, the organized opposition had ended, although Congress continued to receive petitions against Sunday mail up to and during the Civil War; Christian lobbyists would revive the issue in the 1880s.[8]

Johnson's reports on Sabbath mail expressed what had become the dominant conception of the nation's moral polity in the antebellum years. Most Americans thought the federal government had no religious authority and no power to legislate morality, which belonged solely to the states. They consistently opposed the encroachment of government into the realm of religion and remained deeply suspicious of national laws and even some state ones designed to ensure morality because of the threat they posed to individual or personal liberty. Many Americans, especially those like Johnson in the Democratic Party, doubted the power of the majority to tell individuals what to believe or, within limits, even how to behave. Yet these Americans still thought that the stability and success of popular government demanded a moral population. The process of ensuring proper belief and behavior began in the home, where, in what historians have called "Republican motherhood," mothers instilled in their children the virtues needed by the Republic. To supplement their efforts, Americans depended on the voluntary system—the efforts of the churches— and moral suasion. In the first half of the nineteenth century, a host of societies and associations formed to shape individual behavior through various types of moral suasion. Revivals, too, became a major aspect of American life. While serving to recruit church members, revivals also employed an intense form of moral suasion to encourage conversion, which resulted in moral individuals.[9]

If the outcome of the Sunday mail fight in Congress testified to the existence of a moral polity based in personal liberty, states' rights, and moral suasion, the Sabbatarians' crusade, nevertheless, revealed that some Americans doubted that such a moral polity could ensure the moral populace that the nation needed. Two goals of the opponents of Sunday mail would remain central to the crusade for moral legislation over the next century. First, worried about the religious authority of the state, they wanted it to acknowledge God's sovereignty and respect God's laws. Second, they reconceived the federal government's role in shaping individual behavior; they wanted it to have the power to make people follow God's law, in so far as possible, that is, to make them behave morally. The goals were intertwined, since a state with religious authority could have the power to regulate morals and a state that encouraged morality had religious authority.

During the later antebellum period, Congress occasionally passed minor moral legislation. In 1839, Congress prohibited dueling in the District of Columbia. Three years later, having earlier forbidden postmasters to act as agents for lotteries, Congress outlawed lotteries there as well. In 1842, Congress added to a tariff law a section prohibiting the importation of "all indecent and obscene prints, paintings, lithographs, engravings, and transparencies" and, fourteen years later, added obscene "images, figures, and daguerreotypes, and photographs" to the list of banned imports. In 1860, Congress passed a law to protect females immigrating to America from seduction and abandonment by the captains and crews of the steamships that brought them. All of these bills involved clear existing federal powers and evoked little opposition. More dramatic expansions of the federal government's moral powers sparked considerable congressional debate. Attempts to secure legislation to restrict the use of alcohol and the practice of polygamy, both of which the federal government would act against after the Civil War, revealed the difficulty of overcoming opposition to the federal legislation of morality before it.[10]

Although most temperance reformers limited their efforts to curtail or eliminate drinking to municipal or state legislation, a few advocated the use of federal power against alcohol. They petitioned Congress for an end to liquor sales in the District of Columbia and for a ban on the importation of intoxicating liquors. Congress ignored their appeals, but it did consider proposals to end the sale of liquor to Native Americans and to eliminate the spirit ration in the Navy.[11]

Few if any people suffered more from the ravages of alcohol than Native Americans, who learned to drink to excess from the Europeans. Early in the nineteenth century many Native Americans and government officials realized that the problem existed. In a series of measures passed between 1802 and 1827, Congress attempted to limit the sale of liquor to Native Americans within what was termed "Indian territory" and then, in 1832, banned all transportation of liquor there. Later, in congressional acts and treaties, the government adopted additional measures to restrict the use of alcohol by Native Americans. Nothing worked very well. The natives' appetite for liquor, the white traders' desire for profits, and weaknesses in the law, especially the difficulty of defining what constituted the "Indian country," made enforcement almost impossible. Only the fact that relations with Native Americans were clearly under federal control and the fact that white Americans considered Native Americans savages, certainly not citizens possessing liberties, made it possible to try to prohibit sales to them.[12]

In the antebellum period, Congress was asked to stop the distribution of alcohol to one group of citizens, sailors. The Navy's spirit or grog ration, the custom of issuing a daily drink of liquor to all on board ship, predated the Revolution; later the army added liquor to its fixed daily ration as well. Beginning in 1829, Congress debated the merits of furnishing sailors and soldiers liquor. In 1832, the army, where the daily ration was set by its own regulations rather than law, eliminated liquor. Law mandated the navy's spirit ration, so the navy could only adopt a voluntary program that allowed sailors to take cash payments instead of rum. In 1834, the secretary of the navy who had instituted it, asked Congress to end the spirit ration outright, and over the next few years, various temperance associations sent petitions in support of his proposal. In 1842, Congress finally responded, but only by reducing the spirit ration.[13]

Naval officers and temperance groups continued to urge Congress to eliminate liquor from the navy ration, and in 1845, the House Committee on Naval Affairs finally reported a bill that condemned "habitual indulgence in intoxicating liquors" as injurious to both health and morality, but it did not pass. During the next four Congresses legislators received more petitions and continued to discuss abolishing the spirit ration in the navy. In March 1853, Charles Sumner tried once more to end it through an amendment to a naval appropriations bill, but the Senate defeated the attempt, fourteen votes to twenty-eight. Seventeen of the no votes were cast by southern or border state senators; only three southern and two border state senators voted for the amendment. Northern senators split more evenly, eleven against, nine in favor. Voting followed party lines only roughly: Whigs and Democrats voted on both sides of the issue; the Senate's five Free-Soilers, though, voted as a block in favor of the measure. The next year the House voted on a proviso to a naval appropriations bill that prohibited the navy from purchasing and any officer from drinking intoxicating liquors (except for medicinal purposes). It failed when the Speaker broke a tie. In a preliminary vote, thirty-four of seventy-five negative votes came from the South. Only six southerners voted to prohibit the purchase of alcohol.[14]

The second antebellum congressional battle over moral legislation, that over Mormon polygamy, had greater significance but revealed similar sectional divisions. After several moves forced by mob attacks and the murder of their prophet Joseph Smith in Illinois, the Mormons finally settled around the Great Salt Lake in Utah. Under a new leader, Brigham Young, the Mormons established a thriving colony and appealed to Congress for statehood. Entangled in the debates that led to the Compromise of 1850, the request ended not in statehood but in the creation of the Utah Territory. Appointed the territory's governor, Young consolidated power within his and the Mormon leadership's hands. Confident of its control, the Church of Jesus Christ of Latter-day Saints in 1852 publicly proclaimed as revealed doctrine what had been practiced in secret, polygamy. Most Americans were horrified; they regarded plural marriage as a violation of Christian morality, a threat to the family, and therefore subversive of the social order.

Congress soon confronted the problem. In 1854, the House of Representatives debated legislation to allow land sales in Utah. It included a section that granted land there to any white male citizen of the United States, with a proviso that none go to anyone who had more than one wife. The restriction set off a debate over the merits of federal action against polygamy, which quickly involved a discussion of slavery as well. Objecting to limiting the grants to white men, a Rhode Island representative declared that he would just as soon have a polygamous state in the Union as a slave state, where the law did not recognize marriage for much of the population and many citizens practiced concubinage. A Virginia Democrat quickly defended slavery and slave marriage, criticized his colleague from Rhode Island for supporting polygamy, and endorsed the ban on land for polygamists. Another Virginia Democrat also supported the proviso.[15]

Other southerners feared that legislating morality in the territories, even if it involved something they believed to be so clearly immoral as polygamy, would establish a dangerous precedent that could be turned against the South's own peculiar institution. They rested their case against the proviso on broader principles, however. Alexander H. Stephens of Georgia argued that Congress had no power "to establish any religion" or "to touch the question of morals, which lie at the foundation of all systems of religion." "If we discriminate to-day against *Mormons*," he added, "to-morrow, perhaps, we shall be asked to dis-

criminate against Baptists, Methodists, Presbyterians, or Catholics." An Alabama Democrat also condemned the proviso as one more step toward "centralization" and government regulation of "morality." The bill died in the
House.[16]

Two years later, in 1856, the House considered even more drastic action
against polygamy, a motion to instruct the Committee on the Judiciary to report a law prohibiting any married person "from intermarrying or cohabiting
with another within any of the Territories of the United States." The resolution
required a two-thirds vote and failed by eighty-five ayes to fifty-six noes. Five
southerners voted yes; thirty-two voted no. That summer, the Republican
Party's presidential campaign platform proclaimed "the right and the imperative duty of Congress to prohibit in the Territories those twin relics of barbarism—Polygamy, and Slavery."[17]

The next major congressional debate over polygamy occurred in 1860. The
House Committee on the Judiciary reported a bill that made polygamy a crime
and annulled the Utah territorial legislation that had legalized it. Writing for
the committee, Thomas A. R. Nelson, a Tennessee Unionist and former Whig,
condemned polygamy as a violation of the laws of God and of every state of the
Union and bewailed the "open and defiant license which, under the name of
religion and a latitudinous interpretation of our Constitution, has been given
to this crime in one of our Territories." The citizens of Utah laughed at the
Bible and American laws, he continued, and employed American religious liberties as a pretext to "deride" and mock marriage, "an institution which was
honored by the presence of our Savior." Surely, Nelson contended, the authors
of the First Amendment did not intend to honor with the term religion "a tribe
of Latter Day Saints." More likely, they meant by religion "a belief founded
upon the precepts of the Bible" and intended only that there be no discrimination among denominations of Christians. Having dismissed any defense of
polygamy based on religious freedom, Nelson next argued that Congress clearly
had the constitutional power to prohibit polygamy in the territories. Then,
quoting Scripture and breathing fire, Nelson demanded all necessary action be
taken, including force, to eradicate this new Sodom and Gomorrah and to ensure that Utah conformed to the laws of the nation.[18]

Some southern legislators concurred in Nelson's moral condemnation of
polygamy and believed that federal action against it could no longer threaten
slavery because the recent *Dred Scott* decision had declared that Congress had
no power over slavery in the territories. Others considered polygamy such an
immoral and dangerous institution that they voted for the bill even if it did

pose a threat to slavery. In all, twenty-two southerners voted to criminalize polygamy and annul Utah's laws supporting it, which constituted more southern votes against polygamy than in 1854 or 1856. But thirty-three southerners voted against outlawing polygamy. Their votes constituted an answer to the rhetorical question asked by southern fire-eater Lawrence M. Keitt: "Are you prepared to start the Government upon this crusade against manners and morals?" They were not because, as one North Carolinian put it, "if we can render polygamy criminal, it may be claimed that we can also render criminal that other 'twin relic of barbarism,' slavery, as it is called in the Republican platform of 1856." Despite the split vote among southerners, the bill passed in the House by a large margin. In the Senate, where southern Democrats wielded more power, it never came up for debate.[19]

Congress's failure to pass antipolygamy legislation was not surprising; in the antebellum period, it rarely legislated on the issue of personal morality. The small number of laws that it did pass involved the District of Columbia, in the cases of dueling and lotteries, or international commerce, in the cases of obscenity and the protection of immigrant women on steamships. Neither represented a dramatic expansion of the federal government's moral powers. Nor did the attempt to prohibit the sale of alcohol to Native Americans, for the Constitution clearly gave the federal government responsibility for relations with Native Americans. Congress's willingness to prohibit the sale of alcohol among the tribes starkly contrasted with its refusal to stop giving it to sailors. The failure of the movement to end the spirit ration in the navy and the failure to pass federal legislation against polygamy testified to significant opposition to federal involvement in morality.

Opposition reflected the assumptions of the antebellum moral polity that emphasized personal liberty, moral suasion, and the states' responsibility for morality. Yet votes on both the spirit ration and polygamy, like the debates themselves, revealed interesting partisan and regional divisions. On every vote, a significantly higher percentage of Whigs and Republicans than Democrats voted in favor of the legislation. The most substantial support came from New England, with the Midwest and the mid-Atlantic states close behind. Relatively few southerners voted for moral legislation. On one vote on polygamy, 40 percent of the southerners favored legislating morality, but on three other pieces of moral legislation, no more than 15 percent did. At a time when southerners exercised considerable power in Washington and when the states of the future Confederacy constituted the largest regional bloc in each house of Congress, their opposition made legislating morality very difficult.

The varied comments and votes of southerners in Congress reflected their constituents' ambivalence about legislating morality. During the antebellum years, a growing number of white southerners, most associated with the South's evangelical denominations and living in the region's towns or cities, actively supported various reform causes, especially temperance. Like their counterparts in the North, southern moral reformers preached a gospel of self-control but still championed the right of the community to enforce morality and came to conclude that laws would be needed to ensure moral behavior. Many southern ministers joined in crusades for local statutes against Sabbath desecration or drinking. Some local communities did in fact pass such laws, although no southern state passed a statewide prohibition law, perhaps an indication of the limited influence of those who supported community coercion and legal restraint.[20]

Other southerners opposed attempts to legislate morality and instead celebrated a radical sense of individual, white independence that prized liberty and self-assertion. In white southern culture, drinking, gambling, and some of the other "sins" that northern and southern reformers sought to outlaw were considered legitimate expressions of independence and manhood. The South's radical individualism arose out of the region's rural isolation and localism, but slavery facilitated it. Whites could indulge their own freedom from government restraint, could glory in self-assertion, confident that the masters' power would restrain dangerous forms of immorality among the slaves. That confidence lessened southern white fears of workers and the lower class, fears that helped prompt temperance reformers in other regions to seek legal restraints on drinking.[21]

Although white southerners disagreed on legislating morality in general, they united behind a central tenet of the antebellum moral polity, that any legislation of morality should be left to the states. Southern opposition to federal legislation of morality rested in, more than anything else, the politics of slavery—the white South's perceived need to defend slavery from federal attack. As the comments and votes of southern representatives in Washington made clear, southerners feared that any congressional intervention in morality might serve as precedent for federal action against the South's peculiar institution. Since many northern preachers and churches championed abolition, the need to defend slavery even shaped southern rhetoric about religion in politics and government. "What sort of government 'are we to have,'" asked Henry A. Wise during the fight to restrict congressional debate over slavery in 1835, "'if women and priests are to influence our legislation?'" Nearly two decades later, during the debate over the Kansas-Nebraska Act, a petition from 3,500 New England ministers provoked similar outbursts. Although a couple of southerners defended the petitioners' right to even such a wrong opinion, James Mason of Virginia condemned the petition and claimed that "ministers of the Gospel are unknown to this government, and God forbid the day should ever come when they are known to it." Joining in the condemnation, Andrew Butler of South Carolina specifically criticized the ministers' assumption that they spoke for God. Wise's and Butler's comments echoed the position of many southern church leaders who championed the spirituality of the church, a doctrine that held that the church in particular and religion in general had no place in politics.[22]

The centrality of the politics of slavery in shaping antebellum southern attitudes toward religion in government became even clearer during secession and the Civil War. Southern ministers' defense of slavery, in itself a clerical intervention in politics for which southerners criticized northern ministers, helped prepare the way for secession. When the South left the Union and no longer needed to defend slavery from northern attack, religion became extremely important in the attempt to create a Confederate nation. The new Confederacy went further toward establishing the religious authority of the state than the old Republic ever had. The Confederate Congress also considered moral legislation, and, although little of consequence passed, the debates revealed that many southerners accepted the idea.[23]

The Confederacy sought to align the state with God and the church with the state as never before. Ministers and church bodies endorsed secession. In May 1861, the Southern Baptist Convention, the largest denominational body in the region, sent the Confederate Congress a resolution that proclaimed that all moral influences and all institutions should support "rulers" who defended "the endangered interests of person and property, of honor and of liberty." The Baptists' memorial went on to blame the North for the war, praise the Confederate government's action thus far, and invoke "Divine direction and favor" on the new government. In a sermon preached the following month, Benjamin Morgan Palmer, a Presbyterian minister who believed the war was "*between religion and atheism*," went even further. A nation was more than "a dead abstraction, signifying only the aggregation of individuals," Palmer proclaimed; it was "a sort of *person* before God" and God called it, like other persons, to judgment. Southerners therefore needed to confess their sins, the New Orleans minister continued, not individual sins such as intemperance, swearing, and Sabbath breaking (save, Palmer interjected, when the government encouraged them as it did in its postal service) but national sins. He then listed several, including the failure of the founders to make "*a clear national recognition of God at the outset of the nation's career.*" But, Palmer quickly added, he rejoiced that the Confederacy had receded "from this perilous atheism" and formally, solemnly, and unequivocally acknowledged "Almighty God" in its "fundamental law."[24]

The idea of acknowledging God in the Confederate Constitution originated with Thomas R. R. Cobb, a Georgian, a devout Presbyterian, and a temperance advocate. He convinced the committee drafting a provisional document to begin its proposed constitution, "In the name of Almighty God." After rejecting that wording and another offered by William P. Chilton, the provisional Congress voted four states to one to put "Invoking the favor of Almighty God" in the provisional constitution. When the Confederate Congress adopted a permanent constitution, and with no record left of the reason, it invoked not only the favor but the "guidance of Almighty God." The Confederate Congress also put the phrase "Deo Vindice" on the national seal and on three occasions asked President Jefferson Davis to proclaim a day of prayer and fasting in behalf of the cause. On seven other occasions, Davis independently issued a proclamation that invoked God's guidance and help in the war effort. The Confederates proclaimed days of prayer more often than the United States did—but then they were losing.[25]

In addition to endowing the Confederate government with religious authority, some members of its Congress wanted to establish its moral powers as well. Cobb sought a constitutional ban on requiring government employees to work on Sunday and, when he failed to get one, entered a bill to stop the transportation and delivery of mail on the Lord's Day. The Senate divided almost evenly on a series of motions to table Cobb's bill, but refused to pass it, and so sent it to the Committee on Postal Affairs. In 1862, Congress received several petitions in favor of a ban on Sunday mail service; in response the House Post Office Committee presented its own bill, written by Chilton. In defending his bill, Chilton criticized Johnson's 1830 report on Sunday mails. Religious freedom was important, Chilton argued, but preserving it did not mean that Congress must pass laws that "ignore the existence and overruling Providence of the Supreme Being" or that contravene "His known will." Since the Confederate government "professes to 'invoke the favor and guidance of Almighty God,'" it should not" trammel "His statutes" nor defy "His authority." Nor should the government "do violence to religion and the moral sense of the community." Certainly, Chilton wrote, "the Christian people" of "this Confederacy, esteem"

Sunday "a day set apart by Divine appointment for rest from secular employment, and to be dedicated to worship and moral culture." That the nation was
at war only provided "an additional reason" to conform to God's commands.
Chilton apparently could not convince a majority of the House to end Sunday
mails; as in the Senate, nothing ever came of the bill.[26]

In 1864, though, the Confederate House passed a resolution praising military
leaders who recognized the Sabbath and recommended that all officers dis-
pense with military parades and other nonessential activities on Sunday. Most
other Confederate attempts to legislate morality also involved the war effort.
Congress limited the use of foodstuffs in the production of whiskey and, toward the end of the war, prohibited blockade runners from carrying liquor,
seeking to save space for more important cargo. It also passed two laws designed to reduce drunkenness in the military. Yet the Confederacy continued to
provide liquor for soldiers in certain situations, and whiskey remained a part of
the prescribed navy ration. In sum, the Confederacy, either out of principle or
because more immediate war measures commanded legislators' attention, did
little to legislate morality. Southerners at war, however, had not hesitated to
mix religion and politics and, in invoking God in the Confederate Constitution, went further than the prewar Union had in claiming religious authority
for the state.[27]

Northerners, too, debated moral legislation and the relation between religion
and the state during the war, although they never went so far as putting God
in the Constitution. The Union had only to preserve, not create, a nation and
therefore did not need to write a new constitution. The military crisis nevertheless led some to question the religious authority of the state. In August 1861,
after the Union defeat at Bull Run, Horace Bushnell preached a sermon in
which he lamented that the founders had created only a "man-made compact"
without "moral or religious ideas" or any transcendent authority. As a result,
New England political ideals, shaped by religion, had diminished in importance as the theories of Thomas Jefferson, rooted in notions of a social compact, had increased in influence. To that shift in thinking Bushnell attributed
the nation's current problems and broken nationalism. To restore morality and
mend that nationalism, Bushnell added, the nation "might not be amiss, at
some fit time, to insert in the preamble of our Constitution, a recognition of
the fact that the authority of government, in every form, is derivable only from
God; cutting off, in this manner, the false theories under which we have been so

fatally demoralized." Bushnell later backed away from his call for constitutional change. Others did not.[28]

Even before Bushnell's sermon, Congress had received petitions seeking a similar addition to the preamble, and later in the war an organization formed to write God, Christ, and biblical authority into the Constitution. Meeting a few days apart in February 1863, groups gathered independently in Xenia, Ohio, and in Sparta, Illinois, to discuss the crises brought on by the war. In Xenia, John Alexander, a wealthy Pittsburgh industrialist, presented a paper that praised the recent Emancipation Proclamation for ending the nation's involvement in the sin of slavery, blamed the war on the nation's "original sin" of leaving God out of the Constitution, and urged amending the preamble to acknowledge God. Others at the meeting took up the challenge, as did the group assembled in Sparta. Joint conferences followed, out of which emerged the National Association for the Amendment of the Constitution. It prepared a memorial to Congress asking that the preamble of the United States Constitution be changed to read: "We, the people of the United States, humbly acknowledging Almighty God as the source of all authority and power in civil government, the Lord Jesus Christ, as the Ruler among nations, and His revealed will as of supreme authority, in order to constitute a Christian government, and in order to form a more perfect union. . . ." The convention sent its petition to Congress and dispatched a delegation to meet with President Abraham Lincoln. On 10 February 1864, twenty-two people met with the president, and their spokesman, a professor at Princeton, explained the movement and asked Lincoln to send a message to Congress supporting the change in the preamble. Lincoln replied, according to the memory of one of the participants, that he would honor their request just as soon as he could see his way clear to do so. He never did.[29]

At the association's behest, Charles Sumner introduced its memorial in Congress, and other petitions followed. In 1865, both the Senate and House Committees on the Judiciary declined to act on them. Later, the chair of the House committee bristled at newspaper reports that he and his colleagues had thereby "reported against the recognition of God in the Constitution." They had done no such thing, he retorted from the floor of the House. The committee had simply asked to be discharged from considering petitions for and against adding God to the Constitution because such a change "was unnecessary and injudicious, at this time, at any rate." "The committee believes," he continued, "that the Constitution of the United States does recognize the existence of a Supreme Being." After all, it required an oath that implicitly involved an appeal to a supreme being and contained a clause prohibiting any law against the free exercise of religion. Adding God to the preamble was therefore unnecessary. He might also have cited the two proclamations, requested by Congress and issued by Lincoln, calling Americans to prayer and fasting to secure God's assistance in the cause of Union or the addition of "In God We Trust" to the nation's currency during the war.[30]

Although the Union, unlike the Confederacy, rejected the idea of acknowledging God in the Constitution, wartime Congresses proved more willing to legislate morality than their antebellum predecessors or their Confederate counterparts. With southern representatives no longer present to cast votes against moral legislation, Congress passed measures on the use of alcohol, Sabbath observance, polygamy, and of course, slavery.

In 1862, Congress finally abolished the spirit ration in the navy. Later, it passed a series of laws to prevent soldiers from getting liquor in the District of Columbia, to expand the law against selling alcohol to Native Americans, and to amend the internal revenue act to prevent distilleries from operating on Sunday. Another bill touching on Sunday observation led to a revealing exchange in Congress on the role of religion in government, one that hinted at the emergence of new attitudes. District of Columbia officials allowed the railroad company that operated streetcars in the city to operate on Sunday. In a new charter for the line, the House added a section that formally recognized the railroad's right to run on Sunday, although even if Congress did not keep it in the charter, the company could still operate its cars on Sunday. In the Senate, though, some opposed Sunday operation. Waitman T. Willey, a West Virginia Republican, invoking two very different standards, claimed it violated "the Christian sentiment of the city" and "the express word of God." The first assertion linked law to majority opinion, in this case shaped though it might have been by Christianity; the second suggested that laws had to be judged against the absolute authority of the Bible. By the end of moral reconstruction, the difference would prove important—and Christian sentiment would prove more influential than biblical authority. At the time, however, John P. Hale seemed more impressed with the appeal to biblical authority. The New Hampshire Republican praised Willey's speech as the first he had ever heard in the Senate that "openly, boldly, without equivocation or apology, recognized the law of God and the obligations of Christian morality as binding upon him in his legislative capacity." Hale added that perhaps all lawmakers had felt such an "obligation," but none before had stated it so forthrightly.[31]

Other senators criticized Willey's remarks and supported the guarantee of

Sunday operation. If Congress outlawed running the cars on Sunday because it violated Scripture, Justin Morrill asked, how far should it go? Should Congress stop people from walking or riding to church or outlaw innocent amusements? Willey's rather than Morrill's view prevailed; by one vote, the Senate eliminated the section that recognized the right to operate on Sunday. The House, after at first objecting, finally went along. Lawmakers may have realized that by voting against the provision on Sunday operation they took a stand in behalf of their Christian constituents and even the word of God, but still knew that the trains would run on Sunday anyway. Everyone won.

At first glance, it would appear that Congress took a more decisive and substantive stand for morality when it finally outlawed polygamy. In 1862, Justin Morrill entered an antipolygamy bill almost identical to the one the House had approved before the war; it passed again in the House with little debate. In the Senate, where such bills had never made it out of committee before the South left the Union, the Judiciary Committee offered only a few changes and reported the bill. On the floor, only one senator spoke against it, warning that the Mormons might fight rather than submit to an edict from Washington. One other senator joined him in voting against the act, which made polygamy a crime, annulled all Utah territorial laws that recognized the institution, and limited the right of any church in the territories to hold more than $50,000 worth of real estate. The last provision was designed to confiscate the considerable land holdings of the Church of Jesus Christ of Latter-day Saints. The Morrill Act, as it was called, quickly became a dead letter. The nation had enough trouble subduing the South and never really attempted to enforce it.[32]

Wartime laws against alcohol, Sabbath breaking, and even polygamy, as it turned out, had relatively little impact on the lives of Americans or the moral powers of the federal government. The war, however, did lead to emancipation, the exercise of federal power that the South had always dreaded. Emancipation was not solely the result of a moral crusade, of course. American political ideals, as much or more than its Christian principles, provided the justification for emancipation. Moreover, the reason for it also had much to do with the need to defeat the South. Certainly the slaves were freed not because Congress said they should be but because Union armies ensured they were. But for some, slavery had always been a sin to be stopped, and for many postwar reformers, emancipation became a commanding precedent for federal legislation of morality. If the national government could outlaw the sin of slavery, they reasoned, it could also employ its power to end other forms of immorality.

Later, even southerners would cite the antislavery precedent in behalf of moral legislation.

The war, though, had not dramatically increased the moral powers of the national government; nor had the Union, unlike the Confederacy, moved to establish the religious authority of the state. The tension between the need for a moral citizenry and opposition to government involvement in religion persisted. Legislative activity before and during the war demonstrated that some Americans, frustrated by that tension, embraced the idea of using the national government to ensure morality, but the moral polity constructed between the Revolution and the Civil War survived. The national government still accepted little permanent role in shaping morality. Most Americans continued to champion states' rights and individual liberty and to expect Republican mothers, churches, revivals, and other forms of moral suasion to produce a moral population.

CHAPTER TWO

Christ and Prohibition in the Constitution?

I n the first decade after the Civil War, the issues of political, not moral, reconstruction absorbed the nation's attention. In the midst of the battles to define the meaning of freedom for the former slaves and to establish a new political order in the former Confederacy, white southerners and their Democratic allies persisted in, if not intensified, their opposition to federal moral legislation. The first important expansions of the moral powers of the national government, the Comstock Law and effective anti-Mormon legislation, came toward the end for the former and after Reconstruction for the latter. Nevertheless, the campaign for moral reconstruction began almost as soon as the Civil War ended. The unprecedented expansion of federal power during the war and the precedent established when the federal government outlawed the sin of slavery encouraged reformers to seek the national government's aid in combating other sins, while the political issue posed by secession generated new concerns over the religious authority of the state. Conscious of both the potential of and the problems with the national government, the National Association for the Amendment of the Constitution renewed its campaign to put Christ in the Constitution. Temperance advocates, who in the antebellum years had only occasionally turned to the federal government for aid, also sensed the new power of the national government and sought federal legislation in the late 1860s. Within a decade, they had established national prohibition as their goal.

The campaign to recognize God, Christ, and the authority of the Scriptures in the preamble to the Constitution had its roots in the distinctive theology of the members of the National Association for the Amendment of the Constitution. Most of them belonged to either the Reformed or the United Presbyterian churches, denominations with roots in the Covenanter tradition of the Scottish Reformation. Covenanters read certain biblical passages, especially the visions in the seventh chapter of Daniel and chapters eleven and nineteen of the book of Revelation, not in the apocalyptic fashion that many premillennialists did, but as testimony to Christ's kingship over the nations in the present. Each nation, as a moral individual, owed allegiance to Christ, the King of the nations, Covenanters believed. Therefore the state was capable of sin, national sins they termed them, and could expect to be destroyed if it did not repent and conform to God's law. Covenanters also believed that no Christian should pay allegiance to a nation that sinned by failing to recognize Christ's authority, so they refused to vote or participate in politics until the preamble to the Constitution was revised. What they called their "political dissent" notwithstanding, most Covenanters approved of working in a voluntary association such as the one to amend the Constitution.[1]

Although most proponents of what was called the Christian amendment acted from Covenanter beliefs, they also sought to change the Constitution because they feared that secession demonstrated the danger of resting the authority of the state on the theory of popular sovereignty, as many antebellum Americans had assumed. Citizens, the theory held, voluntarily joined together and gave up some of their individual rights in order to form a more perfect union or society. If the government rested on consent, however, why had southerners not been allowed to withdraw from the Union? Why could they not be allowed to retract their consent, to dissolve the contract? Denying them the right to secede as the North had done implied that the Union rested on more than popular sovereignty or a voluntary contract. The fact that the Union had been preserved only by the North's successful exercise of military force made matters worse. Moral reformers wanted a nobler basis for government. One of them, Elisha Mulford, in 1870 published *The Nation*, which argued that the United States was a divinely created nation with an independent existence, answerable to God as well as to the people.[2]

The National Association for the Amendment of the Constitution went a step further, demanding a formal, organic acknowledgment of the state as a moral individual responsible to God. Such an amendment, its supporters claimed, would eliminate the crisis of authority that the Civil War brought by providing the state with religious authority. In addition, it would eliminate the "absurd theory," offered in the attempts to preserve slavery and polygamy, "that every citizen has a veto power over everything in the government which may not accord with his individual belief" and the equally dangerous proposition that majorities had a right to determine morality. If they did, morals would change with every election. The Christian amendment, its proponents made clear, sought to establish the religious authority of the state in part to serve as a basis for an expansion of its moral powers. Placing the authority of the Bible in the Constitution established one moral standard, once and for all and across the land, on which that exercise of moral power would rest.[3]

Petitions asking Congress to write God, Christ, and the authority of the Bible into the preamble trickled in during the years immediately following the Civil War. In late 1868, citing the antislavery movement's success in constitutional reform, the National Association for the Amendment of the Constitution launched a new campaign. Over the next year, it held public meetings and distributed petitions, and in February 1869, memorials began to arrive in Congress in greater numbers than ever before. They varied in form, but the association's printed petition requested the amendment of the preamble to read: "We, the people of the United States, [humbly acknowledging Almighty God as the source of all authority and power in civil government, the Lord Jesus Christ as the Ruler among the nations, and His revealed will as of supreme authority, in order to constitute a Christian government and] in order to form a more perfect union. . . ." The petition also asked Congress to make additional changes in "the body of the Constitution as may be necessary to give effect to these amendments in the preamble."[4]

Congress failed to respond to the memorials, and over the next two years many more were sent. Most Americans, if they had heard of it at all, probably looked upon the proposal to put God, Christ, and the Bible in the preamble as innocuous. Religious liberals did not. Francis Abbot, a leading liberal and proponent of Free Religion, condemned the Christian amendment as the logical result of organized Christianity and the opening salvo in the coming "war against republican liberty." He and his fellow liberals claimed that the amendment would destroy the separation of church and state and lead to the persecution of Unitarians, Jews, and infidels. The amendment's supporters denied both charges. Their proposals would not violate the separation of church and state, they argued, because the state and the church (along with the family) were divinely created institutions that worked together, but separately, to do God's will—an argument opponents of the amendment found far from reassuring. Supporters of the Christian amendment also contended that their proposed changes in the Constitution in no way threatened people's right to worship as they pleased. They denied that they sought any sectarian or ecclesiastical qualification for officeholding, but admitted their amendment might prevent infidels and Jews from holding office or even voting. Many of the amendment's proponents, in fact, did not want to be governed by infidels, Jews, Mormons, or even Roman Catholics.[5]

Frightened by the Christian amendment and its proponents, Abbot and other liberals circulated petitions against rewriting the preamble; the first of them arrived in Congress in January 1872. They condemned the amendment, in the words of students at the Harvard Divinity School, as an "attempt to over-throw the great principles of complete religious liberty, and the complete sep-aration of Church and State, on which the Constitution was established by its original founders." In January 1874, Abbot's own petition against the amend-ment finally arrived; 953 feet long, it bore 35,179 signatures.[6]

The following month, Benjamin F. Butler, reporting for the House Commit-tee on the Judiciary, asked that it be discharged from further consideration of the petitions. The founders expected the nation "to be the home of the op-pressed of all nations of the earth, whether Christian or Pagan," Butler ex-plained, and because they fully appreciated the toll that "the union between church and state" had taken "upon so many nations of the Old World." They therefore decided not "to put anything into the Constitution or frame of gov-ernment which might be construed to be a reference to any religious creed or doctrine." Since that time, Butler added, "our Christian fathers" have repeatedly ratified that decision by rejecting every attempt to put a religious reference into the Constitution. The leaders of the National Association for the Amendment of the Constitution condemned Butler's report and sent to the following Con-gress even more petitions. Unimpressed, lawmakers took no action. The sec-ond attempt to establish the religious authority of the state had failed; a third congressional discussion of the proposal would not occur for another two decades. In the meantime, expanding the moral powers of the national gov-ernment became the primary goal of the forces of moral reconstruction.[7]

Civil War military service, many proponents of moral reconstruction believed, freed soldiers from the moral restraints of their communities and exposed them to temptations never before encountered. The result, some claimed, had been an increase in lewdness, prostitution, and especially the consumption of alcohol. But if the war brought despair over a decline in morals, the wartime expansion of federal power and the antislavery precedent raised the possibil-ity of employing national laws to preserve them. In the antebellum years, temperance advocates had linked slavery and drink, and in the immediate postwar period, drinking became the first immoral activity targeted for federal attack.[8]

In the fall of 1865, the National Temperance Society (NTS) formed to stop the "use, manufacture, and sale of all intoxicating drinks as a beverage." Its first president was William E. Dodge, a wealthy New York copper manufacturer; another founder, Morris K. Jesup, was one of the city's major financiers. Over the next decade, much of the society's financial support came from Jay Gould, Cornelius Vanderbilt, Collis P. Huntington, Russell Sage, and other titans of finance, who objected to federal intervention in their business affairs. Day-to-day operation of the society fell to its secretary, John N. Stearns. Under his leadership, the NTS initially followed the traditional approach of moral suasion, adopting an abstinence pledge for individuals and distributing temperance literature. But in September 1869, Stearns recommended and the NTS Board of Managers voted to undertake a petition campaign to urge Congress to prohibit the sale of intoxicating drinks in the District of Columbia. In choosing this cause, the NTS adopted the abolitionists' tactic of using the District of Columbia as a lens to focus national attention on an evil practice. The society never abandoned moral suasion — it became a leading distributor of temperance tracts — but rather resolved also to seek legal restrictions.[9]

In 1872, the society intensified its efforts in behalf of both moral and legal suasion when it hired as a district secretary Aaron M. Powell, a Quaker and former abolitionist editor. The NTS instructed Powell to "introduce a temperance literature among the Freed People" but also put him in charge of the task of convincing Congress to enact prohibition in the District of Columbia and the territories, everywhere Congress already had the authority to do so. Reformers first sought to employ the existing powers of the federal government in behalf of the control of personal morality. Neither Powell's lobbying nor petitions from various groups, however, convinced Congress to enlist in the temperance crusade. It seemed no more interested in anti-alcohol legislation than it had been before the war.[10]

Between 1870 and 1874, several bills were entered, none passed, and most met with as much merriment as serious consideration. In the case of one prohibition bill for the District of Columbia and the territories, the Senate even had trouble deciding to which committee it should be sent. The chair of the Finance Committee believed the bill "rather a question of morals than a question of finance." Some of his colleagues replied that it could only be considered as a matter of finance since the Constitution granted Congress no power over morals. The Senate knew "perfectly well," said one, "that it is totally out of the scope of the United States" to regulate the manufacture of beverages in the states. Eventually, the Senate referred the bill back to the Committee on Finance, which reported it, but no action on the bill was ever taken.[11]

A similar measure never even got out of committee in the House, although one to deny promotion in the army to anyone who used intoxicating liquors or drugs did make it to the floor. It was quickly tabled, but only after a motion to have it apply to members of Congress evoked laughter. A petition to impose a similar rule on all federal officials and to make drunkenness grounds for impeachment prompted even more merriment in the Senate. Members discussed various committees to which it might be sent. One suggested the Committee on Disabilities; another observed that the proposal "seems to be a very violent change" and recommended "the Committee on Revolutionary Affairs." The laughter that greeted petitions and bills on the alcohol question, not to mention the failure of all the bills to pass, revealed that Congress had no intention of outlawing drinking and considered the attempt "revolutionary," if not absurd. Most legislators still thought that the regulation of morals, the rubric under which they put attempts to control drinking, the province of the states, not the federal government.[12]

In the face of decided, indeed derisive, opposition in Congress even to narrowly focused bills to discourage drinking, the National Temperance Society adopted a new legislative strategy. In 1873, it passed a resolution urging the establishment of a federal commission to study the liquor traffic, a proposal offered in Congress the previous year by a Kansas Republican. NTS support for a federal study of the alcohol industry constituted an acknowledgment that public opinion did not yet perceive a need for legislative action. The evidence a commission produced, its supporters believed, would help convince Americans of the evils of drink. Although in one sense support for a federal commission represented a retreat to moral suasion, the NTS still envisioned a new and significant role for the government in promoting voluntary temperance. Moreover, the society had not abandoned its hopes of employing federal power. At the time that it passed the resolution in favor of creating a federal commission, the society's board of managers expressed its belief in government's responsibility, "after the Divine model, . . . to restrain and prohibit that which tends to the demoralization of the people, and to promote the general welfare." The society continued to believe in both the religious authority of the state and its responsibility to regulate moral behavior. The NTS had executed only a strategic retreat in its attack on the liquor traffic and clearly envisioned the commission

CHRIST AND PROHIBITION IN THE CONSTITUTION?   33

less a neutral body than a means to build support for prohibition, which remained the society's ultimate goal.[13]

The commission proposal made it to the floor for the first time in January 1874. In calling for its passage, the Senate Committee on Finance cited "the great number of petitioners, their respectability, and the very clear justice of what they ask." Following the society's suggestion, the bill called for the appointment by the president, with the approval of the Senate, of a five-member commission to investigate the liquor traffic in its "economic, criminal, moral, and scientific aspects, in connection with pauperism, crime, social vice, the public health, and general welfare of the people." In addition, the commission was to evaluate the effectiveness of license laws and other means of stopping the use of alcohol. In the debate over the bill, one supporter raised the possibility of additional national legislation, which the NTS and the temperance forces clearly hoped the commission would promote. Another advocate frankly stated he did not want an unbiased study but rather one that established that legislation against the alcohol traffic would succeed. Most of the bill's supporters, however, only bewailed the evils of drink, cited constitutional authority to promote the general welfare to justify the commission, and argued it would generate useful information that would not necessarily be employed in passing laws Congress had no authority to enact.[14]

Opponents feared a temperance Trojan horse. An Ohio Democrat predicted that the officers of the National Temperance Society would staff the commission, and therefore it would be unlikely to provide reliable information. He and others repeatedly pointed out that the federal government had no authority over matters that fell within the police power and warned that the commission was part of a trend toward, as one put it, "gathering into the Federal jurisdiction . . . all State functions and all matters of State police." Another warned that the creation of a commission would lead to attacks on gambling, extravagant female dress, or even indigestion, which contributed to family distress. He followed his sarcasm with a serious critique of prohibition. Any attempt to stop a practice that can have an innocent use would fail, he argued. "Human nature is so constituted that it wants, and will seek, pleasure, relaxation, social enjoyment."[15]

The most sustained attack on the bill came from Thomas F. Bayard, a Democratic senator from Delaware described by one historian as "a Border spokesman for the South." Bayard reiterated several of his fellow opponents' arguments but grounded his opposition on more fundamental principles. Neither the state nor federal governments, he proclaimed, had the right to legislate morality. Bayard drew a sharp distinction between the "domain of morals" and that of law. All "sumptuary laws" fell within the domain of morals and had long been considered "odious," he observed. They violated the "right of individual action, that control of personal tastes guided by personal predilection and by individual constitutional peculiarities, which each man should be left to judge for himself, and the interference with which he justly considers an unauthorized invasion of his personal liberty." Not only did laws that entered the domain of morals violate personal liberty, Bayard continued, they did not work. Experience had shown that government cannot compel moral behavior; it had to "proceed from within the human heart." In addition, Bayard criticized what he termed "a narrow-mindedness" in attempting to enforce "the same class of habits to one man as to another." Some could drink moderately; others could not. The state should not try to force everyone to act alike but rather "allow each man to become his own guide as to these questions affecting his own happiness."[16]

Bayard, in sum, championed the antebellum moral polity. He considered federal moral legislation a violation of states' rights, an attack on personal liberty or individual freedom, and a certain failure. Instead, Bayard advocated individual moral suasion, but even had reservations about that. He questioned not just the right of government to set standards but the very existence of an universal standard of moral authority. He thereby endorsed at least a limited form of moral relativism. Bayard's speech anticipated most of the arguments that would be offered against later attempts to create a commission, to pass prohibition, and to legislate against other forms of immorality. Bayard secured some modifications, but the commission bill still passed the Senate on a close vote, as it did again during the next Congress. On both occasions, however, the bill died in the House.[17]

Congress's refusal to create a commission revealed considerable opposition to laws on alcohol in particular and the legislation of morality in general; it also testified to the persistence of antebellum divisions over the issue. In the two Senate votes, Democrats almost unanimously opposed the creation of a commission; they voted fifteen to zero and twenty-two to one against it. Republicans, conversely, voted twenty-five to five and thirty-one to zero in favor. The regional alignment, too, reflected antebellum patterns. Support for the commission came from the New England and midwestern states; representatives of the southern and border states consistently opposed the measure; those from the mid-Atlantic and western states split. The House divided along regional and party lines similar to those in the Senate. In both chambers, a majority of the relatively few no votes cast by Republicans were by southerners, adding further evidence of the strength of opposition to moral legislation in the former Confederacy. Representatives from districts with higher percentages of Roman Catholics were also more likely to vote against the bill.[18]

The proposal for a national commission on the liquor traffic dominated congressional debates over alcohol for the next three decades. One or more bills to create a commission were introduced, almost always by a northern Republican, in every Congress from the Forty-second to the Fifty-fourth. They sometimes passed in the Senate, but never in the House. Just voting on the creation of a commission, with its assumption of a federal role in the control of alcohol, constituted a change from the immediate postwar years when proposals for limiting the use of alcohol evoked laughter and were summarily dismissed as outside the scope of federal power. But Congress, especially its Democratic and southern members, remained fundamentally opposed to any federal role. Early failure, however, led only to expanded efforts. Two developments in the mid-1870s, the emergence of the Woman's Christian Temperance Union and the introduction of a constitutional amendment for national prohibition by Henry W. Blair, reshaped the congressional debate over the control of alcohol.

In December 1873, women in towns in southern Ohio met in churches, listened to speeches against the evils of drink, prayed for success, and then marched off, two-by-two, to confront the saloon. When they reached their destinations, they first tried to convince the bar owners to sign a pledge to stop selling alcohol. A few did; most did not. When liquor sellers refused, the women sang and picketed their establishments. During the next few months, over 900 similar demonstrations occurred in thirty-one states or territories. Perhaps as many as 143,000 women participated, most of them in Ohio, but many in Indiana, Illinois, Michigan, New York, Iowa, and Pennsylvania as well. Both the National Temperance Society and the *Christian Statesman*, the voice of the movement to write Christ into the preamble of the Constitution, endorsed the women's effort. Some of the veterans of the women's crusade issued a call for a convention to form a national organization. In response, in November 1874 some 300 women from sixteen states gathered in a Presbyterian church in Cleveland, formed the Woman's Christian Temperance Union, and elected Annie Turner Wittenmyer president. By the next annual convention, the WCTU had organized in twenty-one states, and by the end of the decade, it boasted 1,117 unions, as local groups were called, with a membership of over 26,000.[19]

From the beginning, not just the name but the participants proclaimed the group's Christian roots. The orator who opened the first national convention assured the delegates that "this is simply and only a religious movement" and prayed for a fresh baptism of the spirit. Frances E. Willard, who would become the group's first corresponding secretary, offered a resolution at that meeting urging prayer for a general revival of religion, which would be needed for the movement to succeed, and the convention adopted a statement that the movement came from God.[20]

Probably most of the WCTU's membership opposed drinking alcohol primarily because they believed it a sin, a violation of God's law to be renounced and fought. Members of the WCTU also opposed drinking because of the problems it brought, especially into the lives of women. They acted in part as women protecting women, their homes, and their children from drunkards who abused and neglected them. Their plea for action became, as Willard put it, "the last cry of the defenseless going up to the ear of God." The pleas went up to government as well; women's unequal status in society and, for many, within their own homes made women more likely than men to turn to government for protection, especially from men. The WCTU sought not only "home protection" but, as Willard put it, "*to make the whole world* HOMELIKE." Its members fought to protect their husbands and their sons in communities increasingly plagued by drink and campaigned to force society to conform to their Christian conceptions of moral order, a goal they shared with the NTS and many other groups or individuals who advocated moral legislation.[21]

In working toward their objectives, members of the WCTU continued to celebrate motherhood and moral suasion, two central components of the antebellum moral polity. The WCTU relied on lecturers and literature to convince children and adults of the dangers and evils of drink, and it dedicated much of its effort to persuading both women and men to take a pledge of total abstinence. From the very beginning, though, these Christian women did not think mothers or moral suasion alone could eliminate the alcohol evil or create a moral social order. They believed the state must be employed to ensure the morality of citizens. "Moral force," explained an editorial in the WCTU's newspaper, the *Union Signal*, "is the persuasion of the human will to act in accordance with intelligent conviction. Legal force is the compulsion of the human will when intelligence and conviction are wanting."[22]

From its first convention in 1874, the WCTU sought to enlist the legal force of the national government in the fight against alcohol. Delegates passed a resolution to petition Congress in behalf of the creation of the commission to study the liquor traffic. President Wittenmyer prepared and circulated 10,000 copies of a memorial that instead called for prohibition in the District of Columbia and the territories. Over 40,000 people signed it, and the consolidated petition was over fifty feet long when presented to the Senate on 1 February 1875.[23]

Frances Willard supported the petition, but she never believed that "prayer, persuasion, and petition" to the "strongholds of power" would suffice. At the WCTU's second national convention, she advocated laws that would prohibit the sale of intoxicating liquor without the consent of the majority of women over eighteen years of age in the effected area. The convention did not endorse her proposal, but in early 1878, Willard testified before a congressional committee in behalf of a bill incorporating that principle. It allowed the sale of liquor in the territories or the District of Columbia only if a majority of men by their votes and women by their signatures requested it. Nothing came of the bill. Asking that women express consent through their signatures represented a compromise on Willard's part. She believed that women had a right to the vote and could accomplish their goals only if allowed to exercise that right. Wittenmyer disagreed, and tensions between the two leaders grew. In 1879, the WCTU's national convention elected Willard to replace Wittenmyer as president of the WCTU. As leader and guiding spirit of the WCTU, Willard became unquestionably the best known of the people who lobbied for federal legislation of morality and, arguably, the most prominent American woman of her time.[24]

Born on a farm in western New York in 1839, Willard grew up on another in Illinois and later in the Chicago suburb of Evanston. She graduated from that city's North Western Female College and set out to create an independent life for herself. The distinguished career that followed rested on two fundamental precepts. As a woman, Willard held to what today might be called difference feminism. She lived a life supported by women, including a series of homoerotic relationships, and steadfastly advocated the rights of women. She also championed the ability of women, especially those she called "mother-hearted," to make men and society better. At the same time, Willard remained, until the last years of her life, a devout and relatively orthodox Christian, who believed Christians, too, had a responsibility to shape their society. After she died, one of the women Willard had lived with, Lady Henry Somerset, an English temperance advocate, wrote that to "be 'about her Father's business' always seemed to be the mainspring of" Willard's life. She saw more clearly than most, Somerset added, "that the things which people call secular are bound up with religion. She was the pioneer of 'religion in politics' in America." Willard never perceived any conflict between her concern for women's rights and her belief in Christianity, and indeed the two driving forces in her life rarely came into

Frances E. Willard—longtime president of the Woman's Christian Temperance Union and "pioneer of 'religion in politics'" in America" (Courtesy of the Library of Congress, Prints and Photographs Division, LC USZ61-790)

conflict as prohibition and woman suffrage became the central causes of her public career.[25]

For Willard and many in the WCTU, the vote became as important a goal as prohibition. Once Willard took over the presidency of the WCTU from Wittenmyer, she worked to convince the WCTU to endorse woman's suffrage, which it did in 1881, and then to adopt a partisan political strategy as the best means of securing both the vote and prohibition. In 1885, the WCTU formally endorsed the Prohibition Party. Willard was already active in the party's affairs, but whether large numbers of the WCTU's rank and file joined her is questionable. In any case, even after the WCTU endorsed the Prohibition Party, neither Willard nor the WCTU abandoned the approach begun by Wittenmyer—nonpartisan, interest-group politics waged in behalf of national legislation to control the consumption of alcohol.

Before Willard became president, the WCTU had created a legislative committee, and the year after she assumed power, it became a department, which reflected an increased importance within the organization. J. Ellen Foster, a Republican partisan, and then Mary A. Woodbridge, a supporter of the Prohibition Party, first directed the WCTU's legislative efforts. During the period of their leadership, Willard and other WCTU officials occasionally went to Washington to testify before congressional committees, and the union itself undertook several national petition drives. Neither Foster nor Woodbridge ever stayed in the capital over the course of a session, and neither really functioned as a full-time lobbyist. Sara Doan (Sallie) La Fetra, who owned a temperance hotel in the city and served as president of the District of Columbia union, did some lobbying, though mostly on issues concerning the District.[26]

Within a decade of its organization, the WCTU had nevertheless laid a foundation that later rendered it an influential component of the Christian lobbying presence in the capital. By the late 1870s, its primary legislative goal became national, constitutional prohibition, first proposed in Congress by a man who for a time was the WCTU's primary congressional ally and the Capitol's leading advocate of moral reconstruction, Henry W. Blair.

Blair was born around the same time Willard was, in 1834, in New Hampshire. He grew up in a small town there, raised by another family after his parents died. He received some formal education, then read law, and became a solicitor. After heroic service in the Civil War, he returned to New Hampshire to practice law and entered politics, serving in succession in the New Hampshire

Assembly, the U.S. House of Representatives, and then the Senate, where he became chair of the Committee on Education and Labor. A Republican, Blair held fast to party orthodoxy on sound money and the tariff but devoted much of his effort to education and moral reform. A Methodist, Blair thought moral citizens essential to the survival of the republic, which in part was why he spent almost a decade trying, unsuccessfully, to convince Congress to provide federal grants for public schools. Blair had imbibed wartime nationalism, he even talked of the nation as a "living soul," and also thought the national government could legislate morality.[27]

In December 1876, he introduced a resolution to send to the states a constitutional amendment for national prohibition. Blair later claimed he entered the resolution to please "Almighty God." He acted from political calculation as well, though; he wanted to express his appreciation to a group of ministers who belonged to a temperance party but had supported his election. Blair's prohibition amendment forbade the manufacture, sale, importation, exportation, and transportation only of "distilled alcoholic intoxicating liquors," not beer or wine, and none of its provisions were to take effect until 1900. In a speech in behalf of his plan, Blair argued that society had a right to protect the general welfare but individuals had no right to indulge in a practice, like drinking, that inhibited their powers. When they did, government could and should intervene. Blair did not make a moral argument; rather, he cited medical evidence on the dangerous effects of alcohol. He did, though, explicitly reject the idea that moral suasion alone could solve the problems alcohol produced. Moral suasion and law must work together, he explained; the first brought about and made the second enforceable. His experience as a prosecutor trying to enforce New Hampshire's state prohibition law convinced Blair that only national prohibition could be effective. Yet the police power clearly rested with the states, Blair concluded, so the Constitution had to be amended in order for the federal government to act.[28]

In 1877, the year after Blair introduced his amendment, the wctu for the first time endorsed and petitioned Congress for the "prohibition of the importation, manufacture, and sale of alcoholic liquors" as "demanded by the spirit of our Christian civilization." The next year the group expressed its appreciation for Blair's amendment but urged him to add fermented liquors to the alcoholic beverages that would be banned. When the wctu held its annual meeting in Washington in 1881, Senator Blair presented his amendment to the convention. The executive committee pledged to secure one million names on a petition for prohibition and asked Blair to write it. From that point on, the wctu formed a de

Henry W. Blair—senator from New Hampshire and ally of the Christian lobbyists
(Courtesy of the New Hampshire Historical Society)

facto alliance with the New Hampshire Republican. Blair and his wife, a WCTU member, became good friends with Frances Willard; she and other leaders of the WCTU frequently stayed with the Blairs when they were in Washington.[29]

Both the WCTU and the National Temperance Society, however, wanted prohibition applied to beer and wine, not just liquor, and to have it take effect immediately upon ratification, not in 1900, as provided for in Blair's proposed amendment. For a few years, rival prohibition amendments were entered, but in 1887, the WCTU and the NTS convinced Blair to change the form of his proposal to make prohibition both total and immediate. The Sons of Temperance, the Good Templars, and the Prohibition Party endorsed it, and petitions for national prohibition, which had steadily arrived in Congress for several years, incorporated the broader approach as well. In December, Blair entered the revised amendment, and his Committee on Education and Labor held hearings on it, at which representatives of both the WCTU and the NTS testified. Each stressed the need for a national solution to a national problem. Powell cited the antislavery precedent but also warned of the dangers liquor posed among new immigrants and the "colored people of the South," who were "ignorant" and "easily duped" by "liquor demagogues" into supporting the saloon. Society had to protect them, Powell added. Blair's committee agreed and reported the resolution, but the Senate took no action. At the very end of the session, Blair tried to get unanimous consent to consider his resolution but mustered only thirteen votes, all from Republicans. Earlier, in the House, the Committee on the Judiciary reported adversely on a similar resolution, saying only that a prohibition amendment was "unwise and inexpedient."[30]

The WCTU and its allies met with a more positive response in Congress with less ambitious legislation. In 1879, Mary H. Hunt, a science teacher convinced that the public lacked sufficient knowledge of alcohol's terrible physiological effects, proposed to the WCTU a program for scientific temperance education in the schools. With Hunt in the lead, the WCTU launched a campaign to have each state adopt a curriculum that taught the dangers of alcohol. The WCTU also urged the secretary of the interior to adopt an alcohol education program in schools for Native and African Americans as well as in reform or industrial schools.[31]

In 1885, Hunt went to Washington to convince Congress to mandate scientific temperance instruction in every school under its control. Henry Blair entered Hunt's bill that December, and in late January 1886, his committee held hearings on it at which Hunt took center stage. Addiction to alcohol, she began, constituted a worse form of slavery than that in the South before the war, because the latter left the slave's soul free, which the former did not. Moreover, the people held in bondage to drink were not "an alien race" but were "our own sons and brothers, husbands and fathers." Through the efforts of the WCTU and the cooperation of the American Medical Association, Hunt continued, people had begun to realize that alcohol was a "powerful drug" and that even moderate drinking led eventually to dissipation that rendered its victims "moral idiots" incapable of self-government. If they ever became the majority, the nation would descend into "anarchy and misrule." The remedy Hunt actually wanted was national prohibition. "God's law concerning alcohol as a beverage is prohibitory, written from the crown of the head to the sole of the foot of every human being made in His image," she told the committee. "Our law should be in harmony with God's law." But, she explained, when a majority of the people opposed a law, it proved difficult to enforce; for prohibition to work, the people must be educated. When they had been, she added, they will rise up and "denounce evil," and when they do "a *vox populi* is a *vox Dei*."[32]

Only a little over a week after Hunt's presentation, Blair's committee reported a revised bill that required all schools under federal control—those for Native Americans, African Americans, other public schools in the territories, those in the District of Columbia, and the military and naval academies—to provide instruction on the effects of alcoholic drinks and narcotics on physiology and hygiene. The following month, the bill passed in the Senate with little debate; however, it remained in a subcommittee of the House Education Committee for three months. During that time, the chairman received petitions from 87,000 people, many of them clergymen, physicians, and other professionals, 77,000 of whom acted at the behest of the Hunt and the WCTU. Despite the outpouring of petitions and personal lobbying by Hunt, the committee still did not act. Finally, following the advice of her allies, Hunt had her bill brought up on a suspension day, which meant it required a two-thirds vote to pass. With little or no discussion, the scientific temperance education bill passed 209 to 8; the president then signed it into law.[33]

Hunt met with equal success at the state level; by 1895, all but three states had created programs of scientific temperance education in the schools. The campaign appealed to the authority of science to promote abstinence, but as Hunt's congressional testimony showed, the program's champions believed science ultimately reaffirmed God's law. Many temperance reformers thought that Hunt's programs also became "the greatest factor in securing a Federal prohibitory law" by schooling a generation of Americans in the dangers of alcohol and the merits of abstinence. The federal program had limited impact since the national government controlled so few schools. Its passage did demonstrate, though, the WCTU's growing influence as well as the merits of personal lobbying.[34]

In 1887, the year following Hunt's success, and perhaps because of it, the WCTU decided to send a temperance attorney to the nation's capital, and Frances

Willard selected Ada M. Bittenbender to fill the post. Born in 1848, in Pennsylvania, of Presbyterian stock, Ada married Henry Clay Bittenbender, a lawyer. Fearful that she faced a fashionable life that would never allow her to contribute to society, the new bride convinced her husband to move to Nebraska. There she taught school, then edited two newspapers, read law, and became her husband's partner. Always a temperance advocate and after 1881 a supporter of woman suffrage, Bittenbender joined the WCTU. As head of her state's legislative department, she helped guide several bills through the Nebraska legislature. Bittenbender "is a marvel," Willard claimed, "to carry a bill she has no superior."[35]

Bittenbender first arrived in Washington in January 1888 and remained through that session of Congress. She followed the same schedule for the next three years. After the first year, she established an office in the headquarters of the District of Columbia WCTU. Her calling card read: "N.W.C.T.U., Department of Legislation and Petitions, National Supt.," but Bittenbender functioned as a lobbyist. She studied the issues, kept the WCTU membership informed about legislation, circulated and then entered their petitions, wrote legislation, talked with lawmakers, appeared before congressional committees, and generally worked to get bills passed. Her efforts combined an indirect lobbying approach (bringing grassroots pressure to bear on lawmakers) with a direct one (meeting with legislators personally to sway their votes).[36]

During her years in Washington, Bittenbender lobbied for various types of anti-alcohol legislation that had already been proposed, but her and the WCTU's primary cause remained national constitutional prohibition. In 1889, Willard proclaimed Blair's revised constitutional amendment "the keystone to the arch; the goal toward which every eye is strained." That same year, Bittenbender published a plan to secure it, one that called for cooperation with the National Temperance Society and other organizations and included detailed instructions regarding local organization as well as guidelines for petitioning Congress most effectively. Bittenbender, however, did not stay to see her plan carried out. During her years in Washington, she remained interested in the law and—sponsored by Blair—joined the Supreme Court bar, becoming one of the first women to be admitted. In 1891, she went back to Nebraska to run for its supreme court. She lost but remained in the state, practicing law and again working as a journalist. It would be several years before another lobbyist took her place in Washington.[37]

By the time Bittenbender left Washington, temperance forces had settled on goals and tactics that would shape the battle against alcohol, indeed most at-

Ada M. Bittenbender—the WCTU's first full-time lobbyist in Washington
(Courtesy of the National Woman's Christian Temperance Union)

tempts to enact moral legislation, over the next three decades. Both the NTS and WCTU, from their origins during Reconstruction, advocated employing the existing powers of the federal government to discourage the use of alcohol and by the late 1870s, sought to expand its powers to include stopping the sale of alcohol across the nation. Although committed to national prohibition, the reformers worked to pass less drastic measures—prohibition in the territories and the District of Columbia, the creation of a commission to study the liquor traffic, and the establishment of alcohol education programs. The WCTU and NTS sought such legislation in and of itself but also as a means to build both popular and governmental support for further action against alcohol. By 1890, despite twenty years of work by the NTS, the WCTU, and others to convince Congress to pass laws against drinking, their only victory came in the passage of a bill requiring scientific temperance education in federal schools. Hardly precedent setting, it did not expand federal moral powers or even directly involve the government in the legislation of morality. The plan only increased government involvement in a key component of what had been the antebellum moral polity, education. The creation of a commission to study the alcohol problem, which would have involved a similar expansion of the government's role in moral suasion, had substantial support in Congress. However, Democrats and southerners, traditional opponents of legislating morality, blocked its passage.

The attempt to write God, Christ, and the Bible into the preamble of the Constitution had met with even less success in Congress than legislation to expand its powers over the consumption of alcohol. Both efforts, however, testified to the new interest in establishing the religious authority and in expanding the moral powers of the state, interrelated goals central to moral reconstruction. Willard, Blair, and, though a bit younger, Bittenbender had all come of age during the Civil War, and the war and the antislavery precedent clearly played a role in the reformers' new willingness to use federal power. The NTS sought congressional action as early as 1869, and it and the WCTU adopted national, constitutional prohibition as their goal in the late 1870s, when the postwar wave of state prohibition laws had barely begun. From the very beginning of their efforts, moral reformers saw federal power as a means to accomplish their ends and became early, important advocates of expanding the power and influence of the nation-state. The National Association for the Amendment of the Constitution, the NTS, and the WCTU had all also come to realize the importance of influence in Congress. At various times, each had lobbied in the capital and, in seeking a prohibition amendment, had begun to work together. Such cooperation in lobbying Congress would help drive moral reconstruction.

The process would proceed slowly, however. Not until 1917 would Congress endorse national prohibition, the crowning achievement of moral reconstruction. By that time, the partisan and regional divisions over legislating morality had shifted, and a more extensive Christian lobby had developed on the base created by the NRA, the NTS, and the WCTU. By then, too, Congress had already expanded the moral powers of government over sexuality and the family, issues on which, unlike drinking, a public consensus existed.

CHAPTER THREE

Sexuality and the Family

L ust defiles the body, debauches the imagination, corrupts the mind, deadens the will, destroys the memory, sears the conscience, hardens the heart, and damns the soul," railed Anthony Comstock, late-nineteenth-century America's best-known antivice crusader. No doubt many of his contemporaries succumbed to, maybe even relished, lust, but most of the champions of moral reconstruction agreed with Comstock. Lust—unrestrained sexuality—frightened them even more than drinking, which led to a similar loss of self-control. It set loose disruptive forces in society and threatened the family, an institution central to the reformers' conception of a stable, moral social order. The reformers believed government had a responsibility to promote and preserve the family by outlawing polygamy and restricting divorce and to restrain sexuality by eliminating from public life publications or practices that encouraged it. The states had long played a role in regulating marriage and controlling sexuality, but Comstock and other proponents of moral reconstruction, like the NTS and WCTU, lobbied to have the national government assume greater responsibility for families and sexuality.[1]

Congress had banned the importation of obscene matter before the Civil War and passed an act to end plural marriages in Utah shortly after the South left the Union. Enactment of a domestic anti-obscenity law and an effective antipolygamy statute owed less to these antebellum precedents, however, than to the postwar dynamics of moral reconstruction. Efforts to pass both benefited from new attitudes toward national power and the efforts of Christian lobbyists, including Comstock, the first of them to achieve prominence. The fight against polygamy was led by Republicans, who had linked the fate of slavery with that of polygamy in their 1856 platform, but they did not succeed in passing strong legislation until the 1880s, after receiving support from the Christian lobbyists and, in a sign of things to come, from some southerners who felt

freed from the politics of slavery. Unlike anti-obscenity and antipolygamy legislation, a contemporaneous campaign to give the federal government power
over marriage and divorce, linked to the fight to preserve the family in Utah,
revealed the limits both of the precedents and the nation's willingness to reconstruct the antebellum moral polity.

Before the Civil War, most pornography came from Europe, so a ban on importation sufficiently curtailed its distribution. Shortly before the war began,
domestic production increased, and during it, soldiers took a liking to dirty
books and risqué prints. Citing the danger that the rapidly expanding circulation of "obscene books and pictures" posed to men in the ranks, the Post Office
Department in January 1865 asked Congress for the power to ban obscene matter from the mails and to punish people who posted it. A few senators expressed reservations about the idea. A Democrat from Maryland objected to
authorizing postmasters to open and throw out first-class letters. The bill's
sponsor agreed that granting them the power to refuse mail might lead to
abuses; postmasters could conceivably "discard matter which was not satisfac-
tory, politically, to some party." Ohio's John Sherman offered a compromise, an
amendment that forbade postmasters from opening a sealed envelope but allowed them to discard letters they knew to carry obscene matter. Since most
obscenity was mailed from New York City with the sender's name on the envelope, Sherman contended, the change would not undermine enforcement. It
obviously would have, since people in the business would have quickly learned
not to put a return address on their mailings. Sherman's amendment attempted
to balance the perceived need to stop the distribution of pornography with a desire to protect the privacy of first-class letters, a tension between enforcing
morals and preserving privacy that would persist in debates over moral legislation. The Senate chose to protect privacy and accepted Sherman's amendment.[2]

With no further debate in the Senate, and apparently with none at all in the
House, the bill became law in March 1865. It made "knowingly" mailing any
"publication of a vulgar and indecent character" a misdemeanor punishable by
a fine of not more than $500 or imprisonment for up to a year. Seven years
later, in 1872, Congress briefly debated but then reaffirmed the ban on obscenity in the mails during a revision of the postal code. The next year, Comstock
convinced Congress to expand and strengthen the law.[3]

In 1872, Anthony Comstock had just begun his career as an antivice crusader.
Born in Connecticut in 1844, Comstock served in the Union army and, not too

Anthony Comstock—full-time antivice crusader and part-time lobbyist (Reprinted from Trumbull, *Anthony Comstock, Fighter*)

long after he left it, moved to New York City and took a job as a clerk in a dry goods store. In 1868, outraged that a friend had been debauched by an obscene book, Comstock tracked down the man who had sold it and had him arrested. Over the next few years, Comstock spent more and more of his time fighting vice. He tried to stop people from selling obscene books or materials, including "rubber goods"—condoms, diaphragms, and possibly what today would be called "sex toys." He also went after people who performed abortions or even provided information about them or birth control.[4]

Comstock undertook his crusade against obscenity because he feared that exposure to pornography would corrupt the young and force them into a life of sexual dissipation. He objected to the dissemination of information about birth control and abortion for much the same reason. Reading about them encouraged sexual license, he believed, and their actual practice facilitated fornication and adultery. Comstock on rare occasions referred to abortion as murder, but his opposition to it was rooted less in concern for the life of the fetus than his broader fear that abortion, along with the availability of birth control (he drew little distinction between the two) and pornography, encouraged lust.[5]

In explaining Comstock's motivation, contemporary critics and subsequent scholars often stressed his personal psychology or class bias. No doubt both helped explain Comstock's zeal, but an emphasis on either obscures what he had in common with more respected advocates of moral legislation. Like Willard, Comstock clearly acted from a deep, conservative Christian faith. Comstock lived and built his career in that complex, contested borderland between sincere Christian devotion and dangerous religious fanaticism. He hated sin with a consuming passion. He loved and listened to God, saw and despised the devil's influence in the world. His conversations with God or sightings of Satan sometimes took a literal form that would place Comstock, in the minds of many, close to if not over the line into religious fanaticism. Other times, his religious faith seemed little different from that of most of the other Christian lobbyists. He shared with them the belief that unrestrained sexuality was a sin and a threat to the moral order as well as a conviction that moral suasion must be combined with legal sanction. Laws had to be passed to make the social environment safe by eliminating temptations that threatened the young, other Americans, the institution of the family, and thereby the stability of the nation. Laws, in Comstock's mind, should ultimately rest on biblical Christianity. His faith in it as the source of moral authority led Comstock to battle not just purveyors of vice but also religious liberals and others who questioned the Christian faith. In fact, it was an unsuccessful attempt to silence two women he thought guilty of purveying vice and promoting godlessness that prompted Comstock to seek stronger federal legislation against obscenity.[6]

In November 1872, Victoria Woodhull, a popular advocate of unorthodox religious views, free love, birth control, and other reforms, and her sister, Tennie C. Claflin, published in their newspaper an exposé that led to one of the great ministerial scandals of the time. The article charged Henry Ward Beecher, a nationally known pastor in Brooklyn, with seducing Elizabeth Tilton, a parishioner and wife of a good friend. In the same issue, another story told of a virgin seduced and taken to a house of prostitution; it included a reference to the seducer's "*exhibiting in triumph*" on his finger "*the red trophy of her virginity*." Such language combined with attacks on a Christian minister proved too much for Comstock. But when he had the two sisters arrested for mailing an obscene publication, a judge ruled that the existing federal statute did not apply to mailing newspapers.[7]

The failure of the judge to convict Woodhull and Claflin convinced Comstock that current laws against obscenity had to be strengthened. For some years, Comstock had conducted his work under the auspices of a committee of New York's Young Men's Christian Association (YMCA), so he approached its members about seeking to change the federal law. Most of them tried to discourage him, but Morris K. Jesup, a New York financier active in the National Temperance Society, provided money for Comstock to go to Washington. Another wealthy committee member who was the first president of the NTS, William E. Dodge, provided moral support.

Comstock and two associates arrived in Washington in December 1872 during the Credit Mobilier scandal and, apparently, accomplished little. Comstock brought with him a proposed new federal obscenity law, written with the help of Benjamin V. Abbott, a lawyer and brother of Lyman Abbott, the prominent editor of a religious magazine. Either on this trip or the next, Comstock consulted with William Strong, a Supreme Court justice who had served as a vice president of the National Association for the Amendment of the Constitution. Strong helped Comstock tighten his bill and also provided a letter of introduction to Senator William Windom, a Republican from Minnesota. During Comstock's second trip to Washington, in January 1873, he talked with several legislators, including Representative Clinton L. Merriam, a New Yorker who had earlier introduced an anti-obscenity statute for the District of Columbia. Comstock carried a large cloth bag filled with various obscene writings, pictures, and objects that he had confiscated, and when discussing the need for a new law, he would pull out one or two to substantiate his points. Encouraged both by the response of lawmakers and by his supporters in the New York YMCA, Comstock made a third trip to Washington in February. He received permission to set up a little shop of obscenity horrors in the vice president's office in the Senate. There senators examined the displays and listened to Comstock's accounts of vile and disgusting matter mailed to schoolboys and -girls. Once they had, Comstock reported, they quickly promised to vote for any bill that he wanted and that they could convince themselves was constitutional.[8]

By Comstock's third trip, several bills had been introduced, and Abbott agreed to consolidate them. Sponsored by Senator Windom, the revised bill was reported on 14 February 1873, only to be recommitted. The Post Office Committee then rewrote the sections of Windom's bill, using an English obscenity statute as a guide. The revised bill dramatically expanded federal involvement in sexuality. Where Congress had the authority to, in the District of Columbia and the territories, the bill outlawed the sale, and even the possession for sale, of obscene material and information about or articles employed for birth control and abortion. It also extended the existing ban on importing and mailing "obscene, lewd, or lascivious" writing and images to include anything "intended or adapted for any indecent or immoral use or nature," anything "designed for or intended for the prevention of conception or procuring of abortion," and "any written or printed card, circular, book, pamphlet, advertisement or notice of any kind" informing people how to acquire these things. In addition to expanding dramatically the definition of obscene goods, the bill tightened enforcement of obscenity statutes. A judge in any district court could order the seizure of obscene matter and issue a warrant of arrest for violating the new law, and anyone subsequently convicted faced a fine of from one hundred to five thousand dollars or imprisonment at hard labor from one to ten years.[9]

The committee reported the revised bill, but a Democratic senator from Ohio, who agreed with the principle of the bill but questioned some of its provisions, delayed its consideration. When the bill came up again, another senator complained that he did not really understand what was in it and reminded his fellow lawmakers that noble motives sometimes led to unfortunate legislation. Few of his colleagues seemed to share his concerns; the bill passed without further debate.[10]

As the bill worked its way through Congress, Comstock continued to lobby legislators, took time out for a White House reception, and even relaxed by writing letters trying to ensnare ten abortionists he had been pursuing. Despite Senate passage of the bill, he soon became discouraged. Comstock contacted Jesup and Dodge, who intervened with the Speaker of the House, James G. Blaine. Blaine then assured Comstock that he would allow the matter to reach the floor. Far from reassured, Comstock endured a spiritual crisis in which, by his account, he battled the devil and heard the voice of God. Late one Saturday night, his despair became so severe that he could neither sleep nor pray; the next morning he could not even sit through church. Finally, on Sunday afternoon, Comstock broke down, dropped to his knees, prayed for forgiveness, and, as always after bouts with sin or the devil, felt a joyful surrender. He later learned that the bill had passed.

Success owed much to Blaine, who, true to his word, let the bill come up that Sunday morning, only two days before the session ended. Merriam asked the

House to suspend the rules and adopt the Senate bill without referring it to committee. One member objected that the bill should not be passed "in such hot haste," but he was informed that there would be no debate. The first attempt to suspend the rules failed, on a close division of 72 to 79. Merriam demanded the tellers, and the motion passed 100 to 37. The House then passed the bill, and the president signed it the same day.[11]

The "hot haste" in which the Comstock Law, as it became known, passed resulted in imprecise legislation that, in 1876, Congress had to revise. After only brief debate, Congress reaffirmed its earlier decision to use the power over the mails to limit the dissemination of information about sexuality. By that time, the Comstock Law had attracted the opposition of some (but by no means all) religious liberals and unbelievers. Robert G. Ingersoll, late-nineteenth-century America's best-known agnostic, sent Congress a petition, signed by 50,000 Americans, that claimed that the Comstock Law threatened freedom of the press, personal liberty, and other basic constitutional and American principles as well as facilitated religious persecution. Moreover, Ingersoll's petition contended, Congress had passed the law "without the knowledge of any great number of citizens."[12]

When the Senate Post Office Committee considered the petitions in February 1878, Comstock went back to Washington to appear before the committee. He stood, as he described it, alone in a room "crowded with long-haired men and short-haired women, there to defend, obscene publications, abortion implements, and other incentives to crime." They hissed, cursed, and jeered him, but Comstock stood firm, taking comfort in the Scriptures and his faith. What else, Comstock added, could he do "as a man and a Christian"? The opponents of the law testified first, and then Comstock replied. He charged the liberals with fraud in securing names on their petition but devoted most of his testimony to a celebration of the good accomplished under the law. He recounted at length his efforts against smut dealers who collected the names of college students and mailed them demoralizing articles. When Comstock finished, the liberals asked for time for rebuttal, but the committee said it had heard more than enough. It reported to the House that "the post-office was not established to carry instruments of vice or obscene writings, indecent pictures, or lewd books" and that the "statutes in question do not violate the Constitution."[13]

The passage and Comstock's subsequent defense of broad anti-obscenity legislation constituted the first great victory in the Christian lobbyists' attempt to expand the moral powers of the federal government and highlighted many of the factors that would shape moral reconstruction. The initial commitment of the post office to a role in preventing the circulation of pornography came as part of the wartime increase in federal powers. Comstock's subsequent efforts received help from Strong, who had already demonstrated his concern for the religious authority of government by supporting the Christian amendment. Comstock also received crucial support from Jesup and Dodge, who had ties to the National Temperance Society, another group interested in moral legislation. Without their appeal to Blaine the bill might never have passed. That Windom, Merriam, Blaine, and other legislators working with Comstock were all Republicans duplicated the pattern of partisan support of the early legislative campaigns against alcohol.

Like later legislation of moral reconstruction, the anti-obscenity law proved paradoxical. It unquestionably constituted a significant expansion of federal power; it curtailed, along with pornography, the dissemination of knowledge about sexuality, restricted the practice of birth control and abortion, and in doing so, affected the lives of many Americans. Yet Congress directed the law more toward the control of commercial activity than private behavior and, in preventing postmasters from opening sealed letters, even respected personal privacy. Lawmakers also proved cautious in expanding the role of the national government. They employed existing powers over the mails, the District of Columbia, and the territories to justify the expansion of the federal government's role in policing obscenity. Even more telling, rather than create a new bureaucracy to oversee enforcement of the act, the federal government relied on private individuals. Comstock's legislative allies got the postmaster general to appoint him a special agent to enforce the new law; it was in that position that Comstock waged his subsequent antivice campaigns that rendered him the best known, and most notorious, of the Christian lobbyists. Until late in his career, he was paid by the New York Society for the Suppression of Vice, a group formed out of the YMCA the same year the law passed and funded by elite New York business and social leaders. Similar groups operated in Boston, St. Louis, and San Francisco, and each had a special agent of the post office working with it. The use of officials paid by private societies to enforce a federal law typified the halting process of state building in late-nineteenth-century America as well as revealed Congress's reluctance to expand the size of government in behalf of the control of morality.[14]

While Congress quietly expanded the government's power to control the flow of information about obscenity, birth control, and abortion, it renewed the antebellum debate over another issue involving sexuality and the family, polygamy. The 1862 Morrill Act outlawing polygamy had never really been enforced, in part because of Mormon domination of courts and juries in Utah and because the Church of Jesus Christ of Latter-day Saints kept records of marriages secret. The practice of plural marriage continued, even grew, in Utah. Beginning in 1865, Republicans in Congress entered bills to ensure enforcement of the antipolygamy laws. They acted from fears, not unlike those of Comstock, that polygamy encouraged licentiousness, "the lustful and unbridled passions of man," as one legislator put it, and endangered the family, especially by degrading women and mothers. Republicans also criticized the Church of Latter-day Saints for exercising political control in Utah and defended their proposed legislation as necessary to ensure national authority, a theme with considerable public resonance during Reconstruction.[15]

Members of Congress who opposed antipolygamy legislation, like those who fought legislation to control alcohol, attacked it as an attempt "to turn the great law-making power of the nation into a moral channel, and to legislate for the conscience of the people." They also charged it violated the principle of the separation of church and state and claimed that the Constitution prevented the government from judging "the truthfulness or error of any creed," a claim that echoed statements made in Richard Johnson's reports against Sunday mail and Thomas Bayard's speech against a commission on the alcohol traffic.[16]

Most of the early bills to enforce the antipolygamy law rarely made it to the floor or, when they did, passed one house of Congress but not the other. In 1874, the year after passage of the Comstock Law, Congress did enact a law designed to improve enforcement of existing antipolygamy laws by giving exclusive jurisdiction over civil and criminal cases to federal courts and providing a method to limit the number of Mormons on juries. Opponents succeeded in removing more stringent antipolygamy measures from the bill, including a section that allowed the challenge of any potential juror who believed in polygamy. Even before the changes, the bill had been far less severe than earlier antipolygamy bills, which probably explains its easy passage. In the Senate, it passed without a recorded vote and, in the House, received overwhelming support among Republicans, including those from the South, and even from a few Democrats. Most Democrats still opposed the attempt to legislate against polygamy, and from 1875 to 1881, with Democrats in control of the House of Representatives, no additional legislation on polygamy was passed.[17]

The Republicans continued to pursue the issue, however, perhaps in part because, with political Reconstruction drawing to a close, the party needed new issues to mobilize its followers. In 1876, for the first time since 1856, the Republican platform mentioned "that relic of barbarism, polygamy" and demanded legislation to secure "the supremacy of American institutions in all the territories." When Rutherford B. Hayes became president in 1877, he appointed a governor and other officials for the Utah Territory who shared his outrage at polygamy and his party's goal of eradicating it. Over the next decade, these federal officials, especially the U.S. attorneys, became the most influential lobbyists for tougher national legislation. Their efforts would meet with success in the 1880s, in part because of a favorable Supreme Court ruling but also because of a new public campaign against polygamy.[18]

A test case of the Morrill Act had been working its way through lower courts, and in 1879 the Supreme Court issued a decision, *Reynolds v. United States*, that granted the federal government broad powers over morality. Writing for the court, Chief Justice Morrison R. Waite argued that to permit polygamy "would be to make the professed doctrines of religious belief superior to the law of the land, and in effect to permit every citizen to become a law unto himself." It would mean, he observed, that someone who believed in human sacrifices or who wanted to burn herself on her husband's funeral pyre could claim that she did so for religious reasons, and the government could do nothing to stop her. Waite considered that absurd and contended that the First Amendment protected only belief, not conduct. Since polygamy, the conduct at issue in the *Reynolds* case, subverted marriage and threatened the social order, Waite concluded, it was a proper subject for federal control. George Reynolds, an influential Mormon who had agreed to test the law, went to jail, but few other successful prosecutions of polygamy followed. By itself, the *Reynolds* decision did not remove the obstacles to enforcement; new laws were still needed. By the early 1880s, public pressure for them had increased.[19]

Some of the pressure originated in Utah, where economic development had resulted in an increase in the non-Mormon, or gentile, population in the territory. Some of the new gentile residents organized the Liberty Party to challenge the entrenched power of the Mormon-controlled People's Party. The new party aligned itself with the Republicans, since the Mormons worked with the Democrats, who shared their suspicion of federal power over morality. Among the new settlers were many Protestant missionaries who established churches and then sought to convert the natives and to reform the moral environment of Utah. In 1879, one of them, Presbyterian Robert G. McNiece, demanded "The Christian Reconstruction of Utah," by which he meant an end to polygamy, the overthrow of Mormon political power, and "*the establishment of a Christian commonwealth.*" McNiece and other Protestant missionaries in Utah sought to mobilize public support outside of Utah for their crusade against Mormonism and polygamy. One historian has concluded that "their influence, direct and indirect," in generating a public outcry over conditions in Utah "can hardly be exaggerated."[20]

In mobilizing national support for antipolygamy legislation, another group within Utah proved even more important, an association of women. Spurred by the plight of a Mormon woman who regretted and fled a plural marriage, 200 gentile women in Salt Lake City held a meeting in 1878 that adopted a protest, addressed to Mrs. Rutherford B. Hayes and the women of the United States, condemning polygamy as "degrading to man and woman, a curse to children and destruction to the sacred relations of family, upon which the civilization of nations depends." That the practice existed "under the cloak of religion" and that polygamists were permitted to serve in Congress only made the situation "more revolting to our common Christian principles." The association called on women throughout America to petition Congress to abolish this "great sin" and asked Christian ministers to urge women to sign such petitions. A committee distributed them to preachers and other likely allies throughout the nation. Within a month, petitions from women began to arrive in Congress, and their numbers increased in January and February 1879. They came primarily from the midwestern (50 percent), mid-Atlantic (27 percent), and New England (16 percent) states. Dramatically more Republican districts generated petitions than Democratic, at a time when the latter outnumbered the former in the House.[21]

The efforts of both the Protestant missionaries and gentile women in Utah spurred some churches to action. In the early 1880s, many petitions for further legislation against polygamy came from synods, conferences, and other church bodies, more often from Presbyterians and Methodists, but from Baptists and Episcopalians as well. In 1882, the General Assembly of the Northern Presbyterian Church, for example, sent Congress a resolution severely condemning polygamy and Mormonism. This "enormous wickedness," the memorial claimed, had organized "itself into a government" for the defense of polygamy and in defiance of the national government, which had oversight over Utah. The assembly's resolution urged all Presbyterians to fight for legislation and a constitutional amendment to obliterate "this vice, whether as an organized system or as an individual practice."[22]

The campaigns of the missionaries and the association of women helped spur the groups already lobbying Congress on other moral issues to embrace the cause of a federal attack on polygamy. The *Christian Statesman*, voice of the movement to put God, Christ, and the authority of the Bible in the Constitution, ran a series of sermons by McNiece. One of its editors called polygamy "a foul system of licentiousness practiced in the name of religion, hence heinous and revolting" and argued that it "should not be reasoned with, but ought to be stamped out." He and his fellow editors did not believe that schools and churches, two key institutions for moral suasion, alone could destroy Mormonism. Both institutions "are indispensable factors in the reformation of society. But right laws are equally indispensable." Slavery, they added, had not been abolished without laws, and temperance forces were finding the same to be true regarding drunkenness. The *Christian Statesman* therefore demanded congressional action against polygamy. As early as 1868, it endorsed legislation to "reconstruct the society and morals of the Mormons" and, over the next decade, objected to seating a polygamous delegate in Congress, insisted that Utah never be permitted statehood "while she tolerates this other twin relic of barbarism," and sought a constitutional amendment banning polygamy. Although usually in less inflammatory rhetoric, the wctu joined in the condemnation of Mormon polygamy. Its 1879 convention protested "against the abominations of Mormonism practiced upon our sisters in Utah," and three years later, Frances Willard provided an introduction for a pamphlet written by one of the Utah women involved in the antipolygamy crusade. Along with the *Christian Statesman* and the wctu, Joseph Cook, a man who became their ally in moral reconstruction, joined the public clamor for legislation against polygamy and Mormonism.[23]

Cook was born in 1834, the only son of a prosperous farmer in upstate New York. Educated at Yale, where during the Civil War a nervous breakdown forced him to drop out, Harvard, and Andover Theological Seminary, Cook prepared to be and served briefly as a minister. Always ambitious, Cook abandoned the parish ministry to become a public lecturer. From 1875 to 1892, he delivered what he called the Monday Lectures each week from January to March in Tremont Temple in Boston. In April and May and again from October to December, he traveled across the country giving paid lectures. He made a great deal of money, both from his lectures and their publication, and became a prominent public figure. One obituary claimed that between 1875 and 1890 "few men . . . exerted a more powerful and more beneficent influence on public opinion in this country." Cook, like Comstock, Willard, and the other Christian lobbyists, combined an intense, orthodox Christian faith with a commit-

Joseph Cook—public lecturer and part-time lobbyist
(Reprinted from Cherrington, *Standard Encyclopedia of the Alcohol Problem*)

ment to moral reform. "The joy of my life," he wrote his parents in 1879, "is defending good causes & assailing bad ones."[24]

That June, during one of his national lecture tours, Cook went to Utah and discovered what he thought was a very bad cause indeed. Preaching in Salt Lake City, he assailed the Mormons' "false religion & abominable practices." Cook then met with McNiece and the women fighting polygamy, from whom he heard stories of "this special sin of polygamy" that evoked sympathy "for the poor, misguided people" of Utah and made his "blood boil with indignation against their vicious leaders." When he went on the lecture circuit again in the fall, Cook attacked not only polygamy but "Disloyal Mormonism" and called for the disfranchisement of polygamists and a constitutional amendment banning plural marriage. At various stops, he got his audiences to pass resolutions asking Congress to do both. In December and January, back in Boston for his Monday Lectures, he continued his crusade, demanding even stricter laws that would make polygamy a continuous offense and allow conviction solely on the basis of cohabitation, with no need for the government to prove that a marriage ceremony had occurred. Cook also warned that "Bluebeard" sought admission to the Union and urged that Utah never be admitted to a Christian republic. He railed not only against polygamy but "priestly despotism," through which, he believed, Mormon leaders controlled the territory. Their power must be broken, Cook concluded. In March 1880, Cook was in Washington and went to see President Hayes to commend him on his Mormon policy.[25]

The *Reynolds* decision, the efforts of federal officials and gentiles in Utah, the petitions of women and churches, and Cook's national crusade increased the likelihood of congressional action against polygamy. The initiative, however, still remained with the Republican Party. In his 1881 inaugural address, James Garfield called for action in Utah, and after his assassination, Chester A. Arthur, in his first message to Congress, reiterated the call. At the same time, some Republicans in Congress objected to the seating of George Cannon, the territorial delegate from Utah, because he was an admitted polygamist. Despite previous challenges, Cannon had already served four terms. This time he was denied his seat, but not until the passage of new antipolygamy legislation. Twenty-one bills designed to confront the problems in Utah were entered that session, twenty of them by Republicans.[26]

The bill that Congress acted upon was introduced in December 1881 by George Edmunds, a Vermont Republican. Edmunds's bill made polygamy a felony punishable by up to a $500 fine and five years in prison, but, unlike its predecessor, the Morrill Act, it also made cohabitation, which was much easier to prove, a felony punishable by up to a $300 fine and six months in prison. The Edmunds bill also allowed jury challenges of anyone who practiced or believed in "bigamy, polygamy, or unlawful cohabitation." Most important, the bill denied the right to vote or hold office to any polygamist, declared all territorial offices in Utah vacant, and established a five-person commission to oversee new elections to fill them.[27]

Reminded of political Reconstruction and supportive of the Mormons because of their ties to the Democratic Party, one border state and three southern senators led the attack on Edmunds's bill: George Vest, a former Confederate congressmen from Missouri, Joseph Brown of Georgia, Wilkinson Call of Florida, and John Morgan of Alabama. They denounced the Edmunds bill on constitutional grounds and because it threatened local control—even as they affirmed their hatred for polygamy. Brown, though, defended the Mormons' right to believe in it. The Georgian pointed out that polygamy was recognized in three-quarters of the world, tolerated in the Old Testament, and supported, in the Mormons' eyes, by revelation. The government, he added, had no right to disfranchise someone because of what he believed. Edmunds's quick response that the bill did no such thing led to a dictionary duel between the two senators over whether the definition of polygamist included people who believed in it or only those who practiced it. Pressing the attack, Edmunds asked Brown if he really meant to defend "the proposition that in a republican country, a government of the people," that a majority had no right "to say that certain acts, certain conditions, of bodily existence, shall" be a "test of participating in the government of that State[.]" Brown replied that a state had the right "to punish any sort of immorality" but that no federal commission should have the power to disfranchise all who believe in a practice.[28]

Claiming that he could not conceive of anyone who believed in Christianity or republican institutions accepting polygamy as compatible with the American system, Edmunds suggested that opposition to the bill came only from legislators habituated to the defense of slavery. The most vocal Senate opponents were in fact southerners, but southerners were far from solid on the matter. Two other southerners spoke in favor of the bill. With the help of a few Democrats, the Republicans in control of the Senate easily passed the bill, without a recorded vote.[29]

In the House, the debate and vote revealed a slightly more complex alignment of partisan and regional forces. Southerners again were among the most vocal opponents. One of them, Roger Q. Mills of Texas, argued that many supporters of Edmunds's bill really wanted to disfranchise the Democrats in Utah and to take the Mormons' property. But he also urged his fellow lawmakers to remember that the "Pharisees taught their followers to govern other people; Christ taught them to let people alone and govern themselves." The first doctrine led to "despotic governments," he added, the second to liberty and freedom. Mills's views reflected traditional southern thinking as well as the assumptions of the antebellum moral polity.[30]

Southern Democrats proved especially concerned about the provision to create an electoral commission in Utah, which might have served as precedent for intervention in southern elections to enforce black suffrage. The politics of race, if not slavery, still shaped the responses of some white southerners to moral legislation. Despite some opposition, the Edmunds bill passed by a wide margin, 199 to 42. More Democrats voted for the bill than against it, but Democrats cast all of the no votes. Of them, 29 were by southern and another 8 from border state representatives. In all, more southern Democrats opposed the bill than supported it, but 18 southern Democrats did vote in favor of the Edmunds Act.[31]

Edwards and other opponents of polygamy sought still tougher laws. The next year, 1883, President Arthur asked Congress to use "the stoutest weapons which constitutional legislation can fathom" to root out polygamy and advocated replacing the territorial government with a new presidentially appointed commission. The editors of the *Christian Statesman* and other Christian reformers supported Arthur's proposal. Joseph Cook, recently returned from a two-year tour of Europe, devoted his first Monday Lecture of 1884 to the idea. He condemned those who advocated the "use only [of] moral measures against Mormonism" and praised President Arthur's call for the "stoutest legal measures also." Cook made it clear that he wanted legislation directed not just against polygamy but the "priestly despotism" that sustained it. The "twin vices of Mormonism," immorality and disloyalty, must be eliminated, he told his audience. Cook then endorsed Arthur's call for rule by commission as well as a proposal to confiscate some of the church's wealth and use it to build a public school system. He also warned that with Mormon wealth and political influence increasing, if Utah ever became a state and polygamy were therefore protected by states' rights, matters would only worsen, and he reiterated his call for a constitutional amendment granting Congress the power to outlaw polygamy.[32]

In Congress, proposals for a constitutional amendment and a law to replace Utah's territorial government with a commission never got out of committee. A bill to repeal the charter of the Mormon Church and appoint trustees to control its property did pass in the Senate, despite continued southern opposition, but failed in the House. The following summer, the 1884 Republican platform demanded an end to polygamy and a "divorce" of "the political from the ecclesiastical power of the so-called Mormon church"; the statement represented the party's strongest stand yet. Democrat Grover Cleveland, however, won the presidential election, and his party retained control of the House. The new president condemned polygamy but hoped to craft some sort of compromise with the Mormons. The attempt failed. The Mormons had thus far staved off substantial federal interference. Polygamy persisted, although a few polygamists had gone to jail, and, despite a drop in voting by polygamists and an increase in gentile influence, the church still exercised considerable political influence.[33]

As the Mormons held on to their power and their precepts, anti-Mormonism outside Utah increased, fed by many sources. Cook continued his crusade, becoming even more sarcastic in his attacks on polygamy and Mormonism. The WCTU increased its involvement in the antipolygamy crusade. Its magazine, the *Union Signal*, condemned polygamy as a degradation of the home and Utah as "a National brothel, where every year hundreds of young girls and middle-aged women, lured from their transatlantic homes by the sophistry of the Mormon missionaries, are sacrificed upon the altar of American lust." The magazine also condemned Mormonism as a "thoroughly organized system of despotism" that spied on and tried to maintain absolute control over "every individual member." At its 1886 convention, the WCTU created a national department to assist the missionary societies in Utah and to petition Congress in behalf of passage of the "Tucker Edmunds bill."[34]

The bill the WCTU advocated, more commonly known as the Edmunds-Tucker Act, was entered and guided through the Senate by Edmunds in 1887. It amended his own 1882 act by further limiting the power of Utah's courts, adding several provisions designed to facilitate prosecution of polygamy, and expanding the power of federal law enforcement officials in the territory. Its most radical provision sought to destroy not just polygamy but the basis of the hierarchy, the Church of Jesus Christ of Latter-day Saints. It authorized the president to appoint a commission to control the church's considerable financial resources. On the Senate floor the usual southern opponents—Vest, Morgan, Brown, and Call—attacked various aspects of the bill. Nevertheless, it passed by a wide margin. Fifteen Democrats either voted for or expressed their support of the bill; only seven opposed it. Among southern senators, almost twice as many favored as opposed the measure.[35]

When Democrats controlled the House, antipolygamy bills usually died in the Committee on the Judiciary, and its current chairman, J. Randolph Tucker, at first glance seemed unlikely to reverse the precedent. A descendant of an old, proud Virginia family, Tucker was a radical states' rights Democrat. But he was also a deeply committed Presbyterian who believed the union of one man and one woman to be God's will and essential to the stability of society. He therefore considered polygamy both morally wrong and a crime and introduced a constitutional amendment granting the national government power to outlaw polygamy. In the committee report he wrote in favor of sending such an amendment to the states, Tucker argued that one day Utah would become a state and that the nation could not "link in one indissoluble bond" a state that practiced polygamy with others that practiced "Christian marriage." It would be like trying to form a union "between the Asiatic type and European-American type of civilized life" and "would be incompatible and fatal to our peace and progress." A house divided, the southerner seemed to say, could not stand.[36]

Nothing came of Tucker's resolution for a constitutional amendment, but a month later he reported, for the Committee on the Judiciary, the new Edmunds bill. Despite his states' rights views, Tucker acknowledged Congress's right to legislate for a territory (as did most southerners during the debates over polygamy) and its responsibility to prepare Utah for statehood by eliminating polygamy. He and his committee disagreed with the Senate majority on how to do that and dramatically revised Edmunds's bill. The major change, one Morgan had unsuccessfully sought in the Senate, abandoned the idea of a presidentially appointed commission to manage church affairs. Instead, under the new version, the Church of Latter-day Saints would retain its religious authority, but all of its wealth over $50,000 would be seized by the federal government and spent to create a federally controlled public school system in Utah, the proposal Cook and many gentiles in Utah had long advocated as a means to undermine Mormon influence. Tucker's version also reined in some of the Senate bill's enforcement provisions and eliminated a section that denied legitimacy to the children of plural marriages. Although these changes weakened the bill, others strengthened it. The House committee added sections abolishing Utah's militia, the Nauvoo Legion, and, most important, defining polygamy not as an act but as a status, thereby eliminating the problem that the statute of limitations created for prosecuting polygamous marriages entered into years earlier.[37]

Tucker guided his version of the bill through the House, which passed it with no amendments and without a recorded vote. A Senate-House conference committee retained most of Tucker's changes, and its revisions received overwhelming support in both chambers. In the House, all but one Republican voted for the conference report. More significant, Democrats supported it eighty-eight to thirty-nine, with half of the yes votes cast by representatives of the former Confederate states. Slightly over half of southern Democrats voted for the stringent antipolygamy statute. Cleveland then signed the bill. That the Edmunds-Tucker Act became law with a Democratic majority in the House and a Democratic president demonstrated that public opinion, heavily influenced by organized Christians, had managed to make the anti-Mormon crusade far more than a Republican Party project. It also suggested how helpful southern votes could be in passing moral legislation.[38]

In 1890, the Supreme Court upheld the government's right to seize the church's property and the other provisions of the Edmunds-Tucker Act. The decision offered various justifications for the act, including the right of Congress to control the territories. It strongly affirmed the "perfect right" of the "State . . . to prohibit polygamy, and all other open offenses against the enlightened sentiment of mankind, not withstanding the pretense of religious conviction by which they may be advocated or practiced." In a separate case, the Court also upheld an Idaho law that sought to disfranchise polygamists. That decision dismissed any argument that polygamy could be excused because of religious belief. To allow polygamy, it argued, would "make the professed doctrines of religious belief superior to the laws of the land, and in effect to permit every citizen to become a law unto himself." Together, the two decisions went even further than the *Reynolds* decision and made it crystal clear that the Court not only approved of but had enlisted in the war against polygamy. That same spring, a bill was entered in Congress to disfranchise anyone belonging to a church that taught or practiced polygamy.[39]

With the church itself under siege and the possibility of even more stringent legislation to come, George Cannon, Utah's expelled territorial delegate to Congress who became the church's chief lobbyist, went to see James G. Blaine in search of relief. Blaine offered his help but also asked if the Mormons could not "find some way—without disobedience to the commands of God—to bring [themselves] into harmony with the laws and institutions of this country[.] Believe me," Blaine warned, "it's *not* possible for any people as weak in numbers as yours, to set themselves up as superior to the majesty of a nation like this." At about the same time, Democratic senator Vest of Missouri, who had long defended the Mormons, told Cannon's son that he would do nothing more to help the Mormons until they changed their practices.[40]

Cannon's son then returned to Utah to discuss matters with the leadership of the church. After hearing his report and praying about the crisis, Wilford Woodruff, the first president, or leader, of the church, issued a proclamation that seemed to renounce the revelation concerning polygamy. At the government's insistence, the general conference of the church endorsed the Woodruff Manifesto. The following year, 1891, the church acquiesced in the death of its own political party and the creation of national Democratic and Republican parties, with Mormons belonging to both. The church, though, decided that it could exert its influence best through the Republican Party and worked more closely with it. The Utah legislature, which had already outlawed polygamy, created a public school system. Utah seemed to have met all the demands of Congress.[41]

After the election of 1892, Benjamin Harrison issued a general amnesty for polygamists, allowed under the original Edmunds Act, and during Cleveland's second administration, the church got back its property. In 1894, with Republicans in the lead and Democrats feeling they had little choice but to go along, Congress finally passed an enabling act for Utah statehood. It included a statement that "perfect toleration of religious sentiment shall be secured, and that no inhabitant of said State shall ever be molested in person or property on account of his or her mode of religious worship: *Provided*, That polygamous or plural marriages are forever prohibited."[42]

Utah and the Mormons had finally achieved what they had long sought: statehood. The Mormons achieved it without actually abandoning polygamy, at least for a decade or more. Despite the Woodruff Manifesto, polygamists in Utah continued to live with the plural wives they had married before 1890, and even after statehood church leaders sanctioned new polygamous unions. The Republican Party nevertheless claimed a victory for morality and quickly lost interest in the antipolygamy cause as it benefited from new political support within Utah. The *Christian Statesman*, the *Union Signal*, Joseph Cook (who took to referring to Mormonism as "the Latter Day Swindle"), and many other Christian reformers fought statehood to the end and charged that the Mormons had not abandoned polygamy. They would continue the fight against plural marriage—and two decades later helped accomplish what the antipolygamy legislation of the 1880s had sought but not secured.[43]

Many factors contributed to the passage of antipolygamy legislation in the 1880s, which, despite its initial lack of success, constituted an amazing exercise of federal power over morality and religion. Republican partisanship and determination to establish the supremacy of the national government played an important role. Yet significant antipolygamy legislation passed, not in the 1860s or 1870s at the height of Republican power, but in the 1880s, when national outrage over polygamy peaked following campaigns by the Protestant missionaries, the gentile women of Utah, and their allies Cook, the WCTU, and the editors of the *Christian Statesman*. By that time, too, many southerners and Democrats in Congress abandoned their party's traditional politics of morality to support the Edmunds-Tucker Act.

Others did not, and opponents of the legislation offered arguments similar to those employed by opponents of laws to control alcohol. They either argued from a broad conception of personal liberty, claimed that Mormons had a right to believe and live as they chose, or advocated reliance on moral suasion and advancing civilization to convince the Mormons to abandon their immoral practices. Similar arguments during the same period succeeded in blocking

even minor federal action on alcohol but failed to deter the anti-Mormon crusade. Several factors contributed to the greater willingness of Congress and the
nation to act against polygamy than alcohol. No doubt the "otherness" of Mormonism contributed. Utah Mormons were both geographically and religiously
"marginalized"; they lived far away in the West and their beliefs contrasted dramatically with those of most Americans. Since the church had recruited many
of its settlers from abroad, the people of Utah were perceived as "foreign" in a
literal sense as well. At times, antipolygamy agitators exploited anti-immigrant
sentiment; at other times, though, they acknowledged and lamented Mormonism's New England origins. "Otherness" did not fully explain Congress's
greater willingness to act against polygamy than against drink.

Most legislators who voted for federal antipolygamy statutes and the vast
majority of Americans they represented believed plural marriage was blatantly
immoral. They also thought polygamy degraded women and threatened the
family, and, like Tucker, they considered strong families absolutely essential to
the persistence of sound government and a stable social order. Strong families
helped instill morality in the next generation; without them the voluntary system and moral suasion would fail to produce the moral population the nation's
future demanded. Polygamy thereby undermined not just morality but the
moral polity as well. Many supporters of the antipolygamy crusade also associated polygamy with lust and licentiousness; for them, it constituted uncontrolled male sexuality or appetite. In that sense, polygamy involved the same
behavior provoked by obscenity, and fears of obscenity had generated federal
legislation earlier and with less opposition than did the awful practice of
polygamy. Unrestrained sexuality frightened late-nineteenth-century Americans, so much so that they more readily employed federal power to check it
than other immoral behavior.

The crusaders did not limit themselves to polygamy, however; they attacked
the Mormon Church as well. In part, they did so because they believed that
anything that fostered unrestrained sexuality had to be irreligious. Antipolygamy agitators also believed, with good cause, that the Mormon Church intervened in, if not controlled, politics in Utah and therefore violated the separation of church and state. Acting on that principle, and with no appreciation of
the irony involved, they turned the federal government against the Church of
Jesus Christ of Latter-day Saints. Moreover, despite rhetoric about separating
belief and practice, most of the people who supported the war on polygamy
sought to change belief as well as practice. The fact that, as they saw it, Mormons openly celebrated the wanton sexuality of polygamy and even claimed

religious revelation justified it infuriated the antipolygamists. They feared not just what the Mormons did but how the open practice and religious defense of polygamy threatened sexual restraint, family values, and national morality. Christian reformers demanded a single, absolute standard of morality for the nation, one in which competing claims of morality, much less revelation, would not be tolerated.

In the midst of the debate over antipolygamy legislation, Joseph Brown of Georgia proposed a constitutional amendment to make adultery the only legal grounds for "absolute divorce from the bond of marriage" in the territories. If the nation accepted Christ's law on monogamy for Utah, Brown explained, it should adopt it for the rest of the nation as well. He then quoted the tenth chapter of Mark and other Scripture passages to defend his proposed standard of divorce. They showed, Brown contended, that a man who divorced his wife for any reason, save fornication, and then remarried, was just as much a bigamist, just as much "living in a state of adultery," as any Mormon in a plural marriage. Although Brown made his comments in attacking antipolygamy legislation, many of its proponents agreed with him. They equated polygamy, the practice of having plural wives at once, with frequent divorce, which some referred to as having plural wives in sequence. In the 1880s, reformers made marriage and divorce another issue about sexuality and the family that Congress confronted.[44]

In 1880, Joseph Cook invited Samuel W. Dike, whom he had known in seminary, to give a Monday Lecture on the divorce question. Dike had only recently become interested in the cause of divorce reform. A New Englander and a Congregationalist minister, he blamed rising divorce rates on the free black population in the South and the poor and ignorant in New England, but he also attributed them to a fundamental shift in values, a growth in "*selfishness & sensuality.*" For too long, he argued, "society in Christian countries has been making more & more of the *individual* & less & less of the family as an organic unit." On the afternoon of Dike's Monday Lecture, Dike and others met and formed the New England Divorce Reform League. Four years later, the group changed its name to the National Divorce Reform League, but it remained primarily a vehicle through which Dike could agitate issues of marriage and divorce.[45]

Because of Dike's agitation as well as the national debate over polygamy, public calls for a constitutional amendment authorizing a national marriage and divorce law increased in the 1880s. The *New York Herald Tribune* and the *Nation* demanded federal action. Some proponents of stricter laws attributed the rising divorce rate to what they called migratory divorce, in which people, usually of some wealth, secured divorces in states or territories that had lenient divorce laws and a short residence requirement. Other reformers, like Dike, blamed a pernicious individualism for the dangerous rise in the number of divorces. In an 1884 Monday Lecture, Joseph Cook pointed to the "modern spirit of Individualism fostered by Democracy" and went on to offer twelve reasons for rising divorce rates, including a growth in immigration and infidelity, cities, mobility provided by trains, and bad laws. Cook then offered a somewhat shorter list of remedies that included a constitutional amendment. His audience applauded the suggestion and voted to petition Congress to send one to the states.[46]

Such an amendment troubled Dike. He doubted that migratory divorce represented a significant problem. He also realized that southerners would oppose any constitutional amendment on marriage and divorce, claiming it violated states' rights but primarily fearing potential federal intervention in state antimiscegenation laws. In addition, Dike worried that divorce reform would become ensnared in politics.[47]

He therefore moved to head off the attempt to send a constitutional amendment on marriage and divorce to the states by pushing instead for a federal commission to collect and study statistics on the divorce problem. The repeated attempts to create a commission to study the liquor traffic may have inspired the idea, but it differed fundamentally in being intended to avert rather than promote federal legislation. In January 1884, Dike and Elisha Mulford, whose book had made a case for the religious authority of the state, petitioned Congress for a commission on marriage and divorce, and over the next few months, a handful of similar memorials followed. Dike also contacted the Cleveland administration and several members of Congress. He worked principally with Morrill, Edmunds, and Luke Poland, possibly because each had sponsored important legislation against polygamy.[48]

After one attempt at creating a commission failed, Carroll Wright, the director of the Bureau of Labor, volunteered his agency's services in compiling the statistics. In 1887, Congress approved an appropriation for a study by Wright's bureau. Three years later, it completed a study, which Dike and others thought demonstrated a rising divorce rate but revealed migratory divorce to be much less of a problem than many feared. Dike continued to work for changes in state laws, but not a constitutional amendment. Even without Dike's support, agitation for an amendment for federal responsibility for marriage and divorce remained on the agenda of moral reconstruction.[49]

Several factors contributed to Congress's refusal to give the federal government power over marriage and divorce. That Dike, who almost everyone agreed was the nation's leading expert on the question, opposed a national divorce law certainly was a factor. So was opposition from white southerners, worried about federal intervention in antimiscegenation laws. Most important, Americans could not really reach a consensus on standards for divorce. Many women, including some in the WCTU, did not want women trapped in marriages with abusive, drinking husbands and therefore opposed restrictive standards for divorce. Christian reformers argued among themselves over which reasons for divorce the Bible sanctioned; some accepted remarriage of the innocent party after divorce, others did not. The absence of consensus on divorce not only undermined reformers' attempts to give the federal government power over marriage and divorce, it revealed how difficult it could be on some questions to agree on a single, absolute standard of morality, a goal at the heart of moral reconstruction.

Nevertheless, by the late 1880s, often in the cause of restraining lusts and protecting families, Congress had expanded the power of the national government to restrict access to obscenity, abortion, and birth control and had seemingly succeeded in forcing the Church of Jesus Christ of Latter-day Saints to revise its revelation about polygamy. The debate over both types of legislation, along with those over marriage and divorce and alcohol, revealed the fundamental divisions that shaped moral reconstruction. Its proponents, influenced by wartime nationalism and the antislavery precedent, sought to employ federal law as a means to impose Christian morality on a society they saw as threatened by sin and immorality. Opponents, holding fast to the basic tenets of the antebellum moral polity, warned of the dangers such legislation posed to the separation of church and state, advocated moral suasion or state regulation as the means to ensure morality, or even celebrated the liberty of each individual to decide such matters for themselves. Southerners in Congress continued to be the most vocal opponents of moral legislation; their fears of a constitutional amendment clearly helped dissuade Dike from seeking one. But the role of Tucker and other southerners in the passage of antipolygamy laws suggested the beginnings of a shift in the South's role that, over the next three decades, would make the final steps of moral reconstruction possible.

The passage of the Comstock Law and antipolygamy legislation demonstrated the potential power of Christian lobbying. And when Comstock warned of the danger that society posed to the morals of the young, he introduced a theme that became central to the continuation of moral reconstruction. Comstock, Cook, and other Christian reformers soon formed an alliance based on their common analysis of the problems that a rapidly changing America faced and then went back to Congress with a broader agenda of moral legislation.

CHAPTER FOUR

Appetite, Avarice—and an Alliance

B y the time Congress ended its legislative assault on polygamy, many Americans had come to worry far more about other threats to their society. In 1886, Josiah Strong, a Congregationalist minister, published *Our Country*, a book that warned of the danger of Mormonism but cited five other "perils" that threatened America's future—immigration, Romanism, socialism, wealth, and the city. By 1891, the first edition of *Our Country* had sold over 130,000 copies, and within four years, a second sold another 40,000. At about the same time, a whole genre of fiction developed that described the social dangers America faced and called for reform. The most popular was Charles M. Sheldon's novel *In His Steps*, which presented as melodrama many of the problems Strong analyzed and documented. Sheldon's novel told the story of a minister's attempt to follow the example of Christ by bringing moral reform and religious revival to a threatened city. *In His Steps* quickly became an even bigger seller than *Our Country*. The sales of both testified to the fact that in the last two decades of the nineteenth century many Americans shared Strong's and Sheldon's fears of moral decline. These widespread fears helped generate public support for the laws that the Christian lobbyists were able to convince Congress to pass after 1890.[1]

As Strong's list of perils indicated, fears of moral decline were rooted in the massive social changes that the United States experienced in the late nineteenth century. Urban areas grew rapidly, and their expansion created inner cities with saloons and brothels, overcrowded tenements, and crime that frightened many Americans. The equally rapid growth of national industries, which brought with it the degradation of labor, vast new power for distant, impersonal corporations, and tremendous disparities in wealth, did as well. So, too, did the arrival of more and more immigrants, speaking strange languages and practicing different customs. In the face of these disruptive changes, many individuals and communities began a "search for order."[2]

In their own way, the Christian lobbyists were a part of that search, but their way differed and remained distinct from those of better-known reform movements, whose efforts sometimes paralleled the lobbyists'. Frances Willard, the most radical of the lobbyists, briefly pursued an alliance with the People's Party, which championed democratic and radical economic reforms in an attempt to preserve the independence of small producers, especially farmers. Even though Populists in Congress on occasion voted for the lobbyists' moral legislation, most of the lobbyists thought Populism a disorderly and dangerous revolt of the masses. When laborers, for whom many of the lobbyists expressed sympathy and on whose behalf they advocated reform, organized to challenge the power of big business, and especially when they engaged in strikes that turned violent, the lobbyists again saw only dangerous radicalism. The Christian reformers were much more concerned about the moral than the material conditions of workers.

The proponents of moral reconstruction had more in common with two other reform movements of their era, Progressivism and the Social Gospel. Joseph Cook, Wilbur Crafts, and a few of the other lobbyists might logically be considered part of the more conservative end of the spectrum of either Progressive or Social Gospel reformers. But almost all the Christian lobbyists responded to some of the same social changes — immigration, urbanization, and industrialization — as well as sought some of the same reforms as Progressives. Evangelical Protestantism, after all, was an important source of Progressives' commitment to change society, and a least some Progressives made the imposition of morality an important element of their reform agenda. What they shared would make cooperation between Progressives and the Christian lobbyists possible, and in so far as most Progressive reform efforts involved the formation of diverse coalitions, the lobbyists' later efforts might well be considered part of "Progressive reform." Yet Progressives also embraced efficiency, expertise, and other values that were relatively unimportant to the lobbyists and pursued a far more extensive reform agenda. The lobbyists never joined the campaign for democratic reform or economic regulation, often treated as the hallmarks of Progressivism. The Christian lobbyists stood in similar relation with proponents of the Social Gospel. They shared with them a sense of Christian responsibility to make society better, to bring in the Kingdom of God in the here and now, and to use government to do it. But for the most part the proponents of the Social Gospel had a different agenda, one focused on economic reforms not personal morality.

Although the Christian lobbyists had much in common with and sometimes worked alongside the Progressives and Social Gospelers, their efforts are best thought of as independent reform movement. The lobbyists began their campaign to enlist the federal government in their cause earlier than the other two movements, and their cause—imposing or at the very least improving personal morality—was more limited. In addition, the Christian lobbyists operated from a distinctive analysis of the source of the problems American society faced. Where proponents of Progressivism and the Social Gospel focused on the structural and economic flaws in American society, the lobbyists centered their criticism on the individual sins of appetite and avarice.[3]

The "two strongest instincts that to-day defend the liquor traffic and drink habit," Frances Willard wrote in 1888, "are avarice in the dealer and appetite in the drinker." In describing the desire for alcohol as an appetite, Willard chose a word that other Christian lobbyists used frequently. Moralists in the antebellum period had often warned of "passions," and the lobbyists did too, but they more often talked of "appetites," which became their favorite description of the intent to sin. The choice of the trope "appetite" over "passion" marked a subtle but important shift in how reformers described the origin of sinful behavior. Both passion and appetite originated within the individual and were considered natural unless allowed to rage unchecked. Appetite, though, was a more appropriate trope in an emerging consumer economy. It evoked an image of people who desired not to attack, as passion might lead them to do, but to attain, to consume, to seek self-fulfillment and self-gratification. The self was central; appetite was a predominately individual emotion. Divorce was not the only immoral behavior that lobbyists blamed on unrestrained individualism.[4]

Appetite led to sin, and sin seemed especially dangerous to the Christian lobbyists because they considered sins interconnected and believed committing one led almost inevitably to others and, in the end, to total degradation. Some reformers even suggested a physiological basis for the descent into degeneracy. Smoking cigarettes, according to one speech printed in the WCTU's *Union Signal*, "affects the nervous system, weakens the will power and destroys the ability of the boy to resist temptation, and, because of this, he easily falls a victim to those habits which not only destroy the body, mind and soul, but irresistibly lead him into a violation of the laws of his state." The first step down what rapidly became a steep slide into degeneracy did not have to be tobacco; it could be some other form of undue and artificial stimulation. The "stimulation of the nervous system by any artificial means, whether alcohol, opium or tobacco, is morally as well as physically injurious," wrote the editors of the *Christian Statesman.* "Not the least of its evil effects is the grieving away of the Holy Spirit by the deliberate indulgence of a fleshly appetite in opposition to the judgment and perhaps even to the conscience."[5]

Substances did not pose the only danger. "There is a Chamber of Imagery in the heart of every child," Anthony Comstock contended, that served as an "art gallery" or repository for all that he or she had seen. Each child's chamber, Comstock explained, was bombarded with lewd and vulgar images from many sources—newspapers, accounts of society scandals, even novels. When his or her "Chamber of Imagery" became too tainted with obscenity, "the fires of remorseless hell are awakened in the soul. Fountains of corruption, . . . soon . . . break down with volcanic force rending asunder all the safeguards to society." Not all reformers agreed on the physiological aspects of degradation, but all concurred with Comstock that evil influences could overstimulate natural appetites and lead to moral disaster.[6]

The lobbyists used various imagery to describe people who had experienced that decent into hopeless immorality. Wilbur F. Crafts, one of the most important Christian lobbyists, in one sermon called them both "savages" and animals. But he and the other lobbyists often compared their plight to that of slaves. Like Elisha Mulford, whose book *The Nation* they praised, some argued that "action which springs immediately from impulse or appetite is not free. The pursuance of a blind instinct, or the subjection to a strong passion, is the negation of freedom." Drinking, gambling, and many other of the sins that moral reformers opposed negated freedom in just that way, and Christian lobbyists spoke of drunks and gamblers as "slaves" who had lost their freedom. The metaphor dated at least to St. Paul, but the long decades of America's debate over slavery increased its familiarity and emotive power. Thinking of those who succumbed to their appetites as slaves also had another advantage; it made them victims as well as sinners, victims of someone else's avarice.[7]

Avarice was the other major trope, along with appetite, that the Christian lobbyists employed to describe the problems facing American society in the late nineteenth century. On occasion, they blamed avarice for leading individuals directly into dissipation. All people were born with "a desire to posses riches," Comstock argued, and as they grow older, they desire things that their "appetite craves"—a home, luxuries, social standing. Gamblers then exploited their appetites, Comstock continued, and besieged their prey with promises of wealth that overpowered and transformed them. More often, the lobbyists blamed avarice indirectly, claiming that it drove those who, like gamblers, sought to grow rich by exploiting normal human appetites. "The man who is controlled by greed for gold," wrote one opponent of the saloon, "will sell liquor, though he makes brutes of his customers; though he incites them to crime; though he breaks mothers' hearts and deprives wives and children of the necessaries of life." Crafts added tobacco, prostitution, fashion, and magazines to the evil influences that the lust for gold spread through society. He and other moral reformers had no sympathy for sellers of sin who exploited appetites; no one, the lobbyists believed, had a right to profit from human frailties. They therefore harshly criticized the businesses and businessmen who purveyed vice. When they did, though, the Christian lobbyists still attributed the problems of society to the failings of individuals. They did not criticize industrialists involved in the honest pursuit of profit or condemn the American economic order. And, since the lobbyists blamed the problems of society on individual sins, on appetite and avarice, they sought not the reorganization of the American political economy, as many in the better-known reform groups did, but the reconstruction of the antebellum moral polity.[8]

The Christian lobbyists never abandoned the older moral polity's central tenets. Good Victorians, they still celebrated self-control; faithful Christians, they continued to believe individual conversion essential to changing people and society. For example, in his most famous lecture, "Ultimate America," Joseph Cook recounted a dream that included visions of the dangers lurking "under emigrant wharves," in "crowded factories," and along "the poisonous alleys of great cities." Against the gloom, he juxtaposed the efforts of various historic personages who represented the dispersion throughout America of "liberty," "intelligence," "property," and "conscientiousness." The dream ended only after Cook saw all of the personages standing in the pierced palms of Christ, who said of the historical figures and their contribution to society, "Ye are efficient, but I am sufficient." Cook and the other lobbyists continued to believe individual conversion central to the Christian faith and to the creation of a moral society, which also distinguished them from many proponents of the Social Gospel.[9]

Nor had the lobbyists completely lost confidence in republican motherhood, the voluntary system, and moral suasion. They advocated parental instruction, Bible reading, and church attendance. Both the National Temperance Society and the WCTU circulated temperance literature and sought to secure pledges of abstinence. More than antebellum moral reformers, though, the Christian lobbyists no longer felt moral suasion sufficient to ensure the moral citizens necessary to the survival of a republic. Their loss of faith in the sufficiency of the central institutions of the antebellum moral polity paralleled a loss of faith in the people's moral judgment, which resulted from, as so much in moral reconstruction did, changes rooted both in the Civil War and in the new society developing about them in the late nineteenth century.

The lobbyists' loss of faith in individual moral judgment resulted not only from their fear that immorality increased because of the Civil War but also from the postwar expansion in the composition of "the people." Over four million former slaves, freed by the Civil War, constituted a new component of "the people," one that many white reformers feared was not morally ready for citizenship. Some northern reformers blamed slavery for the problem; enslavement, they argued, had, at best, not prepared blacks for freedom or, at worst, degraded them, especially women whose masters had abused them. Others, displaying their own racism that worsened in the years after Appomattox, felt the freed people were simply incapable of controlling their own appetites. Whether the lobbyists blamed slavery or the former slaves, they attributed various moral problems to African Americans in the South. In his testimony before Congress in behalf of prohibition, the NTS's Aaron Powell had blamed blacks for increases in intemperance in the South, and Cook and Samuel Dike had resorted to a similar argument to explain rising divorce rates.[10]

Immigrants in the North, more and more of whom were from regions and cultures very different from those of most middle-class Americans, were a second new component of "the people" that worried the Christian lobbyists. Like Strong, whose *Our Country* they praised, the lobbyists thought that immigrants had only "meager or false" "moral and religious training" in their native lands and, in a strange new country, all too quickly succumbed to appetites and avarice. Both immigrants and African Americans, like Mormon polygamists, represented the "other," people so different that the Christian lobbyists, like many other Americans, readily associated them with evil and sin. In arguing that laws would be needed to make all dangerous "others" behave morally, the white middle-class Christian lobbyists displayed their class, racial, and ethnocentric biases. Their efforts became attempts at "social control" of the lower classes, but not simply that.[11]

The Christian lobbyists had lost confidence in the moral judgment not only of the "others" but of their own. At the WCTU's first national convention, one member proclaimed that all "sons of this land are liable to become drunkards, the high in life as well as the low. None are exempt." Crafts agreed that the rich could also become slaves to their appetites. He and other reformers attributed the rising divorce rate, in part, to self-indulgence. Even as they spoke of the immoralities of the high and low, middle-class lobbyists never spared sinners within their own ranks. Comstock worried about the impact of gambling and obscenity on clerks, a position he himself held when he first moved to New York, and all classes. Crafts, in a sermon on the moral perils society offered, focused on the danger they posed not to the rich or to the poor, nor to the immigrant or dandy, but to a generic "youth." "Our boys" generated special concerns among most of the lobbyists. WCTU members sought "to help the mother in her unequal warfare with the dram-shop for the preservation of her boy," Willard wrote in 1883. Almost twenty years later, a prohibition petition to Alabama's senators complained that there "is no way to save our sons from a drunkard's grave but to demand the voice of the moral people shall be heard and not only heard but *obeyed* by the federal government."[12]

The repeated use of "our boys" or "our sons" testified to the Christian lobbyists' fears for their own, but it also indicated they worried more about males than females. Moral reformers knew that women as well as men yielded to their appetites; on occasion, they added "our girls" to "our boys" or, more rarely still, singled out young females for special attention. The woman who at the first WCTU convention warned of the danger drink posed for all classes also reminded her listeners that young women, too, "are tempted by the monster Intemperance." Three years later, WCTU representatives passed a resolution stating that in their "zeal for the reformation and salvation of men," they should "not neglect, an earnest effort for the redemption of women who are victims of the same and kindred vices." For a time, the WCTU even had a department for "Work Among Intemperate Women."[13]

Nevertheless, in the fight for prohibition and other moral crusades, references to males vastly outnumbered those to females. In large part, the lobbyists' emphasis on "our boys" reflected social realities. Young males apparently did drink at a much higher rate than women, and no doubt they succumbed more frequently to the other vices that the Christian lobbyists condemned, smoking and gambling especially. Women, obviously, participated in polygamy and prostitution, but generally reformers did not attribute their participation to their "appetites" but treated them as victims of male lust. Portraying women as victims rather than perpetrators of these sins reflected the persistence of cultural assumptions about the moral superiority of females as well as the late-nineteenth-century demographics of public sin.[14]

The emphasis on the danger to "our boys" and the inclusion of all social classes in their rhetoric of endangerment reflected the other major factor behind the lobbyists' loss of confidence in individual moral judgment, their sense that American society had become a far more dangerous place. In the early years after the Civil War, reformers feared that the war had fostered immorality, but by the 1880s they feared changes in society more. With Comstock, they believed it filled with—in the words of the title for one of his books—*Traps for the Young*. Saloons, gambling dens, decadent theaters, and houses of prostitution were only the most obvious traps; others, like obscenity and information on birth control, came in the mail or the newspaper. All of them had a subtle, cumulative effect by appealing to the "appetites and passions."[15]

Other reformers, again like Comstock, warned that American society had become filled with things that perverted the normally healthy appetites and passions of youth. Mary Livermore, a wctu activist, pointed to the "ten thousand saloons, gambling hells, and houses of vice, made attractive by art and wealth, and all under the protection of law" in which the young faced temptations rarely confronted by their fathers and grandfathers. Crafts cited "the indecent pictures of theaters, of tobacconists, and news-dealers, and by the fashions borrowed from the Paris *demi-monde*, and by the American *demi-monde* themselves, whose dens are as well known and as quickly accessible to tempted youth as any kind of business in our cities." Cities exacerbated the problem because they harbored so many "traps" in an environment that overstimulated appetites.[16]

Convinced that new people, former slaves and immigrants, could not be counted on to exercise moral choice and that society had developed so many temptations that their own boys might not be able to either, the lobbyists believed that the antebellum moral polity's means of ensuring a moral citizenry—Republican mothers, the churches, revivals, moral suasion—had to be reinforced by strong moral laws. They rarely claimed that laws alone would make individuals moral. Christian lobbyists would occasionally promote laws, as they had in the antipolygamy statutes, that actually sought to control individual behavior. More often, as in the Comstock Law that sought to end the distribution of obscene matter, they championed laws to control appetites by outlawing commercial activities or removing the traps that endangered the young. Christian lobbyists argued only that moral laws made society a less dangerous place, thereby giving moral suasion and individual conversion a better chance to succeed and protecting individuals, especially young males, from that first sin that led to dissipation and slavery.

The increased emphasis on law, especially on federal law, to ensure moral citizens and a moral environment was the most radical change to the moral polity that the lobbyists advocated. New laws, even when directed primarily against commercial vice, still restrained personal liberty, one of the values that the antebellum polity had celebrated. The lobbyists often obscured the issue by calling sinners victims or slaves, to whom moral laws brought freedom. On other occasions, though, they admitted the need to restrict liberty by contrasting it with license. "Personal liberty that means entire freedom from restraint is absolute foolishness," said the editors of the *Christian Statesman.* "The insane cry of 'personal liberty,'" echoed Willard, "is clarifying thoughtful minds by the perception than none of God's creation has so little liberty as man to do as he pleases, unless he pleases to obey God's natural laws." Unlike license, in the minds of reformers, liberty operated within the laws of God and respected the rights of others. One's liberty to extend one's arm, in a popular analogy of the time, ended where someone else's nose began. All of society, not just individual noses, needed protection from evil doers. However they defended it, the Christian lobbyists accepted the necessity of some restrictions on personal liberty. Legal restraints were essential to maintain, even more to advance, civilization—to preserve and perfect the moral order. Many believed that if that moral order were properly constructed, as Willard put it, "a man's personal liberty will never be consciously to him, restricted by law."[17]

In constructing a proper moral order, or polity, the Christian lobbyists acted from their fears of appetite and avarice, their sense that both a new people and a changing, more dangerous society demanded additional means to ensure a moral citizenry. The lobbyists' emphasis on individual failings, sins they called them, led them to embrace a distinctive agenda; they never lobbied for changes in labor laws or industrial reform, for instance. Instead, when the National Association to Amend the Constitution and the Woman's Christian Temperance Union broadened their legislative agendas in the 1880s, they included only issues of personal morality—drinking, divorce, sexuality, gambling, and such. During the 1880s, the two groups also solidified their organizational base and, at the end of the decade, formed an alliance with each other as well as Anthony Comstock, Joseph Cook, and others interested in legislating morality.

After Congress in the early 1870s rejected calls to rewrite the preamble of the Constitution to include God, Jesus, and the authority of the Bible, the National Association for the Amendment of the Constitution redefined its goal to be "to *christianize the government.*" In recognition of the new agenda, in 1875 the group changed its name to the National Reform Association (NRA) and later pledged to address every "moral and religious issue which presents itself before the nation." The NRA supported the rights of the Chinese, Indians, and African Americans, opposed secret oaths, worried about the fate of laborers, fought to keep the Bible in the schools, and advocated arbitration to end war. When, in 1881, the NRA asked its supporters to petition Congress in favor of amending the Constitution and keeping the Bible in the schools, it also urged petitions calling for an end to Sunday mails, a national law on marriage and divorce, a commission on the alcoholic liquor traffic, and a prohibition amendment. For a time, securing laws to ensure personal morality became the NRA's primary goal.[18]

With a new name and an expanded agenda, the National Reform Association sought to build popular support. It held annual national meetings and established a few district associations, but they proved short-lived. Organizing fell to district secretaries, usually around seven in number, not all of them full time, who traveled about the country, contacting pastors and churches, and holding public meetings in behalf of the cause of Christian government. The district secretaries also distributed the many pamphlets and tracts that the NRA prepared; national headquarters also mailed them to ministers, college professors, and congregations. The NRA's most influential, although unofficial, publication was the *Christian Statesman,* founded and edited by David McAllister and T. P. Stevenson, both ministers in the Reformed Presbyterian Church who became the NRA's most important leaders.[19]

Despite these efforts, the NRA never fully succeeded in establishing a popular or national base of support. It boasted of its diverse membership and did attract a few prominent supporters from outside of the Covenanter tradition: William Strong, a mainline Presbyterian and the Supreme Court justice who helped Comstock with the preparation of his law; Sylvester A. Scovel, another mainline Presbyterian and president of Wooster College; Charles Hodge and his son A. A. Hodge, theologians at Princeton Seminary; Felix B. Brunot, an Episcopalian whom Ulysses S. Grant appointed to head his Board of Indian Commissioners; and Julius Seelye, a Congregationalist and president of Amherst College who served one term in Congress. Strong, Scovel, and Brunot were each president of the NRA at one time. Most of the leaders and district secretaries, however, were members or ministers in the small Reformed Presbyterian Church or the United Presbyterian Church, both denominations with roots in the Scottish Reformation. A large part of the NRA's relatively small budget, between five and ten thousand dollars during the nineteenth century, came from the Reformed Presbyterian Church or the group's founder, Pennsylvania industrialist John Alexander, a member of the United Presbyterian Church.[20]

Much of the NRA's membership also came from these denominations. The group's strength lay in Pennsylvania, Ohio, New York, Iowa, Illinois, Kansas, Indiana, Nebraska, and Vermont—states where the two denominations were strongest. At first all-male, in 1875 the NRA invited women to participate, and a few became quite active. The NRA also welcomed African American members and sent agents, including one prominent African American, to the South to recruit them. Many of the leaders of the NRA had been abolitionists and continued to be very critical of the white South after the war. In the late 1880s, though, the antisouthern rhetoric began to wane. By the early twentieth century, one of its leaders included the acknowledgment of God in the Confederate Constitution as an important step toward passing the Christian amendment. Long before that, the NRA sent emissaries south to recruit white southerners as well as black. Only a few southerners—white or black—became active in the NRA, however. Despite efforts to broaden it, the NRA's institutional base was limited to New York and a few midwestern states, and its membership remained overwhelmingly white, male, Covenanter, middle class—and small.[21]

National meetings usually attracted around 400 delegates, and the NRA's total membership was probably somewhere between two and three thousand. Subscriptions to the *Christian Statesman*, which had as much as or more public influence than the organization itself, may at times have exceeded that. In 1876, it claimed to have 3,000 subscribers and a readership of at least 10,000, since copies went to churches and libraries. The editors also sent additional copies of certain issues of the *Statesman* to YMCA reading rooms, college and theological libraries, and other institutions through which they hoped its message might be spread. A 1905 compilation showed that the magazine was mailed to forty-four states or territories but that most went to the six or seven states where most NRA members lived.[22]

Even though both the readership of the *Christian Statesman* and the membership of the NRA remained very small, the association had greater influence than the numbers would suggest. Stevenson, McAllister, and other indefatigable NRA leaders willingly worked with moral reformers who did not always em-

T. P. Stevenson (above) and David McAllister (right)—editors of the *Christian States-man* and leaders of the National Reform Association (Reprinted from Glasgow, *History of the Reformed Presbyterian Church*)

brace their theological perspective or even their attempt to put Christ in the Constitution but who shared their belief in the need for a Christian government that legislated morality and created a moral order.

In the 1880s, under Frances Willard's leadership, the WCTU developed a national organization and popular base only dreamed of by the NRA. An inspiring orator possessed of amazing personal charisma, Willard traveled across the country organizing local WCTU unions. Her efforts contributed to the success of the WCTU, but she did not build the organization alone. Her charisma not only at-

tracted, it inspired; she perceived and nurtured the latent leadership of women new to public life. Together, they created an effective national organization, kept relatively harmonious by Willard's willingness to compromise and hesitancy to confront, but one with a modern, hierarchical organizational structure. Willard ran the wctu through an executive committee, composed of Willard and other national officers, and through national superintendents who directed functional departments. In addition, the wctu paid national organizers to recruit members and form state and local groups. State organizations mirrored the national structure, with a president and functionally organized departments headed by a superintendent; local groups, called unions, had similar organizational structures, although they were usually less well developed.

With Willard's leadership, traveling lecturers, and an efficient organization, the wctu began to create a national base. The group had begun in the Midwest, and throughout the nineteenth century its strength lay there and in the mid-Atlantic states; over half its membership lived in those two regions. The New England states had fewer members, but the percentage of WCTU members there was almost double that of the region's percentage of the nation's population. The number of members, in absolute and relative terms, in the West, which was only beginning to be settled, and the South lagged well behind those in other regions.[23]

The WCTU, even earlier than the NRA, perceived the need for southern support. Its first president, Annie Wittenmyer, put the case succinctly: "We can never gain a decided national victory till we secure the co-operation of the South." Early efforts to organize the South, however, met with little success. Matters improved in the 1880s, when Willard made several tours through the region. Her charisma proved almost as powerful below the Mason-Dixon line as above it, and she recruited a cadre of leaders and many new members. Willard and the WCTU also made concessions to secure southern support. "We cannot ask the South with its different population and rearing" at the present time to endorse the vote for women, Willard told the 1886 WCTU national convention. Nor could southerners, with their intense loyalty to the Democratic Party, be expected to support the Prohibition Party. In 1887, the WCTU decreed that no state union had to endorse any aspect of the national group's work, save "the total abstinence pledge" and the constitution of the national union. As Willard's reference to the South's "different population" suggested, she and the organization also became somewhat sympathetic to white southerners' views on race relations and gave them most of the responsibility for work among southern blacks. Despite the concessions, opposition to the WCTU among white southerners persisted, especially among church leaders and many others who opposed women taking such a public role.[24]

The WCTU was even less successful in recruiting black southerners than it was with white southerners. Over the years, three or four African American women and a few whites, some of them southerners, strove to recruit black women to the cause. Several all-black state organizations formed, but their membership remained small. The WCTU's constituency not only was made up overwhelmingly of whites but was limited in other ways as well. Most members came from the middle and upper classes and the evangelical denominations. Nevertheless, the WCTU became the largest organization of women in the country and, among the Christian lobbyists, the first group to establish an extensive national presence. In 1892, when its nineteenth-century membership peaked, the WCTU had 154,213 members in over 7,800 local unions located in every state.[25]

The WCTU's success cannot be explained solely by Willard's charisma or a successful organizational strategy; surely a large number of American women embraced the cause. Some, like Willard, sought to enhance the rights and role of women. Most worried about the danger males, especially males who drank, posed for women and their children. Gendered perceptions of their lack of power to defend themselves influenced their support for the use of government to protect them. Yet many members wanted government to protect boys and men as well. Although their status as women made members of the WCTU more willing to seek government aid, their convictions as Christians probably had more to do with why they campaigned for moral legislation. The women of the WCTU shared with male Christian lobbyists concerns about appetite and avarice as well as a vision of a moral society resting in Christian government. The WCTU's most rapid growth occurred in the late 1880s when the WCTU, like the NRA, embraced the cause of Christian government and expanded its reform agenda.

In early 1883, Willard wrote of the miraculous way in which the light of Christ had entered and changed individual hearts, homes, and churches. Now, she continued, Christ was entering the widest circle of all, the government, and better laws would be the result. All Christians, she urged, should work for Christian government. Four years later, in an address to the national convention, Willard more explicitly enunciated her vision of her organization's role. "The Woman's Christian Temperance Union, local, state, national and world-wide, has one vital, organic thought, one all-absorbing purpose, one undying enthusiasm, and it is that *Christ shall be this world's king.*" Christ's reign, Willard went on to explain, would bring a world of equality between men and women in which separate spheres would disappear. The new society, however, could emerge only after the destruction of intemperance, impurity, and the tobacco habit—the three great enemies of females and males. Willard then asked the national convention to pass a resolution declaring that "Christ and His law" are "the true basis" of the law and the supreme authority in the government. That year, 1887, and for the following three years, delegates endorsed such a declaration. The 1890 version, for example, stated: "While discountenancing all union of church and state, we do affirm our belief that God in Christ is the King of Nations, and as such should be acknowledged in our government, and His Word made the basis of our laws."[26]

By the mid-1890s, Willard herself shied away from talk of Christian government, but the WCTU as a whole did not. The 1896 national convention resolved that "Christian citizenship" is "one of the great needs of the day. Christian prin-

ciples and ethical standards must be introduced and maintained in all political relations." To further that end, the WCTU created a "Department of Christian Citizenship." Its first superintendent defined the term to mean "Christ in
each citizen, in the primary or the convention, at the polls and in all offices, legislative, executive, judicial." She also proclaimed "Jesus Christ . . . the Savior and
the Lord of the state as well as of the individual" and called for the incorpora-
tion into the state "the principles of His divine government."[27]

At about the same time the WCTU embraced the goal of Christian government, Willard enunciated what came to be called the "Do Everything" policy,
an expansion of the group's reform agenda well beyond woman suffrage and
temperance. Whereas in 1882, only three of the WCTU's twenty national departments involved anything other than temperance work, by 1896, twenty-five out
of thirty-nine dealt with other issues. They included a variety of projects, such
as securing police matrons for jails, providing flowers for prisoners, and helping laborers. Several departments concentrated on reforms embraced by the
movement for the federal legislation of morality: suppression of prostitution,
impure literature, and the use of cigarettes and narcotics as well as the promotion of sexual purity and Sabbath observation.[28]

Aware of their similar agendas of moral reform, the National Reform Association began to move toward a tacit, possibly formal, alliance with the WCTU. In
1883, Mary A. Woodbridge, president of the Ohio WCTU and the WCTU's legislative superintendent, spoke at the NRA's national convention. She became a
vice president of the NRA and later a national officer in the WCTU, and as a result, played an important role in bringing the two groups together. In 1884,
Willard sent a pro forma letter of support to the NRA convention, but, more
important, the NRA's T. P. Stevenson addressed the WCTU's national meeting.
He praised the WCTU for its role in restoring "woman to her original place as
man's helper in all the work of life—in the care of the commonwealth as well
as in the care of the family"—and for committing itself to the full panoply of
reforms sought by the NRA.[29]

In 1885, the NRA declared that it "naturally allies itself" with other reform
groups working to promote temperance, the Sabbath, and revisions in marriage and divorce laws, as well as with those seeking to suppress polygamy, obscene literature, and gambling. NRA leaders probably had the WCTU in mind,
and cooperation between the two groups increased. Stevenson and Willard
began to meet in 1886, and in 1887, she allowed him to send a letter to the mem-

bership of the WCTU urging support for the Christian amendment to the Constitution. That same year, Willard gave an address on God in government at the annual meeting, much to the delight of the NRA leadership. The WCTU's 1889 convention not only heard from an NRA representative but praised his organization's "noble work for Christ in our Nation's government and law." Later that year, the NRA convention reciprocated with a statement of praise for the WCTU. In 1893, the WCTU again saluted the National Reform Association, whose "aim is identical with that" of the WCTU, "to enthrone Christ the King of the cloister, the camp and the court."[30]

In 1894, the NRA approached the WCTU's general officers about the possibility of merging the two societies, but the WCTU leaders rejected the idea. They may have had reservations about the NRA's distinctive theological doctrines and certainly preferred to remain an all-female association. Earlier, Willard had explained the need for a single-sex effort. When men opened the halls of Congress to women, she said, then females and males could work together in a new republic. Until then, women had to have their own associations in which to develop the skills necessary to hold their own with men. Women had to "first show power, for power is always respected whether it comes in the form of a cyclone or dewdrop." Despite their rejection of a merger, the WCTU again in 1895 and in 1896 passed a resolution extending its "hearty sympathy to our brothers of the National Reform Association, whose efforts are parallel to ours on many lines."[31]

As the NRA and the WCTU established close ties, they both reached out to Anthony Comstock, who like them saw himself as battling for morality in a society where appetite and avarice raged out of control. The *Christian Statesman* first praised Comstock's efforts in 1872, later referred to him as a "heroic guardian of the public virtue," and in 1878 wrote that he had a "stronger claim than any other American citizen in the last five years on the gratitude of his countrymen." The *Statesman* published an article by Comstock, and he spoke at one NRA convention. The WCTU forged even closer ties with the nation's leading crusader against vice. In 1883, its annual meeting extended its "tender heartfelt thanks" to Comstock and pledged him their "hearty co-operation." Two years later, he addressed the WCTU annual meeting, and Willard praised his efforts in behalf of social purity. The WCTU department to promote purity in literature and art for a time made Comstock an official adviser. Its longtime superintendent, Emilie D. Martin of New York City, consulted often with Comstock; her husband served on his executive committee.[32]

The NRA, WCTU, and Comstock all had ties with Joseph Cook. Cook invited

Comstock, Willard and other WCTU leaders, and at least one representative of the NRA to deliver Monday Lectures. Cook, in turn, addressed an NRA convention and agreed to write articles for the *Christian Statesman*. Cook also spoke to the WCTU national convention, which he referred to as "the 'feminine Congress of the United States.'" Willard introduced Cook, who weighed over 200 pounds at the time, as "our largest brother-in-law." As such banter suggested, the contacts among the Christian lobbyists developed into personal friendships. Cook and Comstock were particularly close; they had summer homes in upstate New York across Lake George from each other. Cook and his wife, Georgiana, an active WCTU member, also became friends with Willard, Mary Hunt, and other leaders of the WCTU. Cook's ties with Stevenson of the NRA were not as close, but the two not infrequently consulted on reform matters. On at least one occasion, Willard and Stevenson spent a weekend together at Cook's summer home, where the three discussed reform strategies.[33]

In the mid-1880s, Cook decided to found a religious journal. He would publish his Monday Lectures in it, but it would also serve as a forum in which to discuss all the "great-issues of *Our Day*," which he quickly settled on as the title for his magazine. *Our Day*, he explained in late 1886, would "bring together in its support a syndicate of specialists who will combine aggressive & scholarly views of Evangelical religious truth with the most strategic & advanced principles & purposes as to practical reform." Cook discussed his plans with many religious leaders and publishers, among them Stevenson, Comstock, and Willard.[34]

With Willard and Comstock on the board of editors, the first issue of *Our Day* appeared in January 1888. In the next volume, Wilbur F. Crafts, who had become prominent in Sabbath reform, joined the board, as did, later still, James B. Dunn of the National Temperance Society, Mary Hunt of scientific temperance fame, and R. G. McNiece, the antipolygamy Presbyterian minister from Utah. The first issue included articles on Mormonism, prohibition, Jesuits in the schools, and the responsibility of pulpit and pew in reviving religion. It also included pieces by Willard on women preachers, Comstock on indecent art, and Samuel Dike on the National Divorce League. In subsequent monthly issues, *Our Day* became what Cook had envisioned — a magazine that defended evangelical orthodoxy and promoted a host of reforms, many but not all them on the agenda of the Christian lobbyists. Willard, Comstock, and Crafts remained on the editorial board and contributed frequent articles. Cook did some of the editing, but when he was on the lecture circuit, his wife, Georgiana, took over most of it.[35]

Our Day's influence remained limited and its financial stability precarious. Circulation never rose above 3,300, and in 1895, Cook, who had tired of the magazine's demands on his financial resources and time, sold *Our Day*. The new management did not pursue its reform agenda. For seven years, however, *Our Day* served as a resource for and voice in favor of several of the Christian lobbying campaigns, including anti-Mormonism, divorce reform, prohibition, Sabbath observance, and the fight against gambling.[36]

Cook's "syndicate" of reformers working together on *Our Day* was as close as the Christian lobbyists came to formal, institutional unity. In the late 1880s and early 1890s, though, an informal alliance of reformers, all committed to Christian government and a broad agenda of moral legislation, had clearly emerged. The allies shared a deep Christian faith and, at least in broad terms, similar fears about their society's declining morality. They considered America threatened by a host of perils, none more dangerous than that which commercial vice, driven by avarice, posed to blacks, immigrants, "our boys," and other individuals plagued by appetites. To protect them and to eliminate the resulting moral crisis, the lobbyists continued to seek to save souls and to change individual behavior through moral suasion. But they also campaigned to enact laws to restrain appetites and avarice and thereby create a moral society. Passing the necessary laws at the national level entailed expanding the moral powers of the federal government and establishing its religious authority, or putting God in government as the lobbyists often phrased it. A national Sunday law would entail both, and as the new alliance of lobbyists campaigned for one and to prevent a national desecration of the Sabbath at the Chicago World's Fair, they realized attaining their goal of a Christian government would also necessitate not just an informal alliance but a permanent Christian lobby in Washington.

CHAPTER FIVE

The Sabbath and Religious Authority

O nce, when Wilbur F. Crafts warned Americans what would happen if the nation continued to allow public amusements and, worse, public drinking on Sunday, he chose typography that suggested a descent not just into dissipation but despotism:

> Holy Day, . . .
> Holiday,
> Work day,
> Devil's day,
> Despot's day.

"With the Sabbath our Christianity and our country stand or fall," Crafts maintained. "A republic cannot endure without morality, nor morality without religion, nor religion without the Sabbath, nor the Sabbath without law." Crafts's comments reflected the Christian lobbyists' fears of moral declension and their conviction that morality continued to be essential to the survival of the nation. Sunday observance was one of the moral issues that both the National Reform Association and the Woman's Christian Temperance Union added to their legislative agenda in the 1880s.[1]

At about the same time their alliance began to form, the two groups cooperated with others in a crusade for, first, a national Sunday law and, later, congressional action to close Chicago World's Fair on Sunday. Like laws on sexuality and divorce, blue laws, as those to stop work and other public activities on Sunday were often called, had long existed, but at the state or local level. The lobbyists therefore sought another significant expansion of the moral powers of the federal government, one that Congress had adamantly rejected before the Civil War. The campaign for national Sunday legislation revealed again the link in the lobbyists' minds between the moral power and religious authority of the state. Adopting a Sunday law would help establish the religious authority of the state, since it constituted an implicit recognition of God's commandment by the nation, but an acknowledgment of the state's responsibility to God also served as a justification for a national Sunday law. When Congress refused to offer such an acknowledgment, the lobbyists made another attempt to put Christ in the Constitution. At the same time, they became convinced that passing their newly expanded agenda of moral legislation would require not just the national organizational base they had begun to build in the 1880s but an institutional presence in Washington, one that they established in the 1890s.

The lobbyists and others who supported new federal laws to preserve the Sabbath believed Sabbath observation had declined since the Civil War. During the war, they pointed out, troops drilled, marched, and fought, trains and telegraphs operated, and newspapers were published on Sunday. They also blamed social changes in the late nineteenth century as well. And, of course, they believed that behind both wartime and postwar desecration of the Sabbath lay avarice and appetite. "It is the Greed Bothers," explained Crafts, "the two sons of Selfishness, the miserly greed for gold and the prodigal greed for pleasure that prompt every movement to overthrow the Sabbath." A Chicago minister active in the campaign for Sunday laws agreed when he challenged the principle that the success of Sunday newspapers demonstrated people wanted them. If society accepted the contention "that what the people want the people must have," he argued, it will "play sad havoc with our morals." After all, he observed, white southerners wanted slavery and people in Utah wanted polygamy. Besides, before the war, people had not demanded Sunday newspapers; newspaper owners had used that "great national exigency" to create an "appetite" for them. Herrick Johnson insisted that the real reason Sunday papers developed was the money to be made from them.[2]

Along with Sunday papers, the lobbyists focused their criticism of Sabbath desecration on Sunday mail, trains, and amusements. All obviously violated biblical proscriptions against work on the Sabbath, but, in the lobbyists' minds, they had other pernicious effects. Trains and commercial amusements kept those who patronized them away from church and disturbed the worship of Christians who attended. Even reading a Sunday paper—which, critics pointed out, contained little about Sunday and much about crime, fashion, amusements, business, and commerce—took time better spent reading the Bible and diverted the mind from worship. "One day in seven I want news of another world," wrote Joseph Cook, "and a seventh portion of my time is none too much to be used as a rudder for eternity." In short, all four of the great Sunday sins forced many to violate God's law of rest, spoiled the sacredness of the day for others, and subverted the day's moral purpose. The lobbyists defended Sunday laws, like other moral legislation, primarily as means to encourage individual morality but maintained it was also necessary to a proper moral society. More was involved, however, as a discussion over what to call the day revealed.[3]

Most members of the National Reform Association insisted on the use of the term Sabbath, which indicated the institution's divine origins, and emphasized that keeping the Sabbath was the duty not just of individuals but of the government as well. Crafts and others, however, preferred the "Lord's Day," which, as Crafts put it, "is the more positive, the more regnant term. One day in the week our Lord halts business and pleasure and politics, as a 'sign' that He is always Lord of our business, our pleasure, our politics." Some lobbyists even talked of a "civil sabbath," which justified Sunday laws not as the government's religious responsibility but something government did to preserve Christians' right to rest and worship. They also cited scientific findings that people needed a periodic day of rest to ensure their health and happiness. Having all citizens rest on a common day, proponents of a civil sabbath emphasized, brought immigrants into a shared culture and created a bond between rich and poor. By unifying society and providing a time for moral and spiritual uplift, Sunday thereby served a civil function; it helped prevent unrest and preserved the republic. "Strikes would not so easily pass into riots if laborers were not so many of them demoralized by being deprived of the Sabbath's humanizing home fellowship and its culture of conscience," wrote Crafts in 1890. "In a very literal sense our nation is 'laying up *wrath*' by its delay to emancipate our three millions of 'white slaves' from their Sunday slavery. Sunday work is unpaid toil in a deeper sense than that of the slaves of the South."[4]

Yet Crafts and many others who advocated a civil sabbath still believed that Sunday observance rested on and taught acceptance of God's authority. They hoped a national Sunday law would help establish the religious authority of the government, but they consciously chose not to emphasize the religious reason for keeping the Lord's Day. One proponent compared their strategy to that of a farmer who put up a sign in his melon patch, " 'Boys, don't touch these melons, for they are green, and God sees you.' Thus," the speaker explained, the farmer "presented two reasons, hoping that if the higher and weightier one should be disregarded, perhaps the lower one might have some restraining influence." Realizing that their higher argument allowed opponents to claim that Sunday laws violated the separation of church and state, Sabbath reformers sought to preempt their objections by basing their demands on the need for a day of rest, relaxation, and moral betterment.[5]

Although agitation for Sabbath observance had waned during the Civil War and Reconstruction, it never stopped entirely. A few local Sabbath associations persisted through the war years, and in the 1860s and 1870s, several cities debated enforcement or repeal of local blue laws. The first national controversy after the war occurred in 1876 when the Centennial Exposition in Philadelphia announced it would open on Sunday. The Congregationalists, northern Presbyterians, Methodists, Baptists, and six other denominations sent protests, but the National Reform Association led the fight to convince the Centennial Commission, the oversight board appointed by Congress, to close the exposition on Sunday. The NRA's representative, T. P. Stevenson, appeared before the commission; so, too, did Francis Abbot of the National Liberal League, who had fought the NRA's attempt to put Christ in the Constitution and opposed Sunday closing. The commission sided with Stevenson. In voting to close on Sunday, the chair claimed, the commission helped "form a bulwark" for "religion and morality for centuries to come."[6]

The successful campaign to close the Centennial grounds on Sunday helped revive interest in Sabbath agitation. In 1879, the International Sabbath Association formed in Philadelphia, with Yates Hickey as its secretary. Two years later, Hickey prepared a petition, which the NRA endorsed and circulated, for a federal law against carrying or delivering the mail on Sundays. In 1883, the NRA executive committee made the cause a priority and created a special fund to distribute an anti–Sunday mail pamphlet to all pastors, postmasters, and WCTU groups. Most important, in 1884, Frances Willard recommended and the WCTU national convention created a "Department of Effort to Prevent Sabbath Desecration." To head it, Willard appointed Josephine C. Bateham, a graduate of Oberlin College and former missionary to Haiti who then lived in Ohio. Bateham held a similar post in the National Reform Association and shared many of its views on the Sabbath. She termed it the "nerve centre of a Christian nation" and interpreted financial disasters, forest fires, strikes, and riots as God's judgment on the nation's continued Sunday desecration. Preservation of the Sabbath, she thought, was "absolutely *vital* in our land," as much so as temperance. Many members of the WCTU agreed; only two years after the establishment of a department on Sunday observance, twenty-one states had appointed superintendents for Sunday work, and by 1889, forty-one had done so.[7]

Bateham and her growing band of WCTU Sunday crusaders worked with the NRA, Hickey, and local Sabbath associations. They continued to pursue various forms of moral suasion but also petitioned Congress to stop Sunday mail service. In new petitions, Hickey included Sunday military parades, and he and others sent separate protests to railroad lines asking them to stop running trains on Sunday. Believing only the national government could stop rail traffic, Crafts in 1885 developed a petition to Congress that asked it to ban interstate trains, military parades, and mail on Sunday and, for good measure, requested a general Sunday law for the territories. Bateham and the secretary of the Illinois Sabbath League did much of the work of circulating Crafts's petition.[8]

In April 1888, as the petitions for restrictions on Sunday behavior arrived in Congress, Henry Blair, the WCTU's ally and advocate of national prohibition, held a hearing on the issue before the Committee on Education and Labor, which he chaired. Crafts took charge of presenting the witnesses. Bateham could not be there but sent a letter that was read, in which she claimed that over a million people, either directly or through their representatives, had signed the petition to stop Sunday mails, military parades, and interstate commerce. "Doubtless the largest share" of them, Bateham admitted, "believe, first of all, that we are bound so to maintain" the Sabbath "because God commands it, and his commands are disobeyed at our peril, but we confine ourselves to asking it on humanitarian grounds." She then provided a fairly typical defense of a civil sabbath.[9]

After Bateham's letter was read, Crafts spoke. He compared the request for a national Sunday law to Blair's proposal for national prohibition. Crafts then linked the violation of the Sabbath with intemperance, "impurity, anarchy, and political corruption." "The war on all these evils must be national," Crafts explained, "for they are all as national as slavery was; indeed, they constitute a new slavery that extends through North and South alike, from which we must have a new and national emancipation." After fending off hostile questions from an Ohio Democrat, Crafts introduced Hickey and later the representatives of several local Sabbath associations who, even as they acknowledged the religious basis of Sunday observation, argued for the law's importance in providing rest for workers and a foundation of morality for the nation. At the end of the hearing, Blair announced that Congress had received nearly 21,000 petitions, but as yet no Sunday bill had been introduced.[10]

Sabbath reformers asked Blair to prepare one. About a month later, he entered a national Sunday law titled "To secure to the people the enjoyment of the first day of the week, commonly known as the Lord's day, as a day of rest, and to promote its observance as a day of religious worship." As the wording indicated, Blair straddled the imagined line between a civil and religious Sabbath. His bill, though, proved sweeping. In the territories, District of Columbia, and all other places under "the exclusive jurisdiction of the United States," it banned all Sunday work, save that "of necessity, and mercy and humanity," and all plays, games, or amusements that would disturb others. Blair's bill also provided for an end to the collection, handling, and transportation of the mails, a ban on military and naval drills and parades, and a prohibition on interstate commerce on Sunday. The restrictions placed on the post office and the military allowed exceptions for work necessary for life, health, or mercy, and those put on interstate shipment also made exception for unavoidable delays, emergencies, and cargoes of perishable fruit and necessary food.[11]

Pleased with Blair's bill, Sabbath reformers intensified their efforts. At Blair's suggestion, Crafts presented it to the Knights of Labor and other unions, and they endorsed it. The WCTU, along with the various Sabbath associations and the NRA, circulated new petitions in its behalf. Crafts, however, decided that the campaign demanded a new organization. In the spring of 1888, he convinced the Methodist Episcopal Church to create a committee on Sabbath reform and to invite other denominations to join in working for proper observance of the Sabbath. The main northern and southern Presbyterian churches, the American Baptist Home Mission Society, the Congregationalists, and other denominations endorsed the idea. That November, a small planning group met at the home of Elliott F. Shepard. Shepard, who had once been a railroad lawyer, was a journalist and, no doubt of some importance to his role in financing the new movement, the husband of a Vanderbilt. A month later, at a meeting in Washington, the group formally organized as the American Sabbath Union (ASU). Shepard became the president and Crafts, the field secretary. The ASU's constitution called for a full range of activities in behalf of Sabbath reform, but its organizational meeting was held in conjunction with efforts in behalf of Blair's national Sunday law.[12]

During the ASU's national meeting in December 1888, Blair's committee held a second hearing. Crafts, Bateham of the WCTU, T. P. Stevenson of the NRA, and others testified. Crafts and Bateham both claimed that the petition campaign demonstrated that the churches and many individuals supported Blair's bill.

Bateham justified it primarily on civil Sabbath grounds but also condemned current Sunday practices as untrue "to the principles of the forefathers who established this as a Christian government on the rock-bed of the Sabbath as the bulwark of all morality." The NRA's Stevenson, in answers to questions from the chair, went much further. He proclaimed Sabbath observance a "sacred obligation" rooted in the "law of God" that "binds nations and governments as well as individuals." Other supporters who testified never made such a strong religious case for a national Sunday law, but a few did acknowledge that they drew their conceptions of the Sabbath from the Bible.[13]

In this hearing, unlike the earlier one, opponents of a national Sunday law testified. They included a representative of religious liberals and several from the Seventh-Day Adventists, Seventh-Day Baptists, and other denominations that recognized Saturday as the Sabbath. Unconvinced by proponents' occasional defense of a civil Sabbath, and not satisfied with the WCTU's proposal to exempt from the penalties of the law those who recognized another day as the Sabbath, the liberals and other opponents of the bill contended that keeping the Sabbath was a purely religious matter and that Blair's bill would interfere in religion and thereby violated the First Amendment. Alonzo T. Jones, a Seventh-Day Adventist who had long battled the NRA, tried to convince the committee that a "theocratical theory" underlay the attempt to pass a national Sunday law. He cited the WCTU's statement about Christ being this world's king, the *Christian Statesman* on the necessity for a Christian state, and other evidence.[14]

An exchange among Jones, A. H. Lewis, another of the seventh-day supporters, and Blair proved the most revealing of the hearing. Jones's defense of observing Saturday as the Sabbath prompted Blair to comment that Christians disagreed even among themselves about which day to celebrate and therefore the state could not decide on a day based on religious authority. It should instead choose the day that was best for society, with the majority determining what that was, and everyone else conforming to it. When Lewis interjected that Sunday worship was a purely religious matter, Blair asked him if he thought God commanded Sunday observance. Lewis admitted that he did, and Blair launched into a defense of the government's right to reenact the will of God, as he said it had in the debate over slavery in the territories. At another point, when Jones said the Seventh-Day Adventists just wanted to be left alone in their religious practices, Blair dismissed his statement as "the common Mormon argument." Later, he attacked the appeal based on individual belief: "There is a good deal of humbug about the sometimes so-called dictates of one's own conscience. If a man is to set up his conscience against the obligation to do what is right, and refuse to perform his duty toward society, an unintelligent, uninformed conscience of that kind might be allowed to destroy all society."[15]

Blair's comments typified the new suspicion of individual judgment and personal liberty common among the Christian lobbyists. They also revealed a paradox at the heart of the lobbyists' crusade. Supporters of the federal legislation of morality shifted easily between religious and civil defenses of their bills. They unquestionably based their definition of morality on God's will as revealed in the Bible. In defending bills in the secular forum of government, however, they were beginning to learn to downplay their religious motives and resort to arguments about the good of society and the rights of the majority. Their arguments therefore led logically, though unintentionally, to Blair's conclusion, that the authority of the law lay in the power of the majority. If that were the case, however, morality would ultimately become only what a majority of Americans judged it to be, and the people's sense of morality might not always conform to what the Christian lobbyists felt was the absolute standard they found in the Bible. Confident that they were right and that a majority of Americans shared their moral values, the lobbyists did not fret about the potential implications of Blair's analysis; instead they worked to mobilize the majority.

Crafts traveled the country promoting the bill. Bateham, who had spent December in Washington interviewing members of Congress, called for and received additional petitions. Many arrived, but the lobbying and petitions either had little effect or were counteracted by petitions sent by the opponents of the bill; Congress took no action. Blair could not even get his own committee to report it. In March 1889, on the last day of the session, a final attempt was made to discharge and pass the bill, but one senator objected, which was all that was necessary to defeat such a parliamentary motion. Any chance that Blair's bill would pass died. The Sabbath forces nevertheless claimed some success because during the debate, the administration had responded to a few of their concerns. President Benjamin Harrison ordered the army to move its formal inspection from Sunday to Saturday, and Postmaster General John Wanamaker, an active Presbyterian laymen, issued orders to reduce the amount of work his department did on Sunday. Wanamaker also instituted a procedure by which residents could petition to stop service at their local delivery windows, a sort of "local option" system for Sunday mail. In the next Congress, Blair introduced a renamed national Sunday law, dropping the "Lord's Day" from the title, but nothing came of it despite continued efforts by the WCTU and others

as well as more petitions to Congress. By that time, the forces of Sabbath reform had a new cause, closing the World's Columbian Exposition on Sunday.[16]

To be held in 1893, the Chicago World's Fair, as it was also called, commemo-
rated the anniversary of Columbus's voyage but also served as a model city on
Lake Michigan, a shining image of how America envisioned itself and its future. The Centennial in Philadelphia and all the intervening world's fairs held
in the United States had closed on Sunday—save for the New Orleans World's
Fair of 1884, which was explained away because of the French and Catholic
influence there. To reverse the precedent and open the Chicago fair on Sunday,
in the view of Sabbath reformers, would offer a dangerous example of Sabbath
desecration and raise questions about the religious loyalty of the nation. The
fight to close the fair on Sunday therefore took on enormous importance in the
minds of Sabbath reformers. Bateham proclaimed it "a turning point in our
nation's career. If the Christianity of the nation can control this question, they
can control the career of this country."[17]

In 1889, with planning for the fair begun but before Congress even authorized an exposition, Bateham called on the wctu to oppose opening it on Sunday. The next year, the NRA sent Stevenson to talk with several members of
Congress about putting a clause requiring Sunday closing in the legislation authorizing a fair, but nothing came of his efforts. Once Congress selected Chicago as the site for the exposition, a local group formed to prevent Sunday
opening. The Illinois Sabbath Association, the National Reform Association,
Crafts (who by that time had quit his job as a field secretary for the ASU), and
a special committee of the American Sabbath Union, headed by its secretary,
James P. Mills, who had previously worked for the NRA, took up the cause. An
intense campaign by these combined forces convinced neither the fair's local
directors, worried primarily about its financial success, nor the commission
appointed by Congress to oversee its operation to close on Sunday.[18]

Undeterred and convinced that they battled for the soul and future of America, the Sabbath forces turned to Congress. The executive committee of the
wctu made Sunday closing a special project and asked wctu members to send
petitions to Congress and to secure resolutions by their state legislatures demanding that the fair close. Several state legislatures sent memorials, and many
petitions, solicited by the wctu, the NRA, Crafts, and the ASU, arrived in Washington. Eighty-eight percent of House members received at least 1 petition, 50

percent received 3 or more, 30 percent, more than 7. Since most petitions came from within the representatives' districts, it is clear that people over a large part of the nation had participated in the campaign. States where the WCTU and NRA boasted strength sent the most. None of the petitions was recorded as actually coming from the NRA, but three-quarters were identified as being from other religiously affiliated groups. About 6 percent came from the WCTU and nearly 5 percent came from Christian Endeavor societies, youth groups associated with individual congregations. The vast majority were submitted by churches, with Presbyterians sending almost 25 percent, Methodists, 11 percent, Baptist, around 5, and Congregationalists, 2 percent of the total.[19]

The campaign to close the fair had mobilized grassroots support, which reflected, in part, the lobbyists' success in establishing an organizational base in the 1880s and, with it, their growing ability to mobilize the churches. The strength of the grassroots campaign remained, as it had in the earlier fight against polygamy, in the mid-Atlantic and midwestern states; in both petition drives, around three-quarters of the petitions came from those regions. The percentage of petitions to close the World's Fair from New England, however, declined by almost half, while those from the border and western states almost doubled. The percentage from the South went up from 1.55 percent to 6.02 percent, but the southern and border states still lagged well behind the other regions in the actual number of petitions sent.[20]

In the fight to close the fair, even more than in the antipolygamy campaign, reform forces did not rely solely on petitions but sent lobbyists to Washington. Primary responsibility fell to H. H. George, the field secretary of the American Sabbath Union. A minister in the Reformed Presbyterian Church, George had attended the original meeting of the movement to put Christ in the Constitution and had remained active in the NRA ever since. On various occasions, Shepard, Crafts, Joseph Cook, Stevenson, and others helped him. George and his fellow lobbyists sought to convince Congress to include in the appropriation for the fair a statement, prepared by former Supreme Court justice and NRA vice president William Strong, that the Columbian Exposition would not receive the money unless the commission stipulated in writing that it would close on Sunday. The lobbyists failed to convince the House committee to include such a provision. After listening to George, Stevenson, and a representative of railroad trainmen, the Senate Committee on the World's Fair did approve the idea, but the Finance Committee disagreed. Cook, Crafts, George, and Stevenson nevertheless continued to lobby individual members in hopes of a victory on the floor.[21]

H. H. George—lobbyist for the American Sabbath Union and the
National Reform Association (Reprinted from Glasgow,
History of the Reformed Presbyterian Church)

In the House, George Johnstone, a South Carolina Democrat, tried to restore
the amendment making the appropriation dependent on Sunday closing. In
the debate that followed, other members introduced amendments to prohibit
obscene art at the fair and lotteries or other gambling on its grounds. At that
point, one member asked if there had "been an amendment offered prescrib-
ing the amount of lunch that every individual should take" to the fair. All
amendments on moral issues failed, except for one, that which would close the
government's own exhibits on Sunday. Sabbath reformers' hopes then lay in the
Senate, where aid came from a surprising source, Matthew Quay, a senator

more often associated with machine politics than moral reform. Quay's home state of Pennsylvania, however, had sent more petitions than any other, and the preacher's son offered an amendment that required Sunday closing. Quay even had the Senate clerk read the Fourth Commandment from the Bible. That moment, Crafts observed later, deserved to be made into a painting that could be hung along with one of Columbus landing with "cross in hand" or one depicting the arrival of the Pilgrims. Several senators defended Quay's motion and cited many of the reasons for closing offered by Sabbath reformers. The most vocal opposition came from southerners—John W. Daniel of Virginia and three who had fought earlier moral legislation, George Vest of Missouri, Wilkinson Call of Florida, and John Morgan of Alabama.[22]

Morgan, for example, condemned Sunday closing as persistent Puritanism and warned of the danger of returning "to the days of the blue laws of Connecticut, Maine, and Massachusetts, when it was an offense by statute . . . for a man to kiss his wife on Sunday." He reminded his colleagues that a Virginian, Thomas Jefferson, had first established the separation of church and state and that Jefferson's efforts, not the blue laws of Connecticut, had led to liberty and freedom. The attempt to close the fair, in contrast, sought to establish not just "a union of church and state, but . . . of politics and religion." Morgan's speech combined sectional antagonism, Democratic doctrine, the assumptions of the antebellum moral polity, and traditional southern suspicion of religion in national politics.[23]

In yet another sign that southern attitudes were beginning to change, a Georgia Democrat, not a New England Republican, rose to challenge Morgan's assertions. Alfred H. Colquitt, who served as an officer in the ASU, criticized Morgan's invocation of liberty in defense of Sabbath breaking and denied that closing the exposition threatened the separation of church and state. Like Morgan, Colquitt said, he believed in both principles. Too often, however, liberty was poorly defined or assumed to be the "liberty of the immoral" rather than the freedom of Christians to enjoy the Sabbath. Although the United States kept church and state separate, Colquitt continued, Americans had always recognized "religion as the basis of our civilization." Colquitt went on to quote Lincoln, to champion the rights of Christians, and to argue that Sunday laws helped prevent social unrest. The Georgian closed by saying that if he had "a voice of power" he would, "with trumpet of the apocalyptical angel," shout across the country, " 'Righteousness, righteousness, righteousness exalteth the nation.' "[24]

An attempt to table Quay's amendment failed, with only eleven negative votes, eight of them from Democrats, but only two by southerners. Later, Quay and the Senate substituted Justice Strong's wording in order to put the ban on Sabbath opening in an independent section that would help protect it in the House. The Senate at first accepted but then reversed itself on another amendment, one that would have banned liquor sales from the exposition grounds. The bill then went back to the House for another debate on the issue. This time, on a recorded vote, the House voted 147 to 62 in favor of the ban. Of members who voted, every Populist, over 90 percent of the Republicans, but only 62 percent of the Democrats voted to uphold Sunday closing. Seventy-four percent of southerners voted in favor of the measure; only the West and the mid-Atlantic states had a higher rate of support. The major opposition came from the Midwest, probably because its representatives still anticipated financial benefits from opening on Sunday. In addition, representatives from industrial districts were slightly more likely to favor closing the fair; those from districts with a high percentage of foreign-born residents and blacks more likely to oppose it.[25]

Crafts proclaimed the ban on Sunday opening "the greatest moral victory since emancipation." He and George gave southerners some of the credit for its passage, but they also claimed that their lobbying efforts and petitions had played crucial roles. The petitions Congress had received did come up during the debate, and lawmakers clearly seemed influenced by them. House members who received no petitions voted against the provision requiring Sunday closing considerably more often than the House average. Members who received from one to six petitions voted yes at roughly the same rate as the House as a whole. Lawmakers who received from seven to fourteen petitions voted yes slightly to dramatically above the House average, and the twenty-two Congressmen who received more than fifteen petitions voted unanimously in favor of closing the fair on Sunday.[26]

Voting to close the Columbian Exposition on Sunday proved simpler than actually closing it. At first the fair's directors announced they would comply but then went back to Congress to try to get the ban repealed. Sunday forces mobilized again. George, Shepard, Cook, and others testified at hearings on the request, and the committee voted against a reversal. Crafts later claimed that a letter-writing campaign he orchestrated among ministers and Christian Endeavor societies in the district of one wavering member convinced him to cast what proved the crucial vote. Foiled in their attempts to repeal the ban, fair officials decided to defy it. They maintained that the federal government had not provided all the money that it had promised and, in any case, that the ban violated the separation of church and state. The Sabbath crusaders and the Christian Endeavor societies urged Christians not to attend the fair; Sunday attendance proved disappointing, and the commissioners reversed themselves. Lawsuits by various parties followed and resulted in competing injunctions and considerable legal confusion before, finally, an Illinois state judge, upholding the rights of stockholders and denying the right of the federal government to require Sunday closing, directed that the Columbian Exposition once more open on Sunday. Attendance remained small, which some reformers found a consolation. For the next two decades, similar fairs did close on Sunday.[27]

The Christian lobbyists' accomplishment in convincing Congress to close the Columbian Exposition on Sunday appeared less impressive when compared to what they initially sought, a comprehensive national Sunday law. Blair's bill would have dramatically curtailed interstate commerce on Sunday, which would have led to a far more radical change in public behavior than simply closing a temporary exhibition. More important, in the minds of the Christian lobbyists, the government itself broke the Sabbath by carrying the mails or training its soldiers and, in the process, undermined any claim to religious authority. A national Sunday law would have both dramatically expanded the moral powers of the national government and helped establish the religious authority of the state. Congress, however, never even debated Blair's law; it did not get out of committee, despite the fact that the committee's chairman had introduced and supported it. Only a few years later, given the chance to please their petitioning Christian constituents, lawmakers happily passed less expansive, less permanent legislation recognizing the Sabbath. In other words, members of Congress were willingly to make a symbolic statement associating the state with God but not to imbue it with religious authority.

The Christian lobbyists drew two somewhat different conclusions from the fight over closing the fair. Most of them agreed that their success in Congress demonstrated the influence that organized Christians could wield in the corridors of power. Crafts praised what he saw as an "aggressive attitude assumed by all the leading evangelical Christian denominations and organizations of the country" and predicted that Christians "in their organized capacity are coming more and more into line for aggressive efforts on behalf of righteousness." The success of the petition campaign to close the World's Fair had demonstrated that members of Congress would respond to aggressive pressure from organized Christians. Both Crafts and George concluded that further success in Congress would necessitate not only the grassroots organization the lobbyists had developed in the 1880s but also a permanent, institutional presence in Washington.

George and the NRA, however, still worried about leaving the definition of morality to a political majority, and for them the court's refusal to close the fair demonstrated once again the absolute necessity of a formal acknowledgment of the authority of God, Christ, and the Bible in the Constitution. The lobbyists acted on both conclusions. The NRA revived its attempt to amend the Constitution, and a Christian lobby formed in Washington.[28]

The NRA first renewed its efforts in behalf of the Christian amendment during the Sunday closing fight. In 1890, H. H. George and other supporters had presented the idea to President Benjamin Harrison, and, two years later, the NRA sought unsuccessfully to have each of the three political parties endorse it. In 1893, hoping to benefit from the expertise he had developed when working with the American Sabbath Union, the NRA sent George back to Washington to promote an amendment to the preamble. He, Crafts, and others convinced Elijah A. Morse, a Republican from Massachusetts, in the House and William P. Frye, a Maine Republican, in the Senate to introduce a resolution to send to state conventions for ratification a long, convoluted addition to the preamble of the Constitution that acknowledged God's authority and mentioned Christ and the Bible. Frye's support was at best tentative, but Morse, the son and grandson of Congregationalist ministers, who had once run on the Prohibition Party ticket and as a Republican advocated prohibition and other forms of moral legislation, worked to pass it.[29]

In January 1894, George and T. P. Stevenson went to Washington to lobby in behalf of Morse's resolution. Their efforts were reinforced by many petitions and public meetings held in various small towns as well as in Pittsburgh and in Boston, where Joseph Cook spoke. Some supporters who attended the rallies and others encouraged by the *Christian Statesman* came to Washington for a House Judiciary Committee hearing on changing the preamble. George took charge, and Stevenson opened the meeting by reading a letter from Cook, who supported the amendment but dissented from what he considered Covenanter justifications for it. Cook based his endorsement on the recognition of the Creator in the Declaration of Independence, references to God in forty state constitutions, and the addition during the Civil War of "In God We Trust" to some American coins. He also cited an 1892 Supreme Court decision in which Justice David Brewer proclaimed the United States "a Christian nation," a pronouncement often invoked by advocates of moral reconstruction. Stevenson also read letters from Herrick Johnson, the Chicago minister active in the fight over the fair; Francis E. Clark of the International Society of Christian Endeavor; and others. The NRA had hoped William Strong would testify, but he was too old and frail. All of the people who did speak were supporters of the NRA, and all but one were ministers in the Reformed Presbyterian Church.[30]

After the hearing, Morse advocated sending the rewording of the preamble to the floor, as did a Pennsylvania Republican who had many NRA members among his constituents. The Judiciary Committee as a whole disagreed and tabled the resolution "indefinitely." Morse's resolution and the hearings on it had generated many counterpetitions and much hostile comment in the press, some of it from Christian leaders who thought the proposal too revolutionary a change in the existing system of church-state relations. George went home, but despite the opposition and the failure to get the resolution out of committee, the NRA was encouraged. In neither of the NRA's two previous attempts had the proposed revision of the Constitution even been introduced in Congress.[31]

The next year, in 1895, the NRA Executive Committee sent George back to Washington to lobby for an amendment with revised wording: "We, the people of the United States, [acknowledging Almighty God as the source of all authority in civil government, the Lord Jesus Christ as the Ruler of nations, and the revealed will of God as of supreme authority in civil affairs,] in order to form a more perfect union. . . ." Morse and Frye again entered resolutions that incorporated the NRA's new wording. By early 1896, petitions from local WCTU women, Christian Endeavor societies, and other groups arrived in Congress, as did letters to the Judiciary Committee. But so too did memorials opposing the Christian amendment, many generated by the Seventh-Day Adventists, who led the opposition to the NRA's efforts.[32]

In March 1896, the House Committee on the Judiciary held another hearing on the Christian amendment during which proponents and opponents confronted each other in a raucous meeting marked by applause and cheering by both sides. Stevenson opened the hearing with prayer, and then George posed the choice before the committee as between a Christian and a secular government. Other speakers in favor of the amendment offered the various arguments that had been made many times before. One NRA activist stressed the importance of the Christian amendment in providing a source of authority: "It asks the Bible to decide moral issues in political life; not all moral questions, but simply those that have become political questions." Religious liberals, Seventh-Day Adventists, Jews, spiritualists, and Unitarians spoke in opposition to the amendment. They criticized the attempt to put God in the preamble as a revolutionary attack on what had always been a secular Constitution and as a dangerous threat to the separation of church and state. One opponent expressed the fear that recognizing the authority of Scripture in the Constitution would lead to the army, navy, and police enforcing religious laws. Another forced one proponent to admit that the amendment would probably prevent a Jew from serving in Congress.[33]

Toward the end of the hearing, David McAllister, an editor of the *Christian Statesman* and leader of the NRA, spoke; members of the committee "wheeled their chairs around to face" him and "plied him repeatedly with questions and objections." When McAllister said Congress had no right to enact laws that were out of "harmony with the justice of God," one representative asked whether "the Protestant or Catholic, the Hebrew or Mahammedan" would determine what constituted justice. McAllister replied that, as now, the people would. "Do you, then, believe the voice of the people is the voice of God?" asked another. "When it is right," McAllister replied. Some of the Republicans on the committee then posed a series of questions about who decided what was right and what happened when the majority was wrong. One argued that making the Bible the standard of morality would render the Supreme Court the arbiter of biblical interpretation. McAllister disagreed and cited Quay's having the Fourth Commandment read to Congress during the debate over Sunday closing of the World's Fair to illustrate his contention that it would be the people who interpreted it. But, countered another member, if someone tested a Sunday closing law in court, the Bible would be cited. Members next questioned whether the amendment would lead to forced baptisms, since the Bible said that all should be baptized, or to bans on women talking in public, since it included a statement that women should be quiet in church. McAllister said no, such biblical statements had never been applied to civil affairs but were ecclesiastical matters and would be left to the churches. Committee members were not convinced by this or McAllister's other replies. As their hostile questions revealed, they feared imbuing government with religious authority and the repercussions for religious liberty if the preamble was amended. The committee again tabled the resolution. Neither the House Judiciary Committee nor its Senate counterpart reported such a resolution.[34]

Undeterred, the NRA continued the crusade for the Christian amendment. Between 1894 and 1919, twelve resolutions with various wordings designed to put God in the Constitution were introduced. None ever made it out of committee. Congress clearly had no interest in writing God, much less the authority of the Bible, into the Constitution. As the hearings revealed, most legislators thought the government a secular state and feared entangling government and religion. Some of them even questioned whether any absolute moral standard could exist in a pluralistic republic. The efforts in behalf of the Christian amendment by Crafts, Cook, and some members of the WCTU demonstrated the existence of the lobbyist's alliance and a shared desire to establish a single moral standard and the religious authority of the state. But unlike the leaders of the NRA, most of the Christian lobbyists quickly lost interest in the Christian amendment. They still sought to Christianize the government but believed it could best be accomplished not by appeals to religious authority but by organized political pressure, which, they had concluded from the fight to close the fair, necessitated a permanent Christian lobby in Washington.

The major proponent of a Christian presence in the capital was the veteran of the Sunday law campaign, Wilbur F. Crafts. Slightly younger than Comstock, Cook, or Willard, Crafts was born in Maine in 1850. The son of a Methodist minister, he graduated from Wesleyan University in 1869 and, three years later, from the School of Theology of Boston University. He served first a Methodist, then a Congregational, and finally a Presbyterian congregation. Like the other lobbyists, Crafts combined an intense, orthodox Christian faith with a commitment to moral reform. He left the parish ministry to take part in the crusade for federal Sunday legislation, and after that he became, for two years, editor of the *Christian Statesman*. Convinced that Christians needed a permanent presence in Washington, Crafts in September 1894 announced the formation of the National Bureau of Reforms. It would lobby "to promote such moral reforms as the Christian churches generally approve by securing the enactment and enforcement of good laws and the defeat of bad ones in regard to Sabbath reform, gambling, purity, temperance, public schools, immigration, civil service reform, ballot reform, voluntary industrial arbitration, etc." The bureau, he added, would serve as both "the watch-tower of Christian reform, to send out swift alarms, and . . . the channel by which the swift protests, petitions and letters of the people can be brought to bear in the interest of righteousness upon the lawmakers, both of the nation and the states." Like other Christian lobbyists, Crafts worked for laws at the local and state as well as federal level.[35]

All of the reforms he listed in his announcement, Crafts argued, constituted "parts of one great reform—the reform which is the consummation of religion—namely the Christianizing of society, which is 'the kingdom of God.'" "The heart of Christian sociology," Crafts continued, "is the Kingship of Christ. The individual is saved by his cross, but society is saved by his crown, that is, by

Wilbur F. Crafts—founder of the Reform Bureau and self-proclaimed
Christian lobbyist (Reprinted from Cherrington, *Standard
Encyclopedia of the Alcohol Problem*)

the application of the law of Christ to all human associations—to the family,
the school, the shop, the Church, the State." "*The Kingship of Christ rather than
the Saviorship of Christ, is the Bible's ultimate theme.*" The Bible demanded the
creation of "the New Jerusalem '*let down from God*'—the kingdom of heaven,
a divinely ordered, divinely promised, human and humane society of purity
and justice and brotherhood and humanity, in which God's will is done on
earth as it is heaven."[36]

Creating the New Jerusalem, Crafts added, required that the church play a
much more active role in society and that the state answer to God just as the
church did. It also entailed an abandonment of the mistaken idea that developed during the Middle Ages of "the unwarranted, unscriptural division of life

into 'sacred' and 'secular.'" Crafts expansive list of reforms and his rhetoric about the Kingdom of God resembled that of many proponents of the Social Gospel. But unlike them, Crafts endorsed the Christian amendment to the Constitution and advocated employing government not to ensure economic justice but to eliminate what he termed "the 'Big Four' evils, intemperance, impurity, Sabbath breaking and gambling."[37]

Crafts advocated attacking "the 'Big Four'" with four methods—lectures, letters, literature, and legislation. He set up an office in Washington, eventually in a building at the corner of Second Street and Pennsylvania Avenue, across from the recently opened National Library. There he operated what he first called the Reform Bureau, and later, the International Reform Bureau. In the early years, it operated on a budget of under $4,000 a year, but spending grew steadily until it passed $10,000 by 1910 and peaked in 1920 at around $18,000. Crafts raised most of the money himself, principally through collections taken during speaking tours. Although he had a few large contributors, the bureau remained a grassroots operation; almost half of the individual contributors gave a dollar or less a year. Contributions came from almost every state, but nearly half of them from three—New York, Pennsylvania, and Ohio.[38]

As the contributions grew, Crafts expanded his operations. He added several part-time office workers and usually had one or two field secretaries who traveled in behalf of the bureau and did some lobbying as well. Numerous people served on his advisory board. Some were prominent public figures—Booker T. Washington, O. O. Howard, and John Eaton—who did not play a particularly active role. More and more active members came from the ranks of the Christian lobbyists—Cook, Comstock, Bateham, Woodbridge, Hunt, Blair, and the National Temperance Society's Aaron Powell. Nevertheless the Reform Bureau remained pretty much a two-person operation, run by Crafts and his wife, Sara J. Timanus. She worked in the office and continued her own reform and Sunday school work. He traveled about the country making speeches in behalf of reform and the bureau; most years he averaged five lectures a week. At home in Washington, Crafts and his wife sent out press releases to various religious magazines and letters and circulars explaining bills before Congress to ministers and other supporters across the nation. Crafts also met individually with legislators; one year he claimed to have talked with a hundred of them.[39]

Most important, Craft cooperated closely with the WCTU, to which his wife belonged. After he founded the Reform Bureau, Crafts frequently addressed the WCTU's national convention. At its 1897 meeting, Willard praised Crafts's "admirable work of reform" that "has been greatly strengthened by our Society, even as we have profited by his wise counsels." By that time, the WCTU again had its own full-time lobbyist in Washington, Margaret Dye Ellis. A native of New York, Ellis had become active in the WCTU, first in California and then, after she moved back east, New Jersey. In 1895, Willard recruited her to be the national legislative superintendent; the following year, Ellis went to Washington for the first time. Each year, from then until Prohibition passed in 1917, Ellis and her husband, who usually helped her in her work, moved to Washington for the duration of the congressional session.[40]

She maintained an office at the District WCTU headquarters and later at the Driscoll Hotel. There she went each day, spending more time with the *Congressional Record* than her Bible, she complained. During most of her years in Washington, she wrote a regular column for the *Union Signal*, the WCTU's magazine, that kept members informed of legislation and other aspects of her work. She also coordinated the efforts of the state legislative superintendents. She represented the interests of the WCTU in the capital and cooperated with Crafts and other temperance leaders. Through it all, she kept her Bible near and always felt that she did the Lord's work.[41]

Ellis and Crafts functioned as direct and indirect lobbyists. They, and the organized Christians they represented, were part of a larger transformation of the American political system, one that began in the late nineteenth century and culminated in the 1920s. After the Civil War, many Americans, not just the Christian lobbyists, expected the national government to accept greater public responsibilities. A suddenly overextended Congress did not always meet these expectations. Lobbyists became a means to overcome the problem, and their numbers and influence increased in late-nineteenth-century Washington. At the same time, farmers, labor unions, and other interest groups became disillusioned with political parties. They formed voluntary associations that, operating outside of partisan politics, employed public education and interest-group politics to influence Congress.[42]

Crafts, Ellis, and their allies were pioneers in the new form of interest-group politics. They went to Washington because they realized someone needed to promote and monitor the progress of moral legislation within Congress, to serve as "the watch-tower of Christian reform," as Crafts put it. Neither the legislators nor the parties were performing that task. Ellis and Crafts therefore worked very hard to promote moral legislation by contacting the president, members of the administration, and individual legislators. They also helped stage what one historian argues was becoming "an indispensable, ritualistic part of the process of legislation," the congressional hearing. Over the course of

Margaret Dye Ellis—longtime Washington lobbyist for the
Woman's Christian Temperance Union (Courtesy of the
National Woman's Christian Temperance Union)

their careers in Washington, Crafts participated in (and often presided over, because the committee let him present the witnesses) at least twenty-five hearings
and Ellis, twenty-three. Few other individuals participated in so many.[43]

Crafts and the others, however, had learned in the fight to close the fair that
members of Congress would respond to their appeals only if they felt the people, or more accurately their constituents, demanded it. "On the doors of the
Capitol one sees the words, 'Push' and 'Pull,'" explained Crafts, "and the greatest
of these is 'Push,' for ours is a wheelbarrow government which will go forward
to almost any moral reform which the sovereign people really 'push,' despite the
politician's contrary 'pull.'" To provide the push, the Christian lobbyists continued to emphasize grassroots organization and participation.[44]

It primarily took the form of petition campaigns. The NRA distributed *A Manual of Christian Civil Government* that provided detailed instructions on how to arouse public sentiment and to petition Congress. The Reform Bureau and the WCTU often prepared printed forms for individuals or groups to fill out; other local activists drew up their own memorials. In either case, they were instructed to prepare one for their representative—Ellis quickly learned legislators cared only what their own constituents thought—and one for each of their state's senators. Crafts also recommended that public meetings be held to pass resolutions calling for legislation. Although groups sometimes sent the petitions or memorials directly to their legislators, both Ellis and Crafts collected them and delivered them to the Capitol. Much effort went into the process, yet Ellis and Crafts realized that personal letters and contacts had a greater impact than petitions and encouraged local supporters to write or visit their representatives personally. For mobilizing the grass roots, the Reform Bureau never developed the extensive network of activists that the WCTU did. The WCTU's hierarchical structure, with state and local leaders specifically responsible for legislative work, proved very effective in generating letters and petitions. The WCTU also had dedicated members who took the petitions to church or circulated them door to door.[45]

Most petition drives brought together the efforts of the lobbyists' organizations with those of individual congregations, pastors' associations in local communities, an occasional Young Men's Christian Association, and other religious groups. One of the most important was the United Christian Endeavor Society, which had sent petitions during the campaign to close the fair. Founded by Francis E. Clark in 1881, the society was a national, interdenominational association that helped organize youth groups, called Endeavor societies, in local congregations. The societies focused their efforts primarily on religious instruction and individual conversion, but they also taught the importance of Christian service. At first wary of working with the Christian lobbyists, who frequently sought their support, the national leadership in the 1890s decided to devote greater emphasis to developing citizenship and putting "God in politics." The group adopted a "Pledge of Good Citizenship," in which members promised not to use intoxicants, tobacco, or bad language, or to violate "Social Purity or the Sabbath." They also pledged that when they started to vote "it shall be as I think Christ would have me vote."[46]

Cartoon from the *Union Signal*, 27 January 1916
(Courtesy of the National Woman's Christian Temperance Union)

With both Crafts and Ellis established as lobbyists in Washington, and with several national organizations and many churches willing to respond to their calls for petitions, a full-fledged, national Christian lobby had emerged. Its leaders, of course, considered themselves God's agents, and their deep faith and sense of doing God's will explained their persistence in seeking the moral reconstruction of the state. But the fight to secure a national Sunday law and Congress's rejection of the Christian amendment, for the third time, had revealed how few in Washington accepted the government's responsibility to God or even responded to an appeal solely to divine law. The lobbyists, like Henry Blair, continued to believe that the government could reenact the will of God, but after their success in getting Congress to close the World's Fair on Sunday, they realized as never before that political pressure from Christians offered the best hope of enacting their expanded moral agenda.

CHAPTER SIX

The Lottery and the South

S outhern support and leadership would be crucial to the Christian lobbyists attempts, after 1895, to pass a broad agenda of moral legislation
and, especially, to achieve the goal they had adopted in the late 1870s,
national, constitutional prohibition. Some southerners in Congress
had demonstrated their willingness to vote for federal moral legislation during
the attempts to outlaw polygamy and to close the World's Fair on Sunday. The
new southern openness to federal legislation of morality became even clearer
over the course of a long-running congressional debate over lotteries. Southerners at first opposed legislation to deny lotteries the use of the mails, but by
1890, many Louisianians demanded federal aid in freeing their state from the
grasp of the Louisiana Lottery. With crucial help from a few southern members, Congress enacted two antilottery laws in the early 1890s. The second
banned lottery materials from interstate commerce, which established an important legal precedent for much of the federal moral legislation that followed.

Lotteries, which had been condemned and outlawed in most states during the
antebellum years, had revived during the Civil War. Several states, most of
them in the South or West, once more legalized these games of chance. The lottery companies established under state laws then opened outlets in large cities
in other states and advertised in newspapers, distributed circulars, sold their
tickets, and delivered prizes by mail—thereby expanding their business across
the nation. Opponents of lotteries and other forms of gambling believed they
excited young minds, fed an unnatural appetite for wealth, and, like other sins,
often led to a life of crime and dissipation. If the gambler somehow avoided a
descent into degeneracy, the habit still undermined his or her work ethic by

promoting a gospel of wealth without toil and subverted religious faith by en-
couraging a reliance on chance rather than God's providence.[1]

With lotteries employing the mails to operate across state lines, the Post
Office Department took the lead in combating them, just as it did with obscenity. Department officials at first relied on their authority to refuse to deliver
mail to anyone participating in a fraudulent activity, but shortly after the war,
the department sought additional power to combat lotteries. In 1868, Congress
responded by making it illegal to mail "any letters or circulars concerning lotteries, . . . or other enterprises offering prizes of any kind." Congress eliminated
a provision in the bill that allowed postmasters to remove such matter from the
mails. Lawmakers did so because of their continued sensitivity to abuses of
power and threats to individual privacy, but the change nevertheless rendered
attempts to outlaw lotteries more difficult. Already weak, antilottery statutes
were further weakened in 1872 when Congress added the adjective "illegal" before "lotteries" in a section forbidding them access to the mails.[2]

In 1876, during a debate on a bill preventing the mailing of obscene matter,
lawmakers recommended extending the ban to material of legal lotteries. Rod-
man West, whose home state of Louisiana had a legal lottery, opposed the
measure and drew a distinction between them and obscene publications. No
state, he explained, permitted the transmission of obscenity, but some did
allow lotteries. Definitions of morality should be left to the states. West spoke
not only for a home-state interest but from the South's traditional view of
moral legislation. Several senators, including one from Texas, disagreed. They
cited the fact that almost all the states had made lotteries illegal and pointed
out that gambling encouraged vice and ruined the lives of many people, especially among the poor. One invoked the antislavery precedent and dismissed
the idea that Congress should defer to the beliefs of people or states that considered lotteries moral. Another argued explicitly for a single national standard
of morality: "if it is wrong in one place it is wrong in another place." Whether
or not senators concurred with the idea of a single standard, they at least
agreed that the government had the power to act. In 1876, Congress banned the
material of legal as well as illegal lotteries from the mail. The Supreme Court
upheld the statute. It asserted that the government's responsibility over the
mails included the right "to determine what shall be excluded." The decision,
however, added that that right could not abridge freedom of the press and
reaffirmed the ideal of personal liberty. The Court, like Congress, drew a distinction between sealed matter, which could not be opened without a court
order, and other materials in the mail, which could.[3]

Illegal lotteries persisted, but state and existing federal statutes proved sufficient to curtail, though never eliminate, them. The national legislative battle therefore came to center on the Louisiana Lottery, the only one that retained state sanction. Originally chartered and granted a monopoly by Republicans during Reconstruction, the Louisiana Lottery had survived by forming an alliance with one faction of the Democratic Party when it took power after Reconstruction. The Lottery then countered several attempts to outlaw it, secured a new charter in 1879, and sustained its position in Louisiana with well-placed bribes and well-publicized generosity. It could afford both; the Louisiana State Lottery Company was fantastically successful, in part because, critics charged, many of the drawings were fixed. If true, crime paid—and paid handsomely. Estimates of the Louisiana Lottery's annual gross revenues ran as high as $28 million a year, with less than half of that paid out in prizes. Most of its phenomenal income, 97 percent of its sales according to some estimates, came from outside of Louisiana, mostly through its mail operations.[4]

Two successive postmaster generals, David M. Key and Walter Gresham, attempted to employ the 1876 law to stop the Louisiana Lottery from using the mails. But the Lottery checked their efforts in court and avoided the law by having a New Orleans bank transact its mail business. Meanwhile efforts to strengthen the law continued. Anthony Comstock, who devoted almost as much of his attention to ending gambling as he did to stopping the distribution of obscenity, tried to close down the Louisiana Lottery's operations in New York City and asked Congress to enact further legislation. In 1879, he urged the Post Office Department to strengthen the postal statute on lotteries by, among other ways, increasing the penalties and allowing the prosecution of both the people who mailed the material and the people who told them to, the managers of the Lottery. Key, then the postmaster general, concurred with Comstock's suggestions and forwarded his letter to the chair of the House Post Office Committee. The committee took no action.[5]

The Committee of the District of Columbia did report a bill that restricted lottery advertisements within the District, where, despite a ban on lotteries there that dated to the antebellum years, newspaper and other advertisements for lotteries were still allowed. The Ohio Republican who introduced the new restrictions cited the precedent of early antipolygamy laws. Opposition came, as it had in the fight against polygamy, primarily from Democrats and southerners. Only three Republicans but ninety-five Democrats voted to table the bill, in effect to kill it. Over half the votes against it were cast by southerners, who split fifty-three to five against the measure. Two years later, the Senate passed a similar ban on lottery ads in the District of Columbia, but it died in the House without debate.[6]

In the following Congress, in 1883, Edward W. Robertson, a Democrat from Louisiana, entered a much broader bill that denied the use of the mails to newspapers or other publications that contained lottery advertisements. In a speech in its behalf, the Confederate veteran urged the federal government to deliver his state from "the poisonous fangs of the deadly reptile which has been fastened upon" it by Republicans during Reconstruction. Nothing came of Robertson's bill, but over the next few years many more antilottery bills were introduced. In 1884, the Senate, controlled by Republicans, passed one that prohibited delivery of registered letters and money orders to lotteries and three years later passed another to ban from the mails newspapers that published lottery ads. Southerners split equally on passage of the latter bill. The House proved more hostile to antilottery legislation; a few bills died on the floor; others never made it out of committee. John H. Rogers, an Arkansas Democrat on the Post Office Committee, spoke for many southerners when he explained that to give "the Postmaster-General" the power "to destroy" or even "to impair as much as he can" the operation "of institutions" recognized as legal by the states, "because Congress regards such institutions as *immoral*," is "to coerce the States to adopt the standard of Congressional morality." Rogers's comments echoed both antebellum southern opposition to moral legislation and contemporary southern fears of federal intervention in race relations. But as Robertson's introduction of an antilottery bill signaled, southern attitudes toward lottery legislation were changing.[7]

During the same Congress in which the Senate passed a newspaper ban, the House Post Office Committee reported a similar measure, and the Committee on the District of Columbia sent to the floor a bill to tighten antilottery laws in the capital. The report for each was written by a southern Democrat, John J. Hemphill of South Carolina and James H. Blount of Georgia. Blount's District bill passed with almost no discussion and only four opposing votes; Hemphill's stronger, more important legislation never came up for debate. In 1888, Hemphill again reported a bill forbidding advertising of lotteries in the District, but the House voted 119 to 114 to return the bill to the Committee on the Judiciary for further study. Democrats and southerners again provided most of the votes to block lottery legislation. Forty-nine southerners voted for referral; only thirteen opposed it.[8]

In the late 1880s, most southern legislators continued to oppose antigambling legislation, but the fact that some had begun to vote in favor of it and that a few—Robertson, Blount, and Hemphill—had even begun to lead the call for it again revealed changes in attitudes among at least some white southerners. Southern support for antilottery legislation constituted an even more dramatic change than votes for antipolygamy or Sabbath legislation because southerners worked for a federal law that would be enforced against an institution, the Louisiana Lottery, based in the South.

In his 1883 speech calling for federal legislation against the Louisiana Lottery, Robertson had criticized ministers in Louisiana for failing to attack the Lottery. Within a few years, and in marked contrast to the traditional southern strictures about preachers in politics, Louisiana ministers helped lead the anti-Lottery cause. One of the early calls for action was delivered in a Methodist pulpit in New Orleans. In February 1889, Beverly Carradine preached a sermon that condemned the Louisiana Lottery and defended preachers in politics. Carradine said he felt justified, as a minister, in attacking the Louisiana Lottery because it was "one of the monster evils of the day," ranking only behind "Mormonism and Impurity and Intemperance." Ministers, he continued, had a responsibility to "warn the people" of evil, "rebuke . . . iniquity," "arouse conscience, create public opinion, and awaken moral sentiment." As a precedent, Carradine cited the antislavery crusade.[9]

Carradine then went on to condemn the Lottery's fraudulent practices and the way it hurt legitimate businesses, undermined "*the spirit of labor*," and subverted morality. In response to people who claimed the lottery was legal and allowed in "a free country," Carradine responded that if God said something was wrong, laws could not make it right. Like many of the Christian lobbyists, he also questioned whether the nation was "a little too free," whether freedom had become license to do evil and to hurt other people. Carradine even compared the lottery to feudalism and slavery, where a "few masters" lived "in ease and plenty, while a multitude of slaves toiled and groaned and died in the fields." "We," he told his fellow Louisianians, "whether we realize it or not, are nothing but the slaves of the Louisiana State Lottery Company."[10]

In early 1890, a year after Carradine's call to arms, an Anti-Lottery League organized. It, along with the Louisiana Farmers' Alliance and a Women's Anti-Lottery League, led the fight against the Louisiana Lottery's attempt to secure a new charter from the state legislature when the old one ran out in 1894. The new organization brought together people who opposed the Lottery because of its corrupt influence on state politics, its support of a competing political faction, and its impact on the state's economy. Most also condemned it for preying on the poor and promoting a reliance on chance rather than hard work for success. They also believed it a violation of the laws of God. Though never simply a moral crusade, the Louisiana antilottery movement clearly had a religious dimension, and ministers actively participated. A Methodist (Carradine), a Presbyterian, and a Baptist minister along with an Episcopal bishop and a rabbi were among the fifty-seven vice presidents of the Anti-Lottery League. Their participation demonstrated that some Louisiana ministers were willing to intervene in politics, and the Anti-Lottery League itself showed that some white Louisianians favored moral legislation—and not only at the state level.[11]

In a speech at one of the league's first meetings, the Presbyterian minister who served as a vice president, Benjamin Morgan Palmer, condemned the Lottery and called on the people of Louisiana to deny it a charter. He wanted the "redemption" of his state "to be accomplished by her own act," Palmer said. But if it were not, the onetime champion of secession, states' rights, and the spirituality of the church quickly added, "the appeal must be made to the virtue and intelligence of the entire country." Louisiana, Palmer said to applause, could not continue as an "isolated community" living "against the moral convictions of the world." Its citizens had scarcely "recovered . . . from the blow inflicted upon" them when "the moral sentiment of the world, right or wrong, was arrayed against the institution of slavery and it went down." Now the world opposed lotteries; those who had once tried to preserve them "found that" they "exhausted the resources of the land" and abandoned them. Louisiana, Palmer predicted, would be an outcast among the states if it did not do the same.[12]

The Anti-Lottery League did not wait to see if the state would redeem itself; the league created a committee to seek national aid. It prepared an "Appeal to the Nation" that requested help in arousing "national sentiment" against the Lottery and in securing a federal statute that would "free the people of the United States from the Louisiana Lottery Company." That law, the appeal continued, should ban from the mails newspapers carrying lottery ads and make it illegal for anyone to deposit knowingly a lottery ticket, circular, or prize in the mail. Mailing such materials should be defined as a "continuous offense," which meant federal officials could try the case in any district through which the material passed, not just New Orleans, where convictions were difficult to secure. Stronger than any bill thus far debated by Congress, the committee's proposal also asked that lotteries be denied the use of railroads, express companies, and public carriers on post roads. The committee forwarded its appeal to leading magazines in the North. It also sent a copy and a personal letter requesting assistance to the president and to all members of Congress. In addition, the Anti-Lottery League hired George D. Johnston, a former Confederate general, and dispatched him north to mobilize antilottery support. For two years, Johnston met with prominent individuals and conducted public meetings there in behalf of the antilottery cause.[13]

Johnston and the Anti-Lottery League's appeals found a receptive audience in the North; after all, Congress had been considering antilottery bills for a decade. Moreover, new calls for legislation by Christian lobbyists and Republican leaders began about the same time. In November 1889, Anthony Comstock published an article in Joseph Cook's *Our Day* that asked Congress to ban newspapers with lottery ads from the mails and all lottery materials in interstate commerce. That same month, Frances Willard, citing Carradine's sermon, persuaded the WCTU to condemn the Louisiana Lottery. The next month, in his first message to Congress, President Benjamin Harrison endorsed the request of his postmaster general, John Wanamaker, for additional antilottery legislation.[14]

In July 1890, Georgia's Blount again reported a strong bill. The chances of its passage improved when the legislature of the recently admitted state of North Dakota barely defeated an attempt by the Louisiana Lottery to secure a charter there. Referring to this latest threat and warning of the dangers posed by the Louisiana Lottery, Harrison and Wanamaker again requested action on the antilottery bill. The national press, too, took up the cause, and Congress acted on legislation written by Blount's House Post Office Committee. Rogers and another southerner opposed it, but other southern representatives, including two from Louisiana, spoke in its favor. After limited debate, the House passed it, as did the Senate, without debate. The bill banned from the mails newspapers with lottery ads as well as registered letters and money orders sent to the Lottery or its agents, a provision intended to stop a New Orleans bank from collecting the Lottery's money. The bill still preserved "the sanctity of the seal"; it prohibited postmasters from opening private letters. It attempted, however, to make enforcement easier by allowing the Post Office Department to try cases in any state through which lottery matter passed. Using that provision, Wanamaker and his department at once began vigorous enforcement of the new law.[15]

Even so, Louisianians appealed to Congress for additional antilottery measures. In early 1891, Palmer and other Presbyterian ministers of New Orleans petitioned Congress in support of a constitutional amendment to prohibit the chartering of lottery companies and the selling or drawing of lottery tickets anywhere in the United States. The Anti-Lottery League, the Louisiana Conference of the Methodist Episcopal Church, South, the Democratic Anti-Lottery State

Executive Committee of Louisiana, and, at the instigation of some Louisiana members, the national convention of the Farmers' Alliance sent similar petitions. Nothing came of them or of a resolution for an antilottery amendment entered by Henry Blair, ever the friend of moral reform. As it would demonstrate in later campaigns to control morality, Congress had little interest in changing the Constitution.[16]

The next year, 1892, the Supreme Court upheld the antilottery law, once more affirming the government's right to exclude material from the mails. But the justices also ruled that the new law did not abridge "the freedom of the press" because Congress did not stop "the circulation of newspapers" but only prevented them from becoming agents "in the circulation of printed matter which it regards as injurious to the people" or injurious to "the public morals."[17]

The Court's ruling ensured that enforcement of the antilottery law would continue, and with the Lottery's allies in Louisiana politics apparently headed for defeat, the company suspended its Louisiana operations in February 1892. Shortly thereafter, antilottery forces there took control of state government and won the vote against rechartering the lottery. Rather than go out of business altogether, however, the Louisiana Lottery moved its headquarters to Honduras and continued to operate in the United States through a company it founded in Florida to print and distribute its tickets, a scheme made possible by a loophole in that state's antilottery law. Wilkinson Call, a senator from Florida who in the past had fought moral legislation, asked the Senate to investigate the Louisiana Lottery's influence within his state, including its corruption of Florida elections. An amazing request from a white southern Democratic politician, other Democrats made sure it was not granted.[18]

Opposition to the Lottery operations persisted, although Louisianians, apparently satisfied once the cursed institution had left their state, played little role in the second phase of the movement. *Our Day*, the *Christian Statesman*, and the wctu still continued the fight, as did several churches, including the Southern Baptist Convention and the largest southern and northern Methodist general conferences. Wilbur Crafts, who had taken credit for getting Wanamaker interested in 1890, again claimed to have exerted some influence.[19]

Crafts and almost everyone else, however, acknowledged that Lyman Abbott and S. Homer Woodbridge did the most to convince Congress to take additional action against the Lottery—to do what the Louisiana Anti-Lottery League asked, deprive it of the use of interstate commerce. Woodbridge, a Congregationalist and professor at the Massachusetts Institute of Technology, first became interested in the cause in December 1890. He had fallen ill while on a visit to New Orleans and, during his recovery there, learned of the antilottery fight. He wrote Abbott, editor of the influential magazine the *Christian Union*, to urge him to join the fight against the Lottery. By chance, the letter arrived while George Johnston, the Anti-Lottery League's representative, was in Abbott's office, and soon the three began to cooperate. In January 1892, Joseph Cook organized an antilottery meeting at Tremont Temple, where he, Johnston, and Abbott spoke against the lottery. Two years later, with the Louisiana Lottery then operating in Florida, Abbott circulated a petition calling on Congress to employ federal power over interstate commerce to stop express companies from transporting lottery materials.[20]

In the spring of 1894, many such petitions, far more than during the earlier lottery debates, arrived in Congress, most of them from New England, mid-Atlantic, or midwestern states. While Abbott mobilized public opinion, Woodbridge worked with Senator George Frisbie Hoar of Massachusetts to prepare and guide legislation through Congress. Rewritten in committee, Hoar's bill extended to all mail the restrictions of the 1890 act that had applied only to registered letters and money orders and, more important, denied lotteries the use of all forms of interstate commerce. It passed in the Senate with only a few changes and without a recorded vote. After revisions in committee, the bill was placed far down on the House calendar and attempts to consider it under unanimous consent failed (twice on objections from a New Orleans representative). With the aid of a southerner who supported the bill, Speaker Charles F. Crisp of Georgia, and with ministers recruited by Woodbridge pressuring doubtful members of the Rules and Judiciary Committees, the bill was brought up at the very end of the session. It passed with no discussion or recorded vote; after a renewed fight, the Senate concurred with the House changes. President Cleveland signed the bill.[21]

In 1903, a divided Supreme Court—the decision was five to four—upheld the law. "As a State may, for the purpose of guarding the morals of its own people, forbid all sales of lottery tickets within its limits, so Congress, for the purpose of guarding the people of the United States against the 'widespread pestilence of lotteries' . . . may prohibit the carrying of lottery tickets from one State to another." When Congress acted to stop such commerce, added Justice John Harlan, it did not violate "any one's liberty" since no one had a right to "introduce into commerce among the States an element that will be confessedly injurious to the public morals." Harlan's decision upheld the ban on lottery materials in interstate commence and recognized an implicit federal police power over interstate commerce; it would be used to justify other laws that expanded the moral powers of the federal government.[22]

Meanwhile, the Louisiana Lottery, denied access both to the mails and to the express companies, tried to conduct its operation from Honduras, but finally closed in 1907. Federal laws had driven the Louisiana Lottery out of business and, in conjunction with various state laws, destroyed all legal lotteries within the United States. Although the federal assault on lotteries was less dramatic than the attack on polygamy, it was as and maybe even more significant. For the first time, Congress employed the federal interstate commerce power in legislating morality. It thereby established an important legal precedent, a federal police power over interstate commerce.

The campaign against the lottery also proved significant because it revealed how far the reconstruction of the politics of morality had progressed. Whereas southerners almost uniformly opposed antilottery legislation in the years immediately after the Civil War, during the 1880s a few began to support it, and in the early 1890s, southerners provided crucial leadership and votes in the passage of the legislation that killed the Lottery. Moreover, white Louisianians, even arch-secessionist Benjamin Morgan Palmer, demanding national laws to rid their state of a peculiar institution was a compelling demonstration of the evolution in southern attitudes toward the use of federal power to ensure morality. That Palmer, other ministers, and two major southern denominations played a very public role also testified to a reversal of southerners' pre–Civil War hostility toward ministers in national politics. Several factors contributed to a change of attitudes in Dixie.

In the antebellum period, white southerners had divided over whether to legislate morality at the local and state level. Some supported it and others celebrated individual assertion and personal liberty. That division persisted after the war and throughout the era of moral reconstruction, but by the 1890s, the forces of moral order were coming to dominate the region. A growth in the number of towns and a slight rise in the size and influence of the middle class expanded the social base for moral reform and for government intervention of various types. Advances in transportation and communication helped make southerners aware of the social changes throughout the nation that worried the Christian lobbyists. Just as northerners did, some southerners feared the effects of appetite and avarice. In addition, evangelicals became more numerous in the postwar

South and, as the antilottery movement in Louisiana showed, more willing to exercise their moral authority—an authority rooted in the region's distinctive religious demography. Methodists and Baptists, and to a lesser extent Presbyterians, dominated the South's public life as in no other section of the country. The South received few of the many Catholic and Jewish immigrants who came to America at the turn of the century, people who brought different conceptions of personal morality, especially on issues like drinking and keeping the Sabbath. White southerners prided themselves on their region's religious homogeneity, and many Americans, including some of the Christian lobbyists, perceived an almost uniformly Protestant South as an important moral resource in an increasingly heterogeneous society.[23]

Along with the modernization of the South and the rise in the influence of its evangelicals, the legacy of emancipation played an important role in shifting the balance in southern attitudes toward moral legislation, at both the state and the federal level. Emancipation broke the subtle link between black slavery and white liberty. Under slavery, responsibility for ensuring proper moral behavior by blacks rested with the masters, not the government. Faced with what they perceived as a growing threat to the moral order from blacks and, after emancipation, no longer able to rely on the masters to control them, southern whites became more willing to turn to government to control black behavior, even though passing laws inevitably curtailed the freedom of whites as well.

The role of race in the change can be seen most clearly in the temperance crusade. Predominately black counties in the South led the nation in the adoption of local option laws, and when states began to enact prohibition in the twentieth century, southern states again led the way. Between 1907 and 1909, Oklahoma, Georgia, Mississippi, North Carolina, Tennessee, and Alabama (although it later reversed itself) enacted statewide prohibition. Not by coincidence, this burst of prohibition laws came as whites' postemancipation fears of "dangerous," "immoral" blacks peaked and southern states consolidated a system of racial control.[24]

Emancipation not only led white southerners to support moral legislation at the state and local levels, it eliminated the politics of slavery, which before the war had led them to oppose federal actions. They no longer needed to oppose federal legislation of morality as a possible precedent for a national attack on slavery. However, the politics of race, which replaced the politics of slavery and encouraged state laws to regulate moral behavior, still left southerners suspicious of federal moral legislation, which might set a precedent that could later be used to justify federal intervention in southern race relations. Over time, various developments eased white southern fears of federal intervention. Many of the Christian lobbyists came to share the South's view of the danger and immorality of free blacks and made it clear to the South that they favored leaving southern whites alone to deal with African Americans as they pleased. More important, beginning in 1883 and culminating with the *Plessy v. Ferguson* decision in 1896, the federal courts approved the South's emerging system of racial oppression. In 1890, Congress refused to pass the Lodge Force Bill, which provided for federal observers during southern elections, and four years later repealed many of the Reconstruction-era enforcement acts. The legislative branch and the Republican Party thereby signaled white southerners that they no longer intended to intervene in southern race relations.

Some southern members of Congress remained unconvinced and continued to oppose moral legislation for reasons that echoed those offered by Morgan, Call, Vest, and other of their predecessors from Dixie. But increasing numbers of them, as congressional votes against polygamy, for closing the World's Fair on Sunday, and finally against the Lottery showed, no longer worried that federal legislation would set a dangerous precedent. In fact, in the 1890s, as they had in fighting the Lottery, white southerners began to seek federal involvement in regulating morality. The percentage of bills to regulate morality entered by southerners rose steadily, and after 1907, southerners introduced over 36 percent of the bills for moral legislation, more than legislators from any other region. The types of bills that southerners introduced reflected the politics of race. They most often sought regulation of behavior that white southerners associated with blacks—drinking, gambling, and the distribution of obscenity—and that could be controlled by laws that entailed little possibility of federal challenge to southern racial norms. On marriage and divorce or purity and prostitution, issues where federal involvement might have created opportunities or only a precedent for intervention in antimiscegenation laws or other southern racial practices, southern legislators less often requested or supported federal action. Southern petitions to Congress displayed a similar pattern of interest in certain types of legislation.[25]

Nevertheless, removing the issue of slavery from debates over religion in politics and the legislation of morality made it easier for white southerners to accept both. Whereas before the Civil War, the politics of slavery had undermined southern support for the legislation of morality, the politics of race—the white South's determination to establish and preserve a repressive racial order—could and often did work in tandem with the politics of morality.

CHAPTER SEVEN

A Broad Agenda of Moral Legislation

On 8 December 1897, the second day of the Fifty-fifth Congress, the House of Representatives recorded thirty-nine petitions asking it to enact five different types of moral legislation. These petitions asked Congress to raise the age of consent in the District of Columbia, to restore the Sabbath law in the capital, to prohibit the sale of liquor in all government buildings, to forbid interstate betting, and to prevent the transmission across state lines of pictures or descriptions of prizefights. They came from towns or cities across the nation, from New Hampshire to Iowa to California, and were among the first of over seven thousand such petitions sent to the House during the Fifty-fifth Congress.[1]

Seven thousand was more than twice as many petitions as Congress had received during the fight to close the World's Fair in the Fifty-second Congress and almost fourteen times the number received during the antipolygamy fight in the Forty-fifth. Christian Endeavor societies sent around 8 percent, the WCTU, roughly 35 percent, and individual churches, over 45 percent of the petitions to the Fifty-fifth Congress, roughly 1897 to 1899. Quaker and Lutheran congregations sent a few; Presbyterians, Congregationalists, and other denominations within the Reformed tradition contributed more but did not dominate the campaign as once they had. Methodists (over 14 percent) and Baptists (6 percent) sent more than any other denomination. Like the denominational base, the geographical base of the petition campaign had also broadened. New England, the mid-Atlantic states, the Midwest, and the West sent roughly equal numbers of petitions (between 20 and 27 percent each). Only the southern and border states sent very few (1.4 and 3.5 percent, respectively), which may have reflected continued opposition to moral laws among some southerners, the lobbyists' relative failure to organize in the South, or maybe simply those regions' lack of enthusiasm for petitioning.[2]

The increased number of petitions, the broad geographical base from which
they came, and the heavy participation of the churches testified to the success
the alliance of Christian lobbyists had in creating a national base in the 1880s.
By the mid-1890s, a permanent Christian lobby to focus the power of that national base had been established in Washington, and southerners in Congress
had demonstrated a new willingness to vote for moral legislation. The con-
fluence of these three developments propelled an expansion of federal power
over morality in the twenty-five years after 1895 far greater than that during the
early stages of moral reconstruction after the Civil War. Led by Wilbur Crafts of
the Reform Bureau and Margaret Dye Ellis of the wctu, the Christian lobby
sought to enact the broad agenda of reform their organizations had embraced
in the 1880s. It included a renewed effort to control alcohol, which became the
central cause of the Christian lobbyists by 1910 and will be discussed in subsequent chapters. The lobbyists also continued to pursue legislation on other
issues that Congress had already debated—gambling, Sabbath observance, polygamy, marriage and divorce, and the control of sexuality. But Congress, usually though not always at the request of the lobbyists, also considered legislation to control narcotics, cigarettes, prizefighting, and obscenity in the movies.

Crafts arrived in Washington in 1895 shortly after the victory over the Louisiana
Lottery, and antigambling legislation initially commanded his "chief energies."
During his first year in the capital, he and Anthony Comstock worked to prevent the creation of a racing commission in the District of Columbia. Crafts,
Comstock, the wctu, the Christian Endeavor societies, and many churches next
campaigned for a bill to make it illegal to use the "telegraph or telephone or
mail or express" or any other means to "bet or report on a race, prizefight, or
other event." In 1898, the House Judiciary Committee, citing the precedent of
the antilottery legislation, reported such a bill, but it never came up for debate.
During the next four Congresses, other bills banning interstate gambling were
introduced but none were reported. In 1906, Congress refused to establish an
antigambling statute for the territories. The lobbyists' only success against gambling came in 1908 when Congress passed a bill, entered by Thetus Sims of Tennessee at Crafts's request, that outlawed all betting in the District of Columbia.
Between 1910 and 1916, Crafts and Ellis did convince Congress to hold a series of
hearings on interstate gambling, but no legislation resulted.[3]

On another old issue, Sabbath legislation, the lobbyists had only marginally more success. After getting Congress to close the Columbian World's Fair on Sunday, the Christian lobbyists revived efforts to enact a national Sunday law. In 1894, Ida Hinman, a reporter who worked with the NRA and sometimes lobbied Congress on behalf of the WCTU, had introduced in Congress a bill very similar to Blair's national Sunday law, and Josephine Bateham planned a major lobbying campaign. By the end of the year, however, the WCTU's chief lobbyist on Sabbath matters concluded that her efforts were doomed and dropped them. Crafts took up the cause, but the bill he had introduced in the next Congress never got out of committee. Crafts, Ellis, and the other Christian lobbyists finally accepted the fact that Congress had no interest in passing a national Sabbath law and therefore sought more restricted legislation, a Sunday law for the District of Columbia and an end to Sunday mail delivery.[4]

An 1886 change in the structure of its government and legal technicalities had left the District of Columbia without a general Sunday law. The absence of one appalled Bateham and Crafts because they believed the nation's capital should serve as a model of Sabbath observance for the nation. The Reform Bureau, the WCTU, and other religious groups sent petitions to several successive Congresses in favor of one, but their efforts were countered by petitions against it from the Seventh-Day Baptists and Adventists. In 1904, the House finally passed a Sunday law for the District, although not the restrictive one advocated by Ellis and Crafts. It failed in the Senate, however. Similar legislation, sponsored by J. Thomas Heflin and Joseph F. Johnston, both of Alabama, remained before Congress for the next several years.[5]

Opponents of Johnston's bill revived the old arguments against moral legislation in general and Sabbath laws in particular, claiming that Sunday laws violated the rights of Jews and established a religious test. They also challenged the exceptions allowed under the bill: hotels, restaurants, and livery stables were allowed to operate on Sunday; people could play baseball and golf; and stores could sell "milk, fruit, confectionery, ice, soda and mineral waters, newspapers, periodicals, cigars, drugs, medicines, and surgical supplies." Opponents asked why cigars but not tobacco could be sold or why shoes could be shined but faces not shaved on Sunday. One questioned how golf could be considered a religious exercise. The exceptions, however, pointed to major new threats to Sunday observation, consumer convenience and modern leisure, which many Americans did not want to give up, even on Sunday.[6]

Concessions to an emerging leisure and consumer society troubled the Christian lobbyists. They sought a more consistent policy of Sabbath observation and wanted it grounded on religious authority. Nevertheless, the lobbyists supported Johnston's bill because they felt it an improvement and because, along with the *Christian Statesman*, they believed that it would help "many . . . now deprived of their weekly rest" as well as lend "support . . . to our national Christianity." Yet the lobbyists failed to secure even so limited a law. The Senate passed Johnston's bill in 1910, but the House never acted on it. Sunday laws for the District of Columbia were introduced in subsequent years, but none ever became law.[7]

Christian lobbyists had more success on their second campaign, one that had begun before the Civil War: ending Sunday mails. Throughout the 1890s and into the 1900s, the Reform Bureau, the WCTU, and especially local Christian Endeavor societies petitioned to close individual post offices on Sunday. In 1904 and 1905, Ellis and Crafts tried but failed to get Congress to end what they called "Sunday banking" in post offices, the handling of money orders and registered letters. More important, as it turned out, postal carriers and clerks pressed for a reduction in the hours that they had to work on Sunday. In response to their pressure as well as that of Sabbath reformers, in 1912 Congress finally outlawed Sunday mail delivery in all first- and second-class post offices, those in towns and cities. The few local experiments in Sunday home delivery had already been abandoned. Rural post offices still operated for limited hours on Sunday, and special delivery continued everywhere, as did the shipment and handling of mail on Sunday. However, the post office delivery window, for a century condemned by many Christians as a sign of the government's disrespect for the Lord's Day, had finally closed.[8]

The Christian lobbyists' limited victory in the battle against Sunday mail came in part because of the efforts of the postal workers; as was often the case, the lobbyists could not work their will alone. They failed to secure a Sunday law for the District of Columbia, much less a national one. These bills failed because some objected to the indirect assertion of religious authority they involved and because other religious groups, even other Christians, opposed the choice of Sunday as the day of rest. The emerging consumer society also posed a formidable challenge to the passage of Sabbath laws.

Even as the Christian lobbyists continued their campaign for antigambling and Sabbath legislation, they revived their crusade against polygamy. In 1898, Utah elected Brigham H. Roberts to the House of Representatives; nine years earlier,

Roberts had pled guilty to polygamy and served time in jail, but he subsequently received a presidential pardon that restored his political rights. Nevertheless, his political opponents in Utah called on Congress to deny him a seat in the House.[9]

The Christian lobbyists, along with churches, women's groups, and other organizations, urged Congress to exclude Roberts. Crafts, in an article in the *Union Signal*, damned Roberts as a "confessed polygamist, living with three wives," and claimed that he was elected because he championed polygamy "as a defiant repudiation of Utah's covenant" to abandon polygamy in return for statehood. The *Union Signal* not only published Crafts's article but took up the fight; Ellis told its readers to send personal letters to their legislators, and Lillian M. N. Stevens of the WCTU warned that if Roberts were seated, the practice of polygamy in Utah would return to former proportions.[10]

When Congress convened in December 1899, petitions against seating Roberts were wrapped in red, white, and blue and piled high in front of the Speaker's desk. The House of Representatives voted to delay seating Roberts and created a special committee to investigate him. It concluded that he continued to practice polygamy and by electing him, Utah had violated its implied agreement with Congress to abandon polygamy in return for statehood. Most representatives accepted the committee's findings and agreed that a polygamist should not serve in the House. The only real debate centered on whether Roberts should be excluded or admitted and immediately expelled. Some southerners, perhaps remembering the exclusion of southern representatives after the Civil War or worried about a precedent that might in the future be turned against representatives from states that defied the Fifteenth Amendment, favored expulsion. In the end, however, the House voted overwhelmingly to exclude Roberts.[11]

The Roberts case revived interest in a constitutional amendment against polygamy and polygamous cohabitation; the later provision would have outlawed living with plural wives married before the Church of Jesus Christ of Latter-day Saints presumed reversal on polygamy. Over the next few years, many resolutions or bills in behalf of a broad antipolygamy amendment were entered; none ever passed. Frank J. Cannon, son of a high Mormon official who broke with his father and became an anti-Mormon agitator, claimed that in 1900 a representative of the Republican Party reached an agreement with Mormon leaders in which they promised to support William McKinley's reelection in return for the party's pledge to block a constitutional amendment that would give the federal government power over marriage and divorce. Such a deal, if in fact it was made, would surely have applied to an antipolygamy amendment. Nevertheless, the WCTU, the NRA, and other Christian reformers continued to lobby for a constitutional amendment against polygamy.[12]

Late in 1902, the Christian lobbyists confronted a new challenge from Utah when its legislature elected Reed Smoot, a high official in the Mormon Church, to the Senate. He was allowed to take his seat, but a four-year congressional investigation of Smoot and a public debate over a Mormon's fitness to serve in the Senate followed. The WCTU, the NRA, and other Christian groups shifted their efforts from passing an amendment to preventing Smoot from remaining a senator. Petitions began to arrive almost at once, and Ellis actively lobbied against Smoot. She made it clear that the WCTU opposed not "the individual Reed Smoot" but "Apostle Smoot," the "sworn, obedient tool" of "the Mormon hierarchy" and "a system so unnatural, so inhuman and abhorrent, so debasing to womanhood," "occupying the exalted position of United States Senator."[13]

As public clamor grew and the investigation of Smoot proceeded, Mormon leaders realized how much their church's reputation was being damaged. They issued a second manifesto against polygamy and, after talk of disfranchising Mormons revived, forced two officials to resign for performing plural marriages. Spurred primarily by the Smoot hearings, these actions, not the earlier Woodruff Manifesto, actually marked the end of the church's commitment to polygamy. The practice did not end, for various polygamous sects persisted, but the church hierarchy abandoned it.[14]

Perhaps the church's additional measures against polygamy reassured some of its critics. Or, perhaps, as Frank Cannon claimed, church leaders made deals with eastern financial interests to secure Republican support and promised Theodore Roosevelt convention votes in return for abandoning opposition to seating Smoot. Cannon offered no evidence to substantiate his claim, and Roosevelt denied it vehemently. But for certain, a refocusing of the debate proved important to its outcome. The Senate investigation concluded that Smoot had violated the separation of church and state by helping the church wield political influence, had as one of its leaders even taught polygamy, but had not himself practiced it. Opponents of seating Smoot stressed the first two conclusions and revived all the old arguments against Mormonism. His supporters, most of them Republicans, tried to keep the debate focused only on the question of whether Smoot practiced polygamy and argued that since the evidence indicated he did not, he should be a senator.[15]

Philander Knox, a Pennsylvania Republican, proffered an even broader defense for Smoot's being allowed in the Senate. Seating Smoot would, he maintained, preserve a state's right to choose its own representatives, prevent an expansion of the basis for exclusion, as well as protect the American ideal of freedom of religion. All the questions about Smoot's fitness, Knox explained, "grow out of the charge that Senator Smoot is a Mormon." Yet all Christians, Knox continued, pray "to God for guidance in matters both spiritual and temporal, and particularly in times of perplexity and doubt, and many believe that they receive such guidance." He was not prepared to attack the belief that God revealed his will to men, Knox added, and neither were the Founding Fathers.[16]

Whether or not senators agreed with Knox's defense of everyone's right to revelation, they did concur that Smoot should be in the Senate. A resolution to deny Smoot his seat failed. Only nine Republicans voted against Smoot, and only three Democrats voted for him—a dramatic reversal of party lines from the votes on polygamy in the 1880s. Southerners were among the Democrats who opposed seating Smoot; fourteen voted to exclude him, and only one voted to let him keep his seat. Perhaps that reflected their growing support for legislating morality, but, like the Republican vote, it probably had more to do with partisanship. The Democratic and Republican reversals showed how, on occasion, partisanship overruled the politics of morality.[17]

The public clamor and the lobbying of Christian groups had nevertheless managed to do what the Republicans had failed to do in the 1880s and seemed to have lost interest in doing, forcing the Church of Jesus Christ of Latter-day Saints to abandon polygamy. At the same time, the vote on Smoot marked a turning point in congressional attitudes toward Mormonism. Seating Smoot offered implicit acknowledgment that Congress believed that the Mormons had kept their covenant with the nation and that no further action needed to be taken against polygamy. The fact that the debate over seating Smoot centered on whether or not he practiced polygamy also suggested that legislators, and perhaps the public, had lost what little willingness they had earlier displayed to challenge Mormon revelation. Like the failure to put God in the Constitution or pass a national Sunday law, the waning of anti-Mormon zeal suggested Congress was not comfortable judging religious authority. At the very least, Congress had decided to treat the Church of Jesus Christ of Latter-day Saints as just another American denomination, not the danger to morality or threat to the separation of church and state many had believed it to be in the

1880s. Even the more limited issue of polygamy never again commanded national attention. The Christian lobbyists remained convinced that the Mormons still practiced polygamy and for another decade continued their crusade for a constitutional amendment—but to no avail.

The lobbyists had no more success with their efforts to secure a constitutional amendment on marriage and divorce. Calls for one had increased after Carroll Wright's 1889 compilation of statistics, the result of the last attempt to secure a national divorce law, which generally substantiated fears of a rising divorce rate. Even so, all the Christian reformers did not agree on the need for a national law or even on standards for divorce.

Frances Willard and the WCTU believed in the importance of the family, the ideal of Christian marriage, and the need for laws to preserve, in Willard's words, "the mutual, life-long loyalty of one man and one woman to each other, which is the central idea of every home." Some WCTU women, including Willard, saw the threat to the family not in divorce but in existing conceptions of the family. They demanded equality between husband and wife. Even moderate members of the WCTU, who did not propose full equality in marriage and generally supported restrictions on divorce, still believed that women should not be forced to live with dangerous men, especially drunkards who threatened them or their children. The WCTU's ambivalence about the availability of divorce may have explained why WCTU lobbyists played little role in the battle for national divorce reform.[18]

The Christian lobbyists' crusade for a national divorce law also suffered from a dispute between Samuel Dike, the nation's leading authority on divorce, and the NRA. Dike sought to build a consensus for divorce reform by promoting the compilation and study of statistics on the problem and advocated a uniform law for the states rather than a constitutional amendment. The leaders of the NRA, in contrast, believed divorce legislation had to rest on the authority of the Bible and suggested a constitutional amendment granting the federal government authority over marriage and divorce.[19]

In 1892, with three resolutions for such an amendment entered in Congress, the NRA lobbied in their behalf. Dike opposed its efforts, dismissing the NRA's leaders as "parties . . . not fully informed regarding the problem." The Senate Judiciary Committee took no action, and the House committee, despite a minority report on the need for uniform laws, reported adversely a resolution for a national law. The committee majority considered the proposal too great an expansion of federal power into an area long reserved to the states. If Congress had authority over all domestic relations, the majority added, "who can doubt that there soon would be a law enacted securing the right of marriage between any man and woman of lawful age, without regard to race, color, or previous condition," which would "encourage the mixing of races." A year later, a commission, dominated by lawyers, formed and wrote a uniform law for each state to adopt; from that point on, Dike worked more with the commission than the Christian lobbyists.[20]

When Crafts opened his Reform Bureau in 1895 he sought to breach the divisions among the lobbyists. Although Crafts favored stringent divorce laws based on scriptural grounds, he acknowledged the concerns of many in the wctu by advocating that legal separation without divorce "be allowed for drunkenness, desertion and cruelty, not less, but more frequently than it is." Despite some tension between them, Crafts also managed to work with Dike. Together, they lobbied not for an amendment but only a divorce law for the territories and the District of Columbia.[21]

Oklahoma, the Dakotas, and other territories had short residence requirements, and rich people from states with stringent divorce laws could move to them and secure a quick end to their marriage. These "divorce mills," as such places were called, remained a central concern of many Americans; divorce was one moral issue where publicized sinning among the rich generated more interest in reform than the failings of the poor. In 1896, with urging from Dike and Crafts, Frederick Gillett, a Massachusetts Republican, entered a divorce law for the territories that limited divorce to people who had lived in them for one year. Crafts, who wrote the bill, actually favored a longer residence requirement but figured a year was the best he could get. The *Christian Statesman*, the unofficial voice of the NRA, called for petitions and letters to be sent to the judiciary committees in behalf of Gillett's bill. The committees reported it favorably, and the bill passed easily in both houses. When the president signed it, he gave the pen to Gillett, who passed it on to Crafts.[22]

Crafts then turned his attention to a divorce law for the District of Columbia. In 1900, after a Washington judge condemned the capital as a mecca for divorce, Crafts promoted a bill that allowed divorce only for adultery, but separation from bed and board (a legal separation without the right of remarriage) in cases of cruel treatment endangering life and health, willful desertion and abandonment for two years, or habitual drunkenness for three years. Crafts and others sought the provision for separation, long a practice in the law, as a means to protect women while still upholding the sacred bond of marriage.

Offered as an amendment to legislation establishing a code of laws for the District of Columbia, Crafts's proposal passed with little discussion.[23]

Having passed tougher laws for the territories and the capital, where it had clear authority, Congress steadfastly refused to consider federal regulation of marriage and divorce. None of the forty-two resolutions introduced in Congress between 1892 and 1920 ever received a favorable committee report. Congress clearly had no intention of turning over responsibility for setting standards of marriage and divorce to the federal government. Several factors contributed to Congress's refusal to act. White southerners, whose support for moral legislation was often crucial, opposed an amendment because they feared it might lead to federal action against state antimiscegenation laws. The influential American Bar Association and the Interchurch Conference on Marriage and Divorce, called together by the Episcopalians and composed of representatives from many leading denominations, preferred to work for uniform state laws rather than for federal control. Its representatives, and apparently Dike as well, did so in part because they feared a federal amendment would lead to an easing of restrictions in states like New York or South Carolina, which had the most stringent divorce laws. And even the Christian lobbyists could not agree on a strategy or legitimate grounds for divorce because they disagreed over what the Bible allowed. Divisions among the Christian lobbyists, the absence of a moral consensus on standards of divorce, and a hesitancy to expand federal power made it difficult for Congress to pass anything but the narrowest laws on marriage and divorce.[24]

When the Christian lobbyists turned their attention to the control of sexuality, they benefited from more widespread agreement on moral standards. Most Americans considered sex outside of marriage both a sin and a threat to the family and feared that young women who had sex before marriage all but inevitably fell into prostitution and ruin. The lobbyists also got help from the New York Committee for the Prevention of State Regulation of Vice, the National Purity Alliance, and other groups that organized after the Civil War to campaign for sexual purity. In the early twentieth century, additional groups formed, among them the National Purity Conference and the National Vigilance Council. These Progressive Era reform groups sometimes worried less about the decline of morals and more about the spread of venereal disease. They campaigned against prostitution in the rhetoric of social efficiency and placed their faith in rational decisions drawn from carefully collected evidence.

The Christian lobbyists sometimes worked with them but operated from very different assumptions.[25]

Frances Willard, who became concerned about prostitution after reading William T. Stead's reports on the prevalence and dangers of prostitution in England, developed a sophisticated analysis of the problems of impurity, which resembled her views on divorce. She attacked the double standard, the dominant cultural ideal that sex outside of marriage was a devastating sin for women, who lost all social and moral standing if they succumbed to its temptations, but a necessary evil if not fully permissible for men, whose reputations easily survived what some termed an "indiscretion." In opposing the double standard, Willard argued that to save women, men needed to be raised "above the merely brutal or even worse than brutal mire of animalism into which" they had "sunk, in all save Christian homes." However, Willard contended, a single moral standard could exist only when women had political power, control over reproduction, and the economic resources to make marriage a true matter of the heart. As she often did, Willard combined her radical analysis with more traditional moralistic rhetoric. At times she blamed the prevalence of impurity on very different influences—the excitement of the ballet, women who wore revealing clothes, theatrical and cigarette advertisements, and, as with almost every failing, the pernicious influence of the saloon.[26]

Few Christian lobbyists embraced Willard's call for full equality of males and females within marriage, but most shared her concern about impurity and agreed on the necessity of holding males to the same standard of sexual purity as women. The *Christian Statesman* endorsed the WCTU's purity crusade; so too did Joseph Cook in a Monday Lecture. Crafts did as well, and his explanation for the growth in impurity and prostitution proved more typical than Willard's. Crafts blamed the prevalence of "this vice" among blacks on the heritage of slavery and their religion, "which, in many cases—there are a few noble exceptions—gives undue attention to emotion, and provides too little ethical instruction and discipline." A similar problem arose among immigrants, Crafts added, because the Roman Catholic faith "neglects ethics to exalt ritual." Even "Americans," Craft admitted, gave in to lust and participated in prostitution. He attributed their failings to "the growth of luxury," in which "pleasure becomes the chief object of life." Like Esau, licentious Americans lived "for the present, ready to sell the birthright of purity for the momentary gratification of passion." Crafts also blamed liquor, "[i]mpure literature and art," plays, tobacco (which he considered "a sexual irritant"), and the "foulest pictures" put in cigarette cases and tobacco store windows, as "if the tobacco itself were not whip enough to passion." To combat so many dangers, the Christian lobbyists sought laws to expand government control over obscenity and to regulate various forms of sexuality.[27]

In the early 1890s, Anthony Comstock, Emilie D. Martin, who headed the WCTU's department on impure literature, her husband, the *Christian Statesman*, the national YWCA, and various Endeavor societies petitioned and lobbied Congress to expand the Comstock Law's definition of unmailable material to include various newspapers and magazines that featured crime stories, in particular the *Police Gazette*, which they believed led the young into crime and immorality. The Senate Post Office Committee, however, reported the bill adversely. Later, Crafts and the WCTU sought to toughen enforcement of obscenity statutes by denying second-class postal rates to newspapers or magazines that had ever been found to include an obscene story or a lottery ad, but Congress again refused.[28]

Congress was willing to apply the federal police power over interstate commerce, established by the antilottery law, against materials already defined as obscene by the Comstock Law, including anything related to birth control and abortion. Lobbied hard by Crafts, Ellis, Martin, and her husband, Congress in 1897 banned both giving such material to and taking it from an express company. The law, however, made "taking" illegal only "with intent to sell, distribute, or circulate," once more demonstrating that lawmakers were more comfortable regulating commercial vice than private behavior.[29]

In addition to trying to expand existing laws restricting the distribution of obscenity, the Christian lobbyists joined purity reformers in campaigns for direct government regulation of sexuality, laws that raised the age of consent and curtailed prostitution. Age-of-consent laws made it illegal for males to have sex with females under a certain age, then as young as ten or twelve. These laws were sometimes used by parents to restrain their daughters' voluntary sexual activity, which would have pleased the Christian reformers. But the lobbyists called for age-of-consent laws in rhetoric still shaped by assumptions of innate female purity; they believed that young, single women would not wish to have sex unless seduced or coerced. Many WCTU women, in fact, objected to the term "age of consent" and preferred "age of protection," which reflected their belief that innocent young girls needed to be safeguarded from predatory males. The term "consent" reflected the advocates' assumption that below a certain age females were incapable of making a rational decision about their sexuality or were so impressionable that evil influences would overpower their natural innocence. It reflected the same thinking that shaped the Christian lobbyists' equally common rhetoric about "our boys" being so easily overcome by stimulation of their appetites for drink, gambling, or obscenity. Either "protection" or "consent" still cast the government in the role of helping victims and preserving individual liberty rather than curtailing it.[30]

The campaign for congressional action on the age of consent began in the late 1880s when the wctu, the New York Committee for the Prevention of State Regulation of Vice, several churches, and other groups and individuals petitioned Congress in behalf of an increase in the age of protection. With their support and the efforts of Ada Bittenbender, the wctu's first lobbyist, Congress in 1889 finally passed a law that set the age of consent in the District of Columbia at sixteen. Bittenbender had sought to make the age of consent eighteen as a model for cities and states to follow, but sixteen was higher than the age in most states, where the campaigns to raise the age of consent had only begun. Ten years later, and after several attempts, Crafts and a local District of Columbia judge, with help from Ellis and the wctu, the *Christian Statesman*, the recently formed National Purity Alliance, and other groups, convinced Congress to raise the age of consent to twenty-one. The act, though, limited the law's application to the seduction of a girl "of previous chaste character."[31]

Congress had passed two strong age-of-consent laws for the District, but only for the District. That testified to the willingness of Congress to act on the issue of age of consent; it had, after all, refused to pass a Sunday law or, at that time, prohibition for the District. Yet because these age-of-consent laws applied only to Washington, they involved no substantial increase in federal powers. The really significant expansion of federal involvement in sexuality involved prostitution, clear cases of coercion, and the use of the interstate commerce power. It came primarily through the efforts of others, not the Christian lobbyists.

In the first decade of the twentieth century, the United States experienced a "white slavery" panic over reports that organized gangs and syndicates imported foreign prostitutes and kidnapped American country girls, who were then forced to work in urban brothels. The hysteria produced a host of city vice commission studies, novels, plays, and motion pictures. Although coercion of women into prostitution occurred, it happened nowhere nearly as often as would have justified public fears. The hysteria had many sources, but it incorporated several themes commonly employed by the Christian lobbyists. Cities served as the stage and immigrants as the villains in the hysteria's stories of moral degradation. "Fallen women" were victims in need of rescue, not sinners to be punished; legislation would be directed at commercial vice, not personal behavior. Even the term "white slavery" echoed the Christian lobbyists' practice of employing the slavery analogy in discussing other immoral behavior.[32]

Congress had already acted to keep foreign prostitutes from being brought into the country in laws passed in 1875, 1903, and 1907, and Ellis had convinced Congress and the executive branch to appoint female inspectors in New York harbor to protect female emigrants from procurers. In 1908, the United States signed a treaty that committed it to help suppress the international "white slave" trade. In late 1909, with the "white slave" panic at full throttle, the U.S. district attorney in Chicago convinced Congressman James R. Mann of Chicago to enter a bill not just to stop the international but also the interstate transportation of prostitutes. Although Ellis mobilized the WCTU and the NRA supported the bill as well, their help was hardly needed. Congress was so anxious to appease the popular clamor that it passed another bill against transporting prostitutes even as it debated Mann's.[33]

Mann's bill was the more important and comprehensive of the two, however. It contained a provision to stop the emigration of prostitutes, but, more important, made it a federal crime for anyone to transport or to "knowingly persuade, induce, entice, or coerce" or even to "cause" or to aid, a woman to cross state lines for "the purpose of prostitution or debauchery, or for any other immoral purpose." Violations of the law carried a fine of $5,000 and a possible jail term of five years; both could be doubled if the woman involved was under eighteen. No matter the age of the woman, she did not commit a crime by crossing state lines; the person who took her or induced her to make the trip did. The distinction reflected the assumptions of the panic and the age-of-consent laws, that innocent women were being tricked or forced into immoral behavior.[34]

Making the crime the crossing of state lines acknowledged that the federal government could interfere only if interstate commerce was involved. By 1910, when Mann's bill was debated, federal power over interstate commerce had already been employed in quarantine legislation and regulation of food and drugs. Mann and his allies pointed to both precedents but also cited earlier moral legislation, the bans on lottery materials and obscenity in interstate trade. Opposition to using the commerce power to allow government intervention in yet another area of life came primarily from southern Democrats. Several of them on both the House and Senate committees reporting Mann's bill signed minority reports against it.[35]

On the floor of the House, four southerners and one midwestern Republican proved the most vocal opponents of Mann's bill. All stressed the importance of maintaining states' rights and preserving constitutional limits on federal power. William Richardson of Alabama, for example, questioned the wisdom of giving the federal government authority to enforce an international treaty within the United States. He mentioned that treaties had been the justification for the pressure put on Louisiana after the lynching of Italians in New Orleans and for Theodore Roosevelt's efforts to force California to allow Japanese in its schools. Richardson may have worried less about the two incidents he mentioned, however, than the creation of a precedent for federal intervention in the lynching of blacks or in southern school segregation. The fact that Mann's bill involved morality proved especially troubling for Richardson, who distinguished it from the regulation of drugs or food, which he found more acceptable.[36]

As had happened in debates on closing the World's Fair on Sunday, southern opponents were challenged by southern supporters of Mann's bill. Edward W. Saunders of Virginia and Thetus Sims of Tennessee both argued that Congress had a responsibility to protect "public morals." Certainly, Sims added, the plight of defenseless girls treated so brutally overrode any constitutional reservations. Gordon J. Russell of Texas made much the same point, but by quoting Tom Watson on how Chicago blacks bought white wives captured in the South, he invoked racial fears in behalf of federal action. Russell also offered a racist variation on the antislavery analogy: "More than forty years ago this country was drenched in fraternal blood and offered up the lives of nearly a million of the very pick and flower of its citizenship in the struggle to abolish the slavery of the black man. In God's name, can we do no less now than pass this bill, which will be a step toward abolishing the slavery of white women?"[37]

Congress could do no less and could not do it fast enough. The House passed Mann's bill without a recorded vote, which hid southern division on the issue; the four-against, three-for split during the debate suggested a rather even one. The Senate, too, passed the bill without a recorded vote, but also without debate. President William Howard Taft quickly signed it. Rapid passage clearly reflected the political pressure created by the "white slave" panic, but it also resembled the enactment of the Comstock Law forty years earlier, when fears of commercialized vice also silenced debate.

Haste made for confused legislation. No one seemed sure whether the Mann Act applied to interstate travel only for purposes of prostitution or also when it involved noncommercial sex, between a man and his mistress, for instance. The act included in the list of purposes for which a woman could not be transported "debauchery, or for any other immoral purpose." The latter part of that phrase had first appeared in the 1907 immigration law, and an intervening

Supreme Court decision had held that it applied to men bringing mistresses into the country, a point reiterated in the Senate report on Mann's bill and once during debate on the House floor. Expanding the language and acknowledging the precedent suggested Congress intended a broad reading of the act to include all sex other than that of husband and wife, not just prostitution.[38]

For three years, federal authorities never clearly established whether they would pursue noncommercial prosecutions, but then a high-profile case brought the issue to national attention. Two married men, sons of politically prominent families in California, took two young women across state lines for a tryst. Purity reformers, women's clubs, and church groups besieged President Woodrow Wilson and the Department of Justice with requests that the Mann Act be applied to noncommercial "escapades," as they termed affairs like those of the two Californians. Among the people pushing the Justice Department was Crafts, who claimed that the Mann Act "distinctly prohibits" men taking women across state lines, "whether for their own carnal indulgence or to fill their pockets." The Supreme Court eventually concurred in Crafts's reading of the law and held that the Mann Act did allow prosecution of cases other than those involving prostitution. During the 1920s, the law was frequently used in instances of illicit but not commercial sexual activity, but enforcement later centered on prostitution, save in cases involving women who were very young or married and, more often, men who were gangsters, political dissidents, or for some other reason, targets of government harassment. During the same period, enforcement of the Mann Act grew more erratic. It nevertheless constituted a dramatic expansion of federal power over morality in general and sexuality in particular.[39]

At about the same time it passed the Mann Act, Congress also took dramatic action to end the sale of narcotics. In the late nineteenth century, Americans had not worried much about drug use. A few bills to stop the importation of opium into the United States were entered in Congress. None passed, except for one to carry out a treaty banning the importation of opium from China, and it had little impact. The Christian lobbyists did not sponsor any of this legislation, although some of them did campaign against drug use. The WCTU created a department on narcotics problems, and its leaders expressed concern about the use of hard drugs. Crafts and his Reform Bureau became more active in the antidrug crusade. In 1902, he led a protest that forced President Theodore Roosevelt to end government-approved sales of opium to the Chinese in the new

American colony, the Philippines. Two years later, the Reform Bureau organized a hearing at the State Department where Crafts and representatives of the Christian Endeavor Society, WCTU, National Temperance Society, and Anti-Saloon League urged an end to the opium trade to China. After that, Crafts devoted much of his time to the opium problem in Asia, primarily through efforts there rather than in Washington. He and other reformers played at most a small role in the passage of federal antinarcotics laws.[40]

The pressure for narcotics laws came primarily from diplomats, who sought to curry favor with the Chinese by suppressing the worldwide trade in opium. Their primary goal was a stronger international treaty, but they realized that for the United States to have any credibility in negotiating one, it would have to strengthen its own drug laws. The diplomats' efforts led, in 1909, to a very weak law banning the importation of smoking opium. Five years later, Congress passed two bills to regulate the importation and sale of opium and coca leaves; they restricted the sale of narcotics to licensed dealers and limited the amounts they could sell to individuals. The more important of the two bills, the Harrison Act, did not make clear whether doctors could prescribe drugs to people who were already addicted. When federal agents tried to stop doctors from maintaining addicts, courts initially rejected such an application of the law. In 1919, however, the Supreme Court ruled that the Harrison Act did not allow prescriptions for maintenance of an addiction.[41]

Many WCTU members and others linked drugs and tobacco, believing both were addictive and dangerous. People had condemned the use of tobacco since its introduction in England during the time of King James, and in the United States antitobacco crusades began before the Civil War. In the 1880s and 1890s, with automated production and expanded advertising, the consumption of cigarettes rose, and Christian lobbyists focused their antismoking efforts on this relatively new form of tobacco use. It involved both appetite and avarice, and cigarettes were most popular among the groups that the Christian lobbyists thought most in moral peril—immigrants in the cities, the young, the poor, and workers everywhere. That tobacco manufacturers sought to stimulate sales by including pictures of scantily clad women in cigarette packages only made matters worse in the minds of Christian lobbyists.[42]

The lobbyists thought cigarettes evil in themselves but also believed smoking led to other sins. "Cigarettes, drink and lust are the devil's trio," proclaimed one reformer in the *Union Signal.* "Cigarette smoking destroys not only bodily and mental health, and refinement of manners, but it also aids materially in the destruction of our moral and spiritual life." To substantiate that claim, reformers offered evidence that smoking among schoolboys led to poor moral choices or that a high percentage of men in prison smoked. The lobbyists also emphasized the health dangers posed by "coffin nails," a term already in use. In 1885, for example, the WCTU superintendent of the "Department for the Overthrow of the Tobacco Habit" reported that the "fatal results of cigarette smoking are rapidly multiplying" and specifically mentioned "cancer of the mouth and throat" as well as "paralysis, heart disease, nervous debility, and insanity." Emphasizing smoking's role in causing disease never precluded condemning it as a sin; the body, activists reminded everyone, was the Lord's temple and God commanded that people " 'cleanse' " themselves " 'from all filthiness of the flesh and spirit.' "[43]

The Christian lobbyists nevertheless found it difficult to make as clear-cut a case for the sinfulness of smoking cigarettes as they did for taking drugs, drinking, or indulging in sex. To label cigarettes but not pipes or cigars sinful seemed contradictory, but respectable men, including many ministers, smoked cigars or pipes. Preachers were not without sin, but they were also not without influence and hardly likely to lead crusades against their own habits. Reformers also had a hard time finding a direct biblical basis for their opposition to cigarettes; as one preacher put it, the Bible never said " 'don't smoke.' " Nor did the results of smoking ever seem quite so terrible as some of the other failings that drew reformers' ire. One article in the *Union Signal* compared tobacco to alcohol and opium and concluded that, although evil, smoking was the least evil because it did "not directly put an enemy in the mouth to steal away the brains at once." Nor did it "directly transform a mild and gentle man into an incarnate fiend" or "rob his wife and children" of financial and emotional support. People who used tobacco, an article in the *Christian Statesman* put it, were not as bad as those who drank rum, because tobacco "injures the user, but does not drive him to attack others, and, therefore, except in the case of minors, it is probably beyond the province of law to prohibit" the use of tobacco.[44]

Despite the ambiguities in the moral condemnation of smoking, the WCTU always opposed the use of tobacco and in 1885 began to seek federal laws to curtail it. The WCTU turned first to the exception cited by the *Christian Statesman*, banning sales to minors. After a petition campaign and support from three stalwart veterans of congressional campaigns for moral legislation—Elijah Morse, George Edmunds, and Henry Blair—Congress in 1891 banned the sale of cigarettes to minors in Washington.[45]

Pleased but not satisfied, Eliza B. Ingalls, a St. Louis woman who for many years directed the WCTU effort against tobacco, organized another petition campaign to convince Congress to prohibit the sale, importation, and manufacture of cigarettes throughout the United States. Ingalls's memorial referred to various ill effects of smoking but stressed its hazards to health. When the Senate received the petitions in 1892, it debated what to do with them, finally decided they concerned a health issue, and sent them to the Committee on Epidemic Diseases. The committee reported back that its investigation had shown that tobacco was a threat to health but that stopping the manufacture or sale of the cigarette "evil" was not within the powers of Congress. The committee recommended that the petitioners get states to pass laws banning cigarettes; if they did, Congress might then consider stopping their importation and their manufacture and sale in the District and the territories, the only places where it had the authority to act.[46]

The WCTU and other anticigarette crusaders did convince a few states to end the sale of cigarettes, and early in 1896, William L. Terry, a Democrat from Arkansas, a state that had passed such a law, entered a bill to ban the shipment of cigarettes to any state that prohibited their sale. Despite many petitions from the WCTU, the House Judiciary Committee reported against the bill. A minority report written by Terry and signed by four other representatives, three of them southern- or border-state Democrats, supported the ban, citing both the danger cigarettes posed to the health of the young and the many petitions by the WCTU and other "religious bodies." Over the next two years, the WCTU continued to petition in behalf of Terry's bill; Ellis tried to convince the chair of the Judiciary Committee to abandon his opposition, even soliciting petitions from his home state, but to no avail. During the next decade, several similar bills restricting the interstate shipment of cigarettes were introduced in Congress, but none ever made it to the floor.[47]

The anticigarette crusade continued; after 1900, Lucy Page Gaston, who had been a member of the WCTU, founded a new organization to spread its message. Congress took no more action, however, and even the Christian lobbyists seemed to lose interest. With no consensus on smoking's sinfulness and with smoking defined more as a health threat than a moral failing, it never commanded their attention the way other behavior did. A few activists raised the issue of what later would be termed second-hand smoke, but most people believed cigarettes harmed only the smoker, if anyone. They certainly did not pose a serious threat to families or the social order. Their consumption seemed to be solely a matter of personal choice—of personal liberty—and most agreed that Congress could prohibit it only among minors, those not yet old enough to make the decision for themselves. All these factors made it difficult to mobilize the lobbyists' usual constituency, much less convince legislators to act. The Christian lobbyists' crusade against cigarettes proved one of their most half-hearted and ineffectual.[48]

The lobbyists had more success in their campaign against another new item on their agenda, prizefighting. Like smoking, it had long drawn opposition from moralists. By the 1890s, however, prizefighting had begun its transformation into modern boxing—with gloves, talk of scientific strategies, and more rules to ensure greater order. Moral reformers did not appreciate the refinements and opposed all fights as "the glorification of merely physical strength—or, worse than that, of a bragging and debauching animalism," as an article in *Our Day* put it. The physical brutality of the prizefight especially upset the Christian lobbyists, for whom it exemplified men out of control, degraded, already descended to the worst forms of degeneracy. Reformers worried, too, about spectators at fights, because watching the brutal contests, like looking at obscene publications, increased the appetite for brutality and perverted spectators as thoroughly as it did the combatants.[49]

In 1870, the Senate considered a bill to prevent prizefighting, only to postpone it indefinitely. The issue did not arise again until 1896, when New Mexico's territorial delegate, seeking to prevent a fight scheduled in his territory, introduced a bill to ban prizefighting, pugilism, and fights between men and animals in the territories and District of Columbia and to punish those who staged them. With the scheduled bout already advertised, the House and Senate passed and the president signed such a bill in only four days. Promoters had to move the fight from New to old Mexico; Wilbur Crafts praised this "rare example of swift legislation for moral ends."[50]

The following year, 1897, Crafts learned of another championship bout scheduled for Carson City, Nevada. Since prizefights were legal in that state, he could do nothing to stop it. Fearful that newspaper accounts and pictures would bring its brutality into the states that had outlawed fights, Crafts wrote a bill that made sending a picture or description of, as well as a proposal or record of betting on, a prizefight through the mails, by telephone, or in interstate commerce a crime punishable by imprisonment or a fine. The House Committee on Interstate Commerce favorably reported Crafts's bill, explaining that prizefights "have been sent to the limbo of condemned customs with dueling, slavery, lotteries, and polygamy" and bemoaning the harm "pugilism" wreaked on "our youth." On the floor, the bill's sponsor read several petitions from churches, ministers' associations, a YMCA group, and a local branch of the WCTU in favor of the ban. A few members spoke against it, but Elijah Morse strongly defended it. In response to people who decried the bill as censorship, he claimed that the laws against mailing obscenity, information about abortion, and lottery materials established the principle of "censorship of the press in the interest of public morals." Other members of the House disagreed; the measure was tabled. In the next session, Crafts and the WCTU renewed the campaign, although they dropped their demand for a ban on newspaper stories about fights, which had generated much opposition. Congress still refused to prohibit the circulation of kinescope pictures of fights, and Crafts abandoned his efforts.[51]

In 1910, the WCTU took up the cause once more. Ellis, Emilie Martin of its department on impure literature, and the general officers of the WCTU supported a new bill to prohibit the interstate shipment of pictures or descriptions of prizefights. Its author, Walter I. Smith of Iowa, claimed that he sought the ban because it might undermine prizefighting's financial success and eventually force the sport out of business, but he admitted that he also wanted to prevent the distribution of a specific film, the one to be made of the forthcoming bout between Jack Johnson and James J. Jeffries. Johnson was black, Jeffries, white. Prizefights pitting whites against blacks had occurred before, but Johnson had recently become the first African American champion. Jeffries had retired as champion a few years before but succumbed to public demand that he come out of retirement as the "great white hope" to defeat Johnson. Johnson's boxing skills and his defiant lifestyle, which included free spending, flashy clothes, fast cars, and dates with white women, made him a hero for African Americans but infuriated many whites. For them, Johnson symbolized the worst associations of boxing and, more important, challenged white supremacy, both inside the ring and out.[52]

Despite Smith's goal, Congress did not act before the fight. When Johnson easily defeated Jeffries, many African Americans celebrated and many whites seethed. In some towns, whites attacked blacks without provocation; in others, celebrations or just signs of a new confidence among blacks sparked confrontations with whites, who beat up and even murdered blacks. The black victory and social unrest led many people, not just the Christian lobbyists, to talk of abolishing the sport. Emboldened, the WCTU again called for legislation to ban the distribution of the film made of the Johnson-Jeffries fight. Although committee hearings were held in that session and the next, Congress still did not act. Nevertheless, in many local communities, the WCTU, Christian Endeavor societies, and other groups successfully suppressed the film.

With Johnson scheduled to fight another, misnamed, great white hope, Jim Flynn, and arrangements made to film the conflict, in 1912, Representative Seaborn A. Roddenbery of Georgia revived the idea of an interstate ban on the distribution of fight films. The National Reform Association endorsed the idea, and Ellis called on the members of the WCTU to send letters and telegrams in support of Roddenbery's bill. Ellis, who shared Roddenbery's opposition to interracial fights, acknowledged that the Georgia congressman primarily sought to keep "films of fights between black and white pugilists out of the South, where he says, it works to the general disadvantage, by creating racial prejudice and supremacy." Another Georgian, Augustus O. Bacon, led the fight for the bill in the Senate, where it passed easily.[53]

In the House, Roddenbery cited the precedent of laws keeping lottery tickets, "gold-brick schemes," and birth control devices out of the mails and interstate commerce and pushed hard for his bill. By then, the Johnson-Flynn fight had already occurred, and Roddenbery made it clear that his efforts had as much or more to do with the race of the fighters as with moral outrage over the sport. He condemned the recent bout, which Johnson had won easily, as "perhaps the grossest instance of base fraud and bogus effort at a fair fight between a Caucasian brute and an African biped beast that has ever taken place." "It was repulsive," he added, and his bill was "designed to prevent the display to morbid-minded adults and susceptible youth all over the country of representations of such a disgusting exhibition."[54]

A move to recommit Roddenbery's bill to committee mustered only five votes. The House amended but quickly passed the bill, and the Senate readily agreed to the House's changes. The new law made it illegal to import, to mail, to ship with an express company or common carrier, or even to send or carry such films across state lines. The courts upheld the law, and into the 1920s, Congress refused to repeal it. But Congress also refused to strengthen the law. Before long it began to be violated through various subterfuges. Its passage, however, again testified to the South's new leadership in legislating morality and provided a splendid illustration of how the politics of race contributed to white southerners' support for moral legislation.

In trying to stop the distribution of fight films, the Christian lobbyists had confronted a part, albeit a small part, of an emerging national popular culture. The danger posed by commercial entertainment had always contributed to the lobbyists' fears about modern society. Comstock criticized the new urban music halls; he and other Christian reformers had also railed against stage plays and obscene playbills. Moral reformers, however, had rarely sought legislation to regulate or outlaw these and other popular amusements. They had tried to stop newspapers and commercial entertainments on Sunday and to extend the Comstock Law to cover the *Police Gazette*, but failed in both attempts. An emerging popular culture proved a tenacious foe, as the lobbyists learned when they took on one of its newest but perhaps most powerful components, the movie industry.

In 1907, at the behest of Jane Addams and others associated with Hull House, Chicago investigated motion pictures, and the city council passed the first municipal censorship ordinance. That same year, agitation in New York City led to the creation of the National Board of Censorship of Motion Pictures, which received financial support from the Motion Picture Patents Company (MPPC), a major industry group. The National Board's committees, made up of volunteers, viewed films submitted by most of the movie producers and judged their "moral standards" and "taste." If the committee approved of the film, a statement to that effect went on prints before distribution, and the New York group's voluntary censorship came to be recognized across the nation. Not all states or local communities accepted the board's judgments, however. By 1914, Pennsylvania, Ohio, and Kansas had created their own censorship boards, and various cities had, too.[55]

Support for censorship also arose in the District of Columbia, where a commission concluded that immoral movies were being shown. In 1913, on the second try, Congress passed a bill entered by Jacob Gallinger of New Hampshire, an ally of the Christian lobbyists, that allowed the District's commissioners to stop theaters from showing "obscene, lewd, indecent or vulgar pictures." It passed without debate in both houses, but President William Howard Taft vetoed it, citing the District police force's insufficient resources to enforce it without undermining its performance of other duties. That same Congress added a provision to a tariff bill that authorized the secretary of the treasury to stop the importation of immoral movies.[56]

By that time, Crafts had enlisted in the campaign for movie censorship. He perceived the potential educational value in films (at one time he even talked of going into the business of making them) and always thought "adequately censored motion pictures" could serve as an alternative to the saloon. But the power of the medium to shape the behavior of the young, especially teenagers, frightened Crafts: "The devil never could put anything before the minds of children in print so effectively as is done in these vivid moving pictures." For Crafts, movies became the ultimate form of dangerous stimulus on the minds or appetites of the young, a force more powerful than anything Comstock imagined when he worried about dirty books in the 1870s. As early as 1910, Crafts participated in campaigns to drive "corrupt picture shows" out of several cities. Emboldened by his success and encouraged by Congress's passage of his law against distributing prizefight films and the ban on importing obscene movies, Crafts asked Congress for national censorship. Joining him in the cause was William Chase, an Episcopalian from New York City, and, later, the WCTU.[57]

Crafts and Chase advocated legislation to create a federal commission to censor all films shown commercially within the United States. Appointed by the president, the five members of the proposed commission would set policy and have final authority over censorship but hire others to help them preview the films submitted by the producers. For each film submitted, the producers would pay a fee to cover the cost of the process. No film without the approval of the commission would be allowed in interstate commerce or granted a copyright. To enter his bill, Crafts turned to two Georgia Democrats, Senator Hoke Smith and Representative Dudley Hughes. Crafts had recently conducted a campaign for movie censorship in Georgia, which may explain why he chose to work with two lawmakers from that state. In any case, Smith never actively supported the bill, but Hughes became its primary champion.[58]

Hughes chaired the Committee on Education and Labor, Henry Blair's old committee, and since Crafts's bill placed the new censorship commission within the Bureau of Education, his committee held hearings on the proposal in March 1914. Crafts presided; he, Chase, and others testified in behalf of censorship; representatives of the movie industry and of the National Board of Censorship spoke against it. After the hearings, both Harriet Pritchard, who succeeded Martin as head of the WCTU's purity department, and Ellis urged WCTU members to support the bill. Ellis, who had attended but not testified at the hearings, warned that the bill would likely remain in committee if members did not demand action.[59]

Almost a year after the hearings, but only a few months after the WCTU campaign, the committee reported in favor of the bill. Signed by Hughes, its report declared the "necessity for censorship of motion pictures . . . beyond question."

It challenged the efficacy of the efforts of the National Board, both because of its ties to the industry and because it never reviewed the 5 percent of films that were offensive. The report also dismissed state and local censorship as "inadequate" for a national industry. The bill the committee reported retained the essential features of Crafts's commission plan and called for the censorship of films that were "obscene, indecent, immoral, inhuman, or depict a bull fight or prize fight" or that "would tend to impair the health or corrupt the morals of children or adults or incite to crime." Ellis again urged all members of the WCTU to write Hughes immediately in support of the bill. In an interview, the Georgian told Ellis that it would be impossible to pass it so late in the session but that he "expected . . . to push it at the opening of the new Congress." Developments outside of Congress in 1915 increased the likelihood of success. The Supreme Court upheld both the federal ban on prizefight films and state movie censorship laws. It ruled that movies were purely a matter of commerce and therefore not covered by the free-speech guarantees of the First Amendment. Moreover, the telegrams and letters to Congress that Crafts had solicited as well as his personal lobbying had generated considerable pressure to reconsider Hughes's bill.[60]

In January 1916, Hughes wrote his wife, "Our Picture Bill of great notice & raising a storm. Comm. on Ed no longer sleepeth. Now of National Prominence." That month, apparently fearful that Crafts's bill might pass, the movie industry organized to oppose it and requested new hearings. Held in a much larger room than the first one, these hearings stretched over six nights as both opponents and proponents testified at length. A trade group organized opposition to Hughes's bill, and the National Board closely monitored the hearings. Religious liberals and the Seventh-Day Adventists, two traditional enemies of the Christian lobbyists, also opposed movie censorship. So did a rabbi, who admitted movies sometimes treated Jews badly but told the committee that the newly organized B'nai B'rith could take care of that and that national censorship was unnecessary. A representative of the Christian Alliance, several ministers, and various reformers spoke in favor of censorship. In what Ellis called "Mothers' night," she and officers of several women's clubs or groups—supported by "scores" of other women in attendance—told of the danger films posed for the family. Crafts and Chase, however, provided the primary arguments for the creation of a federal motion picture commission.[61]

They and the opponents of censorship disagreed over most things—how many immoral pictures were actually being made, whether larger numbers of children attended the movies, and whether most Americans wanted censorship. At the most fundamental level, however, the two sides disagreed on whether the government should intervene, and this debate echoed those on earlier types of moral legislation, especially in obscuring the lobbyists' attempts to establish moral standards.

Crafts and Chase clearly believed that government had the right to uphold moral standards and to restrain the "personal liberty" of individuals in order to protect the whole community. In a series of articles entered during the 1914 hearings, Chase rested government's power to do so on majority rule but still defended the right of the church "to influence the state to enact God's will into law." The church, he added, had the responsibility to petition, advise, and counsel, although Congress retained the responsibility of "rejecting or accepting our advice."[62]

In the 1916 hearings, however, Chase, Crafts, and the others less often referred to the church and more often spoke of the bill as a matter of licensing and regulation; they even denied the commission would have much to do with determining morality. Crafts said that the president would appoint to the commission not ministers or moral leaders but psychologists and other experts trained to understand the impact of the movies. A commission staffed with psychological experts, Crafts stressed, would not judge a movie's morality. In fact, he and other supporters of the bill often spoke as if they assumed an agreement on moral standards. Chase stated flatly that the commission "has no authority to fix the moral standards of this country" and could only reject "such films as are contrary to the moral law of the people of this whole Nation." At other times, however, Chase and the bill's other advocates made clear that more was at stake. Chase admitted some variations existed between the morality of towns and cities, especially New York. Indeed the lobbyists' opposition to continued reliance on the National Board rested in part on their disdain for moral standards in Gotham. New York, where the values of the stage dominated, should not be allowed to set the moral tone for all of America, Crafts told the committee.[63]

Moviemakers and other opponents of Crafts's bill defended the rights of the industry, pointed to potential problems with the plan, and praised the current system. The movie industry representatives claimed that they did not object to stopping the exhibition of movies found to be obscene; they only opposed prerelease review, which they considered unconstitutional and un-American, a violation of freedom of the press. They stressed that the proposed commission would engage not just in regulation but in censorship and warned of the dangers of bringing politics into the process or of leaving such decisions to a small group of people. They also argued that the National Board of Censorship already did a good job of keeping movies moral. Representatives of the producers, distributors, and, even more adamantly, the board defended its independence from industry control and stressed that the volunteers who actually judged the films represented the public. Opponents of Crafts's bill praised the voluntary aspect of the existing system; one even mentioned that because it was voluntary it was more effective than government control, a variation on the celebration of moral suasion. A committee member who opposed the bill advocated another of the old approaches, leaving censorship to local authorities, on the grounds that moral standards between the rural areas and cities differed. More often in private than in the hearings, opponents of a national commission pointed to the different values prevailing in towns and cities as well as among regions and various groups and questioned whether any single standard could be agreed upon. For the most part, however, the industry argued censorship was unnecessary. The vast majority of moviemakers did not make immoral movies, they maintained, and if they or less scrupulous producers did, not enough people went to see them to make them profitable. Their argument assumed, in contrast to their private statements (they were as capable of contradictory thinking as the bill's proponents), that a moral consensus existed in the nation and that, through the wonders of the market's invisible hand, morality would be preserved.

At the end of the 1916 hearings, Crafts, fresh from meetings with a few moviemakers, announced that he had reached a compromise with the major producers and suggested modifications in his bill to make it acceptable to the industry. Other producers and the exhibitors opposed the compromise and any federal censorship. Committee members could not reach agreement and in the end submitted two reports. A majority report, signed by Hughes and all of the southerners on the committee, cited the endorsements of several producers as well as "the earnest support of the leading moral and religious organizations of the Nation" and called for passage of the bill as modified by Crafts's compromise. Condemning the bill in no uncertain terms, the minority report claimed most pictures were unobjectionable and warned of the danger censorship posed to the development of the industry as well as to the constitutional guarantee of a free press. Hughes's bill, it continued, threatened to force a powerful industry into politics even as it gave too much power to propagandists.[64]

After the committee's report, the movie industry, which some thought initially indifferent to what happened in Congress, increased its efforts against the bill. The board of the National Association of the Motion Picture Industry came out against it. Representatives of the Motion Picture Board of Trade met with Woodrow Wilson at the White House and, afterward, claimed that the president had indicated his opposition to Hughes's bill. That fall, industry groups campaigned against members of Congress who they felt supported Crafts's bill. Exhibitors claimed some, but not all, of the credit for helping defeat Hughes. With more visible opposition from the movie industry, signals from the president, and the defeat of the bill's sponsor, the federal movie censorship bill never even came up for debate on the floor.[65]

In 1920, Congress did amend the penal code to add obscene motion pictures to the list of materials banned from interstate commerce. Industry representatives had suggested the idea early in the debates over Hughes's bill, and Crafts and other supporters of the bill agreed to it, although not as a substitute for the commission. (The commission was for prevention, the obscenity law, for cure, explained Crafts.) The primary congressional sponsor, however, clearly intended it as a substitute for a federal commission; he argued that the addition to the obscenity law covered the small number of films not being submitted to the National Board.[66]

In placing movies with other objectionable material under existing Comstock statutes, Congress had refused to expand federal authority over morals. In doing so, it accepted the movie industry's objections to prerelease review and also limited federal involvement to matters of sexuality and obscenity, rather than expanded it to crime and violence as Crafts and Chase had sought. The proposal for a commission that Hughes had regarded as a popular issue at the beginning of the 1916 hearings had met with substantial opposition and been abandoned in Congress. No doubt the attempt to give the federal government a more active and permanent role in censoring movies failed for many reasons. Some lawmakers opposed censorship on principle. Others, as the testimony at the hearings revealed, agreed on the need for censorship but preferred to leave control over the moral content of films to the voluntary efforts of the industry itself. Some became convinced that the National Board of Censorship provided sufficient oversight.

Another factor may help explain Congress's decision against a commission, although no direct evidence supports it. The ban on prizefight films, which Crafts considered a precursor of his censorship plan, had been passed in large part to stop distribution of fight films in which blacks beat up whites. In that instance, federal censorship supported southern racial mores, and many southerners supported the act, almost a prerequisite for passing moral legislation.

After the passage of the ban on fight films and also after the 1914 hearings, the racial dynamics of movie censorship changed with the release of the movie *Birth of a Nation.* The reverse of a prizefight film, this powerful racist epic glorified white people beating up black people. It offered a demeaning portrait of blacks and, many thought, a dangerous endorsement of white supremacy and violence. The National Association for the Advancement of Colored People demanded that the movie not be shown, and several towns did in fact prevent its screening. Two bills were introduced in Congress to ban it from the District of Columbia. During the 1916 hearings on Hughes's bill, two witnesses cited the film as an example of the need for censorship.[67]

Although *Birth of a Nation* persuaded some congressional advocates of censorship to support a federal commission, the controversy over it frightened others into opposition. They testified that attacks on the film not only revealed the dangers of censorship but also illustrated how the process could be politicized or how censors could be intimidated by the threat of civil violence. Both D. W. Griffith, the film's director, and Thomas Dixon, upon whose novel it was based, telegraphed the committee their opposition to Hughes's bill. Dixon, a minister who supported prohibition and other moral reform, also sent his telegram to other members of Congress, one of whom read it on the floor. By reviving the deep southern fear of federal intervention in race relations, the controversy over *Birth of a Nation* may have undermined southern support for Hughes's bill and thereby contributed to the failure of Congress to act.[68]

Crafts and Chase continued to advocate federal legislation, but Congress had clearly lost what little interest it had. But the continued possibility of federal involvement and mounting public outrage over both the content of movies and scandals in Hollywood led the industry to begin a series of steps that led to the adoption of a rigorous production code in the 1930s.

Despite the failure of the plan for federal censorship of the movies, the Christian lobbyists had accomplished much in the two decades since the Reform Bureau set up shop in Washington. In that time, Crafts, Ellis, and the other Christian lobbyists in the capital had established their presence and kept before Congress a variety of moral issues—prizefighting, smoking, Sunday observation, gambling, polygamy, divorce, seduction, and prostitution. The lobbyists, the groups they represented, and the churches across the nation that they mobilized occasionally succeeded in pressuring Congress into action, but they usually needed the support of other interests to succeed. The most dramatic expansions of federal power into morality, the Mann Act and the Harrison Act, did not even come at their behest.

In Congress, older partisan and regional divisions about moral legislation blurred, if not disappeared, although an absence of very many roll call votes makes it difficult to be sure. That in itself, though, may indicate that moral legislation had become a matter of pressure or interest-group, rather than partisan, politics. Certainly no clear party lines emerged. On polygamy, where a stark, partisan division once existed, the parties reversed positions. On other issues, both Republicans and Democrats entered and advocated moral legislation; members of each party also opposed it.

Regional politics tended to blur as well; the new southern support displayed during the Lottery fight continued. On Sunday laws, gambling, stopping the interstate shipment of cigarettes and prizefight films, and federal movie censorship, southerners led the fight for legislation. If the politics of slavery had passed, however, the politics of race still left white southerners suspicious of some forms of moral legislation. Many southerners opposed a constitutional amendment on marriage and divorce because they feared its potential threat to antimiscegenation laws. With the Mann Act, where race was invoked both in behalf of or against the legislation, some southerners remained true to old constitutional principles while others supported the expansion of federal power.

Congress as a whole, not just its southern members, seemed hesitant to expand the moral powers of the federal government. Of all the proposals, Sunday legislation would have most thoroughly intertwined religious and secular authority. That Congress steadfastly refused to enact a Sunday law for the District of Columbia testified once more to its unwillingness even to appear to establish the religious authority of the state. Other factors contributed to congressional resistance to legislating morals. At the beginning of a new century, some lawmakers still defended the basic tenets of the antebellum moral polity; they opposed any federal role in enforcing morals, advocated moral suasion, or, like Knox when defending Smoot's right to a Senate seat, championed an implied moral relativism. Sometimes conflicting definitions of morality, even among Christians, discouraged Congress from acting, as in its unwillingness to recommend to the states a constitutional amendment on marriage and divorce or to pass Sunday laws.

Finally, many lawmakers, even among those willing to legislate morality, did not want to formalize an expansion of federal power over morals. Congress's refusal to recommend a constitutional amendment providing a federal role in marriage and divorce or polygamy (in the latter case an issue on which Congress had already demonstrated its willingness to act) certainly testified to that fact. Lawmakers were most willing to pass legislation that applied only to the District of Columbia, for which they had unquestioned responsibility and a recognized police power. Save for a Sunday law, they passed District regulations on all the issues that the Christian lobbyists raised—sale of cigarettes to minors, gambling, divorce, age of consent, prostitution, and movie censorship (though it was vetoed). The lobbyists intended the laws to control behavior in the capital but also to establish the national government's opposition to the evils they outlawed and to serve as models for state and local laws. Whether they actually promoted legislation elsewhere can be debated, but surely legislating morality in the District enabled Congress to make a moral statement and placate the Christian lobby without fundamentally altering the government's function or powers. Only when legislators became genuinely convinced of a national danger were they willing to go further, and even then they justified their intervention by appealing to existing powers. They used congressional authority over the territories to try to close down divorce mills in the West; they employed the interstate commerce clause to strengthen the ban on the circulation of obscenity and to try to stop "white slavery."

The overall pattern of legislative activity offered other indications of congressional attitudes toward legislating morality. Like the Christian lobbyists, members of Congress worried that uncontrolled appetites could undermine the social order. In the case of smoking, which was not clearly immoral or a danger to the social order, Congress refused to stop the sale of cigarettes to adults. Even when convinced that a form of behavior was immoral and threatened other people or the moral order, lawmakers seemed uncomfortable in attacking appetite directly, in other words, in outlawing specific immoral behavior. Rather, they preferred to attack the businesses that preyed on or stimulated appetites. Lawmakers were most enthusiastic about legislation that appeared less a matter of dictating behavior and more a matter of eliminating a temptation or saving a victim. They showed no inclination to set federal standards for divorce, for example, but readily closed down "divorce mills" in the territories. They passed a law to arrest men who tricked or coerced women into prostitution, not the prostitutes themselves. Lawmakers clearly preferred to legislate against commercial vice rather than to regulate private behavior. Yet, their willingness to attack commercial society had clear limits. Congress refused to close businesses operating on Sunday or to review the products of the moviemakers.

No matter how carefully focused it was, however, the moral legislation the

Christian lobbyists helped convince Congress to pass between 1895 and 1915 significantly expanded the moral powers of the federal government. Like the lobbyists, many members of Congress had lost confidence in the basic tenets of the antebellum moral polity. Although they never abandoned them, lawmakers doubted that, alone, the voluntary system and moral suasion could preserve the moral order or ensure a moral citizenry. Congress also agreed with the Christian lobbyists that, given the existing problems in the moral environment of a changing nation, society could not allow unlimited personal liberty. They therefore enlisted the federal government in establishing morality. The fight over alcohol, the most extensive moral crusade of the era, involved the same issues and resulted in an even more dramatic change in the moral polity.

CHAPTER EIGHT

Aligning the Government against Alcohol

E ven as the Christian lobbyists campaigned for a broad array of moral legislation, they continued their crusade against alcohol. The temperance crusade has had many able historians, but putting the final push for national prohibition in the context of the longer and larger campaigns for moral reconstruction subtly revises parts of the accepted historical narrative. It restores religion, always mentioned but not always emphasized, to a central role in the cause. It shows that the goal of a constitutional amendment emerged early in the crusade, not only after successes with statewide prohibition. It suggests that the women of the WCTU, whose lobbying after 1900 often gets less attention than their efforts before it, remained important even after the rise of the Anti-Saloon League, which not without cause is often given almost all the credit for the passage of national prohibition. And, in the context of the earlier lobbyists' long emphasis on commercial vice, the league's stress on the saloon rather than drinking seems more a means to an absolute end to drinking than an embrace of a more moderate or regulatory approach to the alcohol problem.[1]

Most of the leadership of the league and the other Christian lobbyists, although not all Americans who supported prohibition, wanted to end all consumption of alcohol because it was their prime example of the dangers of appetite and avarice. The appetite for alcohol, the Christian lobbyists stressed, led people to a dependence upon it, a slavery that then dictated and destroyed their lives. Such slavery, in their view, was slavery to sin; as with cigarettes, though, the biblical case against drinking was shaky. The Bible included several strong condemnations of drunkenness but offered few unequivocal texts demanding total abstinence. Instead, it presented stories of patriarchs imbibing and Jesus turning water into wine or serving it to his disciples at his last meal. Most of the Christian lobbyists explained away such references by relying on translations of various Hebrew and Greek words to distinguish between fermented and unfermented wine. Jesus and the godly consumed only unfermented wine, they concluded; trouble arose and sin occurred when people got into the hard stuff. In addition to explaining away troublesome biblical texts, temperance reformers also referred to passages that provided indirect support for total abstinence. As they did with cigarettes, they cited verses about the body being God's temple, which was not to be defiled. An unsigned editorial in the *Union Signal* even cited the commandment "Thou shalt not kill" to support prohibition because, it said, the commandment "embraces within its scope the preservation of the human race from destruction and from all destructive agencies used by one man against himself or another."[2]

Laws against smoking and other forms of moral behavior passed or failed in Congress less on the strength of biblical authority than on the case that could be made that the behavior threatened others and society. The lobbyists stressed that the indulgence of an appetite for drink hurt not just the drinker but his family—through psychological pain, physical abuse, neglect that led to starvation and want. It also endangered all of society as well since alcohol was, in their view, the leading cause of poverty, vice, and crime. In fact, as the debate over prohibition proceeded, alcohol became the mother of all evils. In 1912, the cover of the *Union Signal* featured a cartoon that had a tree, labeled "Alcohol," gripping a globe. Its branches were labeled: "Forgery, Wife Desertion, Assault, Murder, Robbing, White Slave Traffic, Vagrancy, Death, Disease, Accidents, Destitution, Wife Beating, Drunkenness, Neglect of Family, Child Labor, Burglary." Three years later, a story in the same magazine maintained that the liquor traffic "accentuates the difficulty in settling every national question" and went on to explain how it complicated reconciliation of the races, hurt industrial relations, demoralized business and politics, exacerbated problems with the gambling den and brothel, undermined attempts to Christianize America, and curtailed the "evangelization of the world."[3]

As in other of their campaigns, the lobbyists emphasized the dangers of avarice, focusing much of their rhetoric, and almost all of their legislation, on those who sold alcohol. In their greed for gold, the lobbyist argued, saloon keepers, brewers, and distillers—what together the lobbyists condemned as the liquor traffic—fed the appetite that led so many to destruction and cost society so much. In emphasizing the danger posed by an avaricious liquor traffic, the Christian lobbyists presented anti-alcohol laws, as they did other moral legislation, not as a limitation on personal liberty but as a means to free individuals from bondage to their appetites and other people's avarice.

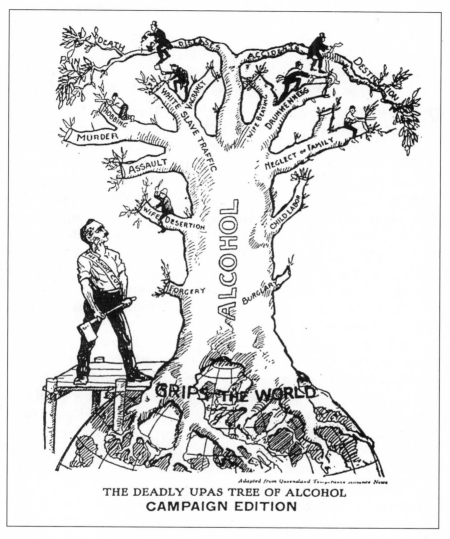

THE DEADLY UPAS TREE OF ALCOHOL
CAMPAIGN EDITION

Cartoon from the *Union Signal*, 22 August 1912
(Courtesy of the National Woman's Christian Temperance Union)

Not surprisingly, the lobbyists still relied on the slavery analogy. "The Saloon business cannot exist without slaves," declared Congressman Richmond P. Hobson, quoted on the cover of a 1912 *American Issue*. "Is not the man who is addicted to the drink habit a slave? There can be no question about it." The one million slaves of the saloon in the United States "go out and work a week or a month, draw their pay, go into the saloon and hand the saloon keeper their money for something which ruins their own lives." The lobbyists relied even more on a new but similar metaphor when they condemned "King Alcohol." It evoked the memory of the American Revolution and the despotism against which Americans had rebelled. Both the slavery and the King Alcohol metaphors served two functions. They acknowledged the entrenched power of the liquor traffic within American society and the total domination alcohol exercised over the life and morals of the individual drinker. At the same time, they reminded Americans of earlier, successful battles to free people from tyranny.[4]

In attacking King Alcohol, most of the Christian lobbyists continued to advocate national, constitutional prohibition, the goal they had first adopted in the 1870s and pursued throughout the 1880s. In 1890, both a resolution entered by Henry Blair that would have sent a prohibition amendment to the states and a law sponsored by the WCTU that would have prohibited all "importation, exportation and interstate transportation of alcoholic beverages" made it to the floor in the House, but no further. Congress also refused to adopt prohibition for the District of Columbia, a symbolic step it did take in the case of gambling, divorce, and age-of-consent legislation.[5]

Congress did pass some less drastic laws to control the sale of alcohol. In response to a Supreme Court decision that liquor in its original package remained in interstate commerce until sold and therefore not subject to state prohibition laws, Congress in 1890 passed the Wilson Act. It made liquor subject to state law upon its arrival in any state. The Christian lobbyists supported the measure but did not expect much of it. Congress took a similar approach to the sale of beer in army canteens, banning it only in prohibition states. Later, Congress finally authorized a study of the liquor traffic, but one by Carroll Wright limited to its economic not its moral aspects.[6]

Two years later, Congress expanded the decades-old ban on the sale of alcohol in the "Indian territory" to Native Americans who lived on land held in trust by the government under the 1887 Dawes Act or those who in any other way remained dependent on the government. In contrast, as white settlement in Alaska increased, Congress abandoned prohibition there and adopted a system of license that allowed the sale of alcohol but tried to prevent it to the native population.[7]

Nevertheless, by the end of the decade, Congress had made it clear that it had no interest in prohibition, at least for white people. Consequently, the Christian lobbyists did not push for it between 1890 and 1910. Only three resolutions for a prohibition amendment were even introduced in Congress during those years.

Instead, the lobbyists worked to pass less sweeping measures that would align the government against alcohol, which in their view would help make the state Christian as well as lead Congress and the public, step by step, toward national prohibition. The lobbyists realized, too, that to enact prohibition they would have to secure the support of people who did not necessarily share their conviction that drinking was a sin and should be stopped altogether. That political reality influenced the way in which the lobbyists made their case for federal legislation. Because of the resulting obfuscation of the Christian lobbyists' motives and goals, because of the lobbyists' decision to take a step-by-step approach, and because each of the steps raised issues important in moral reconstruction, the debates over attempts to align the government against alcohol demand careful analysis. The efforts of Crafts, Ellis, and the other Christian lobbyists began with an attempt to stop the sale of alcohol in government buildings and on army posts. The fight to keep beer out of army canteens marked the emergence as a force on Capitol Hill of a new organization, the American Anti-Saloon League, which introduced innovations to the campaigns for moral legislation and quickly established itself as a, if not the, central component of the Christian lobby. Yet only after it and the older lobbying groups unified their efforts did they achieve their primary goal in the years between 1890 and 1913, a tougher ban on the interstate shipment of alcohol.

In the late 1890s, with Congress hostile to prohibition and most anti-alcohol legislation, Crafts and Ellis contented themselves with working to tighten restrictions in the existing licensing system in the District of Columbia and to stop the sale of alcohol in the Capitol building. They failed to convince Congress to end sales in the Capitol, but with the help of local district WCTU leaders and the Christian Endeavor societies, they did succeed in preventing the sale of beer and wine in the restaurant in the new Library of Congress.[8]

Emboldened, Crafts and Ellis in 1898 expanded their plans for prohibiting the sale of alcohol from the Capitol to all government buildings, including immigrant stations, soldiers' homes, and those on military posts. The addition of immigrant stations and military installations testified to the lobbyists' fears about drinking among immigrants and the working class, but inclusion of the Capitol established that they worried about drinking among the upper echelons of society, too. They also sought to stop sales on federal property as symbolic politics; the ban would put the government on record as opposing the sale of all alcohol—liquor, beer, and wine. In support of their effort, the Christian lobbyists again mobilized petitions and turned first to the House. Crafts got the bill assigned to a favorable committee, which held hearings and, apparently impressed by the testimony of Crafts, Ellis, and others as well as the large number of petitions that had arrived, reported in favor of the bill.[9]

It never came up for debate, and in January 1899, with the session coming to an end, Crafts and Ellis decided to concentrate their efforts on one part of the bill, the sale of beer in army canteens or post exchanges. They and the other Christian lobbyists had never accepted the approach of the 1890 act, stopping the sale of beer only in canteens located in prohibition states. Crafts prepared an amendment that in one section prohibited the detail of officers and private soldiers to sell intoxicating drinks and in a second forbade the army to require or allow anyone to sell them on any camp or fort. He convinced a North Dakota representative to add it to the army appropriations bill. The House passed it after only twenty minutes of debate. The amendment faced a more difficult time in the Senate but eventually passed there as well and became law.[10]

The secretary of war, the attorney general, and the president agreed on a rather strained interpretation of the new law. Since the first section did not include a statement that prohibited the sale of intoxicating drinks in canteens, they argued, Congress must have meant for it to ban the assignment of soldiers as bartenders in canteens but to allow civilians to sell beer there. The second section stopped the War Department from making contracts to sell alcohol on post but did not apply to sales in canteens, since they were covered in the first section. The army, the administration concluded, would therefore continue to sell beer in its canteens. Outraged by the decision, Crafts and other Christian lobbyists argued that Congress clearly intended to close the canteens, blamed liquor lobbyists for preventing it, and demanded that the policy be reversed. Crafts protested to the secretary of war, and a delegation from the National Temperance Society met with President William McKinley. Ellis, Lillian Stevens, who had become president of the WCTU after Willard's death, and Anna Gordon—bearing over two hundred letters of protest that Ellis had gathered from prominent people across the country—also met with the president. All their efforts accomplished nothing.[11]

Crafts, Ellis, and other temperance advocates wrote a new act with an unequivocal ban on the sale of beer, wine, and liquor in canteens and on military posts. They again mobilized public support for it and, along with others, testified at congressional hearings during the following Congress. They emphasized that Congress had already passed a law against selling alcohol in canteens; celebrated the effects a ban would have on the health, morals, and discipline of the soldiers; and adamantly maintained that the government should not be in the business of putting temptation in the way of the boys who mothers sent to the armed forces. The War Department and many others opposed the lobbyists' efforts; a minority report of the House Committee on Military Affairs, signed by one northern Republican and one southern Democrat, summarized the opponents' views. The bill "would be a calamity to the cause of temperance" because soldiers who were denied beer on post would find stronger drink off post. Moreover, such a law would be an affront to soldiers' "personal freedom." "If we wish to have an army composed of self-controlling, self-respecting men," the minority report continued, "we must give them the opportunity to exercise the virtue of temperance by choice, instead of trying to enforce total abstinence." The government, it concluded, had to treat soldiers like the people at home. The minority's views triumphed; the bill did not come up for consideration.[12]

The Christian lobbyists continued their efforts. In the next session, one of their allies, Charles E. Littlefield of Maine, entered an amendment to another military bill that provided for an outright ban on the sale of "beer, wine, or intoxicating liquors by any person in any post exchange, or canteen, or army transport, or upon any premises used for military purposes in the United States." One House member, who opposed prohibition laws, still called for passage of Littlefield's amendment because Congress had to respond to "such an uprising," such a "great moral determination among the people." An opponent bemoaned the fact that "the Woman's Christian Temperance Union . . . 'doth make cowards of us all' on this occasion." Not all. Some lawmakers continued to fight Littlefield's amendment and voted against it, but the House passed it. The Senate Committee on Military Affairs, despite hearings packed with representatives of the WCTU, reported an amendment to the amendment that dropped beer from the list of banned drinks. In the end, senators voted thirty-four to fifteen to table the committee amendment and thereby let the House version banning beer stand. Party lines blurred on the vote, although Republicans still proved far more willing to vote yes than Democrats. Of the senators who announced their support, twenty-seven Republicans favored it, ten opposed it; among Democrats, eleven favored it, eight opposed it. Among southern Democrats, ten expressed their approval, six, their opposition. As with other forms of moral legislation, southerners remained divided, but a shift toward southern support for anti-alcohol legislation, like other moral legislation, had begun.[13]

In passing the bill on stopping the sale of beer in army canteens, legislators seemed anxious to free the government from responsibility for liquor sales and unwilling to draw a distinction between beer and other alcoholic beverages. They also appeared unmoved by arguments based on a broad conception of personal liberty, although limiting personal liberty may not have been an important consideration in anticanteen legislation since Americans had traditionally restrained soldiers' freedom. Perhaps more clearly than anything else, the debate showed legislators to be more sensitive to public pressure than they were philosophically committed to prohibition. Much of the credit for the public outcry by the "church people," as one lawmaker called them, went to Ellis and Crafts, but also to another Christian lobbyists, Edwin Dinwiddie. He and the organization he represented, the Anti-Saloon League of America (ASL), soon became an important participant in the congressional battle over alcohol and perhaps the most powerful single component of the Christian lobby.[14]

"The Anti-Saloon League movement," according to its founder, "was begun by Almighty God." Its earthly organizational heritage could be traced to two "Anti-Saloon Leagues" that formed independently in 1893, one in the District of Columbia, the other in Ohio. The Ohio group's roots went further back, to an earlier temperance society associated with an old abolitionist stronghold, Oberlin College. In 1895, the Washington group organized a convention that met in that city, but leaders of the Ohio association quickly took control and shaped the new group's philosophy. The convention established a permanent organization, the Anti-Saloon League of America, declared its object to be "*the suppression of the saloon*," and pledged "to avoid affiliation with any political party as such and to maintain an attitude of neutrality upon questions of public policy not directly and immediately concerned with the traffic in strong drink."[15]

The newly formed league reached out to the existing Christian lobbying groups, and after some initial hesitation, the National Temperance Society and the WCTU sent representatives to its conventions. The National Reform Association and the Reform Bureau did not establish any formal ties, although Crafts worked with the league. The ASL represented a second generation in organized Christian lobbying. Its primary leaders had long been active in Ohio temperance crusades but had not participated in any of the existing lobbying groups. They were younger than their predecessors. The Anti-Saloon League's first president, Howard Hyde Russell, and the man who succeeded him and did more to establish it as a national organization, Purley A. Baker, were, respectively, five and eight years younger than Crafts, and almost two decades younger than Comstock, Cook, Willard, and Blair. Younger still were two of the league's other primary leaders, Ernest H. Cherrington, who headed its publishing empire and edited its major journal, the *American Issue*, and Wayne B. Wheeler, its chief lawyer and leading spokesman in the 1920s. Russell, a Congregationalist minister, and Baker, a Methodist preacher, had religious backgrounds and beliefs similar to those of their predecessors. Cherrington, the son of a Methodist minister, developed a more liberal theology; Wheeler, another Congregationalist, seemed to have had a less active faith than the other three. Nevertheless, all four brought an intense commitment to Christianizing the government and a deep hatred of alcohol and its effects on society to their work with the Anti-Saloon League.[16]

The league and its leaders, as might be expected of a second generation, introduced innovations to the Christian lobbying effort; three new approaches in particular helped make the ASL substantially more influential in mobilizing the public and lobbying Congress than its predecessors in the Christian lobby. First, the ASL developed new fund-raising techniques and established a much larger financial and organizational base than the earlier groups. The league was a hierarchical organization; most of its power rested with a handful of leaders, especially the executive committee of the board of directors. Paid state superintendents directed state operations and developed grassroots support. The WCTU and the Reform Bureau had paid organizers, too, but more money enabled the ASL to have a far more extensive professional bureaucracy. The league's wealthy patrons included John D. Rockefeller Sr., who had contributed over $350,000 by 1919, and a few other industrialists who gave smaller but substantial sums. Nevertheless, 98 percent of the league's funds, according to one investigator, came in gifts of less than $100. Most of these small contributions were solicited by league workers when they preached in churches and convinced worshipers to pledge a monthly donation to the league. With a few big givers and many small ones who gave regularly, the ASL's budget dwarfed that of the other lobbying groups, and its staff and organizational structure did as well.[17]

Second, the league proved far more pragmatic than its predecessors. It chose to focus its efforts solely on ending the liquor traffic, not on a broad moral agenda; the Anti-Saloon League proved the very model of a single-issue pressure group. Rather than standing unequivocally in behalf of moral principles, the league tried to position itself "in advance of public sentiment, but not so far as to lose touch with the people," as the *American Issue* put it. Total "devotion to abstract principles which at present have no appreciable following in the churches," it explained, could wreck the organization. A 1903 ASL catechism defined the group's purpose as the "present repression and ultimate suppression of the beverage liquor traffic" and proclaimed that it favored "all measures that will secure advance toward the complete extermination of the beverage liquor traffic." As a result, its leaders held to the ultimate goal of state and national constitutional prohibition but focused their efforts on intermediate steps—even smaller ones than the other lobbyists'. It worked for local option, supported various license plans, and fought hard for statewide prohibition before it ever said much publicly about national prohibition. Its pragmatism extended even to the personal use of alcohol. Although the ASL urged people to take a total abstinence pledge and created the Lincoln-Lee Legion to promote it among children, the ASL never required one for membership and happily worked with people who did not support total abstinence.[18]

Third, and most important, the league adopted what it called an "omni-partisan" approach. Although most of its early leaders were Republicans, the league aligned itself with no party and supported any candidate who embraced its program. It did so for strategic reasons; the league sought to enhance its influence by becoming the balance of power between the two major parties. The strategy may also have been predicated on the realistic assessment of the reconstruction of the politics of morality. Prohibition would find its strongest advocates among Republicans in the North and among Democrats in the South. In any case, the "partisan" proved as important to the influence of the ASL as the "omni."[19]

Intervening in elections at all levels in ways none of the other Christian lobbying groups had done, the league promoted candidates who supported its measures and punished those who opposed them—"retributive political justice" Russell called it. To determine who was who, the league evaluated voting records by incumbents as well as distributed questionnaires to and demanded pledges from both them and their challengers. It then furnished voting instructions to its members and to voters whose names were provided by churches. League leaders pressured both to vote "correctly." One Virginia minister told his state's ASL convention that every "man who knowingly gives his ballot and his influence to the cause of bad government will be punished in this world, and in the next, if he does not repent of the sin and endeavor to repair, as far as possible, the mischievous results of it." Pressure on and organization of voters, honed in local and statewide contests, was increasingly applied to congressional races as the final vote on national prohibition approached.[20]

The league's extensive organizational base, extreme pragmatism, and "omni-partisan" appeal brought new vigor and influence to the Christian lobby, but the league built upon the efforts of and had much in common with the first generation of Christian lobbyists. The ASL brought the churches into politics by securing the endorsement of many denominational bodies and mobilizing the influence of local churches, but it was by no means the first group to do so. The American Sabbath Union brought denominations together in behalf of an effort to secure a national Sunday law, and the WCTU and the Reform Bureau had both long organized local churches. In addition, the Anti-Saloon League's emphasis on the battle against the saloon resembled earlier rhetoric by the lob-byists. In speaking of "the saloon," league leaders usually referred not just to a dark, dangerous, degenerate place in the inner city but to the entire "liquor traffic," a term they used nearly as often. The early Christian lobbyists had long focused their efforts against commercialized vice—whether it involved ob-scenity, prostitution, or alcohol. When ASL speakers condemned the saloon or the liquor traffic more than drinking, they followed the same approach. They did slightly revise the appeal, however. Rather than dwell on the avarice that drove the trade, as earlier Christian lobbyists did, the league's leaders and speakers stressed the costs of the traffic. They also emphasized how brewers and distillers corrupted politics, a theme that proved popular in the anti–big business climate of the Progressive Era.

Most important, the league followed its predecessors in seeking national leg-islation through public pressure and intensive lobbying. It created a national legislative committee at its second convention in 1896 and urged its members to petition Congress in behalf of the proposal to create a commission of in-quiry on the liquor traffic and other bills. Three years later, the league became significantly involved in national legislative issues and actually established a presence in Washington. That year, Edwin Dinwiddie arrived to straighten out the canteen mess, and he stayed until the passage of the prohibition amend-ment. Through all but a brief part of that time, he served as the ASL's national legislative superintendent, its chief lobbyist. He did not work alone. Baker lob-bied the Republican presidents, and as the fight for prohibition proceeded after 1912, Cherrington and Wheeler helped in Congress. All along, state superin-tendents and other ASL leaders wrote letters of introduction to their legislators, making sure that they knew and listened to the ASL lobbyist at the Capitol and, on occasion, personally contacted them regarding specific measures. But Din-widdie did the day-to-day work; he also had the closest ties with legislators.[21]

Dinwiddie's roots, like those of the league's other primary leaders, were in

Ohio, but he came from different religious stock. He was raised in the Evangelical Lutheran Church, which blended the Lutheran and Reformed traditions common among German immigrants of the Midwest. Ordained in that denomination in 1894, Dinwiddie immediately went to work for the Ohio ASL. He brought to the task not only a deep commitment to the temperance cause but also astute political skills. Dinwiddie, one admirer wrote, "understood the eccentricities, the strengths and the weaknesses" of politicians and appreciated the difficult situations electoral politics placed upon them. He "never asked or expected a Congressman elected from a distinctly wet district to misrepresent his constituents by voting dry." Instead he cultivated their friendship—and waited for their constituents' attitudes to change. Such a skilled lobbyist became extremely important to the league's eventual success. William Jennings Bryan was correct when, in 1919, he introduced Dinwiddie at a celebration of the adoption of Prohibition as the man "who has directed the fight in congress for some twenty years."[22]

During the battle against the sale of alcohol in army canteens, Dinwiddie worked closely with Crafts and Ellis, and after it, they cooperated in lobbying successfully to secure appropriations to fund recreational alternatives to the canteen and to preserve the ban. The three did not remain solely on the defensive, however. In 1902, they teamed up again and revived the effort to ban liquor sales in the Capitol and at immigrant stations. The Committee on Immigration held hearings at which Crafts presided and his assistant in the Reform Bureau testified. Samuel E. Nicholson represented the ASL, and Ellis and others spoke for the WCTU. The National Temperance Society sent a statement. Crafts explained to the committee that the "four organizations" together represented "the sentiments of the churches of this country, whose membership is 27,000,000, more than one-third of our population." Having testified to their clout, Crafts and the others justified the ban in immigrant stations in two ways. To sell immigrants beer when they first arrived, the lobbyists argued, taught them that bars were harmless things, a lesson that would eventually lead them to the poorhouse and therefore endangered the immigrants. Crafts also argued that the immigrant stations as "public buildings, in whose ownership all Christian citizens share, should not be rented for a business which most of them despise." Both arguments surfaced during the floor debates and were challenged by opponents, most of whom stressed that the immigrants came from cultures

Edwin Dinwiddie—lobbyist for the Anti-Saloon League and other
temperance groups (Courtesy of the Westerville, Ohio, Public Library)

that accepted beer drinking. Nevertheless, Congress approved the ban on the
sale of beer or other intoxicants in the immigrant stations.[23]

The lobbying team of Dinwiddie, Crafts, and Ellis boasted other small victories. That same year, Congress banned liquor sales in the Capitol and the sale
of alcoholic drinks in government-run soldiers' homes. In 1900, after the Spanish-American War and America's new role as a territorial power heightened interest in the international aspects of the crusade against alcohol, Crafts, Dinwiddie, Nicholson, Ellis, and James Dunn of the National Temperance Society
appeared before a congressional hearing on alcohol sales in the Philippines.
They did not succeed in banning the saloon there, as they had hoped, but in
1902, Congress passed an act, prepared by Crafts, that prohibited the sale of alcohol, opium, and firearms on other Pacific islands. When Roosevelt signed it
into law, Crafts received the pen.[24]

The next major fight in Congress concerned whether to include a prohibition on liquor sales in the enabling act for Oklahoma statehood. The new state would include the Indian Territory, where federal law had long banned the sale of alcohol, but when that area became part of a state, the federal prohibition against sales to Native Americans would no longer apply. The ASL, the WCTU, and the Reform Bureau, along with Christian groups in Oklahoma and societies promoting the welfare of Native Americans, sent petitions and lobbied hard to prevent the sale of alcohol to Native Americans in Oklahoma.[25]

Drawing a distinction between the white people of Oklahoma, who, "being of our blood and our own capacity for self-restraint, can take care of themselves," and the Native Americans, who could not, lawmakers agreed on the need to restrict sale to the Native Americans. They disagreed on whether to extend a ban on sales to them throughout the new state or only in the old Indian Territory as well as on how long a ban would remain in force. The ASL and the WCTU sought a long one extended to the whole state. During the second year of debate, fearful that if they insisted on such a provision they ran the risk of being blamed for delaying statehood, which might cost them and prohibition public support in Oklahoma, the Christian lobbyists supported a change that banned, for at least twenty-one years, the sale of alcohol only in the former Indian Territory and on any reservations in the remainder of Oklahoma. Despite protests on the floor, Congress approved the plan. Dinwiddie then left Washington for Oklahoma, where he led a fight to make all of Oklahoma dry. He and his allies secured a prohibition clause in the new state constitution and succeeded in having it ratified by the states' voters.[26]

Oklahoma proved a major victory for Dinwiddie, the ASL, and the other Christian lobbyists. By 1906, they had secured several new laws that banned the sale of alcohol in army canteens, the Capitol, immigrant stations, soldiers' homes, the former Indian Territory in Oklahoma, and the Pacific islands. In defense of these measures, the lobbyists had offered traditional arguments against alcohol but had also claimed that the government should not be involved in the sale of liquor, both as a matter of principle and in deference to its Christian citizens. Congress seemed willing to defer to Christians' sentiment in the case of people the lawmakers felt not quite capable of "self-control": soldiers, Native Americans, immigrants, Pacific islanders—or maybe only people not likely to vote in the next election. A combination of constitutional conservatism, antiprohibition sentiment, and a conviction that the federal government should not dictate individual moral behavior led many legislators, including many from the South, to shy away from more radical action. Christian lobbyists nevertheless had slowly begun to realign the federal government in opposition to the liquor traffic. As they succeeded, they turned their attention more and more to the problem the Wilson Act was supposed to have solved in 1890, the shipment of alcohol into prohibition areas.

By 1898, the Supreme Court had all but invalidated the Wilson Act's restriction on the interstate shipment of alcohol. The federal government, the Court ruled, could not abdicate its power over interstate commerce, which the Court defined to include the shipment of liquor until its arrival at the consignee. Seizing upon the opportunity the Court's interpretation provided, distilleries and breweries established various forms of trade into "dry" areas. They expanded their shipments to individuals, allowed under most state prohibition laws, by sending circulars to and agents through dry areas to recruit new customers. Using provisions for COD, brewers, distillers, wholesalers, and express companies also sold alcoholic beverages to bootleggers or shipped jugs of liquor to fictitious people, often in care of a rail depot, where agents then sold them to anyone who would pay the cost. Several states adopted laws to try to control the sale of alcohol from outside their borders, but they met with limited success.[27]

Four years after the Court decisions gutting the Wilson Act, bills banning interstate shipment of alcohol into prohibition areas were introduced, but Congress did not debate any of them. The trade had only begun to develop, which may explain the minimal interest, and the Christian lobby still concentrated its efforts on the passage of an anticanteen law. Dinwiddie and Ellis had agreed that they would fight and win one battle at a time. After their victory over the canteen in 1902, they and other Christian lobbyists supported a bill introduced by William P. Hepburn, a Republican from Iowa, that sought to deprive liquor of its interstate character upon arrival in a state, making that, rather than delivery to a buyer, the point at which state law and enforcement took effect. In 1903, Hepburn's bill passed the House with little debate, only to die in committee in the Senate. The next year, a slightly different version of Hepburn's bill was reported to the House but never came up for debate. No similar legislation reached the floor until 1912, although many bills were introduced in Congress as the issue of interstate shipment became central to the anti-alcohol crusade.[28]

The major Christian lobbying organizations—the ASL, the Reform Bureau, the WCTU, and the National Temperance Society—supported a succession of interstate shipment bills as they sought wording that would muster sufficient votes in Congress and pass muster with the Supreme Court. Not only did the

Christian lobbyists work hard in Washington, but as in other campaigns to leg-islate morality, the WCTU and other groups mobilized their members to write and petition Congress. Opponents of prohibition countered with similar ef-forts. Brewing and distilling interests as well as various German American or-ganizations attacked restrictions on interstate shipment and, sometimes, the Christian lobbyists themselves.[29]

With both sides applying pressure, Senate and House committees held ex-tensive hearings on proposals to restrict interstate shipment. At them, sup-porters, especially members of the WCTU, occasionally denounced the liquor traffic. For the most part, though, Dinwiddie and other Christian lobbyists de-nied the interstate shipment bills were prohibition measures at all, claiming they were intended only to protect the police power of the states. Opponents scoffed at the lobbyists' invocations of states' rights and charged that they sought an interstate shipment ban as a step toward prohibition. Opponents then proceeded to attack prohibition. It did not really prohibit, they charged; moreover, it was bad for the economy. Representatives of German American groups occasionally claimed that total abstinence was not biblical. More often they and other opponents raised the old moral suasion argument: prohibition was wrong because morality could and should be sustained only through in-dividual conversion, not legislative action. Most frequently of all, defenders of drink denounced restrictions on the sale of liquor as a violation of an individ-ual's right to "personal liberty" and free choice. Laws that told people what to drink or eat were unconstitutional, they added. Even "a majority of people," as one representative of the German-American Alliance put it, did not have "the right . . . to dictate to a minority in matters regarding purely personal and in-dividual rights."[30]

In part because the Christian lobbyists never let the debate center on prohi-bition, the decade-long dispute over interstate shipment came to focus on two issues: the constitutional question of the dividing line between the exercise of a state's police power and the federal government's control over interstate com-merce and whether or not the law should carry an exemption for personal use. Each related to fundamental tenets of the antebellum moral polity: states' rights and personal liberty.

In its decisions against the Wilson Act, the Supreme Court made the consti-tutional question of states' rights unavoidable. Perhaps the simplest way around the problem posed by the Court's ruling that alcohol remained in interstate commerce until delivery to the buyer was to rely on the federal government's power over interstate commerce and stop all shipments of alcohol into dry

areas. Instead, proponents initially advocated laws that recognized a state's enforcement power by changing the definition of the point at which liquor fell
under state control. Southerners naturally embraced the latter approach and introduced 62 percent (and border state representatives, another 11 percent) of the
bills that sought to end interstate shipment. Before a House hearing, James Cannon Jr., an ASL leader from Virginia, defended the states' rights approach in language reminiscent of that southerners used in the antebellum years to protest
national action against slavery: "no other section of the country should have the
right to project itself into our neighborhood life, and if we do not want the
traffic to go into our State we ought to have our right in the matter protected by
the Government. All we ask is to be let alone." Such rhetoric so obviously res-
onated with southern tradition that a few of the region's legislators who opposed prohibition supported interstate shipment legislation in the name of
states' rights.[31]

The fight for an interstate shipment law was hardly part of a campaign to
preserve the rights of the states, an antiprohibitionist senator warned his
"Southern friends." One of them, Augustus O. Bacon, astutely explained why.
"The question is not going to be limited to whether or not power can be dele-
gated to a State, or whether a State can exercise that power by Congress lifting
its hand, as it were, from the subject," the Georgia Democrat testified during a
1908 hearing, "but it will go still further as to the power of Congress directly to
legislate." That was the real question, Bacon continued, and the "people who
are demanding the legislation are not at all choosey about the particular way
it shall be accomplished, whether by State legislation indirectly, or directly by
Congressional legislation. They had just as like have it one way as the other, and
prefer the one that will be quickest and most efficacious." Bacon understood
the dynamics of the debate quite well.[32]

Although southerners entered a majority of the bills on the question of interstate shipment, the early legislation that the ASL and the other Christian lobbyists supported carried the names of northern Republicans—Hepburn, Dol-
liver, Littlefield, Miller, and Curtis. And in 1906, when the House Judiciary
Committee reported Littlefield's bill, it did so with the votes of northern Republicans as well as southern Democrats. Moreover, the league's leading lobbyists on the matter, Dinwiddie and Nicholson, championed states' rights but
admitted that they believed that the court cases that upheld the antilottery law
firmly established "the right of Congress to absolutely prohibit articles of interstate commerce that interfere with the public morals."[33]

As such statements suggested, the Christian lobbyists undoubtedly cared more about stopping the shipment of liquor than about constitutional issues, just as they had in the canteen fight. The original canteen act of 1890 did exactly what the Christian lobbyists said they wanted in the interstate shipment fight; it stopped the army from selling alcohol in prohibition states and thereby committed the federal government only to respect state law. That approach never satisfied the Christian lobbyists who fought long and hard to ban beer sales in all canteens, regardless of local laws. The constitutional issues differed slightly in the case of interstate shipment, but the precedent seemed telling nonetheless. Respecting the rights of the states appeared more a tactic for the pragmatic ASL and the rest of the lobbyists than a matter of principle.

The same could be said of the lobbyists' stance on the other issue at the heart of the debate over an interstate shipment law, whether to allow individuals in prohibition territory to order alcoholic beverages by mail. Opponents of interstate shipment laws demanded personal-use exemptions because they feared that "the real purpose" was "to prevent the use of strong drink as a beverage." Guaranteeing individuals the right to order beer or liquor from another state would ensure a legal right to drink. Confronted with demands for personal-use exemptions, proponents of the legislation waffled and obfuscated. When the Hepburn bill was reported to the House in 1904, the committee added, apparently with Dinwiddie's acquiescence, a clause guaranteeing an individual the right to purchase liquor from out-of-state companies. After that, however, Dinwiddie and other lobbyists opposed such provisions as unnecessary. They repeatedly pointed out that no state had acted to prohibit people from ordering liquor for consumption in their homes.[34]

If taken at face value, their declarations that personal use was not threatened suggested a certain hypocrisy in the lobbyists' position. In maintaining that they sought interstate shipment laws not to interfere with people ordering liquor by mail but to prevent the sale of liquor at railroad stations to anyone who asked for it, the lobbyists seemed to embrace a double standard of drink. They implicitly distinguished drinking liquor ordered by and shipped to an individual from drinking liquor bought in person at an express company. The distinction rested in their perception of the type of people who did the drinking. They spoke most often about sales to minors, habitual drunkards, paupers, and the insane, but they also worried that sales at railroad stations and by bootleggers would be to immigrants, African Americans, or members of the lower class. "Blind tigers" and other illegal saloons supplied by interstate shipments sold liquor by the drink at a cost of five or ten cents, making it affordable to the poor. Such a double standard of drink did contribute to the willingness of some within the prohibition forces to tolerate personal-use exemptions in state prohibition laws.[35]

Most of the Christian lobbyists, though, accepted exemptions for personal use as much out of pragmatism as conviction. They realized that many people would support prohibition laws that reduced if not eliminated drinking among the lower classes, if they still could secure good liquor and wine for their own use. If the lobbyists had personally supported the double standard, they would have been comfortable with a guarantee of personal use written into federal law. They were not, but their explanations for why they opposed a personal-use exemption were somewhat disingenuous. The claim that they opposed it because it would make enforcement more difficult seemed questionable; their most frequent justification, that the matter should be left to the states, more accurately but no more forthrightly revealed their true motives. Dinwiddie and some of the other proponents of the law believed that states had the power to ban importation of all alcoholic beverages for personal consumption. They therefore opposed a federal personal-use exemption for the same reason other Christian lobbyists opposed a federal marriage and divorce law; they feared the exemption might actually lower the standards, might prevent states from adopting laws banning the importation of alcohol for personal use. The lobbyists acted less from a double standard of drink or a philosophical commitment to states' rights and more from their goal of preventing the largest number of people from drinking.[36]

The lobbyists' response to a bill introduced by one of the opponents of their interstate shipment bill reinforces that conclusion. In 1908, Philander Knox of Pennsylvania introduced a bill that relied on the interstate commerce power and was directed primarily at shipments by railway and express companies, the very activities advocates of an interstate ban contended they sought to end. It forbade COD shipments and assessed large fines on anyone who knowingly shipped beer, wine, or intoxicating liquors to a fictitious consignee or who did not clearly label the package with the name of the consignee as well as the nature and quantity of its contents. The bill also included a provision against mailing liquor, something Ellis had advocated for several years. Knox eventually recast his bill as an amendment to a general revision of the laws, and after limited debate in both houses, it passed in 1909 and became law.[37]

The WCTU and the ASL praised the Knox Amendment as a step in the right direction but claimed that it did not go far enough. Their response proved revealing. Dismissing a law limited to the very kinds of abuses that they complained about most—the jug trade, bootleggers, and the like—as *only* a step in the right direction reinforced the conclusion that they sought an interstate shipment law to stop other aspects of the liquor traffic as well. And their failure to protest such a use of federal power suggested the hollowness of the cries for states' rights during the interstate shipment debates and revealed their determination to reconstruct the moral polity.[38]

By 1909, when the Knox Amendment passed, prohibitionist forces in Congress needed any sort of victory. For seven years they had fought unsuccessfully for their version of a tough interstate shipment bill and would not get one for another four. Their lack of success resulted partly from the disarray of the Christian lobbying effort in Washington; a break between Dinwiddie and the Anti-Saloon League proved the most significant aspect of the problem.

In 1907, while Dinwiddie was in Oklahoma working for statewide prohibition, allegations of sexual improprieties arose. A married man, Dinwiddie had gone to Oklahoma with his secretary, which troubled a California league official, who believed that the two had at least violated propriety and may have committed adultery. No evidence substantiated a charge of adultery, but when the Californian shared his concerns with Cherrington and other league leaders, they may have believed it and certainly worried about the damaging effects of appearances. At about the same time, questions also arose over how Dinwiddie handled the money for the work in Oklahoma. Fearful of scandal, the ASL leadership decided Dinwiddie had to go, although it offered to let him stay on until the end of the Oklahoma campaign if he coordinated all of its finances through the national headquarters and sent his secretary back to Washington.[39]

Outraged by the charges, Dinwiddie refused and resigned at once. He continued to work with the Oklahoma ASL until the passage of statewide prohibition, then he returned to Washington and resumed his lobbying activities. Dinwiddie did so as the lobbyist for the International Order of Good Templars, a post he had held since 1899, and for the National Grand Lodge of Good Templars, a group with which he had long worked and for which he became national legislative superintendent in 1905. Two years later, he also became the lobbyist for the National Inter-Church Temperance Federation, an association that brought together the temperance commissions of the various denominations. It had been organized in 1907 by Charles Scanlon, a Presbyterian temperance activist who had his own disagreements with the ASL. In addition, Dinwiddie was a vice president of the NRA and had close ties with Ellis, the WCTU, and Littlefield, who had left Congress and gone to work for the National Temperance Society.[40]

To replace Dinwiddie as its representative on Capitol Hill, the ASL turned first to William H. Anderson, a lawyer who served as state superintendent in nearby Maryland, and then Samuel E. Nicholson, a longtime foe of alcohol and a Quaker minister with Social Gospel tendencies who had done some earlier Washington lobbying with Dinwiddie. Both Anderson and Nicholson quickly became very hostile toward their predecessor, and tensions between the league and Dinwiddie soon worsened. When Speaker Joseph Cannon, whom many prohibitionists blamed for keeping their bills bottled up in committee, ran for reelection in 1908, the ASL opposed him but Dinwiddie wrote a public letter defending the Speaker's fairness. The ASL attacked Dinwiddie as a "sell out." More important, the split between the league and Dinwiddie extended to disagreements over legislative strategy and came to involve other lobbying groups.[41]

Dinwiddie, the WCTU, and the NTS supported a move in Congress to revive the proposal to create a commission to investigate the liquor traffic, but the league opposed it. The ASL claimed the commission plan was being used by the liquor industry to delay real temperance legislation and as a means to provide jobs for a few recently defeated lawmakers. In private, league leaders accused Dinwiddie of supporting the measure in hopes of securing a salaried position as its secretary. Another dispute arose over prohibition in the District of Columbia. The WCTU lobbied for it, while Dinwiddie and the ASL backed slightly different revisions to the existing licensing system. Both the plan for a commission and prohibition in Washington languished in Congress. A final dispute developed when Congress passed a bill that authorized a referendum on prohibition in Hawaii. Dinwiddie and some other Christian lobbyists had supported the idea, and when the islands voted prohibition down, the ASL blamed Dinwiddie for the resulting harm to the cause.[42]

Despite the league's criticism, Dinwiddie's influence in Congress continued to grow. In 1910, the National Temperance Society made him its national legislative representative. That same year, Gallinger and Littlefield published a circular of support and Littlefield raised funds for Dinwiddie. The following year, when Nicholson began to campaign yet again for an interstate shipment law, legislators told him that the Knox Amendment on COD shipments rendered additional legislation unnecessary. When a frustrated Nicholson tracked down where they got such an idea, the trail led back to Dinwiddie. Several people, including one influential lawmaker, told Nicholson that the ASL would have to either obliterate Dinwiddie's influence or come to terms with him. Nicholson informed Baker, the ASL's president, of what he learned and recommended that the league take "heroic action" to unify the temperance forces. Nicholson did not think that he, Ellis, Crafts, and Dinwiddie could achieve unity by themselves, so he suggested bringing together the major temperance lobbying groups—"the Reform Bureau, the W.C.T.U., the National Temperance Society, the Good Templars, . . . [the Methodist] Temperance society, the Presbyterian Temperance Committee, and the Lutheran Committee." Shortly after Nicholson suggested such a conference, the league also began to worry about losing denominational support when it appeared that the new Federal Council of Church's temperance committee, on which Dinwiddie sat, might ally with his Inter-Church Temperance Federation.[43]

Baker and the ASL's Headquarters Committee therefore authorized Nicholson to begin talks toward unifying lobbying efforts. He met with Littlefield and others associated with the National Temperance Society as well as representatives of the Methodists and Presbyterians, who, with varying degrees of enthusiasm, endorsed the idea of a united effort. Nicholson also discussed it with Ellis, who thought it "highly important," and with Crafts, who, Nicholson reported, "regards it as practically imperative." With their and the Headquarters Committee's support, Nicholson began to seek cooperation. A letter to various reformers from James Cannon, a member of the ASL's legislative committee, explained that the drive for national legislation had been hurt not just by the liquor interests and Congress's hesitancy to act but "in large part [by] the lack of coordination and manifest sympathy on the part of our temperance forces." The league had always stood for unity in fighting for "civic righteousness," Cannon's letter added. He then proposed a conference to bring the groups together. In response, representatives from the league, the Reform Bureau, the National Temperance Society, the WCTU, the Good Templars, and the Inter-Church Temperance Federation met and agreed to encourage temperance education, to foster cooperation in national legislative and statewide campaigns, and to support a specific list of temperance bills in Congress. With unenthusiastic approval from the ASL leadership, Nicholson issued a call for a national conference on the interstate liquor traffic to meet in Washington during December 1911. He sent invitations to various temperance groups and to state governors, twenty-four of whom agreed to send delegates.[44]

There remained the matter of Dinwiddie. Well into the fall of 1911, the leaders of the ASL toyed with the idea of seeking a public humiliation of Dinwiddie, which Nicholson thought pointless. The league's representative in Washington had concluded that despite the ASL's considerable national power and influence, the battle on Capitol Hill could not be won without unity among the temperance forces and the churches, and especially not without the participation of the established Christian lobbyists—Crafts, Ellis, and, above all, Dinwiddie. Finally, in a move that must have galled Baker and other leaders, the ASL Headquarters Committee restored Dinwiddie to his position as the Anti-Saloon League's chief lobbyist. Nicholson moved up to be secretary and assistant general superintendent of the league. With Dinwiddie, the ASL obtained his ties to other groups, most of which he maintained formally as well as informally. Both Dinwiddie's stationery and calling card listed his primary affiliation as the superintendent of "The National Temperance Bureau"; his posts as legislative superintendent of the ASL, the Good Templars, the National Inter-Church Temperance Federation, the Committee on Promotion of Temperance Legislation in the National Congress, and the National Temperance Society were also listed.[45]

The same month that Dinwiddie returned as the league's chief lobbyist, the conference Nicholson called opened in Washington with a banquet for 500, including fifty members of Congress. The next day, around 250 delegates met at Calvary Baptist Church and appointed a committee to study the various proposals for an interstate shipment law. It included five members of Congress: Charles Curtis and Porter McCumber of the Senate and Edwin Webb, Morris Sheppard, and Fred Jackson of the House. Three were Republicans and two were southern Democrats. The eight remaining members of the committee included several associated with the ASL's lobbying efforts: Dinwiddie, Nicholson, James Cannon, and A. James Barton, a Baptist preacher from Texas who served as the committee's chair. The others were J. Franklin Hanly, an Indiana politician very active in Methodist temperance efforts; Fred S. Caldwell, an Oklahoma lawyer and friend of Dinwiddie's; Crafts of the Reform Bureau; and Ellis of the WCTU. The composition of the committee reflected the goal of unifying the temperance forces.[46]

In a day-long meeting, the newly created committee agreed to support a version of the interstate shipment bill written by Caldwell and already entered by Webb. Its selection represented a victory for Dinwiddie; he, Webb, and Caldwell had worked together on preparing the bill and had already lobbied Congress for its passage. On a speaking tour shortly after the meeting, Crafts found that many temperance workers doubted that the bill "will bring us any large relief." But, Crafts reassured Webb, using the phrase so often applied to temperance legislation, "I am generally able to persuade them that it will be a step in the right direction and that we can get it in this Congress by a strong pull altogether."[47]

Dinwiddie and Ellis also worked hard to mobilize the grass roots, summoning petitions in favor of the bill from church, ASL, WCTU, and other groups as well as letters targeted to committee members at key times. Christian lobbyists also testified before committees in both houses. Nothing came of their efforts in that session. When Congress returned in December 1912, Dinwiddie and Baker held another gathering in Washington. Attending were 270 people from thirty-two states and twenty-four temperance organizations—almost everyone important in the movement as well as a number of business leaders. In the mornings, they worked the offices of legislators; in the afternoons, they held meetings. One night, Dinwiddie sponsored a large banquet for congressional leaders.[48]

Dinwiddie and his congressional allies entered identical interstate shipment bills in each house, and the bill came up first in the Senate. The version reported by the committee had two sections. The first incorporated the theory inherent in Caldwell's original bill, which, in order to meet previous Court objections, rested on the interstate commerce clause and assumed that when its authority conflicted with the police power of the states, the commerce clause took precedence. It sought to avoid the Court's objection that the Wilson Law allowed state power to operate on materials still in interstate commerce by arguing that the federal government could ban from interstate commerce anything that a state's law prohibited. Therefore, when the state law began to operate against liquor, it was not operating on anything legitimately in interstate commerce. To sustain this contention, the new bill, like Caldwell's, relied on the precedent set by the lottery cases. To ease fears of violations of states' rights, however, it incorporated no penalty, which meant that enforcement would be left up to the states. Despite the concession to states' rights, Caldwell's contribution to the bill was still rooted in the federal control of interstate commerce.[49]

In another concession to states' rights, and at the suggestion of Tennessee's Newell Sanders, the Senate committee added a second section that reproduced the language of older bills in affirming a state's authority over alcohol upon arrival in its borders. The Senate committee reported, and senators allied with the temperance forces readily defended, a bill that incorporated both theories of control over alcohol entering a state, one based primarily on states' rights, the other on federal power. Perhaps no better evidence existed that the supporters of interstate control worried more about stopping the liquor traffic, by any means necessary, than they did about constitutional principles.[50]

In the Senate debate, Sanders and William S. Kenyon of Iowa defended the bill. Sanders said the issue was no longer the saloon but the mail-order liquor business and defended the bill in words that echoed the constitutional confusion highlighted by his amendment to the act. "The Federal Government can absolutely prohibit all interstate shipments of liquor" if it wants to, Sanders observed, but he added that it had a "moral duty . . . to protect the States in the enforcement of their laws." For the most part, the debate followed that on previous interstate shipment bills, but two southerners made speeches that revealed that region's growing support for federal action against alcohol. John R. Thornton, from north Louisiana, admitted a few constitutional reservations but said that they did not override his appreciation of the need for the bill. He also summarily dismissed claims for the supremacy of personal liberty; it had to be "subordinated to the greater right of the State to control that liberty within such bounds as are considered proper with reference to the well-being of the community at large." After Thornton finished, William Robert Webb, a Confederate veteran only recently elected to the Senate, condemned the evil effects of alcohol and acknowledged federal authority to regulate interstate commerce. He reminded his listeners that the federal government had used its power to prevent sales to Native Americans and urged lawmakers to "do as well for" Tennesseans and their children. To applause from the galleries, Webb then appealed for passage of the bill in the name of, among others, the women of the Tennessee WCTU, "all the Christian churches of America," and "our Father in Heaven, who said that righteousness and not material prosperity exalteth a nation." After Webb sat down, Gallinger asked for and received unanimous consent to substitute the just-passed House bill for the one the Senate was debating.[51]

The House bill preserved the Caldwell/Edwin Webb version, based on the interstate commerce power, without the second section that affirmed the rights of the states. For the most part, the debate in the House proceeded along the lines of those that took place in the Senate and in earlier discussions; it centered on constitutional issues, with both sides invoking states' rights. The bill's opponents warned of the law's potential threat to personal use and personal liberty and continued to attack prohibition itself, although with some new arguments.[52]

Wisconsin's Victor L. Berger, the only Socialist in the House, criticized liquor's influence on workers. One could not reason with a drunkard, so therefore a drunkard could "never become a good Socialist," he explained. "He must stay a Republican or a Democrat, though he occasionally may be a Progressive." Or, interjected another member, "sometimes a sociable Democrat." "Yes," Berger replied, "he may be occasionally a sociable Democrat, but never a Social Democrat." After the laughter died out, Berger attacked the heart of the Christian lobbyists' position on alcohol. He wanted, Berger said, to free the worker from being a "slave" of his boss as well as of "his appetite" for drink. prohibition would not accomplish either, Berger argued. It did not work, and, besides, liquor was not the fundamental problem. "It is economic conditions that make drunkards, and not drunkards the economic conditions." Adolph J. Sabath, an Illinois Democrat, did not go quite so far as Berger, but he, too, observed that drunkenness did not cause misery and want; rather, "misery, want, misfortune, and the unnatural conditions brought about by prohibition are conducive to drunkenness." Thomas Gallagher, another Illinois Democrat, took a different approach, one that would become common later in the twentieth century. He suggested that drinking was more a disease than a habit and should be treated as such.[53]

House supporters of the interstate shipment bill ignored the new arguments but reiterated the old defenses of a ban on interstate shipment. Southern supporters proved more numerous and did not shy away from the employment of federal power. Thetus Sims of Tennessee, for example, scoffed at those who opposed the bill on the grounds of states' rights and cited the Mann Act, which he had supported, as a precedent for federal action against liquor. One of the most important speeches in behalf of the bill was delivered by Webb, the bill's author and chief sponsor in the House. Webb, a North Carolinian and active Baptist layperson, opposed any penalty clause for the bill because police regulations rested with the states, but he also defended the bill by referring to the Supreme Court's ruling that the interstate commerce power included the power to exclude, a power Congress had already exercised earlier with lottery materials, obscene books, and other goods. Webb referred to the ASL, the WCTU, the Reform Bureau, the National Temperance Society, the Federal Council of Churches, and most of the denominations, together constituting "a constituency of more than 35,000,000," all of whom supported the bill. As the constituency count indicated, Webb clearly tied passage of his bill to public support, not religious authority. When challenged on why he opposed an amendment to make the law apply to cigarettes and other items besides alcohol, Webb replied, "I want public sentiment to gradually develop before Congress takes hold of all these questions." His questioner interrupted again to ask if the "gentleman does not want his virtue to run ahead of public opinion?" "I do not," Webb replied, "if you want to put it that way; public opinion often makes virtue, and it is often a virtue to abide by such opinion. You can execute no law successfully except public opinion be back of it." But Webb clearly hoped that public opinion would one day allow a more drastic law. Calling the liquor problem "a public-health problem, a public-wealth problem, a home problem, a happiness problem," Webb concluded, "it . . . should weigh upon the hearts of men until the use of liquor as a beverage shall be stamped out forever."[54]

Most House members agreed with Webb, at least on the need to pass the interstate shipment bill. Opponents offered a number of amendments in hopes of derailing it, but its sponsors and lobbyists urged supporters to vote them all down. House members did and then quickly passed Webb's bill by an overwhelming margin of 239 to 64. Yes votes came from both parties, with the percentage of each voting in favor of the bill almost identical (62 percent). Only the mid-Atlantic states, whose representatives split evenly, failed to provide a majority of its votes in favor of the bill. The West provided the most solid support, with 90 percent of its representatives voting yes; the South was next with 77 percent; the New England, border, and midwestern states provided around 66 to 67 percent. Especially in the Midwest, but throughout the nation, representatives from districts with a substantial manufacturing interest or a large number of Catholics more often voted against the bill. The wide support across party and geographical lines testified to the influence of the Anti-Saloon League and other Christian groups—as well as to the growing public opposition to the liquor traffic.[55]

Shortly thereafter, the Senate substituted the House bill for its own and passed it handily, sixty-one to twenty-three. In the Senate, a substantially higher percentage of Democrats than Republicans voted in favor of the bill; it proved most popular among senators from the South, 90 percent of whom voted to pass the Webb-Kenyon Act. Since the House bill was technically a different bill, it had to pass the Senate again, and did so quickly. Purley Baker and others urged President William Howard Taft to sign the bill. Instead, Taft vetoed it, but Congress quickly overrode his veto. The Webb-Kenyon Act became law, and a quarter-century-long fight to curtail the interstate shipment of alcohol came to an end.[56]

The passage of Webb-Kenyon, together with the success in banning the sale of beer and liquor in army canteens, immigrant stations, and soldiers' homes, went far toward aligning the government against alcohol. Before the 1890s, Congress had repeatedly refused to create a commission to investigate the dangers of alcohol; between 1900 and 1913, it acted on the assumption that they were real. Lawmakers still talked of states' rights and personal liberty—pillars of the old moral polity—but they demonstrated a willingness to ignore both in the cause of restricting access to alcohol. By their actions, the lobbyists made it clear that they questioned people's liberty to drink, opposing personal as well as public consumption of liquor. Their defense of states' rights and personal-use exemptions obscured that, however. Exactly what they sought to do, both in interstate shipment laws and in future prohibition laws remained unclear. The confusion served their political purposes but hardly established a sure moral standard.

Perhaps because of the obfuscation, the WCTU, the ASL, and other temperance supporters had convinced enough legislators and many Americans that, in certain instances, the liquor trade had to be restricted in order to protect not only the "others," those without "our" character and self-control, but also "our boys." If it were not restricted, both would be enslaved and unnaturally stimulated appetites would destroy them and the social order. The Christian lobbyists' critique of appetite and avarice had again contributed to significant moral legislation; however, their justification reflected the changed emphasis that followed the failure of the Christian amendment and Sunday legislation. On occasion, Christian lobbyists still referred to biblical authority, but when dealing with Congress they appealed far more frequently to the power derived from Christians' numerical authority in a democratic society. Mobilized Christians had become a political pressure group, a special interest, and they made sure politicians understood the voting power of church members.

No organization better symbolized that subtle shift than the American Anti-Saloon League. In the Fifty-first Congress, which passed the Wilson Act, the WCTU led the temperance forces; by the Sixty-second, which passed the Webb-Kenyon Act, the league had replaced the WCTU as the most important element within the Christian lobby. In the fight for an interstate shipment law, however, the ASL learned that despite its unprecedented organization and its overwhelming financial clout, it could not work its will in Congress without the cooperation of the other Christian lobbyists and the unified effort of the churches.

The passage of the Webb-Kenyon Act also demonstrated how the politics of morality had changed since the end of the Civil War. New England and the mid-Atlantic states no longer provided the leadership or the votes for legislation against alcohol. Midwesterners and southerners led the floor fight for Webb-Kenyon, and a higher percentage of legislators from the West and South than from other regions voted for it. Following a surge in state prohibition laws in the South, its representatives had come to support the use of federal power to curtail drinking. With the South willing to support federal legislation, with the government already aligned against alcohol, and with a united Christian lobby, opponents of alcohol quickly mobilized to take the next step. It proved a giant step, the very one that opponents of the interstate shipment law had warned about all along.

CHAPTER NINE

The Final Step: Prohibition

little over a month after the passage of the Webb-Kenyon Act, President Purley Baker proposed to the Anti-Saloon League's Headquarters Committee what he called "The Next and Final Step." From its origins, Baker explained, the league had sought "to go just as fast and just as far as public sentiment would justify." Now that all the defenses of the liquor traffic "had been battered down except the defenseless appeal to greed and appetite" and much of the nation had adopted prohibition, "The Opportune Time" had come to push for a national constitutional amendment. The Society of Christian Endeavor and the wctu had a few years before pledged themselves to a crusade for a prohibition amendment, but the final campaign began in earnest in November 1913 when the ASL adopted Baker's proposal and another by Ernest Cherrington for an educational campaign in its behalf.[1]

The next month, December 1913, prohibition forces marched on the Capitol. Their parade began with a boy carrying an American flag, then fifty girls, dressed in white, followed by fifteen hundred women each wearing wide white ribbons a yard long that read "WCTU: Amendment for National Constitutional Prohibition." As they marched from their hotel, they met the "Committee of 1000," organized by the Anti-Saloon League, who had marched from their own hotel, and side by side the two groups walked up Pennsylvania Avenue singing "Onward Christian Soldiers" and "America." When they arrived at the front steps of the Capitol, many of the demonstrators went into the rotunda, where Richmond P. Hobson of Alabama and Morris Sheppard of Texas met them and promised to enter resolutions for national prohibition. Several leaders of the two organizations then spoke to the assembled group.[2]

One of them, the ASL's Ernest Cherrington, told the lawmakers that the marchers came from all over the country and were not fanatics but thoughtful members of the "body politic which you represent." He then reviewed the measures passed by the various states to end drinking as well as legislation to align the federal government against alcohol. "We believe," Cherrington concluded, "that just as the time came when the problem of human slavery compelled recognition at the hands of the federal government, so has the time arrived when the American liquor problem can be dealt with adequately only by the nation as a whole." The "will of the people in all the forty-eight states of this Union should be supreme. If time was when this nation could not exist half slave and half free, certainly time is soon to be when, according to all signs this nation cannot exist half license and half prohibition."[3]

After the speeches, the marchers went outside for a photograph; Capitol guards pronounced it the largest crowd ever to gather on the steps, except for inaugurations. In the afternoon, only a few of the demonstrators stayed to hear Sheppard make a speech on the Senate floor in behalf of his resolution for a national constitutional amendment. More returned the next day to pack the galleries and break House rules by applauding and cheering when Hobson spoke in behalf of his identical resolution. That Hobson and Sheppard, two southern Democrats, met the Christian lobbyists on the Capitol steps and introduced their resolutions for national prohibition in the House and Senate, respectively, marked the culmination of the reconstruction of the politics of morality and exemplified the transformation in southern thinking on moral legislation.[4]

Hobson, an Alabamian and a hero of the Spanish-American War, came to the prohibition cause late and not out of any religious conviction. Rather, his study of the scientific evidence convinced him that alcohol was a toxin of yeast that caused degeneracy. Hobson also blamed alcohol for the downfall of all great civilizations and predicted that if the United States did not prohibit the sale of liquor, it too would collapse. The "yellow men," he warned, were already poised to take America's place. The liquor traffic destroyed nations, Hobson explained, because it sapped economic productivity and undermined the character of citizens. Even among the upper and middle classes, drinking reversed the progress of evolution, but it was especially dangerous among immigrants, Native Americans, and African Americans, all of whom, Hobson believed, started further down on the evolutionary slope toward savagery. Since the state had a duty to protect its citizens, Hobson maintained, it should stop the sale of alcohol. Hobson had especially close ties to the WCTU but also lectured in behalf of the ASL. He led early efforts in the House to pass Prohibition but, de-

feated in an attempt to move to the Senate, left Congress in 1915. He continued
to play a role in lobbying efforts and, especially, in mobilizing public support
through his widely delivered speech "The Great Destroyer," which popularized
his theories of reverse evolution and national decline.[5]

Sheppard, a Texan and a progressive Democrat, remained in Congress. He
had long opposed the sale of alcohol. Although he, too, sometimes based his
opposition on scientific grounds or even appealed to antiblack and anti-Mex-
ican sentiment, Sheppard stressed that drinking threatened "free government"
by lowering "moral standards." His attack on alcohol always incorporated a
strong religious dimension. An ardent Methodist, Sheppard, like the Christian
lobbyists, preached the importance of "Christian citizenship" and "righteousness in government." When President Theodore Roosevelt proposed a new set
of coins that did not include the phrase "In God We Trust," which was first put
on some types of coins during the Civil War, Sheppard was one of the members
of Congress who entered a bill to require the phrase on the nation's money. The
next year, Sheppard entered a resolution to add "In The Name of God" at the beginning of the Constitution. Sheppard was, in many ways, a worthy heir to Henry
Blair and the soul mate as well as legislative ally of the Christian lobbyists.[6]

Along with Hobson and Sheppard, Edwin Webb—the North Carolinian
who led the fight for the interstate shipment law that bore his name—helped
lead the fight for prohibition within Congress. A fourth southerner, James
Cannon Jr. of Virginia, a lobbyist rather than a member of Congress, played a
central role in the legislative maneuvering that led to the adoption of Prohibition. Born in Maryland in 1864 to a Confederate sympathizer, Cannon went to
college in Virginia, attended a Presbyterian seminary, Princeton, but returned
to Virginia to become a Methodist minister and, later, president of a Methodist
school for young women.[7]

A traditional southern Protestant, Cannon supported evangelism and hated
sin—"Not sin," he told the girls of his school, "a sort of indefinite, hazy, misty
something that we cannot define or see, but sin in our hearts, and sin in lives
about us." Cannon included among those sins, as did many of his predecessors
among the Christian lobbyists, Sunday papers and trains, gambling, prizefights, and posters and billboards that "appeal to the passions and appetites,"
but, most of all, drinking. Cannon imbibed antiliquor sentiments with his
mother's milk—she had been one of the first organizers of the WCTU in Maryland—and his own experiences had reinforced her teaching. Cannon's first
sermon as a preacher included a condemnation of liquor sellers that stressed
the dangers of appetite and avarice at the heart of the Christian lobbyists' de-

James Cannon Jr.—lobbyist for the Anti-Saloon League and Methodist
minister from Virginia (Courtesy Rare Book, Manuscript,
and Special Collections Library, Duke University)

fense of prohibition. "In order to make money," he said, dealers sold "intoxicating liquor which steals away their neighbor's brains, and brings to their victims not only physical, mental and spiritual death, but brings sorrow and
poverty to children and wives, fathers and mothers. Their indulgence of physical appetite, their lust for money and power brand them as among those who
St. Paul describes as 'earthly, sensual and devilish.'"[8]

Also like the other Christian lobbyists, Cannon believed that a Christian
should "carry his Christian principles into his civil life." The church, not "as an
organization, but the church as composed of individual citizens," had a re-

sponsibility "for the laws and character of the officials of the State." When Cannon took Christianity into the public arena, he acted with an unflagging zeal and an unflinching sense of moral certainty. He "gave no quarter to the things he believed wrong, nor did he expect anything but the fullest and most bitter opposition from the defenders of evil," explained an admirer. "He drew the line of demarkation so clear that a flying machine 5,000 feet high could discover it, and the head that ventured on his side never forgot the sledge-hammer blow which greeted it."[9]

Yet in his pursuit of absolute morality, Cannon—like the ASL he represented —proved amazingly flexible when it came to tactics and allies. During his campaign for statewide prohibition in Virginia, he formed an alliance with the state Democratic machine, an organization hardly distinguished by its high moral tone. The alliance later contributed to Cannon's national prominence, since the machine's leader, Thomas Martin, was a U.S. senator, and another member, Charles Carlin, was an influential congressman. Cannon had close working relationships with both, and in January 1913, congressional Democrats informed the ASL that they did not want to work through Dinwiddie and the Ohio Republicans. From that point on, Cannon, like his fellow southerners Sheppard, Hobson, and Webb, played a prominent role in lobbying efforts in behalf of prohibition.[10]

In the early months of 1914, right after the December rally where Hobson and Sheppard met the parade of prohibition forces, the WCTU appeared to be more active than the ASL in mobilizing public support for the fight for prohibition. Under Ellis's leadership, the WCTU sent over nine thousand petitions to Congress. They came from across the country, but over half of them were sent by groups in the mid-Atlantic and midwestern states. The WCTU's state officials also wrote letters to members of the committees considering the resolution and kept tabs on how their representatives planned to vote, information that Ellis forwarded to Hobson and Sheppard. The two southern leaders appeared to make the strategic decisions, but they conferred frequently with Ellis and Dinwiddie, who in turn kept in touch with each other. In April and May, Hobson, Sheppard, Dinwiddie, and Ellis all appeared before a Senate Judiciary Subcommittee. In addition, Anna Gordon, Frances Willard's confidant who became acting head of the WCTU when Lillian Stevens died a few days before the hearing, made a statement, as did Cannon, William Anderson, and Wayne Wheeler of the ASL. Most of the others who appeared in favor of the amendment were state heads of either the ASL or the WCTU. Crafts missed the hearings, although someone spoke in behalf of his Reform Bureau. Two representatives of religious liberty associations, sponsored by the Seventh-Day Adventists, also testified in favor of national prohibition. Their organizations had actively opposed Sunday legislation and the Christian amendment, condemning both as violations of the separation of church and state, but they had no such qualms about prohibition. On a second day of hearings, representatives of German American associations and a couple of labor unions appeared in opposition to the resolution, and on a third, the proponents had a chance to rebut their comments.[11]

On the first day of the hearings, Sheppard announced a change in the wording of the proposed amendment—one worked out by members of the House subcommittee considering Hobson's resolution and Hobson, Dinwiddie, probably Sheppard, and possibly Ellis—to allow the federal government to enforce prohibition "only in concurrence with the States." They made the change, Sheppard explained, to reassure proponents of states' rights. Persisting in the pragmatic rhetoric that marked the fight for Webb-Kenyon, Sheppard and other supporters of the amendment claimed that the federal government should cooperate with and reinforce the powers of the states. They also said that they did not intend to interfere with the personal use of alcohol if the states allowed it. As the hearings proceeded, however, temperance leaders again made it clear that more was involved.[12]

Despite the rhetoric of states' rights, several prohibitionists who testified denied a state's right to allow the sale of alcohol. The president of the Tennessee WCTU rejected "a double standard of morals" that held "that what is wrong in one section, or for one person to do, can" be "right and proper" for someone else or some other "section." Sheppard argued that Americans could not allow a narrow localism to interfere with the "national action . . . necessary to exterminate" the liquor traffic. Cannon proclaimed himself an unequaled champion of states' rights but then claimed that the problem was national, that the preamble to the Constitution granted the federal government responsibility for the common good, and that three-quarters of the states could delegate to the national government the right to outlaw the sale of alcohol.[13]

Hobson, though, offered perhaps the most expansive definition of national authority. The federal power to tax included the power to destroy, he maintained, and a state could not create what the federal government chose to exercise its power to eliminate. Pushed by hostile questioners, Hobson went further. The preamble of the Constitution—with its emphasis on promoting domestic tranquility, good order, and the general welfare—bestowed a police power on the federal government. Employing that police power to outlaw the sale of alcohol could not possibly violate the police power of the states since a police power could only be employed to promote the well-being of the people. The sale of alcohol clearly undermined their welfare, reasoned Hobson, therefore no state police power could support it. His thinking typified the conception held by many prohibitionists of the states' role in the moral polity; they assumed a state's right only to legislate tougher control of alcohol, not to defy a national ban on its sale.[14]

The lobbyists' references to personal use during the hearings manifested a similar tendency to obscure issues and attitudes but in the end a willingness to restrict liberty. Dinwiddie told the subcommittee that by banning manufacture and shipment only of alcohol for sale, the amendment did nothing to outlaw personal use or possession, but still allowed the states to address these issues. Cannon, without explicitly mentioning personal use, dismissed any argument for a right to drink. If a form of personal liberty proved dangerous to society, Cannon maintained, it must be eliminated to protect society. Hobson admitted that the amendment rightly did not touch the question of use, thereby preserving the spirit of American institutions by preserving the home. The amendment would work, he explained, by leaving old drinkers alone but stopping the recruitment of new ones. In their comments all three Christian lobbyists denied that the amendment attacked anything other than the sale of alcohol, but at the same time they made clear their expectation that it would prevent its use as well.[15]

Despite the case for prohibition made by Hobson, Cannon, and others, the Senate Judiciary Committee did not report the resolution. In early May, the House committee did but, with members almost equally divided on the measure, offered no recommendation as to whether it should pass. A few days later, the House Democratic caucus decided that for the remainder of the session the House would give priority to other legislation. Temperance forces did not object and later prevented their opponents from forcing a vote. The lobbyists convinced the House Rules Committee to put off a vote until December, when the next session of Congress met.[16]

In early December 1916, the WCTU held a rally in Washington in behalf of prohibition, and its leaders remained in the capital to lobby. It also requested that all Christians pray for the passage of a resolution sending the amendment to the states and that ministers across the country preach a prohibition sermon on 13 December 1914. The ASL Legislative Committee met in Washington that month, conferred with friendly lawmakers, and wrote to all the members of Congress urging them to pass Hobson's prohibition resolution. Hobson arranged for anti-alcohol exhibits to be waiting for his colleagues when they returned.[17]

As agreed upon, on 22 December the House Rules Committee reported a resolution that provided for an immediate vote on Hobson's resolution. Proponents of prohibition urged its passage, but so too did many opponents, who thought it best to confront and defeat so serious a threat to the nation's moral polity. With support from both sides, the resolution passed easily and the most substantial and substantive debate over the national prohibition amendment that Congress ever conducted began at once. One Mississippi representative cited the "proud boast that we are a Christian Nation" and called on members of Congress to "live up to our obligations as such." No one else invoked religious authority, but many representatives referred to the wishes of the Christian and temperance forces and pointed to the numerous petitions they had sent. Congress, they concluded, should respond to the demands of the majority of good people of the nation who favored national prohibition. Beyond that, the debate in 1914 revolved around various interrelated arguments over the practicality of prohibition, the history of moral legislation, and the central tenets of the antebellum moral polity—states' rights, moral suasion, and personal liberty.[18]

Proponents of national prohibition criticized the effects of alcohol and, even more, the nefarious influence of the liquor traffic. They blamed drinking for immorality, crime, the suffering of children, the breakup of families, and poverty. Prohibition reduced all these problems, they claimed. To support their claims, they told of and cited statistics from the many areas of the nation that already benefited from the adoption of prohibition. Their opponents questioned their figures and countered that where prohibition had been tried, it failed. Laws could not overcome appetites; prohibition did not prohibit. Opponents also warned that ending the liquor traffic would deny the federal government much-needed revenue and undermine economic prosperity. It would cost workers who produced beer and liquor their jobs and result in the illegal confiscation of the property of brewers and distillers.

While debating prohibition's success, proponents frequently made references to the history of earlier moral legislation. Edwin Webb, for example, claimed that the problem of replacing lost revenue from alcohol taxes did not concern him; if Americans had worried more about money than morals "we would still have lotteries in this Capital." A Texas representative used another historical analogy to counter the claim that it was illegal to confiscate brewers' property. The Thirteenth Amendment, Finis J. Garrett argued, had come at the cost of thousands of lives and had taken away four billion dollars in personal property as well as many millions of dollars in other kinds of property. He did not bring up emancipation in any spirit of revenge, Garrett quickly added, but only to remind lawmakers of the time when three-quarters of the people "declared that human slavery was a great national moral wrong; that it had no right to exist anywhere in the United States; and abolished it." Today, "as it has been with human slavery, so shall it be with alcoholic liquors." Hobson and another representative also invoked the antislavery precedent in behalf of prohibition.[19]

Yet when southerners willingly supported abolishing alcohol, Garrett complained, northerners hollered at "us about State rights and the preservation of property." Northerners did, in fact, raise the cry of states' rights and warned of the dangers of centralization. In the process, they appealed to the tacit moral relativism inherent in states' rights doctrine. Andrew J. Barchfeld, a Republican from Pittsburgh, cited the "different customs in different parts of the country" and championed toleration of disparate cultural practices. Some southerners, too, championed states' rights. By passing Prohibition, Edward W. Pou of North Carolina said, Congress would violate the "right" "to regulate our State matters, without interference on the part of any other State," which would create a dangerous precedent for forcing an end to segregation in schools, churches, and graveyards, repealing laws against interracial marriage, and enforcing the Fifteenth Amendment. The national government could then send a federal police force into the South, a Louisiana representative added, to reestablish "negro rule," which would, said another from Kentucky, "bring a revolution in the social life of the South." Such rhetoric combined older southern assumptions about the proper moral polity with memories of Reconstruction and racist fears for the future.[20]

In addition to celebrating the rights of the states, congressional foes of prohibition also argued that government had no right to legislate morality; promoting it should be left to individual moral suasion. J. Hampton Moore of Philadelphia told his colleagues that nothing "in our fundamental law nor in the spirit of our institutions . . . justifies the passage at our hands of legislation placing one class above another class or of one creed above another creed." Congress should not substitute government for the preacher, nor law for moral responsibility. "We can not make men good by law." Henry Vollmer of Iowa agreed: "I do not regard the policeman's club as a moral agent. Morality that is not self-imposed is not morality. The faculty of self-control is only developed by its exercise. To remove temptation would not improve character."[21]

Opponents of prohibition also cited the equally old and revered tradition of personal liberty. Hobson and his supporters, Barchfeld charged, wanted to introduce something totally new to the Constitution, "a limitation upon the personal liberties of the citizen." Vollmer, too, denounced the attempt "to invade personal rights and destroy personal liberties," and another representative from Illinois said that "millions" of Americans considered prohibition "absolutely un-American" because they felt capable of governing their "moral habits without limitation or restriction." A "law of this kind . . . is an abridgement of the right originally guaranteed by the fundamental law to the people of the United States."[22]

Supporters of the amendment disagreed. Melville C. Kelly of Pennsylvania dismissed the idea that government action against alcohol infringed upon "personal liberty and individual rights." This "once all-powerful" argument, with "its stark individualism, with its Ishmael-like philosophy of every man's hand against his neighbor, is no longer all-controlling. It divorced politics from morals and declared that might was right." With "developing civilization . . . complex conditions have taken the place of the simple relations of a past era. The Nation is a web and woof of citizenship, and a single torn thread mars the whole fabric." Statesmen had to "end the anarchy of selfish individualism." Kelly's remarks echoed not only much progressive thinking of the era but also the arguments of the Christian lobbyists. Kelly again sounded like them later in his speech when he affirmed, "This Republic is founded upon the moral character of its people. It is a monstrous error to regard politics and morals as separate and distinct from each other. . . . No greater calamity would be possible in America than to have a clear line of division between the dominion of government and the dominion of conscience." Other representatives, too, made sweeping claims for the necessity for government action.[23]

The debate over Hobson's resolution, in sum, involved not only the necessity and feasibility of prohibition but also the nature of the state and its responsibility for morality. Supporters of prohibition raised many of the themes the Christian lobbyists had championed since the 1880s—the need for a moral order, the right of society to protect itself, the importance of morality in and to government. Even as the debate addressed issues at the heart of Americans' conception of the moral polity, it revealed a nation fundamentally divided.

When the time for a vote came, the House readily agreed to Hobson's substitute language allowing concurrent state and federal enforcement of prohibition. Then the resolution to send the prohibition amendment to the states, which required a two-thirds vote, failed 197 to 190. Despite all the rhetoric on the floor about states' rights, more than twice as many southern Democrats voted for as against Hobson's resolution. Even adding those who for some reason did not vote, 61 percent of southern representatives voted yes; only westerners (68 percent of whom did) voted yes more often. The outcome showed prohibition still fared far more poorly among Democrats than Republicans (39 percent of Democrats voted yes as opposed to 54 percent of Republicans) and among representatives from the New England and the mid-Atlantic states (whose representatives voted yes only 12.5 and 25.27 percent, respectively) than among those from the South and West.[24]

Prohibition forces continued the educational campaign begun in 1913, and the ASL campaigned in 1914 and 1916 to elect a "dry" Congress. At the same time, the temperance groups worked to establish better cooperation in lobbying and debated the proper language of the amendment. In July 1915, at the instigation of the league's legislative committee and at the call of the ASL, the WCTU, the Federal Council of Churches, and the Good Templars, supporters of prohibition once more met in Washington to debate plans for, and especially the wording of, a constitutional amendment for prohibition. The key issue was whether to retain the words "for sale." To preserve them would allow the personal use of alcohol, so the discussion over the wording of the amendment continued the debate begun over personal-use exemptions in the Webb-Kenyon Act. After a day-long discussion, the representatives voted 126 to 8 to keep "for sale" in the amendment. The vote was only advisory, however. In another attempt to ensure unity in dealing with Congress, the meeting appointed what was called the Committee of Nineteen with authority to make final decisions on wording and legislative strategy. The creation of such a committee followed the strategy used in the Webb-Kenyon fight, and the Committee of Nineteen not only resembled but drew its core membership from its predecessor. The earlier committee had had only thirteen members, but nine of them also served on the Committee of Nineteen: Curtis, Webb, Sheppard, Hobson, Dinwiddie, Cannon, Barton, Ellis, and Crafts. They included the important lobbyists who had worked in Washington since the 1890s—Crafts, Ellis, and Dinwiddie—and represented the major organizations within the Christian lobby—the ASL, the WCTU, and the Reform Bureau. Of the nine who served on both committees, five were from the South.[25]

To fill out the new committee, one member of Congress was added, Horace Towner. The committee then included two members from the House and two from the Senate; two Republicans and two Democrats; two southerners and two westerners. The inclusion of the four active legislators testified to the fact that the Christian lobby had integrated itself into the legislative process. Of the other new members of the committee, three came from the WCTU and four from the ASL. The new members included the WCTU's new president, Anna Gordon, who spent much of her time in Washington during these years; the ASL's Wayne Wheeler, who after 1915 stayed in Washington to lobby and provide legal advice in the fight for national prohibition; and Charles Scanlon, of the Presbyterian temperance committee, who also had ties to the Prohibition Party.

The Committee of Nineteen met in Washington the following December and, by a vote of nine to three, endorsed the same wording for the amendment that Congress had voted on in 1914, which limited the ban on the manufacture and transportation of alcohol to that "for sale." A letter, prepared by Wheeler at the request of Sheppard and Dinwiddie, defended the inclusion of "for sale" in the national prohibition amendment in purely pragmatic, if not Machiavellian, terms. "This wording," the ASL's chief lawyer wrote, "strikes at the motive and root of the traffic in its perpetuation and extension, and at the same time avoids any controversy concerning the invasion of the home and the so-called sacred right of an individual to conduct his own affairs in his home or castle." If the words "for sale" were eliminated, "every means for securing liquor as a beverage is prohibited, and, therefore by indirection the use itself is prohib-ited." No state had gone that far, nor did every prohibitionist agree that the law should keep a person from obtaining a "limited amount of liquor" for use in his or her "own home." To pass, the letter continued, the amendment had to be phrased so as to maximize the number of people who would support it and to minimize the points on which its enemies could attack it. Besides, Wheeler added, there was little danger "of general home distillation of liquor," and under the amendment, Congress could later define sale in such a way as to please "the most radical prohibitionists." At that point, Congress would be able to change the definition without the necessity of a two-thirds vote. "It is always good tactics to accomplish your result along the lines of least resistance."[26]

Sheppard sent Wheeler's letter to his fellow senators as part of the campaign to convince a new Congress to act. On 2 December 1915, local WCTU groups

again met to observe a day of prayer for national prohibition and asked ministers to pray the following Sunday that God would guide members of Congress to send such an amendment to the states for ratification. Not leaving
everything to the Lord, Dinwiddie had already conferred with many members
of Congress. He and the other Christian lobbyists were quite optimistic in early
1916. The Democrats still controlled Congress, but Republicans, who in 1914
had given greater support to the amendment than the Democrats, had picked
up sixty-nine seats in the House. The Christian lobbyists also hoped that both
parties would want to keep prohibition from becoming an issue in the 1916
election and therefore settle the matter before the campaign began. To convince legislators to act at once, the lobbyists again urged their constituencies to
send letters, resolutions, and petitions in behalf of prohibition.[27]

Little came of the prohibitionists' efforts that spring, however; neither the
House nor the Senate Judiciary Committee sent a resolution to the floor. Democrats, who controlled the committees and Congress, argued that if they attempted to bring up the resolution, opponents of prohibition would filibuster
and delay the passage of more important legislation, including bills to bolster
the national defense at a time when war seemed likely. In addition, Democrats
reached the opposite conclusion from the lobbyists; they feared that sending the
amendment to the states would in fact make prohibition a campaign issue
in the 1916 election, one that might well hurt them, especially in the race for
the presidency, since President Woodrow Wilson had long opposed national
prohibition.[28]

As a result, Dinwiddie, Cannon, and the other ASL lobbyists, after consulting
with their allies in Congress and securing Ellis's consent, made a secret agreement with "the leaders in Congress favorable to Prohibition" that the Christian
lobbyists would curtail their efforts to pass both District prohibition (which
they believed they could pass) and the resolution for a national amendment
(which they did not). In return, these congressional leaders promised to do all
they could during the short session that followed the election "to secure speedy
and favorable reports on all important prohibition legislation then pending in
Congress."[29]

In the 1916 campaign, the ASL continued to focus its omni-partisan efforts
on congressional races, but both national parties remained silent on the issue
in their platforms. In the ensuing election, Wilson was reelected and the Democrats barely retained control of both houses of Congress. The Republicans
gained fourteen seats in the House and two in the Senate. Shortly after the election, the ASL's legislative committee—made up of Cannon, Barton, Dinwiddie,

and Wheeler—met in Washington and called for the submission of the national prohibition amendment to the states, adoption of prohibition for the
District of Columbia and Hawaii, and passage of a ban on mailing liquor ads.
No doubt heartened by the agreement they had reached during the spring, the
lobbyists expected great things not of the newly elected Congress but of the old
one, which gathered in December for a final, short, lame-duck session.[30]

Both Senate and House committees reported resolutions in support of a
constitutional amendment. The House Judiciary Committee, which had never
done that before, was chaired by Webb of North Carolina. He, Cannon's ally,
Carlin of Virginia, four other southerners, and two border-state representatives
provided eight of the twelve votes to report the resolution. Neither it nor the
Senate resolution came up for debate. However, two other antiliquor bills on
the lobbyists' agenda did reach the floor and became law: prohibition for the
District of Columbia and a further ban on interstate shipment of liquor, a
more radical one than the prohibitionists had sought.[31]

Sheppard led the fight for prohibition in the nation's capital. He had dropped
a provision in his original bill that would have prevented importation for personal use or limited how much liquor could be ordered by mail. An attempt to
add a bone-dry provision, in other words a ban on all importation or purchase
of alcohol from outside the District, secured only eight votes. "Most of the
friends of the Sheppard bill," the *Washington Times* reported, "took the view
that however meritorious the . . . substitute might be in the abstract, practically,
it could not be forced through the Congress and certainly would fail." With no
bone-dry provision, however, Sheppard's bill passed the Senate by a relatively
wide margin, fifty-five to thirty-two. Only half the Democrats voted yes;
65 percent of the Republicans did. The highest levels of support came from the
West, Midwest, and South—in that order.[32]

In the House, the Judiciary Committee put a bone-dry provision in the bill,
but Dinwiddie asked representatives to support Sheppard's bill as passed in the
Senate, "despite our personal preference" for the House version, since changing
the bill would mean that it would go to a conference committee so late in the
session that it might be defeated. After opponents first tried to filibuster the
measure and then revived a proposal to hold a referendum (already defeated in
the Senate), the House at last voted to substitute the Senate for the House version. A subsequent attempt to have the bill recommitted failed. On this crucial
vote, voting along party and regional lines roughly followed that in the Senate,
although the South rather than the West demonstrated the most consistent
support. Once the bill passed, President Wilson, who still opposed national

prohibition but had in the past supported prohibition for certain localities, signed the bill.[33]

Temperance forces had sought prohibition in the District for decades, and its adoption signaled their increasing influence in Congress and growing support in the nation. But the debate over the District prohibition bill also revealed a continuing division over importation of alcohol for personal use; in dropping a bone-dry ban from the bill, both lobbyists and legislators demonstrated their hesitancy to attack drinking head on or to have the government intervene in the home. The issue would continue to complicate the debate over prohibition, a debate transformed by the other bill passed in the short, lame-duck session that followed the election of 1916.

During an attempt by the Christian lobbyists to pass another of their legislative goals, a ban on liquor advertisements from the mails, James Reed moved to amend an anti-advertisement amendment to a post office appropriations bill to extend its penalties to anyone who "shall order, purchase, or cause intoxicating liquors to be transported in interstate commerce into any" prohibition state, whether that state allowed exemptions for personal use or not. The Missourian's amendment would make all prohibition states bone dry. Reed, generally considered an ally of the liquor industry, and other opponents of prohibition apparently saw his amendment as a means to force prohibitionists to reveal their hypocrisy. If they opposed it, they showed that they wanted to stop people from drinking in saloons but had no intention of interfering with "respectable" people who bought liquor or wine by mail and drank it in the privacy of their homes. If prohibitionists supported Reed's amendment, they publicly acknowledged that, despite all their obfuscation, they did in fact seek to keep everyone from drinking. If prohibitionists chose the second course, Reed and his cohorts believed, they would lose significant public support. With votes from representatives who both favored and opposed prohibition, the measure passed easily in the Senate.[34]

Confronted with passage of the Reed Amendment in the Senate, some of the Christian lobbyists also perceived its potential to harm their cause. Hobson, convinced that personal-use exemptions were necessary to pass prohibition legislation and personally committed to allowing moderate drinking by the better sort of people, frantically wired Dinwiddie and others to oppose the Reed Amendment. Cannon agreed, at least on the political danger the measure posed, and raced to Washington to rally the prohibitionist forces in the House against the bone-dry provision. Dinwiddie, however, had already begun to ask members of the House to vote for the amendment. When he and Cannon met, they could agree only to send out a letter telling legislators to vote whichever way they thought best. Like Dinwiddie, Wheeler, Anna Gordon, and Ellis seemed comfortable with Reed's amendment. Many other prohibition leaders in Congress apparently thought it unwise to oppose the bone-dry provision and then later to ask Congress to pass a national prohibition amendment. The House passed the amendment by a wide margin, suggesting it had support of both sides in the larger battle over prohibition.[35]

The behavior of the other lobbyists after the Reed Amendment passed suggested that those who opposed it did so not out of principle but for pragmatic reasons—they feared it might hurt the chances of passing the ad ban or later efforts. The ASL Legislative Committee as well as many churches and WCTU groups wrote Wilson urging him to sign the bill that contained the bone-dry provision. The president did sign the law, which included a ban both on interstate shipment and on liquor ads in the mail. Congress postponed the effective date of the bone-dry ban, but in the summer of 1917, the attorney general began to try to stop shipment into all states and localities that had adopted prohibition. "Senator Reed's little joke," wrote the *American Issue*, "will undoubtedly prove a boomerang for the liquor interests." Whether or not it came back to haunt them, the passage of the Reed Amendment did mark the beginning of the end for the liquor interests. Within nine months of its passage in 1917, both houses of Congress had approved a resolution sending the national prohibition amendment to the states for ratification.[36]

The public climate in which the Christian lobbyists labored changed dramatically in those nine months. In January, the Supreme Court upheld the Webb-Kenyon Act. Its decision maintained that many legal precedents established that the government had an "enlarged right . . . to regulate" the sale of liquor because of its special character. The Court also argued that it was "not in the slightest degree disputed that" Congress could prohibit "the shipment of all intoxicants in the channels of interstate commerce" and cited as precedents its earlier rulings that upheld the Mann Act and the ban on interstate shipment of lottery materials. Because of the nature of the federal-state system, the Court continued, Congress also had "the lesser power" "of adapting the regulation to the various local requirements and conditions that may be expressed in the laws of the States." The Court's broad affirmation of federal power and the designation of liquor as a special case heartened those who favored prohibition but doubted the federal government's power to control the sale of alcohol. The same case involved a West Virginia prohibition law that banned importation of liquor for personal use. The Court also upheld it, maintaining that it did not matter whether the state had "the right to forbid individual use, . . . since clearly there would be power, as incident to the right to forbid manufacture and sale, to restrict the means by which intoxicants for personal use could be obtained, even if such use was permitted." The Court's decision therefore also heartened advocates of bone-dry laws. Up until then, only a few states had stopped all importation of alcohol; by the end of 1917, eighteen had.[37]

State efforts to toughen prohibition statutes reflected an increase in public support over the previous few years. Sixteen of the twenty-five states that enacted some form of prohibition before Congress passed a resolution proposing the national amendment did so between 1914 and 1917, indicating a significant shift in public opinion during those years. No doubt the expanded public campaigns by the WCTU and ASL played an important role, but their cause benefited from the help of others, including evangelist Billy Sunday. Progressives, who shared with the lobbyists a commitment to legislating morality and the use of government power, provided important support and votes in Congress. Perhaps most important, William Jennings Bryan began his personal campaign for prohibition. The frequent presidential candidate had always abstained from drinking alcohol, but as a loyal Democrat he had initially opposed prohibiting its sale. Bryan first endorsed prohibition, for his home state of Nebraska, in 1910. After he resigned from Wilson's cabinet in 1915 to protest the president's response to Germany's sinking of the *Lusitania*, Bryan began to speak in behalf of national prohibition. Nevertheless, he tried to keep the issue out of the 1916 campaign, so only in 1917 did he become an ardent, public champion of national prohibition.[38]

The most important factor in increasing public support for prohibition, one mentioned at the time and given great weight by historians since, was America's entry in World War I. Even before American intervention, successful wartime prohibition in other nations convinced some Americans of prohibition's benefits and its feasibility. After the United States declared war in April 1917, a general feeling of patriotism and a wartime willingness to accept greater governmental control over various aspects of life had a more direct and dramatic impact. The darker side of patriotism did as well. Wartime hostilities turned some Americans against German American organizations, which long opposed prohibition measures. The most extreme manifestations of anti-German prejudice, however, came in 1918, after Congress sent the amendment to the states. The war also highlighted arguments that the prohibitionists had been making for decades. They had long contended that drinking undermined efficiency and contributed to a loss of productivity in business and industry. Yet business support for prohibition "crystallized" only in 1915, when labor shortages began and many manufacturers anticipated an even more rapid expansion of the economy. In earlier years, when labor was plentiful, most industries did not need to be too concerned; drinkers could always and easily be replaced. Wartime labor shortages and demands for rapid production changed the situation, and business support for prohibition increased. Prohibitionists and other Christian lobbyists had also long talked about the effect of drinking on "our boys" and argued that the government had a responsibility to protect them. As increasing numbers of "our boys" became "our soldiers," that responsibility became more direct and the need for protection more immediate.[39]

Weighing the war's influence on the adoption of prohibition against other factors is probably futile. To prove the crucial counterfactual claim—that, given the growth in public support and the lobbyists' increasing efforts, prohibition would have passed even had there been no war—is impossible. Two things remained clear, however. Despite the role of the war and the aid of Progressives, the Christian lobbyists and their allies continued to guide the debates in Congress and shape the form prohibition would take. And, at the very least, the Christian lobbyists did not hesitate to exploit the war as an occasion to pass prohibition legislation.

Six weeks before American entry into World War I, the Anti-Saloon League raised the possibility of nationwide wartime prohibition. The day after the Senate voted to declare war, the league's legislative committee endorsed and, shortly after that, publicly called for legislation to prevent the sale of alcohol to soldiers and sailors, to create dry zones around military camps, to prohibit interstate shipment of liquors, to prevent the use of foodstuffs in the manufacture of alcoholic beverages, and to send an amendment for national prohibition to the states. Despite its tradition of pacifism, the WCTU quickly endorsed the war effort, the legislative goals of the league, and a wartime antivice crusade as well. Gordon and Ellis urged their members to write the president in behalf of prohibition and purity, telling them to emphasize "mothers' appeal for sons." In a letter to President Wilson, Cannon struck the same note: "The mothers and fathers of our country . . . insist that while their sons are in the army, the navy, or the training camp, they be protected from the liquor and vice traffic." Parents "fear the possibilities of moral and physical evil . . . more than they fear physical wounding and death by German bullets." One mother, according to Ellis, claimed that she "would rather a thousand times that my son went to the bottom of the ocean unwarned, but clean and pure, than to have him come back home polluted and tainted from drink and sensuality."[40]

Lawmakers seemed to agree. In May, Congress approved a ban on the sale of liquor to anyone in uniform and in September created zones around military installations in which both prostitution and the sale of liquor were forbidden. Not just the WCTU but also the ASL, which temporarily and quietly abandoned its single-issue focus, pushed for the ban on prostitution as well as that on drinking. Congressional proponents of these measures proclaimed the need to protect "our boys" and to ensure wartime efficiency. Yet prohibitionists supported the legislation as much for the advancement of their own cause as for the war effort. Sheppard, for example, praised the passage of one of them "as another step toward the entire abolition of the traffic in alcoholic liquors throughout this Republic."[41]

A wartime ban on using food supplies in the production of alcohol, another goal of the prohibitionists, also offered a means to protect "our boys," to support the war effort, and to take "another step" toward prohibition. In addition to the ASL and WCTU, several governors and six hundred business and university leaders endorsed the ban. Irving Fisher, a Yale economist and veteran prohibitionist who served on the Council of National Defense, was an especially influential advocate of the idea. Whatever one thought of prohibition in peacetime, Fisher argued, during war it would save food and allow workers from the liquor trade to be shifted to vital war industries.[42]

After a heated debate, the House agreed; it passed an amendment to a food-control bill that prevented the use of grains and cereals in the production of any alcoholic drink. In the Senate, Henry Cabot Lodge offered a compromise, one made possible in part by a split between brewers and distillers that undermined later attempts to forestall Prohibition. He proposed banning the use of foodstuffs in the production of distilled spirits (distillers had a two-year stockpile that could still be sold) but allowing breweries to continue to use grain to make beer. Fearful that delaying tactics by the liquor interests would prevent passage of any food-control bill and opposed to prohibition anyway, President Wilson, through Virginia's Senator Thomas Martin, asked the ASL Legislative Committee to drop demands for a total ban. The committee agreed and endorsed Lodge's proposal to exempt beer and wine from the ban on the use of foodstuffs in the production of alcohol.[43]

To ratify its decision, the league committee called a National Legislative Conference made up of representatives of twelve national temperance groups. It included several new members, Fisher among them, but its core came from the Committee of Nineteen—Barton, Dinwiddie, Wheeler, Cannon, Ellis, Gordon, Scanlon, and Crafts. The conference, too, endorsed Lodge's compromise. The prohibitionists portrayed their concession as a grand, patriotic gesture and self-righteously (and gleefully) contrasted it with what they termed the unpatriotic intransigence of their wet foes. Certainly patriotism played a part, but no doubt many, like Webb, agreed to "exempt wine and beer for the present if by doing so we can secure the submission of the Constitutional Amendment." Although apparently no specific deal was cut, the prohibitionists sought the benefits that their patriotic concession promised for the achievement of their ultimate goal. Even after the agreement between the league and Wilson, Senate debate on the food-control bill remained contentious. The upper chamber toughened Lodge's proposal and then accepted the basic compromise.[44]

As they compromised on the food-control bill, the league and the prohibitionist forces made clear their intention to continue the battle for wartime and permanent national constitutional prohibition. The terms of the debate over an amendment had shifted. In 1916, the Senate Judiciary Committee had reported a resolution for a constitutional amendment that dropped "for sale" and simply prohibited the manufacture, sale, and transportation of alcoholic beverages. The House, though, preserved "for sale." In March 1917, as the opening of the Sixty-fifth Congress approached, Anti-Saloon League leaders and the other lobbyists discussed whether to adopt the Senate committee's wording or the House's more restricted language, which they had long endorsed. Despite the opposition of Hobson and others, both the ASL Legislative Committee and the Committee of Nineteen agreed to follow the Senate committee's lead and eliminate the "for sale" after manufacture and transportation. Doing so meant that all making or shipping of alcoholic beverages, even for personal use, would be illegal. The Reed bone-dry amendment, the ASL committee explained, had already nullified the personal-use exemptions granted by many states and thereby eliminated the possibility that states might refuse to ratify a broader amendment in an effort to protect them. Moreover, the committee maintained, rapidly advancing prohibitionist sentiment in the nation made it possible to pass a more radical amendment. The "policy of the Anti-Saloon League of America, which has been consistently followed for the last 24 years," explained the *American Issue,* "has been to go after the best attainable legislation . . . , while constantly pressing toward the ultimate best."[45]

Early the next month, Sheppard introduced a joint resolution providing for submission to the states of a national prohibition amendment that would ban all manufacture, sale, and transportation of intoxicating liquors. In its behalf, the ASL and the WCTU once more mobilized their forces to pressure Congress. After several failed attempts to bring the resolution up, in late July 1917, the Senate, for the first time ever, agreed to debate national prohibition. Its discussions included only a few references to the war but revisited many of the arguments offered during the 1914 House debate. Proponents again pointed to the dangers and the costs of drinking and cited scientific and medical authorities to support their contentions. They also occasionally invoked morality and God's authority but more frequently referred to the growing popular demand for prohibition. In response, opponents proclaimed that the government should not and could not enforce morality, condemned the confiscation of the liquor industry's property, and criticized the amendment as a violation of states' rights. Far more northern than southern congressmen raised the last issue.[46]

One Georgia senator who spoke of states' rights also tried to add an amendment banning not only the sale but also the purchase of liquor; it was hypocritical, he complained, to allow people to buy something that was illegal to sell. Sheppard replied that a constitutional amendment should be stated in as few words as possible and that the existing wording would stop purchases. The Georgian's amendment garnered only four votes. To secure enough votes to reach the two-thirds majority needed to send the amendment to the states, Sheppard and other supporters did accept a proposal, brokered by Ohio senator Warren G. Harding and the ASL's Wheeler, to put a limit of six years on the process of ratification. If enough states had not ratified in that time, the amendment would die. Harding and the wet forces hoped ratification could not be accomplished in that period, but the lobbyists felt confident it could and knew that even if the amendment was not ratified, they could still try again. With the extra votes, the resolution passed sixty-five to twenty. Democrats and Republicans voted yes at relatively equal rates, and again support for national prohibition was strongest among senators from the West, South, and Midwest.[47]

The House Democratic caucus had agreed early in the session to consider only measures related to the war and approved by Wilson, so the prohibition amendment did not come up there until December 1917. The House debate occurred under a strict rule limiting the time allowed each speaker. For that reason or perhaps because attitudes had ossified over the years, the debate proved less a discussion than a series of statements by various House members. Opponents appealed to states' rights and personal liberties more often than their counterparts in the Senate had. The war was mentioned more often as well, although most frequently by opponents of the resolution who argued that passing it would divide the nation in the midst of a crisis. Wets also cited the opposition of organized labor, a point disputed by some proponents. For the most part, however, the arguments for and against prohibition resembled those made in the Senate as well as those in the 1914 House debate—not to mention the debates that had raged in the public arena for many years.[48]

A California representative's attempt to add an amendment exempting wine and light beers failed, but the House did change the resolution in other ways. It expanded to seven the number of years allowed for ratification and added a provision that delayed implementation of prohibition for one year after its adoption, to allow brewers and distillers time to adjust. The House also changed the enforcement clause to provide for concurrent federal and state jurisdiction. With these modifications, the resolution submitting the amendment to the states passed on a vote of 282 to 128.[49]

The vote in the House generally followed the pattern in the Senate, with the percentage of Democrats and Republicans voting yes roughly equal and levels of regional support about the same as well (except in the border states, where a significantly higher percentage of representatives than senators voted yes). Some of the new yes votes were cast by Republicans who had been elected after the 1914 vote and might be attributed to the success of the ASL's campaigning, as Wheeler, who had led it, claimed. Other new yes votes came from legislators who had changed their positions since 1914. New York, whose delegation experienced a significant turn around, had recently enacted woman suffrage, and the ASL's William Anderson later credited that and pressure from female activists with scaring its representatives into changing their votes. Increased support for prohibition among Democrats also contributed to the victory. Even though the party had lost seats, it still provided twenty-three more votes in favor of the amendment than it had in 1914. The percentage of yes votes among Democrats rose from 39.31 percent in 1914 to 65.26 percent in 1917, while among Republicans it rose only from 54.20 to 65.09. Dinwiddie, Sheppard, and others had cultivated and consulted William Jennings Bryan. He in turn had lobbied hard to influence doubting Democrats, and his efforts no doubt helped change votes. The South, where Bryan was extremely popular, provided most of the new Democratic votes for prohibition; in fact, twenty-five more southerners voted yes than had in 1914. Only the level of support in the West, with 79.25 percent of its representatives voting yes, exceeded that in the South, with 78.57 percent. The southerners gave the resolution solid support, as the *American Issue* observed after the vote, despite tremendous pressure on them to oppose it.[50]

In exerting pressure, southern opponents often returned to the themes of states' rights, white supremacy, and the terrors of presumed "negro role" during Reconstruction. In doing so, they again revealed the fear that prohibition would set a precedent for federal intervention in racial segregation or southern elections. Some proponents of prohibition fought racism with racism by citing the danger of drunken blacks who did not work and posed a threat to white womanhood. Others, including Edwin Webb, employed the language of concurrent jurisdiction to dismiss fears of an invasion of federal officials. But Webb also offered a positive argument rooted in nationalism. Government "is but the organized forces of the nation formed for strengthening its power and advancing its life," he declared. It should "suppress those agencies which have a tendency to sap and weaken" its "strength" and should "suppress vice and crime in order that the nation may, unrestrained by these evils, go forward in its efforts for greater liberty, freedom, and achievement." States' rights rhetoric dominated on the floor, but Webb's position attracted four times as many southern votes. The lobbying of Cannon, the legislative leadership of Webb and Sheppard, and the overwhelming southern vote for prohibition in each house of Congress testified once again to the important role a changed South played in moral reconstruction. In the end, support from the former Confederacy proved crucial to the passage of a resolution proposing the most radical expansion of federal authority over morality since emancipation.[51]

Once Congress voted to send the amendment to the states, the ASL, the WCTU, the Reform Bureau, and other prohibition forces worked to secure its ratification. While that process proceeded, their lobbyists in Washington continued the push for wartime prohibition. In late January 1918, with the amendment having been sent to the states, the ASL Legislative Committee and the WCTU urged Congress to enact total, wartime prohibition. A contentious debate over the proposal revealed that more than a few legislators still opposed all forms of prohibition and believed the plan's supporters were only using the occasion of the war to enact their moral agenda. Nevertheless, Congress banned the sale of all distilled spirits after 30 June 1919, the use of grain and other crops in the production of beer, wine, or liquor after 1 May of that year, and the sale of beer and wine after the same date. The bans were to remain in effect through demobilization and until such time as the president declared the war at an end. Since the bill became law after the fighting had stopped, the goal seemed to be to stop drinking not to win the war. In December, Sheppard also introduced a bill for bone-dry prohibition in the District of Columbia, and Congress approved it in February 1919.[52]

By that time, the constitutional amendment for national prohibition had been ratified. Mississippi became the first state to ratify it on 8 January 1918, less than a month after Congress had approved sending it to the states. Virginia and South Carolina soon followed. "Thus," proclaimed the state superintendent of South Carolina's Anti-Saloon League, "does the state of Calhoun, of Rutledge and Pinckney, the first state to secede in 1860, declare for good order and conserved manhood in preference to ancient and respected doctrines which have no relevance and are invoked by those who contend for liquor under the camouflage of states' rights." By the time the required thirty-six states had approved the amendment, all eleven states of the former Confederacy had ratified national prohibition, nine of them by margins in excess of two to one in both houses of their legislatures. Only in both houses of the legislature in Louisiana, with its large Catholic vote, and in the Alabama senate was the margin of victory smaller than two to one.[53]

On 16 January 1919, Nebraska became the thirty-sixth state to ratify the amendment. That day, Sheppard took the Senate floor to announce victory and to point out that ratification had occurred in only thirteen months, more rapidly than with any previous amendment save that abolishing slavery. Kenyon called the crusade for prohibition "the greatest moral battle waged in this country since the abolition of slavery" and gave much of the credit for leading that fight in the Senate to Sheppard. No "greater service has ever been performed to humanity or righteousness and to the real best interest of this Nation," Kenyon added. He then thanked Texas for sending such a man to Congress. Thirteen days later, Sheppard, Bryan, and leaders of the ASL, the WCTU, the Reform Bureau, and denominational temperance committees gathered in the office of the secretary of state to witness the signing of the proclamation of the Eighteenth Amendment. The legislators and lobbyists who gathered to celebrate still faced another battle in their long war for prohibition, the passage of an enforcement act. It would reveal much about national attitudes toward legislating morality.[54]

In December 1918, the legislative conference of the temperance forces had agreed on certain elements essential to the successful enforcement of prohibition: the inclusion of "distilled, malt, fermented, vinous, alcoholic or any intoxicating liquor"; a ban on the sale, manufacture, and "possession of intoxicating liquors"; sufficient federal enforcement power; and adequate search and seizure provisions. Wheeler, who with his legal expertise became more important than Dinwiddie or Cannon in lobbying on the enforcement bill, put these elements into a sweeping measure that set rules for the enforcement of both wartime and national prohibition. As actually passed, the Volstead Act, as the enforcement bill was called after its sponsor, did not include everything Wheeler and the prohibition lobbyists wanted.[55]

The debates over the Volstead Act, in part, reprised the fight over the amendment itself. Opponents attacked the very idea of prohibition. Once again, they maintained that it did not prohibit, claimed that most Americans did not favor it, and charged the Anti-Saloon League with all manner of evils in unfairly securing its passage. As opponents of moral legislation had so often before, they also maintained that the government could not and should not regulate morality and championed individual rights and personal liberties. Proponents occasionally responded to their arguments and praised the role of the ASL and the WCTU. For the most part, however, supporters of the bill, confident in their victory, simply proclaimed that the passage of the amendment demonstrated that the American people wanted strict prohibition.[56]

Along with re-arguing the merits of Prohibition, the debates over the Volstead Act addressed specific issues of enforcement. Despite the amendment's provision for "concurrent powers," the House minority report on the bill concluded that it assumed federal power was supreme. On the floor, opponents therefore revived states' rights arguments. A few questions on the nature of concurrent power arose, but the issue never became central in the debate. Later, Webb wrote that in passing the Volstead Act his colleagues thought of both the state and federal governments as "sovereigns in the enforcement of their prohibition laws." If the federal government had a more expansive definition of what constituted an intoxicating liquor, he explained, it could not make a state enforce it. But, Webb's letter made clear, federal officials would still enforce the more rigorous standard in that state—which certainly made the federal sovereign a good bit more sovereign than the state.[57]

The definition of "intoxicating liquors" became a far more hotly contested issue than the notion of concurrent powers. Wheeler had advocated and the bill defined "intoxicating liquor" by a standard that the government had used for tax purposes, .05 percent alcoholic content. Some opponents claimed that Congress had no right to set a standard, but most devoted their efforts to trying to raise the acceptable level of alcoholic content to 2.75 percent alcohol, which would have made some forms of beer legal. They championed the right of workers to their beer and drew a distinction between the effects of beer and those of liquor, a tactic that opponents of Prohibition had employed successfully in the fight over the first wartime food-control bill. Prohibitionists had treated beer and liquor as equally dangerous since as early as the revision of Blair's proposed amendment in the 1870s and certainly since the army canteen fight in 1900. The Volstead Act defined alcoholic beverages as anything containing more than .05 percent alcohol.

Wheeler and the Prohibition lobbyists met with less success in their attempt to write strict possession and stringent search-and-seizure provisions into the bill. A general statement making "possession" illegal stayed in the act, but critics claimed that outlawing possession went dramatically beyond the amendment since it forbade only manufacture and importation, not use. They prevented the prohibition forces in the House from amending the bill to prohibit use, although only by three votes. The House did include a provision making it illegal to drink on a train or other public conveyance, but a Senate committee eliminated that section and another that involved possession.

Possession in the home proved an especially sensitive issue. Even the tougher House version allowed the storage and consumption of liquor in a private dwelling. Andrew Volstead admitted that many prohibitionists objected to this provision, but contended that it had to remain in the bill if it were to pass. Although the "object of the eighteenth amendment is, no doubt, to prohibit the use of liquor," he added, "there is no express provision against keeping it or drinking it." The House agreed. Many legislators thought that citizens should be allowed to drink whatever they wanted in their homes, that their liberties there could not be abridged. The discussion of the search-and-seizure provision underscored the idea of the home as liberty's castle. Even the ASL maintained that enforcement officers should not have the right to search a house if liquor stored there had been bought before Prohibition went into effect. As finally passed, the Volstead Act allowed a search only if the house were being used to sell liquor and included other protections for homes. As one Virginian put it, "Throughout this act we seek to preserve the sanctity of the home."[58]

Despite some compromises, Congress still passed a strong enforcement code. Wilson vetoed it, but Congress passed it over his veto. In some respects, the Volstead Act proved to be another instance of expanding the scope of Prohibition as public opinion allowed, the final step along the road to the total elimination of alcohol from American society that its most prominent supporters had wanted all along. Yet the lobbyists sought and would have preferred an even more stringent code. They made it clear that they wanted to end the use of alcoholic beverages, not just stop their sale in saloons, but they also tacitly and sometimes explicitly acknowledged that they could not pass a law that did so forthrightly. Buttressed by the persisting antebellum tradition of personal liberty as well as widespread belief in the sanctity and privacy of the home, their opponents had the votes to limit what the prohibitionists could do. To a degree, the debate was a phony one. If liquor could not be purchased, drinking would stop when stocks ran out. The unwillingness of Congress to outlaw personal use along with manufacture and sale probably reflected the will of the people and the persistence of the ideal of personal liberty. They would not take all the steps the prohibitionists would have liked. Their opposition and the resulting ambiguity in the law helped make the enforcement of Prohibition confusing, to say the least.[59]

At the moment of victory, few of the prohibitionists foresaw problems; instead they rejoiced in the better, brighter world that lay ahead and predicted, with the *American Issue*, that "the future historian will accord to January 16, 1920," the day Prohibition took effect, "a place second only to that of the advent of the Redeemer." Other days come to mind, but Prohibition did represent the crowning achievement of the Christian lobbyists' campaign to reconstruct America's moral polity. The Anti-Saloon League, so often given full credit for the achievement, played a central role in the victory. But the fact that the ASL involved the WCTU, Crafts, and representatives of denominational committees in lobbying efforts and in determining the wording of the amendment revealed its continued awareness of the need for support and cooperation. Even acting together, the Christian lobbyists never dictated to Congress but rather worked with Sheppard, Webb, and their other congressional allies. In the evolution of the wording of the amendment as well as on most decisions on legislative strategy, the lobbyists followed the lead of elected officials. Success, then, owed something to their lobbying skills but also to the astute judgment of their allies. Prohibitionists also benefited from the weakness of their opposition. In a polity increasingly dominated by organized interest groups, only three types of organizations opposed them: labor unions, German American associations, and the alcohol industry itself. The influence of the first proved minimal. Anti-German sentiment during the war reduced the already limited clout of the second. A division among distillers, brewers, and vintners undermined the industry's potential influence, as did the obvious self-interested nature of any argument sellers of alcohol offered against prohibition. Disclosures of the industry's attempts to corrupt the political process further reduced their ability to work their will in Congress.[60]

In the final analysis, Prohibition probably passed because most Americans wanted it, even though they might not have fully understood what they were getting. The lobbyists' pragmatic, step-by-step approach obscured the potential impact of Prohibition. Supporters delighted in talking about the onward march of prohibition, giving statistics and drawing maps to show how over the years increasing amounts of territory had become dry. They made national prohibition seem all but inevitable. Until the enforcement of the Reed bone-dry amendment in the summer of 1917, however, individuals in most prohibition areas could still order liquor by mail. Prohibition had not necessarily stopped them from drinking. Most of the Christian lobbyists did want to end all consumption, but many other people wanted to stop sales to "others," not themselves—to close saloons, not "the rum holes under their own noses," as Crafts so delicately put it. With that caveat, however, probably a majority of Americans favored prohibition, at least in some form, and at least at the time. The Christian lobbyists had persuaded them that the liquor traffic acted primarily from avarice. The lobbyists had also convinced many Americans that King Alcohol created the worst of appetites, one that turned drinkers into slaves, took away their liberties, and hurt others as well as themselves. Slavery to alcohol led to poverty, crime, the breakdown of the family, and the abuse of women and children.[61]

Prohibition was the most dramatic expansion of the moral powers of the federal government achieved by the Christian lobbyists, yet the political maneuvering that led to the adoption of Prohibition had resulted in anything but the enunciation of a clear, single standard on the morality of drinking. As in their earlier moral crusades, the lobbyists had stressed the need to control the sale of alcohol, not its use. And in the final years of the debate over Prohibition they repeatedly obscured their position on the personal use of alcohol. In the end, neither the amendment nor the Volstead Act outlawed consumption or really even the possession of alcohol. More important, the demands of organized Christian constituents and a growing public consensus on the evils of alcohol that they claimed existed became the justification for Prohibition, not the religious authority Christian lobbyists had long championed. During the debates over Prohibition, a few legislators cited moral law and resorted to the rhetoric of righteousness, but such appeals were relatively rare. Most lawmakers defended their votes by citing the demands of the people. Most Americans wanted Prohibition, they said, and the majority should get its way. Prohibition proved not the triumph of Christian government but of Christians in government— not an example of government enacting biblical morality but of Congress letting the majority dictate moral behavior.

Prohibition, the crowning achievement of moral reconstruction, became its culmination as well. By the time the nation's most dramatic experiment in legislating morality began in 1920, the alliance of Christian lobbyists that helped pass Prohibition had lost its unity and much of its influence. The first generation of lobbyists who formed it and built its public power had died—or soon would. Frances Willard, perhaps the best known, was the first, in 1898. Her friend who led the WCTU and participated in the behind-the-scene decisions during the drive for Prohibition, Anna Gordon, stayed on to fight for its enforcement but retired in 1925 and died six years later. Margaret Dye Ellis, the WCTU's chief lobbyist, decided that with the passage of the resolution sending the prohibition amendment to the states her work was done. She went home to New Jersey and spent much of the rest of her life, which ended in 1925, as an invalid.[1]

Joseph Cook lived longer than Willard but passed from the national scene even earlier. In the 1890s, Cook turned his efforts from moral reform to world evangelism. He completed one international speaking tour, but at the beginning of a second in 1895 he suffered a stroke from which he never fully recovered. When he died in 1901, his once formidable reputation as a public speaker and moral reformer had all but disappeared. Cook's friend and neighbor Anthony Comstock outlived him, but in the early 1900s his public support began to erode; some of his opponents even tried to have him fired from his post office job. He kept it but died shortly thereafter, in 1915. By that time, all three of the leading lobbyists of the National Reform Association—David McAllister, T. P. Stephenson, and H. H. George—had passed away. Henry W. Blair lived to see prohibition adopted and to receive a bit of public acclaim for being the first to introduce a constitutional amendment, but he died within the year. Wilbur Crafts died two years later in 1922.[2]

The organizations the first generation helped found survived their deaths but never again played so important a public role. With the financial base

Crafts had secured, the International Reform Bureau survived into the 1940s, but without its leader it accomplished little. The National Reform Association's public influence probably peaked in 1913, when it held a large conference on Christian citizenship in Portland, Oregon. After that, most of its efforts went into the fight to put an antipolygamy amendment in the Constitution and to keep the Bible in the schools. As time went on, the NRA became even more closely identified with the Christian amendment and the Reformed Presbyterian Church. It continues to exist, but it never again achieved the influence that George, Stephenson, and McAllister managed to acquire through their alliance with other Christian lobbyists and their own contacts on Capitol Hill.

The WCTU, too, remains active. In the 1920s, it continued to work in behalf of the prohibition cause, promoted strict enforcement, and continued its campaign of moral suasion. The WCTU also persisted in the fight for movie censorship, though it focused on local and state rather than federal efforts in the twenties. It still had a lobbyist in Washington, however, and expanded its lobbying efforts to include child welfare, health, and other broader social concerns. As the twentieth century progressed, however, the WCTU's public influence and profile declined.[3]

The Anti-Saloon League's ultimate fate paralleled that of the WCTU, but in the early 1920s, it was the only association within the alliance that increased its public influence. Two of its major leaders charted different postamendment courses for the group. Ernest Cherrington wanted to shift the league's activities within the United States to an emphasis on moral suasion and, an even higher priority with him, to direct its energies into an international campaign against alcohol. Wayne Wheeler, who had led league lobbying for the Volstead Act, thought the primary focus of the league should be enforcement. Purley Baker and Howard Hyde Russell, the other of the four major leaders of the league, concurred with Wheeler. With their support and from his post in Washington, Wheeler sought to exercise as much power over the enforcement of Prohibition as he possibly could. During the early twenties, he wielded considerable influence in Congress and on the choice of officials appointed to enforce Prohibition, including federal judges. He also intervened openly in politics and tried to block the election of Alfred E. Smith in 1928. Wheeler's blatant use of power tarnished the league's reputation, as did a 1927 investigation of its campaign contributions.[4]

The fate of Edwin Dinwiddie and James Cannon Jr., Wheeler's predecessors as lobbyists for the ASL, did not help any. Almost as soon as the Prohibition resolution passed in Congress in 1917, criticism of Dinwiddie resurfaced within the league. In 1918, Crafts claimed than Dinwiddie had misused government monies appropriated for a 1915 International Congress of Alcohol, a meeting never held because of World War I. Cannon and others within the league joined the attack, and eventually the ASL Executive Committee agreed to pay the government back out of its own funds but claimed it did so "without reflecting in any way upon the character of Mr. Dinwiddie" or accepting "any responsibility for the action" taken by him. A little over a year later, in the summer of 1920, Dinwiddie resigned. Cannon, in contrast, at first went on to greater glory. In 1918, the Methodist Episcopal Church, South, elected this minister-in-politics a bishop. Cannon remained active in league affairs. In 1928, he too tried to stop the election of Smith, organizing a southern rebellion against him that trafficked in virulent anti-Catholicism. That same year, charges surfaced, raised by his political enemies, that Cannon had gambled heavily in stocks at a bucket shop, that he had hoarded food supplies during World War I, that he had misused campaign funds, and that he had committed adultery with a woman whom he later married after his wife died. Cannon denied all the allegations and over the next five years defended himself in court, in congressional hearings, and before church commissions. He was never convicted of anything, and church bodies exonerated him. Nonetheless, the experience compromised his moral authority and did nothing to improve the reputation of the Anti-Saloon League.[5]

The death or discrediting of almost all of the lobbyists who played a crucial role in passing moral legislation, along with the diminished influence of the organizations that they led, obviously helped bring moral reconstruction to an end, but fundamental social changes probably proved more important. The Protestant churches, whose support and petitions had proved crucial to securing moral legislation, had their attention diverted to different issues in the 1920s. What had been a latent divide within the churches in the late nineteenth century became manifest in a stark division between fundamentalists and modernists in the twenties. The battle between the two groups for control of their denominations and the soul of American Protestantism absorbed much of the churches' energy. In addition, neither group shared the Christian lobbyists' commitment to reshaping society through moral legislation. The modernists, or liberals, who had a more positive view of the people's basic goodness, worried less about ensuring personal morality than creating a just society. The fundamentalists, who despite theological differences with the lobbyists would have been more likely to support moral legislation, channeled most of their political energies into a campaign to stop the teaching of evolution in the schools.

Even more than changes in the churches, a transformation in society helped doom further advances in legislating morality. Beginning before World War I but intensifying after it, American culture experienced a revolution in morals. A renewed emphasis on individualism, new cultural currents represented by those who fought Comstock and federal movie censorship, and the increasing power and influence of both urban values and a new national mass culture promoted much of the behavior—smoking, drinking, and more openness about sexuality—that the Christian lobbyists had fought so hard to restrain. Many artists and intellectuals condemned Victorian morality and championed an explicit moral relativism that the opponents of moral legislation had shared but usually left implicit. As a result, the twenties hardly proved hospitable to a major new campaign for moral legislation.

Instead, the Anti-Saloon League and conservative Christians who remained interested in politics had to commit their political energies to preserving Prohibition. Recent historians have shown that the prohibition experiment worked surprisingly well, reducing both individual consumption and the social and health problems associated with alcohol abuse. Especially after 1925, however, enforcement faltered, and Americans increasingly tired of the experiment. Many religious liberals and political conservatives changed their minds about Prohibition. Interest groups formed to fight for repeal and argued, among other things, for states' rights and against laws to regulate individual moral behavior. When repeal occurred in 1933, some bemoaned it; many rejoiced. But very quickly, the public memory defined Prohibition as an abject failure. The Christian lobbyists' crowning achievement became the first thing cited when anyone asserted, "You can't legislate morality." In the end, the prohibition experiment made further attempts to legislate morality, in the twenties and beyond, more difficult.[6]

The reaction against Prohibition that led to its repeal and to reservations about legislating morality resembled the earlier repudiation of political reconstruction. Moral reconstruction, of course, involved different issues and groups, and its links to the Civil War were tangential, though important. A perceived increase in immorality growing out of wartime experiences first spurred some of the Christian lobbyists to seek more stringent controls over moral behavior, and wartime nationalism and the antislavery precedent led them to call on the federal government to legislate morality. The resulting debates in Congress always centered on the wisdom on expanding national power and at times took the form of sectional politics. Sectional divisions changed after emancipation, however, as many white southerners developed a new openness toward moral legislation. There was another link between political and moral reconstruction. Northern support for reconstructing southern politics and labor relations foundered when the growth of industrial capitalism in the North led many Republicans to abandon or at least modify the antebellum free-labor ideology, with its celebration of independence and liberty. Moral reconstruction entailed a similar reduction in respect for personal freedom and loss of faith in self-control. The analogy between political and moral reconstruction therefore remains, if far from exact, at least instructive.[7]

The most important difference, of course, was timing. During political Reconstruction, Congress passed the Comstock Law and began to consider new legislation against polygamy and temperance forces requested federal help in controlling alcohol. Prohibition and most moral legislation was not adopted until much later, however, well after political Reconstruction ended. The Christian lobbyists' success between 1895 and 1920 testified to the importance of late-nineteenth-century social changes—immigration, urbanization, and the very early growth of a consumer economy—in the passage of moral legislation. Moral legislation became part of a second type of reconstruction, the reconstruction of the American state. Historians who have traced the growth of the state in the late nineteenth and early twentieth centuries have focused on the federal government's increasing role in regulating the economy. The expansion of its role in regulating morals first proceeded and then paralleled the growth in economic regulation.

Much of the credit for expanding the moral powers of the federal government rightly goes to the loose alliance of individuals and organizations here labeled the Christian lobby. Its lobbyists did not instigate antipolygamy legislation, the Mann Act, or antinarcotics measures—although they supported all three. Temperance reform had too long a history and too diverse a constituency to grant sole credit to any one group or alliance of groups for its adoption. But the Christian lobbyists first promoted national, constitutional prohibition, guided Congress to its adoption, and shaped the form it took. On other moral legislation, the lobbyists played a central role in prompting Congress to act.

Most of the early leaders of the Christian lobbyists' alliance—Comstock, Cook, Blair, Willard, Ellis, Crafts, George, Stephenson, McAllister—shared similar backgrounds. Born in the late antebellum period, they came of age during or shortly after the Civil War, which no doubt contributed to their tendency to look for national solutions to problems. Most grew up in small towns, usually in New England or the Midwest, but lived their later lives in large cities. No doubt their personal transitions from rural to urban life contributed to their sense that the nation faced a moral crisis. Most of the leaders of the Anti-Saloon League, who were born a generation later, had similar confrontations with a new America, although they often continued to live in small towns. The lobbyists shared their demographic experiences with a host of Americans, though; a common social or psychological profile does not seem crucial to their reform activities or their alliance. Nor does a single theological perspective. Several of them belonged to (or in the case of Dinwiddie and Cannon went to seminaries of) denominations within the Presbyterian or Reformed tradition, with its emphasis on the Christian's responsibility for the state. Other lobbyists and members of their organizations came from Methodist, Baptist, or other evangelical denominations; even Quakers and Episcopalians joined the campaign for some moral legislation. None of these denominations emphasized Christian responsibility for the state as the Reformed tradition did.[8]

The Christian lobbyists did share a sense of Christian mission, a firm belief that God called them to fight sin and to create a moral society. They also shared an analysis of what they fought—the problems posed by appetite and avarice—and a conviction that victory would necessarily entail the establishment of the government's religious authority and an expansion of its moral powers. The women among the lobbyists, especially the leaders of the WCTU who were so central to the lobby's success, supported an expanded role for the state in part because they saw it as a potential ally in protecting females from dangerous males. But all the Christian lobbyists agreed, often well before many better-known reformers, on the potential of the national government to regulate behavior.[9]

Despite their roots in small towns and their suspicions of an emerging consumer society, the Christian lobbyists were not backward-looking champions of small-town America. Most of the lobbyists built or at least participated in national, hierarchal, bureaucratic associations that incorporated the values and methods of an emerging organizational society. The lobbyists and their organizations, especially the WCTU and the ASL, practiced a very modern form of interest-group politics that entailed an exercise of popular power outside of the party structure, one that became typical of twentieth-century politics. The lobbyists were sent to Washington to work in behalf of a moral agenda supported by the members of the organizations they represented. Once there, they worked with members of Congress to enter such legislation—and then the lobbyists called on the members of their organizations to endorse the resulting bills.

The lobbyists' ability to convince Congress to pass their bills rested on their grassroots organization and support. It was initially based in areas where moral reform had always been strong, the New England, mid-Atlantic, and midwestern states. The latter two regions provided at least half (and sometimes more) of the petitions to Congress in support of the lobbyists' bills. Before the late 1880s, all three provided most of the congressional votes for moral legislation as well. That began to change in the 1890s and was not at all the case in many of the crucial votes on moral legislation after 1910, especially Prohibition. During the intervening years, numerous Catholic and Jewish immigrants settled in New England, the mid-Atlantic states, and parts of the Midwest. Many of them feared Protestants' attempts to impose their definition of morality. Representatives of districts with large Catholic populations, for example, were consistently more likely to oppose federal legislation to control alcohol. The growing presence of immigrants may well help explain the reluctance of legislators in the regions where they settled to vote for moral legislation.[10]

During the same years, the new states of the West began to provide many votes for moral legislation. More surprisingly, the South, which had once led the opposition to moral legislation, reversed itself. A few southern lawmakers remained adamantly opposed to federal intervention in morality, but other southerners provided not only many of the votes for moral legislation but leadership in Congress as well. J. Randolph Tucker, Thetus Sims, Seaborn Roddenbery, Dudley Hughes, Richmond Hobson, Edwin Webb, Morris Sheppard, and others introduced and championed important moral legislation. Most southern legislators came from homogeneous districts dominated by evangelical Protestants, which made their votes and efforts in behalf of moral reform easier than those of some of their northern colleagues with Catholic and Jewish constituents. But the Protestant domination of the South existed before 1890, when southerners in Congress had generally opposed moral legislation. Demographic and other changes played a role, but the shift in southern support resulted primarily from emancipation. The politics of slavery, which sought to prevent any precedent for federal intervention in slavery, gave way to a politics of race that, especially as southern whites' fears of federal attempts to change southern race relations declined, allowed, even encouraged, federal laws to control certain types of moral behavior. The resulting southern support not only made moral reconstruction possible it helped transform the national image of the region. Whereas before the Civil War, slavery made the South seem, to many northerners, a moral miasma, a region of sin and sinners, by the passage of Prohibition, the South was becoming the Bible Belt. For the remainder of the century, the South would be seen as the stronghold of religion in politics and a bastion of support for moral legislation.[11]

With congressional support and often leadership provided by the South, the Christian lobbyists sought to reconstruct the antebellum moral polity, which was based primarily on faith in the voluntary system and in moral suasion to ensure moral citizens; on the principle that responsibility for the morals of the people (the police power) lay with the states; and on a strong sense of personal liberty that discouraged moral legislation of any form. The older ideals proved powerful and persistent, and therefore the outcome of moral reconstruction was ambiguous at best. On certain issues, Congress refused to abandon the traditional values of states' rights and individual liberty in order to expand the national government's powers.

Despite appeals by the Christian lobbyists, Congress never enacted a federal Sunday law, prohibition on the sale of cigarettes, comprehensive antigambling legislation, or a commission to censor motion pictures. On two moral issues on which Congress did act, polygamy and divorce, it refused repeated requests for a constitutional amendment to make them a federal responsibility. Only in the case of Prohibition did Congress endorse, and the states concur in, a change in organic law.

Legislators, in short, did not approve federal involvement in every aspect of personal morality that the lobbyists sought and clearly shied away from structural changes in federal responsibility. Some of the lobbyists claimed a federal police power, but Congress never shared their view and evidenced little interest in creating one. It did, beginning with the 1894 legislation against lotteries, establish a police power over interstate commerce, perhaps the most dramatic expansion of federal power the lobbyists' efforts prompted. Other than that, Congress remained content to use federal powers over the District of Columbia, the territories, and the post office to justify moral legislation. Thus the antebellum moral polity's primary reliance on the police powers of the states and local communities survived moral reconstruction.

Another fundamental aspect of the antebellum moral polity, individual liberty, was also undermined, but it, too, persisted. The Christian lobbyists condemned unrestrained individualism and asserted the right of society to restrict liberty; both assumptions were central to their moral vision. The Christian lobbyists, however, focused their rhetoric and directed their legislative efforts on stopping commercialized vice rather than prosecuting individual sinners. The lobbyists' long obfuscation of their goal of ending the personal consumption of alcohol suggested that emphasis reflected a pragmatic decision to accommodate, for a time, public acceptance of personal liberty. But the lobbyists' own analysis of America's moral crisis also played an important role. Their belief that avarice fostered overstimulation of appetites that in turn undermined self-control and resulted in a descent into degeneracy led naturally to the lobbyists' attacks on commercial vice. If greedy merchants of sin caused the problems, government had only to outlaw the activities of people or businesses who exploited the appetites of the weak in order to ensure a proper environment, a moral order, in which moral suasion and self-control could be effective. Focusing on avarice also allowed the lobbyists to portray consumers of pornography or alcohol less as sinners than victims, helpless slaves, in the lobbyists' rhetoric.

Congress clearly seemed more favorably disposed toward moral legislation if it were portrayed as protection from evil forces or an attempt to save victims from avaricious commercial interests. The law then became, in lawmakers' minds, an attempt to preserve freedom, not deny it. Congress certainly never abandoned the ideal of personal liberty or the related ideal of privacy. The Comstock and antilottery laws drew the line at opening first-class letters. The Volstead Act incorporated neither an unequivocal ban on possession and consumption of alcohol nor a strong search and seizure provision for private homes. Whether or not a basic right of privacy existed in the Constitution, the American moral polity at the beginning of the twentieth century certainly recognized one. Persistent respect for personal liberty restricted how far Congress would expand the moral powers of government.

Congress refused altogether to establish the religious authority of the federal government, perhaps the most fundamental way in which Christian lobbyists sought to reconstruct the moral polity. In attempting to put God, Christ, and the authority of the Bible in the preamble to the Constitution, the National Reform Association sought a radical affirmation of the state's responsibility to God. Despite many petitions and three serious discussions of amending the preamble, Congress never acknowledged the authority of God or the Bible. Its members clearly wanted nothing to do with so fundamental a change. Congress even refused to pass sweeping Sabbath laws, in part because they involved an acknowledgment of God's authority. Debates over them and divorce laws as well demonstrated the difficulty of establishing biblical standards. Even Christians disagreed on what the Bible said about Sabbath observation or acceptable grounds for divorce. Why give government the right to decide, at least some in Congress concluded.

Not only the lobbyists' repeated failures to secure a Christian amendment or

Sabbath laws but their successes as well demonstrated how far they were from establishing religious authority as the basis for laws. WCTU leaders and other lobbyists, who talked of putting God in government, wanted Congress to recognize God's law as a clear, absolute authority for moral legislation. However, most of it passed not because of appeals to the Bible but because the lobbyists mobilized churches and Christians across the nation to petition in its behalf and because they themselves lobbied so skillfully within Congress. The most political and least "religious" organization within the alliance, the Anti-Saloon League, became the most successful. With its heavy-handed efforts at influencing voters and its soft but sure touch in cultivating Congress, the league helped pass Prohibition by exercising political influence rather than by establishing religious authority. Moreover, it practiced a political pragmatism and a step-by-step approach that obscured its goals and hardly affirmed a clear, absolute moral standard. With the nation so closely divided over the morality of drinking and the benefits of Prohibition, the adoption of the Eighteenth Amendment seemed a clear case of morality being determined by majority vote, although some of the amendment's opponents charged that the majority actually opposed it.

Yet if Congress would not write God or biblical authority into the Constitution or even respond to religious appeals, it did not hesitate to reassure Christians of a tie between their faith and their government. Shortly after Congress refused to debate a national Sunday law, it voted to close the Chicago World's Fair on Sunday. During the Civil War, the U.S. Treasury put "In God We Trust" on some of the nation's coins, and at the beginning of the century, Congress hastily and decisively insisted that the phrase remain on a new set of coins. The committee that recommended in favor of restoring "In God We Trust" explained that as a "Christian nation" the United States should have the phrase on its coins "'as an outward and visible form of the inward and spiritual grace' which should possess and inspire American citizenship, and as an evidence to all the nations of the world" that republican institutions must rest "upon a Christian patriotism, which, recognizing the universal fatherhood of God, appeals to the universal brotherhood of man as the source of the authority and power of all just government." The term "Christian nation" seemed to take on a life of its own in the late nineteenth century; Christian lobbyists, many legislators, one justice of the Supreme Court, and a host of authors employed it. Few defined it. Most used the term, like the phrase "In God We Trust" on coins, to invoke a special relationship between God and the nation. Although happy with the symbolic affirmation, Christian lobbyists had, after all, sought a more fundamental moral reconstruction.[12]

To summarize, Congress never recognized a federal police power but instead derived one from existing federal powers. The states retained primary responsibility for policing morals. Congress also proved cautious in restraining personal liberty. Not only Congress but the Christian lobbyists themselves continued to champion moral suasion. And, though willing to associate the nation with Christianity, Congress steadfastly refused to proclaim the religious authority of the state. Congress never undertook a radical reconstruction of the moral policy.

It did, however, approve a substantial expansion of the moral powers of the federal government. In the years after the Civil War, the efforts of the Christian lobbyists resulted in a steady enlargement of the role of the federal government in controlling personal morality. Congress prohibited the interstate circulation of prizefight films, lottery tickets, obscene material, and information about or goods designed to be used for birth control or abortion. Congress forced Mormons to abandon polygamy. It attacked prostitution, put the nation's last legal lottery company out of business, made narcotics contraband, and stopped the manufacture and sale of alcohol. Compared to the federal government's role in the antebellum moral polity, these efforts constituted a dramatic expansion of federal power and, in some cases, a significant reduction in personal liberty. To take the most extreme case, before the Civil War, the government denied the liberty to buy alcohol only to Native Americans, people it dismissed as savages not citizens; with the adoption of Prohibition, it treated all of its citizens as it once had only those it considered savages. Moreover, federal moral legislation, in many instances reinforced by state and, in the case of the movies, voluntary regulation, helped mold the public culture of the United States during the first half of the twentieth century, especially on matters relating to sexuality.

The expansion of federal power over moral behavior also contributed to the expansion of the influence of the nation-state after the Civil War. The crusades of the Christian lobbyists for a righteous republic, with their rhetoric of Christian nationhood and God in government, may have helped establish the legitimacy and authority that the Civil War undermined. Christians found it easier to accept and be loyal to a Christian nation concerned about morality. Alfred Colquitt certainly spoke truthfully when, during the debate over closing the World's Fair on Sunday, he said, "Righteousness, righteousness, righteousness, exalteth the nation." Unintentionally, the Christian lobbyists had succeeded in exalting the nation as much as righteousness. They had helped establish the legitimacy and expand the powers of the nation-state, one that, despite their efforts, remained essentially secular.

Despite the real, though limited, accomplishments of moral reconstruction, in the years following the passage of Prohibition, individualism, moral relativism, and other influences against which the Christian lobbyists had battled became more pervasive in American society. Many factors contributed to the change. Certainly a decline in religious faith played a role; so too did a growing public disenchantment with some of the measures the Christian lobbyists had helped pass. The Comstock Law was occasionally turned against art and literature that many did not condemn; its ban on the circulation of information on birth control seemed unreasonable to others. The Mann Act did little to reduce prostitution, much less adultery and fornication, and its enforcement was primarily directed against the unpopular. When the Mann Act and other moral laws were selectively or poorly enforced, the difficulties and dangers of legislating morality became apparent. Significant disregard for Prohibition laws proved an even more glaring example. And the repeal of Prohibition in 1933 suggested that the people had simply changed their minds about what was good, thereby offering a profound and, for some, frightening lesson in the social construction of morality.[13]

An even more important factor behind the rise of relativism and celebration of individual fulfillment was avarice, the danger against which the Christian lobbyists had warned. Sunday observation provides an excellent illustration. During the twentieth century, the demands of a modern economy, the promise of profits, and the lure of commercial entertainment led to an almost complete abandonment of public Sunday observance. The dramatic decline in Sabbath observance may have owed something to the absence of a federal law, but it resulted primarily from the dynamics of a commercial economy and the values of a consumer society. A similar process occurred in popular culture. Although the Production Code forestalled it for a time, by the mid-twentieth century, the movies and television, in competition for customers, featured sex and other behavior beyond anything Crafts or Comstock could have imagined. In the process, these profit-driven, pervasive media helped transform American values.

In response to the apparent triumph of unrestrained individualism and moral relativism, as well as public acceptance of drinking, drugs, gambling, and overt sexuality, in the 1970s another group of Christian reformers turned to politics and the promise of moral legislation. The "new Christian right," as many termed it, differed from its late-nineteenth-century predecessor in fundamental ways. The new leaders of the Christian right did not emphasize the dangers of avarice, commercial values, or ally themselves with women who sought to expand their roles. They found much support for their legislative agenda among Roman Catholics and Mormons, two groups their predecessors had feared. But like their predecessors, late-twentieth-century Christians in politics fought for what they believed to be a proper moral order, wanted to use government to help ensure it, and on occasion even seemed interested in establishing biblical authority as the basis of government.

The story of moral reconstruction provides no sure lessons to be applied to the renewed debate over legislating morality that continues at the beginning of the twenty-first century, but it does provide a useful historical context. For one thing, the earlier moral reconstruction reassures Americans that the present movement is far from unique. Before the Civil War, Sunday, temperance, and antislavery crusades all propelled believers into politics. After the war, the antislavery precedent encouraged religious reformers to turn again to the state with a much more extensive legislative agenda and demands for far more expansive government involvement. Although most nineteenth-century Christian reformers limited their political activities to lobbying, the Anti-Saloon League participated in electoral politics. Later in the twentieth century, other groups took part in both types of politics. A tradition of religion in politics based on faith in law to make right, or at the very least, to create a moral order capable of making people behave morally, has always existed alongside the dominant voluntary and revivalist traditions.

In addition to reassuring Americans that the current involvement of Christians in politics and attempts to legislate morality are not unprecedented, the story of moral reconstruction also suggests that a secular government and a polity that recognizes personal liberty and privacy is no recent development either, but has deep roots in American history. The campaigns of the Christian lobbyists also demonstrate that historians who contrast the moral relativism of the twentieth century with a fixed, universal morality in the nineteenth, and political pundits who look back on that era as a golden age of moral authority, overstate their case. The nineteenth century witnessed three great, public debates over moral issues: slavery, polygamy, and prohibition. In each case, opposing sides were fully confident of their own morality. During congressional debates on other moral issues similar divisions emerged; a few members of Congress offered explicitly relativistic defenses of various moral practices. Definitions of morality differ, they argued, and no one standard has greater authority. Even the Christian lobbyists' victories testified less to an unchanging standard of morals than to a belief in moral progress. On lotteries and drinking, for example, legislation codified an evolution in standards of moral behavior. What most people had once considered moral was later deemed and legislated to be immoral. Nineteenth-century America boasted no moral certainty or authority; it was not some age of innocence that can be restored.

The story of moral reconstruction, in fact, reminds a nation fighting similar battles of the inescapable complexities in the debate over legislating morality. The Christian lobbyists' case for moral legislation cannot be summarily dismissed. Almost all Americans would agree on the need to protect children from the appetites of adults, as age-of-consent legislation was designed to do. The lobbyists' warnings of the dangers of unrestrained individualism and their calls for society to foster moral behavior and a moral order still ring true today, but so too do their opponents' celebrations of personal liberty, moral suasion, and moral choice.[14]

The dangers of appetite and avarice, of unrestrained individualism and commercialism, and the need for a moral citizenry are as real at the beginning of the twentieth-first century as they were at the end of the nineteenth. The tenuous moral reconstruction that followed the Civil War did not alter in any fundamental way the religious authority of the government; it simply became more powerful while remaining secular. In the late twentieth century the government's commitment to personal liberty, never abandoned during moral reconstruction, deepened. With that, the attempt to balance personal liberty and morality, freedom and order, may have become more difficult, but it had never been easy. Nor have the compromises and instability that resulted ever been comfortable. An escape to either extreme, a religious state or unrestrained individualism, would be worse, however. The fundamental tension built into the moral polity of the early republic thus persists two centuries later: a democratic state needs a moral citizenry but cannot force its citizens to be moral. There appears to be no escape from that tension.

Moral Legislation Entered in Congress

The bills proposed to legislate morals compiled in the following tables were found by reading the list of bills and the subject indexes for the Twenty-seventh through the Sixty-sixth Congresses (roughly 1841 to 1921). During the years of the *Congressional Globe*, the list of bills and the subject indexes were printed in the journals of the House of Representatives and the Senate. Its successor, the *Congressional Record*, prints a list of bills and a subject index for each session.

My search for bills likely missed some. In addition to the potential for overlooking some bills when reading a list of 2,000 bills each Congress, other problems arose. The title of a bill does not always indicate its purpose. In addition, amendments to otherwise unrelated bills can easily be missed. Some of the amendments or bills missed in these ways appear in the subject indexes, but the indexes themselves are not always complete. Additional bills and amendments were found through various other references to them. No doubt some were still missed, although not in any way or in sufficient numbers to undermine the validity of the comparisons made here.

Once a bill was identified, its number, its general subject, the member of Congress who introduced it, his party, his state, his district (in the case of representatives), and the legislative history of the bill were entered into a database. The tables that follow were then generated from the database.

The Twenty-seventh through the Thirty-sixth Congresses are grouped together as the antebellum period. The Thirty-seventh through the Forty-fourth Congresses roughly correspond to the Civil War and Reconstruction eras. The three post-Reconstruction groupings reflect stages in the increase in the number of bills entered but primarily offer a means to demonstrate change over time. They are, of course, arbitrary. In order to select blocks that reflect certain changes in emphasis in postwar lobbying efforts as well as to highlight the differences from the antebellum and the Civil War/Reconstruction years, the number of Congresses in each grouping differs. Although the absolute numbers are usually provided, they are not as accurate a reflection of change as are the percentages under each category.

States composing each region:

New England (NE): Maine, N.H., Vt., Mass., Conn., R.I.

Mid-Atlantic (MA): N.Y., Pa., N.J.

South (S): Va., N.C., S.C., Ga., Fla., Ala., Miss., La., Tex., Ark., Tenn., Okla. (Indian Territory)

Border (B): W.Va., Del., Md., Ky., Mo.

Midwest (MW): Ohio, Ind., Ill., Iowa, Minn., Wisc., Mich.

West (W): N.D., S.D., Nebr., Kans., N.Mex., Colo., Wyo., Mont., Idaho, Utah, Nev., Ariz., Wash., Ore., Calif., Alaska, Hawaii

TABLE A1.1. Moral Legislation Entered and Passed, 27th–66th Congresses

Congress	No. Entered	No. Passed
27th (1841–43)	3	3
28th (1843–45)	3	1
29th (1845–47)	1	0
30th (1847–49)	4	0
31st (1849–51)	0	0
32d (1851–53)	1	0
33d (1853–55)	2	0
34th (1855–57)	4	1
35th (1857–59)	1	0
36th (1859–61)	5	2
37th (1861–63)	8	6
38th (1863–65)	5	3
39th (1865–67)	4	0
40th (1867–69)	5	3
41st (1870–71)	14	2
42d (1871–73)	15	2
43d (1873–75)	17	2
44th (1875–77)	13	1
45th (1877–79)	19	1
46th (1879–81)	29	0
47th (1881–83)	43	3
48th (1883–85)	43	0
49th (1885–87)	61	4
50th (1887–89)	56	2
51st (1889–91)	91	7
52d (1891–93)	53	2
53d (1893–95)	39	2
54th (1895–97)	51	5
55th (1897–99)	38	2
56th (1899–1901)	36	3
57th (1901–3)	41	3
58th (1903–5)	38	3
59th (1905–7)	69	6
60th (1907–9)	155	5
61th (1909–11)	105	5
62d (1911–13)	85	4
63d (1913–15)	82	6
64th (1915–17)	113	3
65th (1917–19)	115	8
66th (1919–21)	71	2
Total	1,538	102

TABLE A1.2. Moral Legislation Entered and
Passed, by Type, 27th–66th Congresses

Legislation	No. Entered		No. Passed		No. Passed as % of No. Entered
Alcohol	822	(53.45%)	45	(44.12%)	5.47
Gambling	160	(10.40)	11	(10.78)	6.88
Polygamy	123	(8.00)	7	(6.86)	5.69
Marriage and divorce	114	(7.41)	5	(4.90)	4.39
Obscenity	76	(4.94)	8	(7.84)	10.53
Purity and prostitution	74	(4.81)	12	(11.77)	16.22
Sunday observation	71	(4.62)	4	(3.92)	5.63
Narcotics	53	(3.45)	7	(6.86)	13.21
Cigarettes	19	(1.24)	1	(0.98)	5.26
Prizefighting	14	(0.91)	2	(1.96)	14.29
Christian amendment	12	(0.78)	0	(0.00)	0.00
Total	1,538	(100.1*)	102	(99.99*)	6.63

*Percentages do not total 100 due to rounding.

TABLE A1.3. Party of Legislators Who Entered
Moral Legislation, 26th–66th Congresses

Legislation	Republicans[*]		Democrats		Others		N/A[**]		Total
Alcohol	49.76%	(409)	38.08%	(313)	3.65%	(30)[a]	8.52%	(70)	822
Gambling	51.25	(82)	35.63	(57)	1.25	(2)[b]	11.86	(19)	160
Polygamy	75.61	(93)	13.82	(17)	1.63	(2)[c]	8.94	(11)	123
Marriage and									
divorce	53.51	(61)	25.44	(29)	4.39	(5)[d]	16.67	(19)	114
Obscenity	46.05	(35)	40.79	(31)	2.63	(2)	10.53	(8)	76
Purity and									
prostitution	64.87	(48)	21.62	(16)	0		13.51	(10)	74
Sunday									
observation	43.67	(31)	28.17	(20)	4.23	(3)[e]	23.94	(17)	71
Narcotics	52.83	(28)	32.08	(17)	1.89	(1)[b]	13.21	(7)	53
Cigarettes	57.90	(11)	21.05	(4)	0		21.05	(4)	19
Prizefighting	71.43	(10)	14.29	(2)	7.14	(1)[b]	7.14	(1)	14
Christian									
amendment	58.33	(7)	16.67	(2)	0		25.00	(3)	12

[*]In antebellum period, also includes Whigs, Free-Soilers, and Abolitionists; later, also
  includes Silver Republicans
[**]Not applicable refers to bills introduced by request (which meant the members of
  Congress did not wish to take credit for them) or amendments or committee bills.

[a]Includes 4 by Populists, 2 by Progressives, and 24 by Prohibitionists
[b]Members of Prohibition Party
[c]Members of Opposition Party
[d]Includes 1 Populist and 4 Prohibitionists
[e]Includes 2 Independents and 1 Prohibitionist

TABLE A1.4. Region of Legislators Who Entered Moral Legislation, 27th–66th Congresses

Legislation	NE	MA	B	S	MW	W	NA	Total
Alcohol	137 (16.67%)	30 (3.65%)	50 (6.08%)	233 (28.35%)	109 (13.26%)	194 (23.60%)	69 (8.39%)	822
Gambling	24 (15.00)	12 (7.50)	6 (3.75)	47 (29.38)	31 (19.38)	21 (13.13)	19 (11.88)	160
Polygamy	29 (23.58)	12 (9.76)	2 (1.63)	6 (4.88)	38 (30.89)	25 (20.33)	11 (8.94)	123
Marriage and divorce	15 (13.16)	19 (16.67)	9 (7.90)	10 (8.77)	28 (24.56)	14 (12.28)	19 (16.67)	114
Obscenity	6 (7.90)	15 (19.74)	1 (1.32)	25 (32.89)	19 (25.00)	2 (2.63)	8 (10.53)	76
Purity and prostitution	13 (17.57)	6 (8.11)	3 (4.05)	10 (13.51)	15 (20.27)	17 (22.97)	10 (13.51)	74
Sunday observation	10 (14.09)	10 (14.09)	4 (5.63)	15 (21.13)	5 (7.04)	10 (14.09)	17 (23.94)	71
Narcotics	10 (18.87)	7 (13.21)	1 (1.89)	2 (3.77)	9 (16.98)	18 (33.96)	6 (11.32)	53
Cigarettes	3 (15.79)	0 (0.00)	2 (10.53)	3 (15.79)	5 (26.32)	2 (10.53)	4 (21.05)	19
Prizefighting	3 (21.43)	0 (0.00)	0 (0.00)	2 (14.29)	5 (35.71)	3 (21.43)	1 (7.14)	14
Christian amendment	4 (33.33)	0 (0.00)	3 (25.00)	1 (8.33)	1 (8.33)	0 (0.00)	3 (25.00)	12

TABLE A1.5. Percentage of Types of Legislation Entered by
Lawmakers of Each Region, 27th–66th Congresses

Legislation	NE	MA	B	S	MW	W	All
Alcohol	53.94	27.03	61.73	65.82	41.13	63.40	53.45
Gambling	9.45	10.81	7.41	13.28	11.70	6.86	10.40
Polygamy	11.42	10.81	2.47	1.69	14.34	8.17	8.00
Marriage and divorce	5.91	17.12	11.11	2.82	10.57	4.58	7.41
Obscenity	2.36	13.51	1.24	7.06	7.17	0.65	4.94
Purity and prostitution	5.12	5.41	3.70	2.83	5.66	5.56	4.81
Sunday observation	3.94	9.01	4.94	4.24	1.89	3.27	4.62
Narcotics	3.94	6.31	1.24	0.57	3.40	5.88	3.45
Cigarettes	1.18	0	2.47	0.85	1.89	0.65	1.24
Prizefighting	1.18	0	0	0.57	1.89	0.98	0.91
Christian amendment	1.57	0	3.70	0.28	0.38	0	0.78
Total	100.01*	100.01*	100.01*	100.00	100.02*	100.00	100.00

*Percentages do not total 100 due to rounding.

TABLE A1.6. Moral Legislation by Party of Entering
Lawmakers, 27th–66th Congresses

Congresses	Republicans[*]	Democrats	Others	N/A[**]	Total
27th–36th	10	5	2[a]	7	24
(1841–61)	(41.67%)	(20.83%)	(8.33%)	(29.17%)	
37th–44th	67	3	0	11	81
(1861–77)	(82.72)	(3.70)	(0.00)	(13.58)	
45th–51st	235	54	2[b]	51	342
(1877–91)	(68.71)	(15.79)	(.59)	(14.91)	
52d–59th	229	78	10[c]	48	365
(1891–1907)	(62.74)	(21.37)	(2.74)	(13.15)	
60th–66th	274	368	32[d]	52	726
(1907–21)	(37.74)	(50.69)	(4.41)	(7.16)	

[*]In antebellum period, includes Whigs, Abolitionists, and Free-Soilers
[**]Not applicable refers to bills introduced by request (which meant the members of
  Congress did not wish to take credit for them) or amendments or committee bills.

[a]Opposition Party members
[b]Populist Party members
[c]9 by Populist Party members and 1 by Independent
[d]Progressive and Prohibition Party members

TABLE A1.7. Moral Legislation by Region of Entering
Lawmakers, 27th–66th Congresses

Congresses	NE	MA	B	S	MW	W	NA	Total
27th–36th	11	1	2	2	1	0	7	24
(1841–61)	(45.83%)	(4.17%)	(8.33%)	(8.33%)	(4.17%)	(0.00%)	(29.17%)	
37th–44th	18	10	2	1	29	10	11	81
(1861–77)	(22.22)	(12.35)	(2.47)	(1.24)	(35.8)	(12.35)	(13.58)	
45th–51st	88	22	14	31	90	46	51	342
(1877–91)	(25.73)	(6.43)	(4.09)	(9.06)	(26.32)	(13.45)	(14.91)	
52d–59th	90	37	17	57	70	46	48	365
(1891–1907)	(24.66)	(10.14)	(4.66)	(15.62)	(19.18)	(12.6)	(13.15)	
60th–66th	47	41	46	263	75	204	50	726
(1907–21)	(6.47)	(5.65)	(6.33)	(36.23)	(10.33)	(28.1)	(6.88)	
Total	254	111	81	354	265	306	167	1,538
	(16.51)	(7.22)	(5.27)	(23.02)	(17.23)	(19.90)	(10.80)	(100.01*)

*Percentages do not total 100 due to rounding.

TABLE A1.8. Moral Legislation Entered, by Type, as Percentage of Bills Entered, 27th–66th Congresses

Congresses	Alcohol	Gambling	Polygamy	Marriage and Divorce	Obscenity	Purity and prosti- tution	Sunday Observation	Cigarettes	Narcotics	Prize- fight- ing
27th–36th (1841–61)	50.00	4.17	20.83	8.33	8.33	8.33	0	0	0	0
37th–44th (1861–77)	50.62	3.70	22.22	7.41	8.64	2.47	2.47	0	0	2.47
45th–51st (1877–91)	40.94	19.88	18.13	7.31	3.80	3.51	1.76	1.76	2.92	0
52d–59th (1891–1907)	44.93	10.96	5.48	13.15	6.03	4.66	8.77	2.19	1.90	1.37
60th–66th (1907–21)	64.05	6.61	2.48	4.55	4.41	5.65	4.27	0.69	5.38	0.96

TABLE A1.9. Percentage of Moral Legislation Passed
by Congress, 27th–66th Congresses

Congresses	Percentage
27th–36th (1841–61)	29.17
37th–44th (1861–77)	23.46
45th–51st (1877–91)	4.97
52d–59th (1891–1907)	7.12
60th–66th (1907–21)	4.54

TABLE A1.10. Percentage of Acts Passed that Passed on Recorded Vote

Legislation	Recorded Votes
Alcohol	37.78
Gambling	9.09
Polygamy	71.43
Marriage and divorce	20.00
Obscenity	0.00
Purity and prostitution	0.00
Sunday observation	25.00
Narcotics	0.00
Cigarettes	0.00
Prizefighting	50.00
Christian amendment	0.00

Note: These percentages are for a total of 102 pieces of moral legislation that passed, 26 on recorded votes. There were another 22 recorded votes on moral legislation when the bills did not pass, 12 on alcohol-related issues, 6 on polygamy, and 4 on gambling.

Petitions to Congress for Moral Legislation

Counting petitions to Congress is at best an inexact process. Rules for the introduction of petitions differed over time as did the way in which they were recorded and indexed in the records of Congress. During the period discussed here, first the *Congressional Globe* and then the *Congressional Record* usually referred to or listed petitions. The original petitions are in the National Archives, although some mentioned in the printed records are not there and others that are there are not mentioned in the published record. Still other petitions are sometimes found in the private papers of members of Congress. The numbers of actual petitions do not correspond with the number listed in the *Congressional Record*. No absolute record of all petitions sent to Congress seems possible. The tables below are based on the petitions recorded in the *Congressional Record*, which appeared to be the most convenient, consistent list for comparing the numbers and sources of petitions sent on different issues at different times. Petitions were analyzed only for the House because the printed record on them is more complete and because it allowed analysis by the smaller geographical areas of the congressional districts.

Two problems concerning the data should be acknowledged. First, every petition to any district was assumed to come from that district. A few did not. But because the Christian lobbyists believed that only petitions from constituents swayed lawmakers, they almost always sent petitions only to their own representatives; no attempt was made to eliminate the few petitions that came from other areas. Second, these numbers should be used only to make relative comparisons. They are not exact. Because of the vague wording of some of the brief entries in the *Record*, determining the actual number of petitions was often difficult and sometimes impossible.

Petitions submitted during the Fortieth Congress asking Congress to amend the Constitution to put God, Christ, and the authority of the Scripture in its preamble are counted. Almost all of the entries on these petitions mentioned only a group of individuals, so no attempt was made to analyze the sources of these petitions.

Petitions submitted during the Forty-fifth Congress asking Congress to outlaw polygamy are analyzed. With these, too, entries gave little specificity as to source, save a group of individuals or specifically of women.

Petitions submitted during the Fifty-second Congress asking that the Chicago

World's Fair close on Sunday (and sometimes asking for broader Sunday legislation) are analyzed. With these petitions, the types of groups sending the petitions were often distinguished and are analyzed.

During the Fifty-fifth Congress the House received petitions on a variety of moral issues—alcohol (most for ending its sale in government buildings, but a few for broader legislation), cigarettes (banning shipment into states that prohibited them), gambling (denying the use of interstate commerce to lotteries and other forms of gambling), age of consent (raising the age in the District of Columbia and the territories), prizefighting (banning it in the territories or pictures of fights in interstate commerce), Sunday observation (a law for the District of Columbia), marriage and divorce (an amendment creating a national standard), and a few other issues. Sometimes one group sent petitions on two or three of these issues.

For each of these Congresses, the petitions received, their subject, and their source were entered along with the member's district, party affiliation, and region (with region defined as it is in Appendix 1).

Numbers of petitions in favor of prohibition in the Sixty-third Congress were not derived from individual entries in the *Congressional Record* (which were no longer indexed by that time) but were derived from a table listing the number of petitions from each state, from 63d Cong., 2d sess., 8626. Such a listing did not allow analysis by district or by source.

TABLE A2.1a. Number of Petitions on Selected Issues
to the House of Representatives, by Region

Region	Christian Amendment (40th Cong.; 1867–69)	Anti-polygamy (45th Cong.; 1877–79)	Closing World's Fair (52nd Cong.; 1891–93)	Various Behavior (55th Cong.; 1897–98)	Prohibition (63rd Cong.; 1913–15)
New England	6	80	193	1,453	883
Mid-Atlantic	67	137	889	1,804	2,137
Border	3	13	113	249	882
South	0	8	158	98	1,005
Midwest	52	259	1,061	1,930	2,700
West	0	19	207	1,549	1,689
Unclear	—	—	2	—	—
Total	128	516	2,623	7,083	9,296

TABLE A2.1b. Percentage of Petitions on Selected Issues to the House of Representatives, by Region

Region	Christian Amendment (40th Cong.; 1867–69)		Anti-polygamy (45th Cong.;; 1877–79)		Closing World's Fair (52nd Cong.; 1891–93)		Various Behavior (55th Cong.; 1897–98)		Prohibition (63rd Cong.; 1913–15)	
New England	4.69	(12.80)	15.50	(9.66)	7.36	(7.93)	20.51	(7.37)	9.50	(7.36)
Mid-Atlantic	52.34	(35.98)	26.55	(22.76)	33.89	(21.04)	25.47	(20.40)	22.99	(20.92)
Border	2.34	(10.98)	2.52	(11.03)	4.31	(10.98)	3.52	(10.48)	9.49	(9.20)
South	0.00	(0.00)	1.55	(25.17)	6.02	(25.00)	1.38	(25.50)	10.81	(25.75)
Midwest	40.62	(37.80)	50.19	(27.93)	40.45	(27.44)	27.25	(26.63)	29.04	(24.60)
West	0.00	(0.00)	3.68	(3.45)	7.89	(7.62)	21.87	(9.63)	18.17	(12.18)
Unclear	—		—		.08		—		—	
Total	99.99*	(100)	99.99*	(100)	100.00	(100.01*)	100.00	(100.01*)	100	(100.01*)

Note: Number in parenthesis is the percentage of all House members for that region.
*Percentages do not total 100 due to rounding.

TABLE A2.2a. Number of Petitions on Selected Issues to the House of Representatives, by Party Affiliation of Member Receiving Them

Party	Christian Amendment (40th Cong.; 1867–69)	Anti-polygamy (45th Cong.; 1877–79)	Closing World's Fair (52nd Cong.; 1891–93)	Various Behavior (55th Cong.; 1897–98)
Republicans	122	397	1,370	5,958
Democrats	6	119	1,181	551
Populists	—	—	70	567
Others/unclear	—	—	2	—
Total	128	516	2,623	7,076

TABLE A2.2b. Percentage of Petitions on Selected Issues to the House of Representatives, by Party Affiliation of Member Receiving Them

Party	Christian Amendment (40th Cong.; 1867–69)		Anti-polygamy (45th Cong.; 1877–79)		Closing World's Fair (52nd Cong.; 1891–93)		Various Behavior (55th Cong.; 1897–98)	
Republicans	95.31	(75.61)	76.94	(42.42)	52.23	(26.22)	84.20	(57.23)
Democrats	4.68	(20.14)	23.06	(57.78)	45.02	(71.03)	7.79	(35.98)
Populists	—	—	—	—	2.67	(2.12)	8.01	(5.67)
Other		(4.27)	—	—		(0.61)		(1.13)
Total	99.99*	(100.00)	100.00	(100.00)	100.00	(99.98*)	100.00	(100.01*)

Note: Number in parenthesis is the percentage of all House members from region.
*Percentages do not total 100 due to rounding.

TABLE A2.3. Number of Districts in Which at Least One Petition Was Received

Christian Amendment (40th Cong.; 1867–69)	Anti-polygamy (45th Cong.; 1877–79)	Closing World's Fair (52nd Cong.; 1891–93)	Various Behavior (55th Cong.; 1897–98)
48 (25.00)	119 (40.61)	261 (78.61)	207 (57.98)

Note: Number in parenthesis is percentage of all districts.

TABLE A2.4. Sources of Petitions to House in Favor of Closing Chicago World's Fair on Sunday, 52d Congress, 1891–1893

Source	Number	Percentage
Independent groups	696	26.53
Presbyterians	651	24.82
Methodists	305	11.63
Baptists	140	5.34
WCTU	167	6.37
Christian Endeavor societies	126	4.80
Congregationalists	65	2.48
Lutherans	43	1.63
Epworth leagues	7	.27
YMCA	2	.08
Friends/Quakers	7	.27
Other churches	351	13.38
Other reform groups	26	.99
Others	37	1.41
Total	2,623	100.00

TABLE A2.5. Sources of Petitions, Various Moral Issues, 55th Congress, 1897–1898

Source	Number	Percentage
Independent groups	625	8.82
Presbyterians	407	5.75
Methodists	1,165	16.45
Baptists	473	6.78
WCTU	2,513	35.48
Christian Endeavor societies	594	8.39
Congregationalists	392	5.53
Lutherans	61	.86
Epworth leagues	175	2.47
YMCA/YWCA	61	.86
Friends/Quakers	49	.69
Other churches/church related	511	7.21
Other reform societies	57	.81
Total	7,083	100.01*

*Percentages do not total 100 due to rounding.

TABLE A2.6a. Distribution of Types of Legislation Requested
by Petitions, 55th Congress, 1897–1898

Type of legislation requested	Number	Percentage
Alcohol	1,908	26.94
Cigarettes	1,832	25.87
Gambling	1,387	19.58
Age of consent	1,354	19.12
Prizefighting	352	4.97
Sunday observation	215	3.03
Marriage and divorce	15	.20
Others	20	.29
Total	7,083	100.00

TABLE A2.6b. Distribution of Types of Legislation Requested
by Petitions; South Only, 55th Congress, 1897–1898

Type of legislation requested	Number	Percentage
Alcohol	14	11.42
Cigarettes	20	20.41
Gambling	15	15.31
Age of consent	11	11.22
Prizefighting	24	24.49
Sunday observation	11	11.23
Marriage and divorce	2	2.04
Others	1	.29
Total	98	100.00

NOTES

ABBREVIATIONS USED IN NOTES

ADAH	Alabama Department of Archives and History, Montgomery
AI	*The American Issue*
ASLAP	Anti-Saloon League of America Papers
BHL	Bentley Historical Library, University of Michigan, Ann Arbor
CAH	Research and Collections Division, Center for American History, University of Texas, Austin
CG	*Congressional Globe*
CR	*Congressional Record*
CS	*The Christian Statesman*
DPH	Department of Presbyterian History, Philadelphia, Pa.
Duke	Rare Book, Manuscript, and Special Collections Library, Duke University, Durham, N.C.
FEWL	Frances E. Willard Memorial Library, Woman's Christian Temperance Union Headquarters, Evanston, Ill.
ICPSR	U.S. Congressional Roll Call Voting Records, Inter-University Consortium for Political and Social Research, University of Michigan
LC	Manuscripts Division, the Library of Congress, Washington, D.C.
LSU	Hill Memorial Library, Louisiana State University, Baton Rouge
MHS	Massachusetts Historical Society, Boston
NA	National Archives, Washington, D.C.
NHHS	New Hampshire Historical Society, Concord
NTSPHR	National Temperance Society and Publication House Records
NYPL	Manuscripts and Archives Section, New York Public Library
OD	*Our Day*
RG	Record Group
RPTSL	Reformed Presbyterian Theological Seminary Library, Pittsburgh, Pa.
RRL	Richard Russell Library, University of Georgia, Athens
SHC	Southern Historical Collection, University of North Carolina, Chapel Hill
SL	Schlesinger Library, Harvard University, Cambridge, Mass.
SS	Serial Sets

STFP	Scientific Temperance Federation Papers
THS	Ticonderoga Historical Society, Ticonderoga, N.Y.
T&P	Temperance and Prohibition Papers, joint Ohio Historical
	Society–Michigan Historical Collections (microfilm collection),
	Ann Arbor, Mich./Columbus, Ohio
US	*The Union Signal*
VHS	Virginia Historical Society, Richmond
WCTU Minutes	*Minutes of the Annual Meeting of the Woman's Christian*
	Temperance Union
WCTU Papers	Historical File of the National Headquarters, Woman's Christian
	Temperance Union Papers
W&M	Swem Library, College of William and Mary, Williamsburg, Va.

INTRODUCTION

1. For examples, see Ebersole, *Church Lobbying in the Nation's Capital*; West, *Politics of Revelation and Reason*; Ribuffo, *Old Christian Right*; and William Bennett's introduction to Reed, *Politically Incorrect*.

2. Handy, *Undermined Establishment*, provides an excellent exploration of religion and government during this period.

3. The relationship of the Christian lobby to the social gospel is addressed in Chapter 4.

4. Even Wiebe's brilliant *Search for Order*, 44, 56–57, treats these movements as the last-gasp efforts of older, island communities. For the individual histories of the various reforms, see the references below and the citations in later chapters when the respective types of legislation are discussed. Two important works do bring together the various reform efforts. Boyer, *Urban Masses and Moral Order*, offers a much broader analysis of reform crusades than the one here; however, it does not analyze the ties among the Christian lobbyists or their various efforts to secure federal legislation. Burnham's very helpful *Bad Habits* puts much more emphasis on legislation but deals primarily with developments in the twentieth century.

5. Fredrickson, *Inner Civil War* and "Coming of the Lord." The fears that the war brought an increase in sinful behavior led, during the war, to the creation of the Christian Commission; see Griffin, *Their Brothers' Keeper*, 241–64. For arguments of reform's roots in abolitionism, see Blocker, *Retreat from Reform*, 15, and Pivar, *Purity Crusade*. The lobbyists' effort represented a new reliance on federal power but built upon a resort to law that had begun in the antebellum era when reformers abandoned their faith in moral suasion alone. The Whigs, Know-Nothings, and Republicans all embraced that idea, but most attempts to legislate morality occurred at the local or state level. On the abandonment of moral suasion, see Griffin, *Their Brothers' Keeper*; Tyrrell, *Sobering Up*; and Ginzburg, *Women and the Work of Benevolence*. For a good summary and introduction to the vast literature on religion in antebellum politics, see Carwardine, *Evangelicals and Politics*.

6. Blocker, *American Temperance Movements*, 118, argues that the key to the passage of

Prohibition was an upsurge in drinking. On increased public sexuality, see D'Emilio and Freedman, *Intimate Matters*, 130–38.

7. The classic formulation of the role of the middle class came in Gusfield, *Symbolic Crusade*, but later works continue to stress the reformers' ties to the middle class. For examples, see Bates, *Weeder in the Garden of the Lord*, and Beisel, *Imperiled Innocents*. The idea of social control has more often been employed in discussions of antebellum reform but is still relevant here. For examples of its application to postbellum reform, see Pivar, *Purity Crusade*, and, for a very sophisticated variation that also incorporates the role of gender and other factors, see Odem, *Delinquent Daughters*. For a discussion, although not an endorsement, of the social control model's relevance to postwar reform, see Hunt, *Governing Morals*, 18–19.

8. Bordin, *Woman and Temperance*; Epstein, *Politics of Domesticity*; Tyrrell, *Woman's World/Woman's Empire*, 114–45; Baker, "Domestication of Politics" and *Moral Frameworks of Public Life*. Parker, *Purifying America*, 10, however, points out that the resort to government in the end undermined women's power by replacing it with male-dominated federal power.

9. Tyrrell, *Sobering Up*; Kerr, *Organized for Prohibition*; Pegram, *Battling Demon Rum*; Clemens, *People's Lobby*. In contrast to Clemens, Edwards, *Angels in the Machinery*, emphasizes that women worked through party politics. The literature on temperance stresses not only a reliance on a partisan approach in the early years but the influence of the Prohibition Party. The Prohibition Party played little role in the Christian lobby's efforts. For one thing, it eschewed the lobby's broad agenda in favor of a narrow focus on prohibition. The role of the Prohibition Party is stressed in Blocker, *Retreat from Reform*, which also has an excellent account of its debate over a broader moral agenda. See also Colvin, *Prohibition in the United States*. On the major parties' interest in moral legislation at the national level, see Gerring, "Culture versus Economics."

10. Kerr, *Organized for Prohibition*; Boyer, *Urban Masses and Moral Order*, 162–219; Timberlake, *Prohibition and the Progressive Movement*; Connelly, *Response to Prostitution in the Progressive Era*. For summaries of the literature on Progressivism, see Rodgers, "In Search of Progressivism," and McCormick, "Progressivism." Even the Anti-Saloon League, undoubtedly the most "progressive" of the lobbying groups, probably had more in common with its predecessors in the Christian lobby than with most Progressive Era reform groups and certainly would not have been able to work its will in Congress without the other lobbyists' help.

11. Novak, *People's Welfare*, 149–89.

12. Pegram, *Battling Demon Rum*, esp. xii–xiii; Keller, *Affairs of State*, esp. 507–17; and Keller, *Regulating a New Society*. Where Keller writes of an older polity of individualism, localism, and laissez-faire, the account here describes an antebellum moral polity centered around personal liberty, moral suasion, and states' rights. On the development of the state, see also Bensel, *Yankee Leviathan*, and Skowronek, *Building a New American State*, which uses the term "reconstruction" and provides the best overview of state formation in this period.

13. Sanders, *Roots of Reform*.

14. The phrase "moral reconstruction" was used by contemporaries; see, for example, Gladden, "Moral Reconstruction," 13, and Abbott, *Reminiscences*, 256. Contemporaries, however, used the term primarily to refer to the efforts of northern missionaries and teachers who descended on the South immediately after the Civil War, intent on saving its collective soul and convincing both the former slaveholders and their former slaves to embrace northern values.

CHAPTER ONE

1. Gaustad, *Faith of Our Fathers*, 115–17. Gaustad, "Religious Tests," also stresses the paradoxical nature of the founders' thoughts on religion and the state.

2. The case for a secular Constitution is most forcefully made in Murrin, "Religion and Politics," and Kramnick and Moore, *Godless Constitution*. For a different interpretation that stresses the references to God in the state constitutions, see Botein, "Religious Dimensions." On state regulation of morality, see Novak, *People's Welfare*, 149–89, 151 ("crucial").

3. The account here relies heavily on John, *Spreading the News*, 169–205; Wyatt-Brown, "Prelude to Abolitionism"; and West, *Politics of Revelation*, 137–70.

4. John, *Spreading the News*, 325, n. 76, and West, *Politics of Revelation*, 260–61.

5. *Account of Memorials Presented to Congress*, 8, 17, and 4.

6. Wyatt-Brown, "Prelude to Abolitionism," 335. Johnson's reports were actually written by Obadiah B. Brown, a Baptist minister and Democrat who lived in Johnson's boardinghouse; see John, *Spreading the News*, 199.

7. U.S. Senate, *Petitions Relative to Mails on the Sabbath*, 1 ("proper . . ." and "good citizens . . ."); U.S. House Committee on Post Offices and Post Roads, *Sunday Mail*, 2 ("principles . . ."); 1 ("to inquire . . ."); 5 ("arm . . ."); 6 ("public mind . . .").

8. *Register of the Debates in Congress*, 21st Cong., 1st sess., 427 and appendix.

9. For an introduction to "Republican motherhood," see Evans, *Born for Liberty*, 57–66.

10. *U.S. Statutes at Large*, 25th Cong., 3d sess., 5:318; Thomas, *Law of Lotteries*, 7–8; *U.S. Statutes at Large*, 27th Cong., 2d sess., 5:566–67; U.S. House Committee on Ways and Means, *Tariff Act of 1842*; S. 3 and H.R. 19, *CG*, 36th Cong., 1st sess., 198, 795, 1013, 1140–46, 1194, and 1319. For totals on bills entered, see Appendix 1.

11. For an example of petition on sales in D.C., see *CG*, 31st Cong., 1st sess., 655. Legislators tried to or entered bills to end sale in D.C.; see esp. *CG*, 31st Cong., 1st sess., 388, and 35th Cong., 1st sess., 636.

12. Prucha, *American Indian Policy*, 102–38; Unrau, *White Man's Wicked Water*.

13. U.S. House, *Ardent Spirits–Navy*; U.S. Senate, *Memorial of the Pennsylvania State Temperance Society*; H.R. 62, *CG*, 28th Cong. The account here relies heavily on Langley, *Social Reform in the United States Navy*, 209–69.

14. U.S. House Committee on Naval Affairs, *Spirit Ration in the Navy*; H.R. 342, *CG*, 32d Cong.; H.R. 97, *CG*, 33d Cong.; V359, Senate, 32d Cong., and V19, House, 33d Cong., ICPSR. Party division in 33d Cong. based on my own calculations.

15. H.R. 317, *CG*, 33d Cong., 1st sess.

16. *CG*, 33d Cong., 1st sess., 1094 ("to establish . . .") and 1093 ("centralization . . .").

17. *Journal of the House of Representatives*, 34th Cong., 820–21 ("from . . ."); V199, House, 34th Cong., ICPSR; Donald Johnson, *National Party Platforms*, 27.

18. U.S. House Committee on the Judiciary, *Polygamy in the Territories*, 2.

19. *CG*, 36th Cong., 1st sess., appendix, 198 ("Are you . . .") and 1410 ("if we can . . ."); V124, House, 36th Cong., ICPSR.

20. Hood, *Reformed America*; Loveland, *Southern Evangelicals and the Social Order*, 159–85; Farmer, *Metaphysical Confederacy*, 256–57; Quist, *Restless Visionaries*.

21. Wyatt-Brown, *Southern Honor*; Ownby, *Subduing Satan*; Bardaglio, *Reconstructing the Household*.

22. Simpson, *Good Southerner*, 30 ("What sort . . ."); *CG*, 33d Cong., 1st sess., 618 ("ministers . . .") and 619. Although he does not use "the politics of slavery" exactly as it is here, on that concept see Cooper, *South and the Politics of Slavery*.

23. Many historians have demonstrated the role of the southern clergy in the defense of slavery and indirectly in the justification of secession; for a strongly argued example, see Snay, *Gospel of Disunion*.

24. Goen, *Broken Churches*, 171–76; U.S. Senate, *Journal of the Congress of the CSA*, 1:237 ("rulers . . ."); Thomas Johnson, *Life and Letters of Benjamin Morgan Palmer*, 238 ("*between* . . ."); Benjamin Morgan Palmer, "National Responsibility before God," in Chesebrough, "*God Ordained This War*," 202–8 ("a dead . . ."). Miller, Stout, and Wilson, *Religion and the American Civil War*, contains several essays that reach the same conclusion about a "corporate Christianity" in the Confederacy; see especially the essay by Harry Stout and Christopher Grasso, 313–59.

25. Davis, "*A Government of Our Own*," 98 and 226; Hull, "Making of the Confederate Constitution," 286; U.S. Senate, *Journal of the Congress of CSA*, 1:25, 32, 33, 851, 858–59; Faust, *Confederate Nationalism*, 22–32; "Proceedings of the First Confederate Congress," 451–52; U.S. Senate, *Journal of the Congress of CSA*, 1:218, 3:783, 785, 4:444, 454, 475, 5:390, 6:244, 847–49, 7:448; Nevins, *Messages and Papers of Jefferson Davis*, 1:103–4, 135, 217–18, 227, 268, 324–25, 328, 412–14, 563–65, and 567–68. Chilton's wording was what Cobb had originally suggested. The number of states voting differed because Georgia did not cast a vote since its delegation divided evenly on the issue.

26. U.S. Senate, *Journal of the Congress of the CSA*, 1:892, 121–22, 5:15, 43, 61, 195–98 ("ignore . . .").

27. Ibid., 7:272; Robinson, "Prohibition in the Confederacy"; U.S. Senate, *Journal of the Congress of CSA*, 5:62, 250, 294; 2:127, 161–64, 180, 212; 3:615, 788, 793; 7:260, 293, and 758.

28. Bushnell, *Reverses Needed*, 9 and 26.

29. Petitions for such an amendment were entered in the 36th through 41st Congresses and the 43d and 44th. Alexander, *History of the National Reform Movement*, 5 ("original sin"); *Constitution and Address of the National Association*, 4 ("We . . ."); T. P. Stevenson, "The Origin and Progress of the Movement to Secure the Religious Amendment of the Constitution of the United States," *CS* 5 (15 March 1872): 105–6; H. H. George, "Reminiscences III. Early Conventions in the National Work," *CS* 43 (January 1909): 14–16.

30. *CG*, 38th Cong., 1st sess., 693; *CG*, 38th Cong., 2d sess., 980 and 1272 ("was . . ."); Basler, *Collected Works of Abraham Lincoln*, 4:482–83, 7:431–32.

31. Langley, *Social Reform*, 262–67; H.R. 423, *CG*, 37th Cong.; S. 53, 61, 98, *CG*, 37th Cong.; H.R. 186, *CG*, 37th Cong.; H.R. 522, *CG*, 38th Cong., 1st sess., 149, 3135 ("Christian . . ."), 3136 ("openly . . ."), 3261–65, 5264.

32. H.R. 391, *CG*, 37th Cong.

CHAPTER TWO

1. See Vos, *Scottish Covenanters*, for an introduction to the Covenanter tradition and J. M. Foster, *Reformation Principles Stated and Applied*, for an introduction to the theology and beliefs of the movement. My interpretation rests on reading of the *Christian Statesman* and other sources.

2. Neely, "Elisha Mulford;" Mulford, *Nation*. For another and earlier attempt to provide a religious basis for the state, see Morris, *Christian Life and Character*. My thinking on this issue has been influenced by both my reading of the lobbyists' writings and Royster, *Destructive War*.

3. "National Protection for Citizens of Nation," *CS* 11 (1 November 1877): 76 ("absurd . . ."); Taylor Lewis, "The State and the Mass-Meeting," *CS* 1 (2 September 1867): 1; "The Philadelphia Meeting," *CS* 2 (15 June 1869): 160; Sloane, *State Religion*; J. A. Fischer, "Origin and Providence of Government," *CS* 13 (1 April 1880): 365 and (8 April 1880): 378.

4. "Petitions to Congress," *CS* 2 (15 December 1868): 61. Petitions are reported in *CG*, 40th Cong., 3d sess.; a copy is on 272 ("We . . .") and some of the originals are in Petitions and Memorials, Committee on the Judiciary (SEN40A-H10.1), RG 46, NA. See Appendix 2, Tables A2.1a and A2.1b, for distribution.

5. "The Conflict Coming," *Index* 2 (31 January 1871): 20 ("war . . ."); Arthur E. Bradford, "'God in the Constitution': Would It Be Right to Incorporate Religious Dogmas into the Constitution of the United States?" *Index* 2 (28 October 1871): 337–38; "National Christianity and Religious Toleration," *CS* 1 (1 February 1868): 84–85; R. Z. Willson, "The Proposed Amendment No Infringement of Right," *CS* 2 (1 May 1869): 137–38; "Constitutional Safeguards to Official Integrity," *CS* 1 (15 June 1868): 156–57; "Address of Rev. J. P. Lytle," *CS* 6 (19 October 1872): 49–50; "An Unfortunate Nomination," *CS* 11 (22 November 1877): 112.

6. "Act Promptly!" *Index* 3 (6 January 1872): 5; *CG*, 42d Cong., 2d sess., 580 ("attempt . . ."); *CR*, 43d Cong., 1st sess., 432. See also ibid., 1586, 1254, 2630, and 3892.

7. U.S. House Committee on the Judiciary, *Acknowledgement of God*, 1 ("to be . . ."); "The Present Congress on the Religious Amendment," *CS* 7 (21 February 1874): 197; *CR*, 44th Cong., 1st sess., 4191.

8. Cook, *Relations of the Temperance Reform*, 6–7; Slagell, "Good Woman," 115; "America's Past and Future," in Haven, *National Sermons*, 626–27; Mary T. Lathrap, "The National Woman's Christian Temperance Union," *US* 17 (2 April 1891): 3; Joseph P. Thompson, "The Theocratic Principle; or, Religion and the Bond of the Republic," *CS* 1 (1 August 1868): 182–83; "National Perils and Hopes," *US* 24 (27 October 1898): 9; Wilbur F. Crafts, "What Business Has Church or State with Ethics?" *US* 30 (15 September 1904): 3.

9. 26 October 1865, Minute Book, "Board of Managers, September 26–October 31, 1865," folders 2–5 ("use . . ."); J. W. Cummings to Eleanor DeGraff Coyler, 12 January 1915, Letterbook, 2 November 1914–2 February 1917, box 2; William E. Dodge to My Dear Sir, 3 March 1881, folders 1–2; 14 September 1869, "Board of Managers, Minutes, November 14–, 1865 to Dec. 26, 1882," box 2, all in NTSPHR, DPH. For biographical information on Stearns, see Lender, *Temperance Biography*, 458–60.

10. 19 November 1872, "Board of Managers, Minutes, November 14–, 1865 to Dec. 26, 1882," box 2, NTSPHR, DPH. Petitions indexed in *Senate Journal*, 41st Cong., 2d sess. (SS 1404), and 42d Cong., 2d sess. (SS 1477) and 3d sess. (SS 1544).

11. S. 479, 502, and 543, *CG*, 41st Cong.; S. 1202, *CG*, 42d Cong.; *CG*, 42d Cong., 3d sess., 93 ("rather . . .") and 95 ("perfectly").

12. H.R. 3392, 3391, and 3609, *CG*, 42d Cong.; *CG*, 42d Cong., 2d sess., 401–2 ("seems . . .").

13. 7 January 1873, "Board of Managers Minutes, Nov. 14, 1865 to December 26, 1882," box 2, NTSPHR, DPH; S. 606 and 1336, *CG*, 42d Cong. A copy of the NTS's petition is in Petitions and Memorials, Committee on the Judiciary (HR42A-H.4), RG 233, NA.

14. S. 161, *CR*, 43d Cong.; *CR*, 43d Cong., 1st sess., 798 ("great . . .") and 1581 ("economic . . .").

15. *CR*, 43d Cong., 1st sess., 1581 ("gathering . . .") and 1760 ("Human . . .").

16. Morgan, *From Hayes to McKinley*, 79 ("Border . . ."); *CR*, 43d Cong., 1st sess., 1806–8 ("domain . . .").

17. S. 161, *CR*, 43d Cong.; S. 124, *CR*, 44th Cong.

18. V100, Senate, 43d Cong.; V410, House, 43d Cong.; and V116, Senate, 44th Cong., ICPSR.

For several votes on moral legislation, I ran a logistical regression analysis in which the dependent variable was the vote (no = 0; yes = 1) and in which the independent variables were five social characteristics of House districts—population density, percentage of the population that was black, percentage that was foreign born, percentage that was Roman Catholic, and the total dollar value of manufactured goods produced. (Votes were taken from ICPSR; statistics on the individual districts were taken from Parsons, Beach, and Dubin, *United States Congressional Districts and Data*, and Parsons, Dubin, and Parsons, *United States Congressional Districts*.)

The two votes to create a commission on the alcoholic liquor traffic (one in the 43d Cong., the other in the 47th) indicated an inverse relationship between a vote for creating a commission and both the percentage of Catholics and the percentage of blacks in a district. In the 43d Cong. there was also an inverse relationship between a vote for creating a commission and population density. The only positive relationship was between the percentage of foreign born in the population and the vote in the 47th Cong. The other variables did not produce statistically significant results (in other words, they had a Prob. value of above .05). At a time when an overwhelming majority of African Americans lived in the South, the influence of the variable for black population probably reflects the overwhelming no vote by southern representatives. That the influence of the percentage of blacks in the population is not statistically significant when each region is analyzed independently supports such a conclusion.

V410, House, 43d Cong., ICPSR: "To bring up the bill to create a commission on the alcoholic liquor traffic" (n = 203): percentage foreign born: B = .0686, Wald = 7.0574, Prob. values = .0079; Population density: B = −8.7E−05, Wald = 3.9830, Prob. values = .0460; percentage black: B = −.0231, Wald = 4.9334, Prob. values = .0263; percentage Catholic: B = −.1484, Wald = 6.6049, Prob. values = .0102. V34, House, 47th Cong., ICPSR: "To create a Commission on the alcoholic liquor traffic" (n = 212): percentage black: B = −.0814, Wald = 25.3590, Prob. values = .0000; percentage Catholic: B = −.0947, Wald = 4.1363, Prob. values = .0420.

19. Bordin, *Woman and Temperance*, 15–51; 5 March 1874, "Board of Managers Minutes, Nov. 14, 1865 to Dec. 26, 1882," box 2, NTSPHR, DPH; "The Public Morals," *CS* 7 (24 January 1874): 163; "Woman's Temperance Crusade," *CS* 7 (7 March 1874): 212; David McAllister, "The Temperance Movement," *CS* 7 (14 March 1874): 220–21; *WCTU Minutes*, 1874, 7; 1875, 44, 49; and 1879, 54. Blocker, *"Give to the Winds Thy Fears,"* 24, offers a lower estimate of 57,000.

20. *WCTU Minutes*, 1874, 6 ("this . . ."), 38, 27.

21. Slagell, "Good Woman," 219 ("last . . ."); *WCTU Minutes*, 1884, 50 (*"to make . . ."*).

22. "Two Harmonious Forces," *US* 10 (25 September 1884): 8.

23. *WCTU Minutes*, 1874, 29; Willard to Wittenmyer, 11 December 1874, frames 262–68, reel 11, WCTU Papers, T&P; *WCTU Minutes*, 1875, 53; *CR*, 43d Cong., 2d sess., 867.

24. *WCTU Minutes*, 1876, 103 ("prayer . . ."); "Points for Second Nat. Conv. of Women," frames 426–27, reel 11, WCTU Papers, T&P; Slagell, "Good Woman," 230–36.

25. *WCTU Minutes*, 1888, appendix, 3 ("mother-hearted"); Lady Henry Somerset, "An Impression," introduction to Strachey, *Frances Willard*, 14–15 ("be . . ."). My interpretation of Willard's views rests on a reading of her letters, diaries, and speeches, her autobiography, *Glimpses*, and biographies of Willard: Strachey, *Frances Willard*; Earhart, *Frances Willard*, and Bordin, *Frances Willard*.

26. "Outline Course of Study for Local Unions," *US* 32 (5 April 1906): 14; Ida Hinman, "Mrs. Sara Doan La Fetra," *US* 15 (12 September 1889): 10; Willard, "A Week on the Wing," *US* 14 (8 March 1888): 2–3; Sara La Fetra to Grover Cleveland, 17 February 1887, reel 109; 27 April 1887, reel 112; 20 May 1887, reel 49; 14 November 1887, reel 65; and La Fetra to Mrs. Cleveland, 9 May 1887, reel 112, all in Cleveland Papers, LC.

27. *CR*, 51st Cong., 1st sess., 1547. On Blair's background and life, see Blair Papers, NHHS; Henry W. Blair Questionnaire, 5 March 1867, folder 8, Pecker Papers, NHHS; Leavitt, *Blair Family*, 7, 147, 154–59; and "Henry W. Blair," *Dictionary of American Biography*, 2:334–35.

28. H. Res. 170, *CR*, 44th Cong.; *CR*, 44th Cong., 2d sess., appendix, 5–17. Blair's accounts of the origins of his resolution varied slightly. See Bittenbender, *National Prohibitory*, 1–3; *CR*, 66th Cong., 1st sess., 2478; and "Message from Hon. Henry W. Blair," *AI* 27 (17 January 1920): 4.

29. *WCTU Minutes*, 1877, 171–72, 176 ("prohibition . . ."); *WCTU Minutes*, 1878, 41 and 112; 1880, 71; 1881, 33, 39, 40–41, 49, and 54; Clara L. Roach to Willard, 11 October 1881, frame 622, reel 12, and "Memorandum of Trip to Washington for Convention Oct 1887," frames 329–34, reel 11, both in WCTU Papers, T&P; "Since Our Last Issue," *US* 13 (3 February 1887): 1; "Ex-Senator Blair Writes of Prohibition Movement—Past and Present," *US* 43 (11 January 1917): 4; *WCTU Minutes*, 1890, 40 and 60.

30. 22 November 1881, "Board of Managers, Minutes, Nov. 14, 1865 to Dec. 26, 1882," box 2, NTSPHR, DPH; Bittenbender, *National Prohibitory*, 3; *WCTU Minutes*, 1887, 80; U.S. Senate Committee on Education and Labor, *Report to Accompany S. Res. 12*, 11 ("colored . . ."); U.S. House Committee on the Judiciary, *Sale of Alcoholic Beverages*, 1 ("unwise . . .").

31. *WCTU Minutes*, 1879, 135–36; 1880, 10–11, 102–3; 1881, 38. On Hunt and the campaign, see Zimmerman, *Distilling Democracy*.

32. "The Jubilee at Washington," *US* 12 (10 June 1886): 5; U.S. Senate Committee on Education and Labor, *Report to Accompany Bill S. 1405*, 5 ("an alien . . ."), 8 ("moral . . ."), and 17 ("denounce . . .").

33. *WCTU Minutes*, 1886, ccvi–ccx; S. 797 and 1405, *CR*, 49th Cong.; *CR*, 49th Cong., 1st sess., appendix, 145–46.

34. *WCTU Minutes*, 1895, 209–10; Gordon, *Women Torch-Bearers*, 42–43 ("greatest . . .").

35. *WCTU Minutes*, 1887, 43–44; Willard and Livermore, *American Women*, 1:87–88; Frances E. Willard, "Mrs. Ada M. Bittenbender," *US* 14 (15 March 1888): 10; 4 January 1888, vol. 47, Journals of Willard, FEWL ("marvel . . .").

36. Ida Hinman, "District of Columbia," *US* 16 (1 May 1890): 10; *WCTU Minutes*, 1888, 23; calling card in HR50A-H13.5, file Dec. 6–Mar. 17, 1888, box 147, RG 233, NA; Bittenbender, *National Prohibitory*.

37. *WCTU Minutes*, 1889, 111 ("keystone . . ."); Bittenbender, *National Prohibitory*.

CHAPTER THREE

1. Comstock, *Frauds Exposed*, 416.

2. S. 390, *CG*, 38th Cong.; *CG*, 38th Cong., 2d sess., 661 ("obscene . . ." and "discard. . .").

3. *CG*, 38th Cong., 2d sess., appendix, 141 ("knowingly . . ."); H.R. 2295, *CR*, 41st Cong.; H.R. 1, *CR*, 42d Cong.

4. Biographical material comes from the authorized biography, Trumbull, *Anthony Comstock*, and from Broun and Leech, *Anthony Comstock*; Richard Johnson, "Anthony Comstock"; and Bates, *Weeder in the Garden*. My interpretation of Comstock's motives, however, rests on my reading of his books and an analysis of the records he kept of his arrests. See Records of New York Society for the Suppression of Vice, LC.

5. Bates, *Weeder in the Garden*, 161; no. 92, 1873, nos. 9, 10, and 43, 1876, no. 5, 1878, no. 109, 6 December 1902, Records of New York Society for the Suppression of Vice, LC; copy of letter, Anthony Comstock to James F. Morton Jr., 5 June 1915, frame 473, reel 12, Dennett Papers, SL.

6. Comstock, *Traps for the Young*, 184–207 and 239.

7. Goldsmith, *Other Powers*, 337–45 ("*exhibiting* . . ."); nos. 38 and 39, 2 November 1872, and nos. 45, 46, 47, 9 January 1873, Records of New York Society for the Suppression of Vice, LC. Goldsmith points out that Comstock acted at the request of a member of the district attorney's staff.

8. Comstock, *Frauds Exposed*, 390–93; Trumbull, *Anthony Comstock*, 83–104; Broun and Leech, *Anthony Comstock*, 128–44. These accounts do not always agree; Broun and Leech, for example, found references in Comstock's diaries (which are now lost) to a

trip Comstock does not mention. The history of the bill in *CG* does not always substantiate Comstock's account; I have followed the *Globe*. Merriam's bill was H.R. 2014, *CG*, 42d Cong. On Strong and the Christian amendment, see Teaford, "Toward a Christian Nation." The Credit Mobilier scandal involved the vice president and other politicians who were charged with taking bribes from a railroad.

9. *CG*, 42d Cong., 3d sess., appendix, 297.

10. S. 1572, *CR*, 42d Cong.

11. *CG*, 42d Cong., 3d sess., 2004–5.

12. H.R. 1239, *CR*, 44th Cong.; *CR*, 45th Cong., 2d sess., 1340.

13. Comstock, *Frauds Exposed*, 424–25 ("crowded . . ."); U.S. House Committee on the Revision of the Laws, *Repeal of Certain Sections*, 1373 ("post-office . . .").

14. Comstock, "Helps and Hindrances in the Suppression of Vice," *OD* 1 (March 1888): 222–23. See also Pivar, *Purity Crusade*, and Beisel, *Imperiled Innocents*. Andrea Tone, "Black Market Birth Control," questions whether the Comstock Law actually did much to reduce the flow of contraceptives.

15. H.R. 1089, *CG*, 41st Cong.; *CG*, 41st Cong., 2d sess., 1373 ("lustful. . .").

16. *CR*, 41st Cong., 2d sess., appendix, 173 ("to turn . . ."), appendix, 179 ("truthfulness . . .").

17. H.R. 3097, *CR*, 43d Cong., 1st sess.

18. Donald Johnson, *National Party Platforms*, 54. At the same time, Grant and other Republicans also tried out anti-Catholicism as an issue, a return to antebellum nativism; see Hoogenboom, *Rutherford B. Hayes*, 421–23. On the attitudes of federal attorneys, see Cresswell, *Mormons, Cowboys, Moonshiners, and Klansmen*, 123–28.

19. Firmage and Mangrum, *Zion in the Courts*, 151–59.

20. Lamar, *Far Southwest*; Larson, *"Americanization" of Utah*; Lyman, *Political Deliverance*; R. G. McNiece, "The Christian Reconstruction of Utah," *CS* 12 (24 April 1879): 402–4 ("*establishment* . . ."); Dwyer, *Gentile Comes to Utah*, 181 ("their . . ."); Lyon, "Religious Activities," 292–98.

21. Dwyer, *Gentile Comes to Utah*, 190–214; Iversen, "Debate on the American Home"; Pascoe, *Relations of Rescue*, 61–69; petition, November 1878, Petitions and Memorials, Committee on the Territories (HR45A-H23.3), RG 233, NA ("degrading . . ."). See also U.S. House, *Enforcement of the Anti-Polygamy Act*. For petitions, see Appendix 2, Tables A2.1a, A2.1b, A2.2a, and A2.2b.

22. U.S. Senate, *Memorial of the General Assembly*.

23. Rev. R. G. McNiece, "Government and Doctrines of the Mormons," *CS* 12 (22 May 1879): 449–50; "The Spirit of Mormonism," *CS* 12 (12 June 1879): 484–85; "The Spirit of Mormonism," *CS* 12 (10 July 1879): 532–33; "The Outlook," *CS* 15 (22 September 1881): 1 ("foul . . ."); editorial, *CS* 17 (20 September 1883): 2 ("are . . ."); "Our Washington Letter," *CS* 1 (1 January 1868): 71 ("reconstruct . . ."); "Polygamy in Congress," *CS* 7 (23 May 1874): 300; untitled editorial, *CS* 10 (24 May 1877): 344 ("while . . ."); "The Outlook," *CS* 12 (9 January 1879): 217; *WCTU Minutes*, 1879, 72 ("against . . ."); Dwyer, *Gentile Comes to Utah*, 199.

24. "Joseph Cook," *Zion's Herald*, 3 July 1910, tear sheet in Printed Materials Box, Cook Papers, Duke ("few . . ."); Joseph Cook to parents, 22 December 1879, Letters Home, Cook Papers, THS ("joy . . ."). Biographical material on Cook from Pointer,

Joseph Cook; Bascom, *Letters of a Ticonderoga Farmer*; Cumbler, *Moral Response to Industrialism*; the Cook Papers, Duke (which include an autobiography that is more a biography, written by his wife); and the far more extensive and personal Cook Papers, THS.

25. Georgia Cook to friends, 8 June 1879 ("false . . ."); Joseph Cook to parents, 13 October 1879 ("this special . . ."); Joseph Cook to parents, 22 December 1879, all in Letters Home, Cook Papers, THS; Cook, "Mormonism and States Rights," *Independent* 31 (11 December 1879): 5–6 ("Bluebeard . . ."); "Disloyal Mormonism," *Independent* 32 (15 January 1880): 6–7 ("priestly . . ."); Joseph Cook to parents, 25 March 1880, Letters Home, Cook Papers, THS.

26. Richardson, *Messages*, 8:11 and 57.

27. S. 353, *CR*, 47th Cong.; *CR*, 47th Cong., 1st sess., 1152 ("bigamy . . .").

28. *CR*, 47th Cong., 1st sess., 1204.

29. Ibid., 1212–13 and 1216.

30. Ibid., 1861.

31. V72, V73, and V74, House, 47th Cong., ICPSR. Fifteen southerners voted to allow disfranchisement of polygamists; only one was in favor of the commission.

A logistical regression analysis (described in Chapter 2, note 18) of the vote on the Edmunds Act indicated a positive relationship between a vote for the bill and the dollar value of manufactured goods produced and an inverse relationship between the vote for the bill and both population density and the percentage of blacks in the population. The relationship between the vote and manufacturing probably reflects the overwhelming Republican vote (many Republicans came from districts with a manufacturing base) and the influence of the percentage of blacks probably reflects the strong support from the South. The influence of all three factors becomes statistically insignificant when each region is analyzed independently.

V74, House, 47th Cong., ICPSR: "To Pass Edmunds Act" (n = 245): Population density: $B = -.0002$, Wald = 8.4047, Prob. values = .0037; percentage black: $B = -.0247$, Wald = 4.6837, Prob. values = .0304; total value of manufactured goods produced: $B = .0001$, Wald = 6.9923, Prob. values = .0082.

32. S. 2238, *CR*, 47th Cong.; Richardson, *Messages*, 8:184 ("stoutest . . ."); Joseph Bowles, "Moral Issues at the National Capital," *CS* 17 (20 December 1883): 3; Joseph Cook, "What Shall Be Done with Mormonism?" *Independent* 36 (21 February 1884): 5–6. Cook's sermon was included in U.S. House Committee on the Territories, *Marriages in the Territory of Utah*.

33. H. Res. 12 and 50, S. 404 and 1283, *CR*, 48th Cong.; V231, Senate, 48th Cong., ICPSR; Donald Johnson, *National Party Platforms*, 74; Cannon and O'Higgins, *Under the Prophet*, 73. Every Republican on record and even nine of twenty-six Democrats supported Hoar's bill. Five of those Democratic votes came from the former Confederacy. Even so, half of the Democrats from outside of the South voted yes; only a quarter of those from Dixie did.

34. "Joseph Cook on Polygamy," *CS* 17 (19 June 1884): 8; "Book Notices," *US* 12 (8 July 1886): 3 ("National . . ."); *WCTU Minutes*, 1886, ix, 42, 47 ("Tucker Edmunds"), and 142–43.

35. S. 10, *CR*, 49th Cong.; V88, Senate, 49th Cong., ICPSR.

36. U.S. House Committee on the Judiciary, *Polygamy: Report to Accompany H. Res. 176*, 7 ("link . . ."). Comments on Tucker rest primarily on Tucker Family Papers, SHC; Tucker Papers, VHS; and John Davis, "John Randolph Tucker." See especially paper titled "Domestic Relations" filed in "Sociology, Government, Constitutions," 1890, vol. 9, in Tucker Papers, VHS.

37. U.S. House Committee on the Judiciary, *Suppression of Polygamy*. Van Wagoner, *Mormon Polygamy*, 128, also argues that the Tucker version was more severe and reports that Mormon lobbyists thought so as well.

38. U.S. House Committee on the Judiciary, *Bigamy*, V88, Senate, V284, House, 49th Cong., ICPSR. A logistical regression of the vote on the Edmunds-Tucker Act produced only one statistically significant result, an inverse relationship between a vote for the measure and the percentage of blacks in the population in the district. (B = −.0235, Wald = 5.8392, and Prob. values = .0157; n = 243). That relationship again no doubt reflects the significant southern opposition.

39. *The Late Corporation of the Church of Jesus Christ of Latter-day Saints v. United States*, 132 U.S. 1 (1890), 50 ("perfect right . . ."); *Davis v. Beason*, 133 U.S. 333 (1890), 344 ("make . . .").

40. Cannon and O'Higgins, *Under the Prophet*, 88 ("find . . .") and 32.

41. Lamar, *Far Southwest*; Larson, *"Americanization" of Utah*; Lyman, *Political Deliverance*.

42. *U.S. Statutes at Large*, 53d Cong., 2d sess., 138:108.

43. Cook, "Will Mormonism Capture Washington?" *CS* 25 (2 April 1892): 4; "The Admission of Utah as a State," *US* 19 (11 May 1893): 9; "Utah at the Doors of Congress," *OD* 11 (May 1893): 364 ("Latter Day . . ."). Historians have documented the deception and even questioned whether the leaders of the church had considered the Woodruff Manifesto a new revelation. See, for example, Hardy, *Solemn Covenant*, 127–90, and Van Wagoner, *Mormon Polygamy*, 140–61.

44. *CR*, 48th Cong., 1st sess., 364, 4513, 4553–63.

45. "Draft of Unfinished Autobiography," 2, box 22; "The Divorce Question and Its Problems," 27, box 19; and "An Address on Divorce," 24 and 38, box 19 ("*selfishness . . .*"), all in Dike Papers, LC. Biographical details from autobiography and other materials in these papers.

46. "The Amended Edmunds Bill," *Public Opinion* 1 (19 June 1886): 182; "National Marriage Law," *CS* 13 (4 September 1879): 4; "The Outlook," *CS* 14 (28 July 1881): 554; Cook, "New Proposals on the Divorce Question," *Independent* 36 (20 March 1884): 5–6 ("modern . . .").

47. Samuel Dike, "The National Divorce Reform League," *OD* 1 (January 1888): 49–54.

48. *CR*, 48th Cong., 1st sess., 516; Dike to A. H. Garland, Attorney-General, 4 November 1885, reel 23, and Garland to Grover Cleveland, 23 November 1885, reel 24, Cleveland Papers, LC; Edmunds to Dike, 19 and 21 January 1884, 28 July 1886; L. P. Poland to Dike, 1 and 8 February 1884, 22 March, 13 and 20 June 1884, 3 February 1885; Joseph E. Brown to Dike, 23 July 1886; Nelson Dingley to Dike, 20 November 1886, all in Dike Papers, LC. The few times prior to this that Congress had acted on divorce had concerned the District of Columbia and the liberalization of divorce laws there.

49. S. 1076, *CR*, 49th Cong.; "Draft of Unfinished Autobiography," 13–18, box 22, Dike Papers, LC.

CHAPTER FOUR

1. Strong, *Our Country*; Sheldon, *In His Steps*.

2. Wiebe, *Search for Order*.

3. Willard's efforts to work with the Populists are discussed in the biographies of Willard cited in Chapter 3. For the most part, however, the discussion here is based on my reading of the lobbyists' writings and letters. Henry May, *Protestant Churches*, 163–66, 130, 181, and 127–28, mentions Cook (in a section on conservatives in the Social Gospel movement), Crafts, and Willard, who he apparently considers part of the movement.

4. "Questions to Specialists: Replies by Miss Willard," *OD* 1 (February 1888): 168–69.

5. George Torrence, "The Relation of the Cigaret to Crime," *US* 25 (8 June 1899): 4 ("affects . . ."); "Editorial Notes," *CS* 12 (30 January 1879): 260 ("stimulation . . .").

6. Comstock, "Immoral Imaginationalism," *OD* 16 (April 1896): 191–92.

7. Crafts, "Transfigured Flesh," in *Before the Lost Arts*, 57–79; Mulford, *Nation*, 110. References to slaves will be cited throughout the remainder of the study.

8. Comstock, *Traps for the Young*, 56 ("desire . . ."); A. C. Bane, "Appetite and Greed," *AI* 22 (4 December 1915): 5 ("man . . ."); Livermore, *Story of My Life*, 630–51; Crafts, "Transfigured Flesh," 63.

9. Cook, "Ultimate America."

10. Powell's comments were discussed in Chapter 2, Cook's and Dike's in Chapter 3. For other examples, see "The Outlook," *CS* 14 (11 August 1881): 579–80; Julia Colman, "Temperance for the Freedmen and the Dime Collection," *US* 9 (16 August 1883): 2–3; *WCTU Minutes*, 1884, 55–56; J. W. Clokey, "Questions to Specialists," *OD* 3 (February 1889): 189; and Wilbur Crafts, "Purity," *US* 23 (15 July 1897): 4–5.

11. Strong, *Our Country*, 53.

12. *WCTU Minutes*, 1874, 15 ("sons . . ."); Comstock, *Traps for the Young*, 59; Crafts, "Transfigured Flesh," 62; Willard, *Woman and Temperance*, 237 ("to help . . ."); petition from Ramer, Montgomery County to Senators Bankhead and Johnston, 7 August 1912, folder 5, box 40, Bankhead Papers, ADAH ("is no . . .").

13. *WCTU Minutes*, 1874, 14 ("are . . ."); 1877, 176 ("zeal . . ."); 1881, 7 ("Work . . .").

14. On lower rates for women drinking, see Tyrrell, *Woman's World/Woman's Empire*, 14–15.

15. Comstock, *Traps for the Young*, 238.

16. Livermore, *Story of My Life*, 630–51 ("ten thousand . . ."), 637; Crafts, "Transfigured Flesh," 63. Livermore also pointed to the dangers posed by modern railways, steamships, and telephones that "marvelously quickened" the "pulse and pace of humanity," a point similar to the critique of society offered by George M. Beard. The Christian lobbyists' analysis in some ways resembled Beard's, but rather than the increased pace of society leading to nervousness or paralysis, as Beard argued, their analysis suggested it led to the use of alcohol and other depressants.

17. "Personal Liberty," *CS* 42 (November 1908): 333 ("Personal . . ."); *WCTU Minutes*, 1891, 152 ("insane . . ."); Willard, *Woman and Temperance*, 492 ("a man's . . .").

18. "Righteous Men for Civil Office," *CS* 1 (15 April 1868): 124 ("*christianize* . . ."); "Meeting of the National Association," *CS* 9 (20 November 1875): 92; "National Reform Work during 1878," *CS* 12 (2 January 1879): 210 ("moral . . ."); "Petitions for the Coming Campaign," *CS* 15 (15 September 1881): 1.

19. Glasgow, *History of the Reformed Presbyterian Church*, 574–75 and 694–95; "The Rev. David McAllister, D.D. LL.D.," *CS* 41 (July 1907): 193–99; "The Rev. Thomas Patton Stevenson, D.D. LL.D.," *CS* 46 (November 1912): 321–31.

20. "To the Friends of National Reform," *CS* 22 (18 April 1889): 2; John Alexander, "A Munificent Offer—Shall It Be Accepted," *CS* 24 (11 September 1890): 2–3.

21. *CS* 21 (13 October 1887): 2; "Call for the Columbus Convention," *CS* 8 (6 March 1875): 212; J. F. Quarles, "Letter from the South," *CS* 3 (1 August 1870): 183; "Letter from Secretary Foster," *CS* 20 (18 November 1886): 6–7; "The South as a Field of Reform," *CS* 19 (31 December 1885): 2; "Letter from Secretary Weir," *CS* 20 (2 December 1886): 6–7; "The Annual Meeting of 1887," *CS* 20 (26 May 1887): 6; "Important Meeting of the Executive Committee of NRA," *CS* 21 (19 September 1887): 2; David McAllister, "The Birth of the National Reform Movement," *CS* 36 (October 1902): 107.

22. *CS* 10 (26 October 1876): 90; *CS* 12 (6 February 1879): 268; *CS* 1 (1 October 1867): 21–22; *CS* 39 (August 1905): 249.

23. *WCTU Minutes*, 1880, 92; 1885, 121; 1891, 286; 1892, unnumbered chart. Membership percentages are based on 1891 numbers, with regions defined as they are in Appendix 1.

24. *WCTU Minutes*, 1878, 17 ("We can . . ."); 1879, 16; 1886, 84 ("We cannot . . ."); 1887, 20 ("the total . . ."); Willard, *Woman and Temperance*, 32–33.

25. *WCTU Minutes*, 1892, unnumbered chart; Bordin, *Woman and Temperance*, 3, 163–75; Gusfield, *Symbolic Crusade*, 80–81, 84.

26. Frances Willard, "Christ in Government," *US* 4 (4 January 1883): 2; *WCTU Minutes*, 1887, 71–76 (71, "Woman's . . ."); 1888, 57; 1889, 61–62; 1890, 54 ("While . . .").

27. *WCTU Minutes*, 1896, 38 ("Christian . . .") and 395–96 ("Christ . . .").

28. Willard first used the term to refer to the necessity for employing all means to the prohibition end, but over time it came to stand for a broad reform agenda. See Bordin, *Woman and Temperance*, 95–116. State and local groups could choose which of the expanding number and types of programs to support.

29. Hills, *Life and Labors of Mrs. Mary A. Woodbridge*; W. J. Coleman, "Mrs. Mary A. Woodbridge," *CS* 19 (15 October 1885): 4; "Legal Prohibition and National Reform," *CS* 17 (15 November 1883): 2; "The National Reform Convention," *CS* 17 (20 December 1883): 1; "Letters from Vice Presidents of the National Reform Association," *CS* 17 (31 January 1884;), 6; T. P. Stevenson, "Kindred Reform Movements," *CS* 18 (6 November 1884): 2 ("woman . . ."); *WCTU Minutes*, 1884, 105–7; 1885, 46.

30. "Proceedings of the Annual Convention," *CS* 18 (30 April 1885): 4 ("naturally . . ."); untitled editorial, *CS* 20 (27 January 1887): 2; T. P. Stevenson, "An Open Letter: To the Leaders, Officers and Members of the Woman's Christian Temperance Union," *CS* 21 (15

September 1887): 2–3; "The Annual Meeting for 1887," *CS* 20 (26 May 1887): 3; *WCTU Minutes*, 1889, 64 ("noble . . ."); 1893, 43–44 ("aim . . .").

31. *WCTU Minutes*, 1894, 44 and 66; "The World's Christian Reform Union," *CS* 27 (4 November 1893): 8; *WCTU Minutes*, 1892, 94 ("first . . ."); *WCTU Minutes*, 1895, 50 ("hearty . . ."); untitled, *CS* 30 (22 February 1896): 121.

32. "Editorial Notes," *CS* 6 (9 November 1872): 77; untitled editorial, *CS* 11 (4 April 1878): 342 ("heroic . . ."); untitled editorial, *CS* 11 (7 March 1878): 289 ("stronger . . ."); Anthony Comstock, "Purity," *CS* 25 (2 January 1892): 2; Anthony Comstock, "Christian Reform or National Ruin — Which?" *CS* 27 (25 November 1893): 6; *WCTU Minutes*, 1883, 36 ("tender . . ."); 1885, 33 and 73; 1891, 9; 1892, 53; 1893, 9; 1896, 354–60; 1897, 109; 1898, 329–30; "The Work of a Good Man," *US* 18 (28 April 1892): 8.

33. *WCTU Minutes*, 1891, 68 ("'feminine . . .'"); 1888, 39 ("our largest . . ."). Contacts are documented in Cook's letters and diaries, THS, the Willard Papers, T&P, and *CS*. On joint meetings at Cook's summer home, see Willard, "Four Halcyon Days at Cliff Seat," *US* 12 (2 September 1886): 4–5; T. P. Stevenson, "Editorial Correspondence," *CS* 23 (21 August 1890): 2–3. Various of the lobbyists also met at Ocean Grove and other summer campgrounds for Christians.

34. Joseph to Georgia H. Cook, 13 April 1884; Joseph to Georgia, 9 November 1885 ("great . . ."); Joseph to Georgia, 15 December 1886 ("bring . . ."); and Joseph to Georgia, 16 January, 15 May, and 30 November 1886, all in Letters Home, Cook Papers, THS.

35. *OD* 1 (January 1888); *OD* 2 (July 1888): 89; *OD* 8 (July 1891).

36. Diary, 8 March 1889; Joseph to Georgia Cook, 15 April 1892 and 27 November 1895, Letters Home, all in Cook Papers, THS; Daniel Weever to Cook, 20 October 1893, Cook Papers, Duke.

CHAPTER FIVE

1. Crafts, *Sabbath for Man*, 160 ("Holy . . ."); Crafts, "The Manifold Worth of the Sabbath," *OD* 8 (July 1891): 23 ("With . . .").

2. J. C. Bateham, "Wither Are We Drifting?" *CS* 20 (24 March 1887): 8; Rev. R. D. Harper, "The First Day of the Week," *CS* 20 (14 April 1887): 5–6; "Address of Rev. Wilbur F. Crafts on Sunday Papers," *CS* 26 (11 March 1893): 5 ("It is . . ."); Herrick Johnson, "Sunday Newspapers," *OD* 3 (February 1889): 116–17 ("that . . .").

3. Joseph Cook, "Sunday Newspapers," *Independent* 38 (25 February 1886): 6 ("One . . ."). For examples, see "The Sunday Newspaper," *CS* 20 (18 November 1886): 3; President Jeffers, "The Sabbath Mail Service," *CS* 15 (1 June 1882): 3–4; "Railroads and the Sabbath," *CS* 14 (11 August 1881): 581.

4. Crafts, "The Manifold Worth of the Sabbath," *OD* 8 (July 1891): 14 ("is . . ."); Crafts, "Transcontinental Notes on Sabbath Desecration," *OD* 6 (July 1890): 40 ("Strikes . . .").

5. B. W. Williams, "The Observance of the Sabbath," *US* 14 (12 July 1888): 2.

6. "A Glorious Triumph for the Sabbath" and "Public Morals," *CS* 9 (29 April 1876): 276–77; "The Sabbath and the Centennial Exhibition," *CS* 9 (8 July 1876): 349; "The First Battlefield," *Index* 7 (13 July 1876): 331; "The U.S. Centennial Commission and the Sun-

day Question," *Index* 7 (20 July 1876): 339–40; "Closing the Gates," ibid., 340–41 ("form . . ."). The commission refused to ban the sale of alcohol on the Centennial grounds, despite a request from the National Temperance Society to do so; see entries 30 November 1875 and 8 May 1876, "Board of Managers, Minutes, Nov. 14, 1865 to December 26, 1882," box 2, NTSPHR, DPH.

7. "Annual Meeting of the International Sabbath Association," *CS* 14 (19 May 1881): 438–39; "Petition against the Mail Service on the Sabbath," *CS* 13 (5 February 1880): 268; "The National Reform Association and the Sabbath," *CS* 13 (25 September 1879): 40; *CS* 17 (20 September 1883): 2; "Meeting of the Executive Committee," *CS* 18 (25 June 1885): 5; Crafts, "The Sabbath Question," *CS* 24 (2 October 1890): 5; *WCTU Minutes,* 1884, 42 and 61; "Mrs. Josephine Penfield Cusham Bateham," in Willard and Livermore, *American Women,* 1:62; *WCTU Minutes,* 1887, xxiv–xxv ("nerve . . ."); Mrs. Kate L. Shaw, "Work of the WCTU for Sabbath Reform," *CS* 23 (10 October 1889): 4.

8. "Closing Post-Offices on the Sabbath," *CS* 18 (29 January 1885): 2; "The National Reform Association and the Sabbath Mail Services," *CS* 18 (2 April 1885): 3; *WCTU Minutes,* 1885, xxv–xxvi; Mrs. J. C. Bateham, "Our Sabbath Observance Petition to Congress," *US* 13 (3 November 1887): 12; Crafts, *Sabbath for Man,* 566–67.

9. U.S. Senate, *Notes of a Hearing before the Committee on Education and Labor,* 2 ("Doubtless. . .").

10. Ibid.; "National Sabbath Reform," *OD* 1 (April 1888): 337 ("impurity. . ."). Crafts published this account of his testimony; it did not appear in the printed report.

11. "Since Our Last Issue," *US* 14 (3 May 1888): 1; S. 2983, *CR,* 50th Cong., 1st sess., 4455. Bill appears in U.S. Senate, *Sunday Rest Bill.*

12. "Editorial Notes," *OD* 2 (December 1888): 523–24; "American National Sabbath Reform: The Origin and Organization of the American Sabbath Union," *OD* 3 (January 1889): 44–54; *WCTU Minutes,* 1888, 62; "Public Morals—Sabbath Observance," *CS* 22 (13 September 1888): 4; Chamlee, "Sabbath Crusade," 265–67. On Shepard, see *National Cyclopedia of American Biography,* 1:159–60, and *CS* 26 (1 April 1893): 1.

13. U.S. Senate, *Sunday Rest Bill,* 22–23 ("to the principles . . ."), 31 ("sacred. . .").

14. Ibid., 82 ("theocratical . . .") and 24.

15. Ibid., 63–102 (77, "common . . ."; 101, "There is . . .").

16. *CR,* 50th Cong., 2d sess., 2640; Richardson, *Messages,* 9:29; "Wilbur F. Crafts to the Postmaster-General," *CS* 24 (12 March 1891): 3; *CR,* 51st Cong., 1st sess., 124. Wanamaker informed Crafts, who had written to complain that more local windows had not been closed, that many church members did not practice what they preached and apparently wanted to continue their Sunday mail service.

17. J. C. Bateham, "Sabbath Observance the Next Thing," *US* 17 (12 March 1891): 14.

18. *WCTU Minutes,* 1889, 24; "Shall the World's Fair Misrepresent American Institutions?" *CS* 23 (10 March 1890): 3; "The Outlook," *CS* 23 (14 August 1890): 1; "Memorial of the National Reform Association," *CS* 24 (18 September 1890): 7; untitled, *CS* 25 (6 February 1892): 9; James P. Mills, "Sabbath Reform Notes," *CS* 25 (22 October 1891): 6–7; R. C. Wylie, "The Columbian Exposition and the Sabbath," *CS* 25 (17 September 1891): 5–8. On Mills as NRA secretary, see "Proceedings of the Annual Meeting of the National Reform Association," *CS* 23 (10 April 1890): 2.

19. *WCTU Minutes*, 1891, 186−87, 18. Willard at first suggested a compromise in which the grounds would be open for Christian groups but the machinery of the fair closed on Sunday, but she later had to recant that position. On petitions, see Appendix 2, Tables A2.1a, A2.1b, A2.2a, A2.2b, A2.3, and A2.4.

20. See Appendix 2, Tables A2.1a, A2.1b, A2.2a, A2.2b, and A2.3.

21. Joseph to Georgia Cook, 10 January 1892, Letters, Cook Papers, THS; untitled, *CS* 25 (13 February 1892): 9; "Editorial Letter from Washington," *CS* 26 (21 January 1893): 8−9; "Sabbath Reform," *CS* 25 (2 April 1892): 1; untitled, *CS* 25 (16 April 1892): 5; "Sabbath Reform," *CS* 25 (9 July 1892): 1.

22. *CR*, 52d Cong., 1st sess., 4690, 5941, and 4716 ("been . . ."); Crafts, "Sabbath Closing of the World's Fair," *OD* 10 (October 1892): 701−8 ("cross . . .").

23. *CR*, 52d Cong., 1st sess., 6003−4.

24. Ibid., 6046−47.

25. Ibid., 6096−102; Crafts, "Sabbath Closing," 701−8; "Sabbath Closing of the World's Fair—The Greatest Moral Victory Since Emancipation," *CS* 25 (30 July 1892): 8; *CR*, 52d Cong., 1st sess., 5995 and 6039; V104, Senate, V201, House, 52d Cong., ICPSR.

A logistical regression analysis (described in Chapter 2, note 18) of the vote to concur with the Senate in closing the World's Fair on Sunday revealed a positive relationship with the dollar value of manufactured goods and an inverse relationship with the percentage of foreign born and blacks in the district. Although the percentage of southerners voting in favor of this measure exceeded that on previous votes on alcohol and polygamy, the inverse relationship between the percentage of blacks and the vote probably still reflects southern opposition. The statistical significance of all three factors disappears when each region is analyzed independently.

V201, House, 52d Cong., ICPSR: "To Concur with the Senate amendment making the federal contribution to financing the World's Fair dependent on its closing on Sunday" (n = 209): percentage foreign born: $B = -.0998$, Wald = 8.1209, Prob. values = .0044; percentage black: $B = -.0379$, Wald = 10.6599, Prob. values = .0011; total value of manufactured goods produced: $B = 3.21E-05$, Wald = 4.0094, Prob. values = .0452.

26. Crafts, "Editorial Notes," *OD* 9 (September 1892): 691; "Sabbath Closing at the World's Fair," *CS* 25 (13 August 1892): 3. A logistical regression analysis was run with the vote as the dependent variable and the following independent variables: number of petitions received, party, region (as defined throughout this study), and several demographic characteristics of the congressional districts (population density, the percentage of its population that was black, the percentage that was Catholic, the percentage that was foreign born, and the value of manufacturing). Only the number of petitions showed a strong positive relationship ($B = .1113$; Wald = 5.9810, and Prob. values = .0145; n = 209).

27. Crafts, "Editorial Notes," *OD* 11 (February 1893): 139−44; Crafts, *National Perils*, 142−44; "World's Fair," *CS* 26 (3 June 1893): 1; "Honor or Dishonor," *CS* 26 (3 June 1893): 8; untitled and "Sabbath Reform Work," *CS* 26 (20 May 1893): 1 and 4; Badger, *Great American Fair*, 93−94. Other aspects of the fair also upset the Christian lobbyists, especially obscene paintings in its exhibits, which the WCTU campaigned against, and dancers on its midway, some of whom Comstock arrested.

28. Crafts, "On to Victory," *CS* 26 (8 April 1893): 8 ("aggressive . . ."); H. H. George, "'Government of the People' Being Realized," *CS* 26 (18 March 1893): 4; Felix Brunot, "Call for a National Convention," *CS* 27 (28 October 1893): 4.

29. "Meeting of the Executive Committee," *CS* 24 (18 September 1890): 9; "The King's Daughters," *CS* 23 (17 April 1890): 7; William Weir, "Republican National Convention," *CS* 25 (25 June 1892): 5, "The Democratic National Convention," *CS* 25 (9 July 1892): 3, and "The People's Party Convention," *CS* 25 (30 July 1892): 2; J. M. Foster, "National Reform," *CS* 26 (19 August 1893): 3; H. H. George, "Washington Letter," *CS* 27 (3 February 1894): 4; Crafts, *Practical Christian Sociology*, 416; S. Res. 56 and H. Res. 120, *CR*, 53d Cong.

30. *Minutes of the Synod of the Reformed Presbyterian Church*, 1894, 238, RPTSL; J. M. Foster, "Christian Amendment to the U.S. Constitution," *CS* 27 (10 March 1894): 4; "On to Washington," *CS* 27 (10 March 1894): 8–9; William Weir, "From the West," *CS* 27 (17 March 1894): 4; letters in box 143, Hoar Papers, MHS; "Book Notices," *Our Day–Altruistic Review* 14 (April 1895): 212–13; Diary, 1 March 1894, Cook Papers, THS; "The Hearing at Washington," *CS* 27 (17 March 1894): 8–9; "Death of Justice William Strong," *CS* 29 (24 August 1895): 536; *Church of the Holy Trinity v. U.S.*, 143 U.S. 457 (1891).

31. "National Reform," *CS* 27 (7 April 1894): 1; 27 March 1894, Minutes, Committee on the Judiciary, 45, 53d Cong., RG 233, NA; "God in the Constitution," *Public Opinion* 17 (12 April 1894): 46–47; Cornelison, *Relation of Religion to Civil Government*, 232–33; Will C. Wood, "God in the Constitution," *OD* 12 (December 1893): 473–97.

32. "Meeting of the N.R. Executive Committee," *CS* 29 (5 October 1895): 629 ("We . . ."); S. Res. 28, H. Res. 28, and H. Res. 157, *CR*, 54th Cong.; "Petitions for the Christian Amendment," *CS* 30 (1 February 1896): 72–73; Charles Roads, "Christian Citizenship Work for Christian Endeavors," *CS* 30 (25 January 1896): 57; petitions listed in *CR* and found in Petitions and Memorials, Committee on the Judiciary (SEN54A-J19.2), RG 46, NA.

33. "The Hearing at Washington," *CS* 30 (14 March 1896): 168; "An Outsiders Impressions of the Hearing," *CS* 30 (4 April 1896): 217; *Hearing before the Committee of the Judiciary, House of Representatives, March 11, 1896, on H. Res. 28, Joint Resolution*, 8 ("It asks . . .").

34. T. P. Stevenson, "Report of the Hearing," *CS* 30 (21 March 1896): 184 ("wheeled . . ."); *Hearing . . . on H. Res. 28*, 27–38 ("harmony . . ."); "Action of the Judiciary Committee on the Amendment," *CS* 30 (21 March 1896): 184.

35. "Sabbath Closing of the World's Fair," *CS* 26 (22 October 1892): 3; Crafts, "Valedictory: Five Years of Sabbath Reform Campaigning," *CS* 27 (30 December 1893): 8–9; Crafts, "Practicable Sabbath Reform," *OD* 13 (November–December 1894): 520–24 (523, "to promote . . ."; 524, "watch-tower . . ."); "Circular Announcing the National Bureau of Reforms," frame 392, reel 21, WCTU Papers, T&P. Crafts was also inspired by Mary Hunt's efforts in behalf of scientific temperance education; see, "Mrs. Hunt as a Christian Lobbyist," *CS* 26 (17 June 1893): 8–9. Account of Crafts's life based on his writings; a few personal references in the Crafts Notebooks, BHL; Joseph Cook's introduction to Crafts, *Practical Christian Sociology*; and Lender, *Temperance Biography*, 112–13.

36. Crafts, *Practical Christian Sociology* 16 ("parts . . ."), 23 ("heart . . ."), 28 ("*Kingship* . . ."), 31 ("New Jerusalem . . .").

37. Crafts, *Practical Christian Sociology*, 25 ("unwarranted . . ."); Crafts, *Patriotic Studies*, 62 ("'Big Four' . . .").

38. Ibid., 62. Budget and observations on sources of funds based on an analysis of Cashbooks, International Reform Federation Collection, BHL.

39. Crafts, *Patriotic Studies of a Quarter Century*, 52–53; U.S. Senate, *Moral Legislation in Congress*; International Reform Federation Collection, BHL.

40. *WCTU Minutes*, 1897, 155 ("admirable . . ."); *WCTU Minutes*, 1895, 53; 1897, 26; 1898, 42 and 57; 1899, 47; 1900, 39; 1902, 71. In 1910, Crafts was made a life member of the WCTU; see *WCTU Minutes*, 1910, 54. On Ellis's background, see Gordon, *Women Torch-Bearers*, 103–6; obituary, *Newark Evening News*, 13 July 1925, 6; and Elizabeth P. Gordon, "A Week in Washington," *US* 28 (24 April 1902): 5.

41. Gordon, "Week in Washington"; Elizabeth P. Gordon, "An Interview with Mrs. Margaret Dye Ellis," *US* 29 (22 January 1903): 5; Ellis, "Our Washington Letter," *US* 31 (4 May 1905): 2; Gordon, *Women Torch-Bearers*, 127.

42. Thompson, "*Spider Web*"; Clemens, *People's Lobby*.

43. Rodgers, *Contested Truths*, 201. Rodgers observes that public hearings were unusual in the nineteenth century; if that were the case, the Christian lobbyists pioneered the use of this forum. Number of appearances based on listings in Index to Personal Names, *CIS U.S. Congressional Committees Hearing Index*; Crafts claimed more.

44. Crafts, "Our Day in Review: The March of Progress and Reform," *OD* 16 (April 1896): 181.

45. McAllister, *National Reform Movement*; Crafts, "Reform Bureau's Calendar of Reform Bills in Congress . . . ," *US* 23 (7 January 1897): 8–9; Crafts, "Petition Victories," *US* 24 (17 November 1898): 5; Ellis, "The Battle Is on at Washington," *US* 29 (15 January 1903): 2; "Our Washington Letter," *US* 42 (16 March 1916): 2. For examples of letters to congressmen, see Ellen R. Richardson to Gallinger, 22 September 1904, folder 7, box 2, Gallinger Papers, NHHS; Elizabeth Moore to Simmons, 19 January 1910, Simmons Papers, Duke; Annie K. Weisel to Bankhead, 9 January 1912, folder 5, box 40, Bankhead Papers, ADAH. For examples of WCTU-ers gathering signatures, see Margaret Dye Ellis, "Our Washington Letter," *US* 38 (18 April 1912): 2; Eva Dawson to Willard, 2 December 1891, frame 669, reel 17, WCTU Papers, T&P. On Ellis's role in general, see *WCTU Minutes*, 1914, 313, and Boole, interview, 17–18.

46. "The Christian Endeavor Pledge of Good Citizenship," *US* 20 (16 August 1894): 9; Charles Roads, "Christian Endeavor in Christian Citizenship," *CS* 30 (25 July 1896): 467; Anderson, interview, 130–32.

CHAPTER SIX

1. Ezell, *Fortune's Merry Wheel*. For another study of attitudes toward gambling, see Fabian, *Card Sharps*.

2. Ezell, *Fortune's Merry Wheel*. 235, 237–38; *CG*, 40th Cong., 2d sess., 4412 and appendix, 552 ("any . . ."").

3. H.R. 1239 and H.R. 2575, *CR*, 44th Cong.; *CR*, 44th Cong., 1st sess., 4263 ("if it . . ."); *Ex parte Jackson*, 96 U.S. 727 (1877) ("to determine. . .").

4. Ezell, *Fortune's Merry Wheel*, 242–70; Alwes, "History of the Louisiana State Lottery Company"; Hair, *Bourbonism and Agrarian Protest*.

5. McDaniel, "Frances Tillou Nicholls," 491; "Lottery Correspondence Suppressed in

the Mails," *CS* 16 (19 July 1883): 2; Gresham to W. P. Fishback, 2 November 1883, book 45, Gresham Papers, LC; Comstock, *Frauds Exposed*, 324–87; Comstock to David B. Parker, 10 December 1879, and David M. Key to H. D. Money, 14 January 1880, both in Petitions and Memorials, Committee on the Post Office (HR46A-F26.8), RG 233, NA.

6. H.R. 4000, *CR*, 46th Cong.; V180, House, 46th Cong., 2d sess., ICPSR; S. 1047, *CR*, 47th Cong.

7. H.R. 7563, *CR*, 47th Cong.; *CR*, 47th Cong., 2d sess., appendix, 84–90 (90, "poisonous . . ."); S. 1018, *CR*, 48th Cong.; V191, Senate, 48th Cong., ICPSR; S. 260, *CR*, 49th Cong.; V446, Senate, 49th Cong., ICPSR; U.S. House Committee on Post Offices and Post Roads, *Delivery of Registered Letters*, pt. 2 ("Postmaster-General . . ."). The vote occurred in 1887 during the same Congress that passed the antipolygamy Edmunds-Tucker Act. Of the fourteen southern senators who participated in both votes, eleven voted consistently. Four opposed both expansions of federal power over morality; seven supported them.

8. U.S. House Committee on the District of Columbia, *To Punish the Selling and Advertising of Lottery Tickets*; U.S. House Committee on Post Offices and Post Roads, *Lottery, Gift-Enterprise* and *Selling and Advertising Lottery Tickets*; H.R. 5933, *CR*, 50th Cong.; V41, House, 50th Cong., ICPSR.

9. Carradine, *Louisiana State Lottery*, 4 ("one . . ."), 6 ("arouse . . .").

10. Ibid., 19 ("*spirit* . . ."), 7 ("free . . ."), 33 ("few masters . . .").

11. "The Anti-Lottery League of Louisiana," filed with Charles Parlange to Benjamin Harrison, 14 May 1890, reel 27, Harrison Papers, LC.

12. Thomas Johnson, *Life and Letters of Benjamin Morgan Palmer*, 561.

13. "Appeal to the Nation," *New Delta*, 27 May 1890, 2; Parlange to Harrison, 14 May 1890, reel 27, Harrison Papers, LC. On Johnston, see Owen, *History of Alabama*, 3:916–17. This and other biographical sketches ignore his work against the lottery.

14. Comstock, "The Louisiana Lottery a National Scourge," *OD* 4 (November 1889): 436–42; *WCTU Minutes*, 1889, 153–54; Richardson, *Messages*, 9:44.

15. Richardson, *Messages*, 9:80–81; "The Louisiana Lottery," *Public Opinion* 9 (9 August 1890): 405–8; H.R. 11569, *CR*, 51st Cong.; U.S. House Committee on Post Offices and Post Roads, *Certain Sections of the Revised Statutes Relating to Lotteries*; Cushing, *Story of Our Post Office*, 522–62.

16. U.S. Senate, *In the Senate of the United States: Memorial of Members of the Presbyterian Clergy of New Orleans*; *CR*, 51st Cong., 2d sess., 706, 754, 798, 935, 1121, 2116; U.S. Senate, *In the Senate of the United States: Mr. Stewart Submitted*; S. Res. 85, *CR*, 51st Cong.

17. *In re Rapier*, 143 U.S. 110 (1892).

18. *CR*, 53d Cong., 3d sess., 12, 479, 556, 1884, 1899, 1933–34, 1975–78, 2154–56, 3142–43.

19. *WCTU Minutes*, 1891, 64; "Anti-Lottery Meeting in New York," *CS* 25 (19 November 1891): 4; Ezell, *Fortune's Merry Wheel*, 259; Farish, *Circuit Rider Dismounts*, 357–60; "Since Our Last Issue," *US* 20 (2 August 1894): 1; "Gambling," *CS* 29 (27 April 1895): 258; W. F. C., "Editorial Notes," *Our Day–The Altruistic Review* 14 (April 1895): 214.

20. *Crafts*, "Fraternity of Reforms, III," *US* 21 (24 January 1895): 3; Woodbridge, "Anti-Lottery Campaign," LSU; Diary, 27 January 1892, Cook Papers, THS; "New England Reformers," *CS* 25 (13 February 1892): 4.

21. Woodbridge, "Anti-Lottery Campaign," LSU; Mary Caswell to Hoar, 11 April 1894, and Woodbridge to Hoar, 22 May 1894, both in Correspondence, box 145, Hoar Papers, MHS; S. 1620, *CR*, 53d Cong.

22. *Lottery Cases*, 188 U.S. 321 (1903).

23. Tyrrell, "Drink and Temperance in the Antebellum South"; Bardaglio, *Reconstructing the Household*; William Link, *Paradox of Southern Progressivism*; Ownby, *Subduing Satan*. For an example of praise of the South by Henry Blair, see *CR*, 51st Cong., 1st sess., 1546.

24. Sechrist, "Comparative Analysis of Multi-Dimensional Diffusion Models." For examples of individuals who linked racism and the need for legal restrictions on alcohol, see *WCTU Minutes*, 1881, 25–26, and Scomp, *King Alcohol*, 719. On racist hysteria, see Williamson, *Crucible of Race*, and Litwack, *Trouble in Mind*, 197–216.

25. Southerners overwhelmingly entered bills to control alcohol; but so did representatives from every region (see Appendix 1, Table A1.5). Therefore I looked for types of legislation where southerners entered a higher or lower percentage of the bills introduced than the percentage of total bills entered by southerners (roughly 23 percent). Figures for the types of legislation mentioned in the paragraph are in Appendix 1, Table A1.4. On patterns of petitions, see Appendix 2, Table A2.1b. In the five petition campaigns studied, the South had its highest percentage of participation in those for closing the World's Fair on Sunday and for prohibition. See also Appendix 2, Table A2.6b, for a breakdown of southern petitions within one campaign.

CHAPTER SEVEN

1. *CR*, 55th Cong., 2d sess., 44.

2. For statistics, see Appendix 2, Tables A2.1, A2.5, and A2.6. In large part because so few petitions came from the southern and border states, petitions went overwhelmingly to Republican districts.

3. Wilbur Crafts, "Our Day in Review: The March of Progress and Reform," *OD* 16 (April 1896): 184 ("chief . . ."); H.R. 1294, *CR*, 47th Cong.; H.R. 4964, *CR*, 50th Cong.; S. 5100, *CR*, 51st Cong.; Crafts, *Patriotic Studies*, 258–65; H.R. 10355, *CR*, 54th Cong.; "To Suppress Interstate Gambling by Telegraph," *CS* 30 (29 February 1896): 137; *WCTU Minutes*, 1897, 469; U.S. House Committee on Interstate Commerce, *Interstate Gambling*, 16 December 1898, 44, Minutes of the Committee on the Judiciary, 55th Cong., RG 233, NA; S. 2844 and H.R. 10853, *CR*, 59th Cong.; H.R. 4063, *CR*, 60th Cong.; *Prevention of Transmission of Race-Gambling Bets, Hearings* (this document has record of several hearings); U.S. House Committee on Interstate and Foreign Commerce, *Interstate Transmission of Race-Gambling Bets*.

4. Ida Hinman, "Washington Letter," *CS* 27 (21 April 1894): 3; *WCTU Minutes*, 1894, 374; Wilbur Crafts, "Our Day in Review: The March of Progress and Reform," *OD* 16 (June 1896): 303.

5. Crafts to Dike, 1 January 1896, and clipping from *Capital News* filed with it, Dike Papers, LC; Josephine C. Bateham, "Department Sabbath Observance," *US* 22 (23 January 1896): 12; petitions and letters from Crafts to committee chair in boxes 166–68 (HR55A-H4.5), RG 233, NA; H.R. 11819, *CR*, 58th Cong.; H.R. 16556, *CR*, 59th Cong.;

S. 3940 and H.R. 4929, *CR*, 60th Cong.; S. 404 and H.R. 14619, *CR*, 61st Cong.; S. 237 and H.R. 14690, *CR*, 62d Cong.

6. *CR*, 61st Cong., 2d sess., 1013; *CR*, 62d Cong., 1st sess., 1013, 1599.

7. "The Struggle to Maintain the Sabbath," *CS* 44 (April 1910): 98.

8. Crafts, "Our Day in Review: The March of Progress and Reform," *OD* 16 (June 1896): 302; *WCTU Minutes*, 1897, 53; U.S. Senate, *Moral Legislation in Congress*; Ellis, "Our Washington Letter," *US* 31 (6 April 1905): 2; U.S. Senate Committee on Post Offices and Post Roads, *Handling Money Orders*; "Movement among Postal Employees for Sabbath Rest," *CS* 45 (May 1911): 135–36; *WCTU Minutes*, 1911, 327–28; *CR*, 61st Cong., 2d sess., 2527; U.S. Senate Committee on Post Offices and Post Roads, *Post Office Appropriation Bill*, 23; typed note, case file 490, reel 280, Wilson Papers, LC.

9. Hardy, *Solemn Covenant*, 244–50; Bitton, "B. H. Roberts Case."

10. Wilbur Crafts, "Brief of the Case against Brigham H. Roberts," *US* 25 (12 January 1899): 5 ("confessed . . ."); *WCTU Minutes*, 1899, 97.

11. *CR*, 56th Cong., 1st sess., 1175–77; U.S. House Special Committee, *Case of Brigham H. Roberts*; V20 and V21, House, 56th Cong., ICPSR.

12. H. Res. 354, *CR*, 55th Cong.; Cannon and O'Higgins, *Under the Prophet*, 236–38; petitions in HR56A-H13.4, boxes 94 and 95, RG 233, NA. In fact, Cannon may have had this amendment in mind; there were resolutions entered for a marriage and divorce amendment, but they were not being as hotly debated at the time. Judging the reliability of Cannon's charge is difficult, but scholars have come to credit his book as a whole with greater authority than it once had.

13. Ellis, "Our Washington Letter," *US* 30 (28 April 1904): 2; "Our Washington Letter," *US* 29 (31 March 1904): 2 ("individual . . ." and "occupying . . ."); "The Real Smoot Question," *US* 30 (12 May 1904): 4 ("sworn . . ."); "The Case of Senator Smoot," *US* 29 (31 December 1903): 1 ("system . . ."); *WCTU Minutes*, 1904, 94 and 316–17.

14. Hardy, *Solemn Covenant*, 250–67. Hardy acknowledges the role of the WCTU but gives primary credit to other lobbying groups.

15. Cannon and O'Higgins, *Under the Prophet*, 261–93; N. H. Davis to Joseph Tumulty, 3 September 1919, case file 118, reel 219, Wilson Papers, LC; Ellis, "Our Washington Letter," *US* 30 (12 May 1904): 2; 32 (24 May 1906): 2; and 33 (28 February 1907): 2; Roosevelt to John F. Dobbs, 3 October 1904, in Morison, *Letters of Theodore Roosevelt*, 4:967–68 and 7:222–26; U.S. Senate Committee on Privileges and Elections, *Reed Smoot*.

16. *CR*, 59th Cong., 2d sess., 2936 ("grow . . .") and 2938 ("to God . . .").

17. V118, Senate, 59th Cong., ICPSR.

18. Willard, *Glimpses of Fifty Years*, 611 ("mutual . . ."); "A White Life for Two," in Leeman, "*Do Everything*" *Reform*, 159–71; Livermore, *Story of My Life*, 675–76; *WCTU Minutes*, 1904, 87; "The Marriage Question," *US* 21 (16 May 1895): 8. Partly that was their choice, but in some cases the groups working on divorce reform excluded women's participation, over the protest of the WCTU; see, Rachel F. Avery to Robert C. Ogden, 25 July 1892, Dike Papers, LC.

19. Samuel Dike, "The Future of the Divorce Problem," 27 October 1911, box 19, Dike Papers, LC; "Proceedings of the Annual Meeting of the National Reform Association,"

CS 23 (10 April 1890): 8–9; Samuel W. Dike, "Correspondence," *CS* 23 (5 June 1890): 3; "Divorce Reform," *CS* 30 (29 February 1896): 133.

20. *Report of the National Divorce Reform League*, 1892, 11, box 23, Dike Papers, LC ("parties . . ."); S. Res. 29, H. Res. 23, and H. Res. 46, *CR*, 52d Cong.; T. P. Stevenson to Harrison, 30 November 1892, reel 38, Harrison Papers, LC; U.S. House Committee on the Judiciary, *Marriage and Divorce*, 2 ("who . . ."); "Progress of National Divorce Reform," *OD* 11 (March 1893): 173–81.

21. Crafts, "Marriage and Divorce," *US* 23 (June 3, 1897): 4 ("drunkenness . . ."); Crafts to Dike, 1 January 1896 and 10 February 1896, Dike Papers, LC.

22. Crafts, *Patriotic Studies of a Quarter Century*, 1910, 89; Gillett to Crafts, 7 February 1896, Dike Papers, LC; *Report of National Divorce League*, 1896, 7–8, box 23, ibid.; "Divorce Reform," *CS* 30 (22 February 1896): 116; H.R. 5217, *CR*, 54th Cong.; Crafts, "Our Day in Review," *OD* 16 (June 1896): 303.

23. S. 1514, *CR*, 54th Cong.; Gillett to Dike, 1 February 1896, Crafts to Dike, 28 February 1896, and Crafts to Dike, 19 January 1900, all in Dike Papers, LC; Crafts to George W. Ray, 7 April 1900 (HR56A-H13.4), box 95, RG 233, NA; H.R. 9835, *CR*, 56th Cong.

24. *Documents of the Interchurch Conference on Marriage and Divorce*, pamphlet in DPH; W. Lawrence to Dike, 17 October 1903, Dike Papers, LC; Dike to Taft, 21 June 1905, reel 51, Taft Papers, LC; H. H. George, "A Visit to Washington," *CS* 41 (March 1907): 82–83.

25. On the larger movement, see Pivar, *Purity Crusade*.

26. *WCTU Minutes*, 1883, 32; 1885, 73–74; 1891, 127–30 and 134–35; "Social Purity," 30 January 1887, in box of Leaflets and Timely Talks, FEWL; "A White Life for Two," in Slagell, "A Good Woman Speaking Well," 575–88; *WCTU Minutes*, 1892, 128 ("above . . .").

27. Crafts, "Purity," *US* 23 (15 July 1897): 4–5 ("this . . ."); "Woman's Christian Temperance Union Notes," *CS* 19 (28 January 1886): 3; Cook, "Low Morals in High Places," *Independent* 38 (18 March 1886): 5–6.

28. "District of Columbia," *US* 18 (27 October 1892): 11; "Since Our Last Issue," *US* 18 (31 March 1892): 1; Emilie D. Martin, "Work for the Promotion of Purity in Literature and Art," *CS* 26 (20 May 1893): 2; *WCTU Minutes*, 1894, 444–46; U.S. Senate Committee on Post Offices and Post Roads, *Report to Accompany S. 2834*; U.S. Senate, *Moral Legislation in Congress*, 12; S. 3380, *CR*, 58th Cong.

29. Crafts, "Our Day in Review," *OD* 16 (July 1896): 361–62; *WCTU Minutes*, 1897, 444–45; S. 1675, *CR*, 54th Cong.; H.R. 9493, *CR*, 58th Cong.; *CR*, 54th Cong., 1st sess., 2322 ("with . . ."). Seven years later, Congress extended the law on interstate shipment to include the nation's new territorial acquisitions.

30. Willard, "Social Purity Work for 1887," *US* 13 (13 January 1887): 12. On the use of age-of-consent laws, see Odem, *Delinquent Daughters*.

31. *WCTU Minutes*, 1887, 90; 1888, 35 and 136–46; Ada M. Bittenbender, "Letter from the National Superintendent of the Department of Legislation and Petitions," *US* 14 (8 March 1888): 5; petitions (HR50A-H13.5), box 147, RG 233, NA; H.R. 5870, *CR*, 50th Cong.; Bittenbender, "The 'Protection Bill,' Passes Congress," *US* 15 (14 February 1889): 4–5; *WCTU Minutes*, 1889, cclxiii; "Age of Consent," *US* 22 (16 January 1896): 9; JWL, untitled, *CS* 30 (8 February 1896): 89; "The Age of Protection Bill," *US* 23 (25 February 1897): 9; untitled, *CS* 31 (27 February 1897): 68; Crafts, "Our Day in Review," *OD* 16 (May

1896): 244–45; "District of Columbia," *US* 23 (25 February 1897): 11; letters in "Age of Consent for Girls in D.C." (HR54A-F21.2), box 114, RG 233, NA; U.S. House Committee on the District of Columbia, *Age of Protection*, 1 ("of previous . . ."); S. 2880 and H.R. 1136, *CR*, 55th Cong.; "Notes and Comments," *US* 24 (7 April 1898): 1.

32. Bochnowski, "Muckraker Crusade against White Slavery"; Grittner, *White Slavery*.

33. Ellis, "The Battle Is on at Washington," *US* 29 (15 January 1903): 2; "Our Letter from Washington," *US* 29 (14 January 1904): 3; Ellis, "Our Washington Letter," *US* 35 (16 December 1909): 2; 36 (10 February 1910): 3; 36 (26 May 1910): 1; "Editorial Articles," *CS* 44 (March 1910): 7. On activities of others in passing the bill, see Grittner, *White Slavery*, and Langum, *Crossing over the Line*.

34. U.S. Senate Committee on Immigration, *White-Slave Traffic*, 1.

35. Ibid; H.R. 12315, *CR*, 61st Cong.

36. *CR*, 61st Cong., 2d sess., 810–11.

37. Ibid., 1038, 811, 820–21 ("More . . .").

38. U.S. Senate, *White-Slavery Traffic*, 4; *CR*, 61st Cong., 2d sess., 809. Langum, *Crossing the Line*, traces the history of this controversy and enforcement in general.

39. Langum, *Crossing the Line*, 70–71 ("whether. . ."). The Mann Act was originally upheld in *Hoke v. United States*, 222 U.S. 308 (1913); *Athanasaw v. United States*, 227 U.S. 326 (1913), extended its enforcement to noncommercial sex. For more on these and other cases, see Langum, *Crossing over the Line*.

40. S. 2754 and S. 3044, *CR*, 49th Cong.; S. 375, *CR*, 50th Cong.; S. 947, *CR*, 51st Cong.; S. 470, *CR*, 55th Cong.; Crafts, *Patriotic Studies of a Quarter Century*, 29–30, 72–78, 88; Crafts, *Patriotic Studies*, 204, 234–35, and 237–46. Unless otherwise cited, much of the account that follows relies on Musto, *American Disease*, 1–90, and Courtwright, *Dark Paradise*. Crafts and the others had also conducted hearings on opium at the State Department in 1902 in a failed effort to add it to the law that banned the sale of alcohol in the Pacific Islands.

41. H.R. 1966, 1967, and 6282, *CR*, 63d Cong.; Musto, *American Disease*, 93; *Webb et al. v. U.S.*, 249 U.S. 96 (1919). In regulating drugs, Congress used the power of taxation, a different approach from that of earlier moral legislation. The Christian lobbyists' efforts, however, had played an indirect role. Musto, *American Disease*, 9, credits antilottery legislation, the Mann Act, and the Webb-Kenyon Act with helping to make federal regulation of narcotics possible and argues that the Supreme Court's broad interpretation of narcotics laws in 1919 may have been influenced by the passage of the prohibition amendment.

42. On the history of cigarettes, see Sobel, *They Satisfy*, and Tate, *Cigarette Wars*.

43. "Cigarette Smoking," *US* 17 (25 June 1891): 7 ("Cigarettes . . ."); "An Anti-Tobacco Symposium," *CS* 37 (August 1903): 247–49; *WCTU Minutes*, 1885, cxxviii ("fatal . . ."); Frank L. Templin, "Is the Use of Tobacco a Sin?" *US* 34 (22 October 1908): 5 ("'cleanse' . . .").

44. "Questions to Specialists," *OD* 5 (January 1890): 59–65; "Good Resolutions for 1903," sermon in folder 2-4, Mayhew Papers, DPH ("'don't smoke'"); Ira Gale Tompkins, "Tobacco and the Christian," *US* 18 (1 December 1892): 3 ("not directly . . ."); untitled, *CS* 25 (20 February 1892): 9 ("injures . . .").

45. *WCTU Minutes*, 1877, 176; 1878, 40; 1881, 37; 1884, v–vii; Lydia H. Tilton, "Impor-

tant Work at Washington," *US* 14 (17 May 1888): 5; Emma F. Shelton, "Anti-Tobacco Legislation in Congress," *US* 17 (5 February 1891): 5; Ida Hinman, "District of Columbia: The Cigarette Bill," *US* 17 (19 March 1891): 10; S. 4560, S. 4413, and H.R. 12442, *CR*, 51st Cong.

46. *WCTU Minutes*, 1890, 181; L. C. Kessler, "District of Columbia," *US* 18 (27 October 1892): 11; U.S. Senate Committee on Epidemic Diseases, *Report to Accompany Petition of M. C. Dean*, 5050–51. On Ingalls, see Willard and Livermore, *American Women*, 1:410.

47. H.R. 4057, *CR*, 54th Cong.; U.S. House Committee on the Judiciary, *Sale of Cigarettes*; *WCTU Minutes*, 1898, 246 and 360. Petitions are listed in *CR* during both 54th and 55th Congresses, with originals in boxes 228 and 229, Petitions and Memorials, Committee on the Judiciary (HR55A-H12.9), RG 233, NA.

48. On Gaston and continuing crusade, see Sobel, *They Satisfy*, and Tate, *Cigarette Wars*.

49. Wayland Hoyt, "Newspaper Apologies for Pugilism," *OD* 11 (June 1893): 432 ("glorification . . ."); "Editorial Notes," *CS* 28 (1 December 1894): 3; "Prize Fight Moving Pictures," *US* 36 (21 July 1910): 8. The account of the history of boxing relies on Gorn, *Manly Art*, and Sammons, *Beyond the Ring*.

50. S. 590, *CR*, 41st Cong.; H.R. 5566, *CR*, 54th Cong.; Wilbur F. Crafts, "The Month in Review: The March of Progress and Reform," *OD* 16 (March 1896): 121–22 ("rare . . .").

51. Crafts, *National Perils*, 42–48; U.S. House Committee on Interstate and Foreign Commerce, *Transmission by Mail . . . of Any Description of Prize Fights* ("have been . . ."); *CR*, 54th Cong., 2d sess., 2588 ("censorship . . ."); H.R. 1598 and S. 1187, *CR*, 55th Cong. On petitions, see Appendix 2, Table A2.6.

52. *Hearings before the Committee on Interstate and Foreign Commerce*, esp. 9; Ellis, "Our Washington Letter," 36 (19 May 1910): 1; *WCTU Minutes*, 1910, 346; untitled, *CS* 44 (August 1910): 230. On the fight and its aftermath, see Roberts, *Papa Jack*, 108–13.

53. "Executive Committee Meeting," *CS* 46 (April 1912): 121; Ellis, "Our Washington Letter," *US* 38 (6 June 1912): 3, 12; *WCTU Minutes*, 1912, 348; Ellis, "Our Washington Letter," *US* 38 (13 June 1912): 2 ("films . . ."); Ellis, "Our Washington Letter," *US* 38 (4 July 1912): 2; S. 7027, *CR*, 62d Cong.

54. *CR*, 62d Cong., 2d sess., 9305–6.

55. Lary May, *Screening out the Past*; Couvares, "Hollywood, Mainstreet, and the Church"; "Papers relating to the formation and subsequent history of the National Board of Review, 1916–1951," box 170, and unidentified speech, 1913, in "Papers relating to the formation and subsequent history of the National Board of Review, 1908–1915," box 170 ("moral standards . . ."), both in Records of the National Board of Review, NYPL.

56. S. 7191, *CR*, 61st Cong.; S. 2600, *CR*, 62d Cong.; *CR*, 62d Cong., 3d sess., 2897–98; *CR*, 63d Cong., 1st sess., 4605.

57. Crafts to Cora F. Stoddard, 9 September 1915, box 4, STFP, NYPL ("adequately . . ."); *Federal Motion Picture Commission: Hearings*, 77 ("devil . . ."); Crafts, *Patriotic Studies of a Quarter Century*, 60; Crafts, *National Perils*, 34; Ellis, "Our Washington Letter," *US* 40 (26 March 1914): 2.

58. U.S. House Committee on Education, *Federal Motion Picture Commission*, 1915,

explains the provisions of the bill. Crafts's campaign in Georgia is mentioned in Feld-man, *National Board of Censorship*, 67.

59. *Motion Picture Commission: Hearings*; Harriet S. Pritchard, "A Federal Motion Picture Commission," *US* 40 (21 May 1914): 10; Ellis, "Our Washington Letter," *US* 40 (1 October 1914): 9.

60. U.S. House Committee on Education, *Federal Motion Picture Commission*, 1915 ("necessity . . ."); Ellis, "Work for Smith Hughes Film Censorship Bill" ("expected . . .") and "Our Washington Letter," *US* 41 (25 February 1915): 2; Feldman, *National Board of Censorship*, 91; *Mutual Film Corporation v. Industrial Commission of Ohio*, 236 U.S. 230 (1915); *Mutual Film Corporation of Missouri v. George H. Hodges*, 236 U.S. 248 (1915); *Weber v. Freed*, 239 U.S. 325 (1915).

61. Hughes to Henrietta, 21 January 1916, folder 2, box 4, series 1, Hughes Papers, RRL ("Our Picture . . ."); "Facts and Comments," *Moving Picture World* 27 (22 January 1916): 563; W. Stephen Bush, "Film Hosts in Battle Array," ibid., 566–69; U.S. House Commit-tee on Education, *Federal Motion Picture Commission*, 1916; "Mutual Fights Federal Censor Bill," clipping, *Reel*, 22 January 1916, in folder 2, box 3, Hughes Papers, RRL; Ellis, "Our Washington Letter," *US* 42 (27 January 1916): 2 ("Mothers' night . . ."). Efforts of the New York Board can be followed in "Federal Censorship" file, box 25, Records of the National Board of Review, NYPL.

62. *Motion Picture Commission: Hearings*, 21 ("personal . . ."); *Federal Motion Picture Commission: Hearings*, 167 ("influence . . .").

63. *Federal Motion Picture Commission: Hearings*, 169. See also 170 and 67.

64. U.S. House Committee on Education, *Federal Motion Picture Commission*, 1916, pt. 1, 1 ("earnest . . ."); pt. 2. One member from Kentucky did side with the minority; see W. Stephen Bush, "Our Friends and Our Foes," *Moving Picture World* 30 (14 October 1916): 210.

65. "Facts and Comments," *Moving Picture World* 20 (9 May 1914): 791; "Facts and Comments," ibid., 27 (22 January 1916): 563; "Film Men Firm against Censorship," ibid., 30 (7 October 1916): 51; J. W. Bender to Wilson, 11 August 1916, Crafts to Wilson, 25 Jan-uary 1916, Memo, Wilson to Joseph Tumulty, 17 August 1916, and others letters in case file 541, reel 285, Wilson Papers, LC; *New York Times*, 4 October 1916, 1; "Facts and Com-ments," *Moving Picture World* 30 (14 October 1916): 207; "Facts and Comments," ibid., 30 (7 October 1916): 47.

66. H.R. 14077, *CR*, 65th Cong.; H.R. 7629, *CR*, 66th Cong.; "Censor Bills in Con-gress," *Moving Picture World* 28 (1 April 1916): 57–58; *Prohibiting Shipment of Certain Motion-Picture Films: Hearing*.

67. H.J. Res. 221 and 22, *CR*, 64th Cong.; *Federal Motion Picture Commission: Hear-ings*, 90, 99–101.

68. *Federal Motion Picture Commission: Hearings*, 123–25, 236, and 253–55. See also "Memorandum in Opposition to House Bill No. 456," in "Federal Censorship" file, box 25, Records of the National Board of Review, NYPL, and *CR*, 64th Cong., 1st sess., 1184.

CHAPTER EIGHT

1. There are three excellent syntheses of the temperance crusade: Clark, *Deliver Us from Evil*; Blocker, *American Temperance Movements*; and Pegram, *Battling Demon Rum*. On efforts in Congress, Hamm, *Shaping the Eighteenth Amendment*, is indispensable, but Timberlake, *Prohibition and the Progressive Movement*, is also very good.

2. "Only One Remedy," *US* 11 (8 January 1885): 2. See also "The Scriptures vs. The Liquor Traffic," *Anti-Saloon League Year Book*, 1911, 24–26.

3. Cartoon, *US* 38 (22 August 1912): 1; M. B. Fuller, "The Saloon and National Problems," *US* 41 (19 August 1915): 2 ("accentuates . . .").

4. "Saloons and Slaves," *AI* 20 (June 1912): 1. For examples of King Alcohol, see "Editorial Notes," *OD* 4 (August 1889): 191, and F. O. Blair, "The New Declaration of Independence," *US* 13 (23 June 1887): 7.

5. S. Res. 2, *CR*, 51st Cong.; Ada Bittenbender, "National Interstate Prohibition," *US* 16 (16 October 1890): 4–5 ("importation . . ."); S. 4389, *CR*, 51st Cong.; U.S. Senate Committee on the District of Columbia, *Memorial of the Officers of the Woman's Christian Temperance Union*.

6. Hamm, *Shaping the Eighteenth Amendment*, 56–91; U.S. House Committee on the Judiciary, *Regulation of Commerce*; S. 389, *CR*, 51st Cong.; Sarah A. M'Clees, "Legislation against the Canteen in the Year 1890," *US* 26 (22 February 1900): 4; *WCTU Minutes*, 1890, 189–93; *CR*, 51st Cong., 1st sess., 2821, 2864, 4381–82, and 5477; Ida Hinman, "Washington Letter," *CS* 29 (6 April 1895): 215; U.S. House, *Economic Aspects of the Liquor Problem*. Hamm's book has an excellent discussion of *Leisy v. Hardin*, the Wilson Law, other cases referred to here, as well as later cases on the issue of interstate shipment of alcohol; it renders any case-by-case summary here unnecessary.

7. H.R. 280, *CR*, 54th Cong.; Crafts, *Patriotic Studies of a Quarter Century*, 17–18; U.S. Senate, *Letter from the Secretary of the Interior*.

8. Gordon, *Women Torch-Bearers*, 106–7; *WCTU Minutes*, 1895, 157; 1897, 89; Crafts to Mrs. Hunt, 7 February 1897, folder 11, box 1, reel 2, STFP, T&P; Margaret Dye Ellis, "A Glimpse of Work in Washington," *US* 23 (4 February 1897): 4; H.R. 7083, *CR*, 54th Cong.; "Notes and Comment," *US* 24 (6 January 1898): 1; "Agitation in Washington," *US* 24 (20 January 1898): 2; "An Impetus to Petition Work," *US* 24 (27 January 1898): 2.

9. Ellis to Willard, 19 January 1898, frames 351–55, reel 25, WCTU Papers, T&P; U.S. House Committee on Alcoholic Liquor Traffic, *Sale of Intoxicating Liquors*.

10. *WCTU Minutes*, 1898, 359–61; 1899, 289–90; Ellis, "Army Bill Passed," *US* 25 (9 March 1899): 2; Ellis, "Recent Legislation of Interest to 'White Ribboners' and Others," 17 March 1899, folder 7, box 1, reel 1, STFP, T&P; "Notes and Comments," *US* 25 (30 March 1899): 1; *CR*, 55th Cong., 3d sess., 1315–18.

11. "Beer in Army," *US* 25 (13 April 1899): 2; "Dr. Crafts Replies to Secretary Alger," *US* 25 (15 June 1899): 2; "Notes and Comments," *US* 26 (15 February 1900): 1; "Mrs. Ellis Replies to Attorney-General's Charge of 'False Statement,'" *US* 26 (15 February 1900): 2; "The Anti-Canteen Fight," *US* 26 (22 February 1900): 2; letters and petitions, January 1900, reels 70–71, McKinley Papers, LC.

12. U.S. House Committee on Military Affairs, *To Prevent the Sale of, or Dealing in, Beer*, pt. 2, 1 ("would . . .") and 4 ("If we . . .").

13. *CR*, 56th Cong., 2d sess., 117 ("beer . . .") and 113 ("such . . ."; "Woman's . . ."); *WCTU Minutes*, 1901, 318–20; V112 and V127, Senate, 56th Cong., ICPSR.

14. *CR*, 56th Cong., 2d sess., 694 ("church people . . .") and 766; Edwin C. Dinwiddie, "The Senate Will Put Beer out of the Canteen," *AI* 8 (18 January 1901): 5; U.S. Senate, *American Anti Saloon League*, 1902, esp. 2 and 5.

15. "Our League, God's Plan," folder 34, reel 4, Russell Papers, T&P ("Anti-Saloon . . ."); *National Anti-Saloon Convention, Held at Washington, D.C. December 17, 18 and 19, 1895 . . .* , 13, folder 1, box 1, reel 1, Anti-Saloon League of America Papers, T&P ("*suppression . . .*"). On the formation of the ASL, see Kerr, *Organized for Prohibition*, 66–89.

16. For short biographical sketches of all four, see Lender, *Temperance Biography*. Wheeler is the subject of two studies, Steuart, *Wayne Wheeler*, and Hogan, "Wayne B. Wheeler." I have also relied on the Russell and the Cherrington Papers, T&P.

17. Odegard, *Pressure Politics*, 182–90.

18. "To Our Friends," *AI* 7 (October 1899): 5 ("in advance . . ."); *Proceedings of the Annual Convention of the Anti-Saloon League of America*, 1903, 9 ("present . . ."). On total abstinence, see typescript of brochure of the Ohio ASL, 1894, Scrapbook, 21, Dinwiddie Papers, LC; "Lack of Information," *AI* 9 (11 April 1902): 1–2; *Proceedings of the Annual Convention of the Anti-Saloon League of America*, 1903, 44.

19. "The Two Wings of Every National Political Party," *AI* 8 (2 August 1901): 4.

20. "Christian Endeavor versus the Saloon," folder 32, reel 4, Russell Papers, T&P ("retributive . . ."); J. R. Hawthorne, "Ethics of the Anti-Saloon Movement," 1902, folder 18, box 5, Virginia Anti-Saloon League Papers, W&M ("man . . ."). On questions to candidates, see, for example, "Questions Propounded Candidates for the U.S. Senate in 1911 . . . ," Cannon Papers, Duke; Odegard, *Pressure Politics*, 21.

21. *Proceedings of the Annual Convention of the Anti-Saloon League of America*, 1896, 26–27 and 59; 1898, 50–51, 86, 94–95. For examples of introductions to congressmen, see Baker to Underwood, 8 December 1908, folder 7, box 16, series 1, Underwood Papers, ADAH; R. L. Davis to Simmons, 18 February 1910, Simmons Papers, Duke; Davis to Webb, 18 March 1910, Webb Papers, SHC.

22. William E. Johnson, "Some Remarks about Edwin Courtland Dinwiddie," *AI* 25 (26 January 1918): 6 ("understood . . ."); clipping, "Luncheon to Mr. Bryan," *The Commoner*, February 1919, in "Miscellaneous Correspondence, newspaper clippings, 1901–1919," Scanlon Papers, DPH ("who has directed . . ."). On Dinwiddie, see Lender, *Temperance Biography*, 138–39, and Cherrington, *Standard Encyclopedia*, 2:806–9. Dinwiddie's papers at the Library of Congress include very little personal information.

23. "Important Letter from Legislative Superintendent Dinwiddie," *AI* 8 (1 February 1901): 5; Dinwiddie, "What Was Done," *AI* 10 (15 May 1903): 10; Crafts, "To Hold and Extend the Anti-Canteen Victory," *US* 28 (27 February 1902): 3; Ellis, "The Battle Is on at Washington," *US* 29 (15 January 1903): 2; Dinwiddie, "What Was Done," *AI* 10 (15 May 1903): 10; Crafts, "News from the Firing Line," *US* 28 (3 July 1902): 4–5; U.S. Senate Committee on Immigration, *Foreign Immigration*, 176 ("four . . .") and 180 ("public . . .").

24. Dinwiddie, "What Congress Did," *AI* 14 (31 August 1906): 6; Cetina, "History of Veterans' Homes," 435–56; H.R. 21260, *CR*, 60th Cong.; "Our Country's New Responsibilities: Call for a National Christian Citizenship Convention at Washington, D.C. Dec. 13–15, 1898," in folder 11, box 1, reel 2, STFP, T&P; Ellis, "A Hearing before the House Insular Committee," *US* 26 (12 April 1900): 2; Crafts, *Patriotic Studies of a Quarter Century*, 29; Crafts form letter, 18 February 1902, folder 13, box 2, reel 2, STFP, T&P; *U.S. Statutes at Large*, 57th Cong., v. 32, pt. 1, 33.

25. Ellis, "Our Washington Letter," *US* 31 (9 February 1905): 12.

26. H.R. 14749, *CR*, 58th Cong., 3d sess., 688 ("being . . ."); E. M. Sweet, "Temperance Measures before Congress," *AI* 14 (23 February 1906): 12–13; Franklin, *Born Sober*, 3–35.

27. Hamm, *Shaping the Eighteenth Amendment*, 174–202.

28. U.S. Senate, *American Anti Saloon League*, 1904, 1; H.R. 15331, *CR*, 57th Cong.; H.R. 4072, *CR*, 58th Cong.

29. For examples of statements by brewers, see U.S. House, *Regulating Interstate Commerce*.

30. Ibid., 221–22.

31. Ibid., 92.

32. *CR*, 60th Cong., 1st sess., appendix, 324.

33. Minutes, 14–15, Committee on the Judiciary, 59th Cong. (vol. says 1st sess.), RG 233; U.S. Senate, *To Regulate Interstate Commerce*, 142 ("right . . .").

34. U.S. Senate, *To Regulate Interstate Commerce*, vi ("real . . ."); U.S. House Committee on the Judiciary, *Regulating Interstate Commerce*, 2; "Hepburn Bill," *AI* 11 (8 April 1904): 9. For lobbyists on personal use, see U.S. House, *Regulating Interstate Commerce*, 99–104.

35. U.S. Senate, *To Regulate Interstate Commerce*, 136, 169, 179–80, 242; Bankhead to S. N. Burns, 21 January 1913, folder 6, box 40, Bankhead Papers, ADAH.

36. See especially U.S. Senate, *State Control of Interstate Liquor Traffic*, 7.

37. S. 6576, *CR*, 60th Cong.; *CR*, 60th Cong., 2d sess., 2583–84; "Interstate Bill Passes Congress," *AI* 17 (March 1909): 6; *U.S. Statutes at Large*, 60th Cong., v. 35, pt. 1, 1136–37.

38. Ellis, "Our Washington Letter," *US* 35 (25 February 1909): 2; *WCTU Minutes*, 1909, 352–53; "Report of William H. Anderson," *AI* 18 (January 1910): 3–4.

39. Headquarters Committee of ASL to Dinwiddie, 5 July 1907; Dinwiddie to Headquarters Committee, 5 July 1907; Dinwiddie to Russell, 11 July 1907; S. E. Nicholson to Dinwiddie, 15 July 1907; Dinwiddie to Nicholson, 2 August 1907; "Resolutions by the Board of Trustees of the Oklahoma Anti-Saloon League," April 19, 1908; E. S. Chapman to Laura Church, 8 March 1911; Nicholson to V. G. A. Tressler, 20 November 1911; enclosure, Robert N. Turner to Nicholson, 29 November 1911, all in folders 1–2, box 1, reel 16, Nicholson Subseries, ASLAP, T&P; E. E. McLaughlin to Cherrington, 30 October 1908, and Nicholson to Cherrington, 22–23 October 1908, both in file 15, box 1, Office Files, reel 1, Cherrington Papers, T&P.

40. William E. Johnson, "Some Remarks about Edwin Courtland Dinwiddie," *AI* 25 (26 January 1918): 6; William H. Anderson, "The National Inter-Church Temperance Federation," undated, file 3, box 2, Office Files, reel 3, Cherrington Papers, T&P.

41. Cherrington to Nicholson, 16 October 1908, file 15, box 1, Office Files, reel 2, Cherrington Papers, T&P ("sell out"); Nicholson to J. S. Dancey, 24 October 1908, file 15, box 1, Office Files, reel 2, and Baker to "My Dear Sir and Brother," 26 October 1908, file B, box 1, Office Files, reel 2, Cherrington Papers, T&P; Cherrington to Baker, 22 and 31 October 1908, Russell to J. K. Shields, 12 November 1908, and Cherrington to Nicholson, 8 July 1910, all in folder 1, box 1, reel 16, Nicholson Subseries, ASLAP, T&P; William E. Johnson, "Some Remarks about Edwin Courtland Dinwiddie," *AI* 25 (26 January 1918): 6. On Anderson and Nicholson, see Lender, *Temperance Biography*, 5–7 and 365–67.

42. On the commission, see *CR*, 60th Cong., 2d sess., 3078–82; Ellis, "Our Washington Letter," *US* 35 (25 February 1909): 2; (4 March 1909): 13; Anderson to Brother Superintendent, 19 January 1909, box 3, Virginia Anti-Saloon League Papers, W&M; Nicholson to Dinwiddie, 3 August 1909, and Nicholson to Shields, 19 October 1908, both in file 15, box 1, Office Files, reel 2, Cherrington Papers, T&P; Anderson to George S. Stafford, 27 June 1912, folder 2, box 25, reel 76, Cherrington Papers, T&P. On D.C. prohibition, see H.R. 6016, *CR*, 59th Cong.; H.R. 9086, H.R. 17530, and S. 8465, *CR*, 60th Cong.; Ellis, "Our Washington Letter," *US* 34 (27 February 1908): 1; (19 March 1908): 3; (30 April 1908): 2; Albert E. Shoemaker to Lelia D. Emig, 14 November 1907, folder 12, box 1, reel 2, Anti-Saloon League of the District of Columbia Papers, T&P; "Report of William H. Anderson," *AI* 18 (January 1910): 3–4; and Nicholson to Anderson, 6 July 1911, folder 2, box 1, reel 16, Nicholson Subseries, ASLAP, T&P. On Hawaii, see S. 5253, S.J. Res. 80, and H.J. Res. 155, *CR*, 61st Cong.; and Nicholson to Anderson, 6 July 1911, folder 2, box 1, reel 16, Nicholson Subseries, ASLAP, T&P.

43. 19 January 1910, 258, "Minutes of the Meetings of the Board of Managers . . . ," NTSPHR, DPH; printed circular, 1910, folder 4, reel 17, and Littlefield to Taylor, 29 October 1910, folder 1; Nicholson to W. H. Anderson, 6 July 1911, folder 2; Nicholson to Baker, 27 April 1911, folder 2 ("heroic . . ."), all in box 1, reel 16, Nicholson Subseries, ASLAP, T&P.

44. Nicholson to "Members of the Headquarters Committee," 17 July 1911 ("highly . . ."); Cannon to "Friends," 17 July 1911 ("in large . . ."); Secretary "To the Members of the Headquarters Committee," 7 August 1911; Secretary "To Members of the Headquarters Committee," 4 September 1911; and Nicholson to Cherrington, 13 November 1911, all in folder 2, box 1, reel 17, Nicholson Subseries, ASLAP, T&P; "Suggested Letter to Be Sent in Duplicate to International Reform Bureau, the National Temperance Society, W.C.T.U. and the National Grand Lodge of Good Templars," folder 4, ibid.; untitled handwritten speech, file 4, box 2, Office Files, reel 4, Cherrington Papers, T&P.

45. Nicholson to Cherrington, 12 August 1911; Nicholson to Baker, 18 August 1911; and Nicholson to William I. Haven, 11 December 1911; all in folder 2; and circular, 26 December 1911, folder 4, box 1, reel 17, Nicholson Subseries, ASLAP, T&P; calling card, 13 February 1912, case file 20, reel 357, Taft Papers, LC.

46. Ellis, "Our Washington Letter," *US* 37 (21 December 1911): 3 and 12.

47. Nicholson to Baker, 16 May 1911, folder 2; and Nicholson to Baker, 13 January 1912, and Baker to Nicholson, 10 January 1912, folder 3, all in box 1, reel 16, Nicholson Subseries, ASLAP, T&P; Hanly to Cannon, 4 January 1912, Cannon Papers, Duke; Webb to D. C. K. Wilkinson, 24 March 1914, and Crafts to Webb, 9 February 1912 ("will . . ."), both in Webb Papers, SHC.

48. Ellis, "Our Washington Letter," *US* 38 (8 February 1912): 2; "The Kenyon-Sheppard Bill," *AI* 21 (January 1913): 1; "That National Interstate Conference on Illegal Liquor Shipments," ibid., 6; Ellis, "Our Washington Letter," *US* 38 (26 December 1912): 2.

49. U.S. Senate Committee on the Judiciary, *Regulation of Commerce between the States.*

50. *CR*, 62d Cong., 3d sess., 761–72.

51. S. 4043, *CR*, 62d Cong., 3d sess., 700 ("Federal Government . . ." and "moral . . ."), 2912 ("subordinated . . ." and "do as well . . ."), 2914 ("all the . . ." and "our Father . . .").

52. H.R. 17593, *CR*, 62d Cong.

53. *CR*, 62d Cong., 3d sess., 2814 ("never . . ."), 2836 ("misery . . ."), 2828.

54. Ibid., 2830, 2808–14, 2812 ("constituency . . ."), 2808 ("I . . ."); 2804 ("public-health . . .").

55. V243, House, 62d Cong., ICPSR. A logistical regression analysis (described in Chapter 2, note 18) of the vote on the bill to pass the Webb-Kenyon Act revealed an inverse relationship between a vote for the bill and population density, the percentage of the population that was Catholic, and the value of manufactured goods produced. When the votes for each region were analyzed independently, the relationship held only in the Midwest and only for the percentage of Catholics in the population, although that for manufactured goods is suggestive. The absence of a statistically significant relationship with the percentage of blacks in the population reaffirms that in earlier votes that relationship reflected southern opposition. With the South now in strong support of anti-alcohol legislation, no statistically significant relationship seems to exist between a vote for moral legislation and the percentage of blacks in the population. V243, House, 62d Cong., ICPSR: "To pass the Webb-Kenyon Act" ($n = 313$): Population density: $B = -.0001$, Wald $= 5.2457$, Prob. values $= .0220$; percentage Catholic: $B = -0736$, Wald $= 10.2271$, Prob. values $= .0014$; total value of manufactured goods produced: $B = 1.4E-05$, Wald $= 4.8641$, Prob. values $= .0274$. For Midwest alone ($n = 92$): percentage Catholic: $B = -.1034$, Wald $= 3.9766$, Prob. values $= .0461$; total value of manufactured goods produced: $B = -2.4E-05$, Wald $= 3.3560$, Prob. values $= .0670$.

56. Vote totals compiled from *CR*, 62d Cong., 3d sess., 2922.

CHAPTER NINE

1. 22 April 1913, Minutes of the Meeting of the Headquarters Committee of the Anti-Saloon League of America, folder 1, box 27, reel 82, Cherrington Papers, T&P ("to go . . ."); Baker, "The Next and Final Step," *AI* 21 (June 1913): 4; "Wanted, a Saloonless Nation," *CS* 47 (November 1913): 481–82; "Important Proclamation," *US* 37 (14 September 1911): 3; *WCTU Minutes*, 1913, 87–88; form letter, Promotion Committee, National Council of One Hundred, 10 June 1913, folder 13, box 2, Office Files, reel 51, Cherrington Papers, T&P; "Nation-Wide Prohibition," *AI* 21 (November 1913): 1–4.

2. *Washington Post*, 11 December 1913, 2; *New York Times*, 11 December 1913, 5; "Temperance Forces Gather at Nation's Capital," *US* 39 (18 December 1913): 1–2.

3. "Address of Ernest H. Cherrington," file 4, box 2, Office Files, reel 4, Cherrington Papers, T&P.

4. *Washington Post*, 12 December 1913, 1.

5. Hobson, *Alcohol and the Human Race.* A copy of "The Great Destroyer" appears in *CR*, 61st Cong., 3d sess., 1867–73. Discussion of Hobson's life rests on an account by his

wife, "Notes by Mrs. Hobson," box 75 (AC6196, add. 13), and other material in the Hobson Papers, LC. See also Pittman, *Navalist and Progressive*.

6. Clipping, Walter Raleigh, "The Man Behind Prohibition," file 7, box 2G199; James B. Borrow, "Senator was a 4-Year-Old Orator," 74–75, scrapbook 15, box 3L506; "Morris Sheppard's Speech Yesterday," 61, scrapbook 13, box 3L469; letter to W. J. Estes, released to public, 121, scrapbook 13, box 3L469 ("free government . . ."); "Christian Citizenship," *Athens Journal* 76, scrapbook 10; John Temple Graves, "Morris Sheppard of Texas," 96, scrapbook 14, box 3L504, all in Sheppard Papers, CAH; Bailey, "Morris Sheppard," 49. On coins, see Gaines Foster, "Christian Nation." On God in the Constitution, see H.J. Res. 17, *CR*, 61st Cong. On Sheppard's life, in addition to his papers, see his biography written by his daughter, Keyes Narrative, CAH; Duke, "Political Career of Morris Sheppard"; and Bailey, "Morris Sheppard."

7. James Cannon, *Bishop Cannon's Own Story*; Dabney, *Dry Messiah*; Hohner, *Prohibition and Politics*.

8. 19 May 1907, Sermon, Cannon Papers, Duke ("Not sin . . ."); Spence, "Outstanding Policies," 188–95, 198, 200–203, 206, and 208–9; "In Defense of Decency," typescript, from *Baltimore and Richmond Christian Advocate*, 5 March 1905, box 31, Cannon Papers, Duke ("appeal . . ."); James Cannon, *Bishop Cannon's Own Story*, 8–17; "Study This Question," 30 August 1914, box 19, and "First Sermon in Pastorate," box 28 ("In order . . ."), both in Cannon Papers, Duke.

9. "Methodist in Politics," typescript, 14 January 1904, box 31, Cannon Papers, Duke ("carry . . .)"; E. J. Richardson, "An Appreciation of Dr. Cannon," *AI* 25 (2 February 1918): 7 ("gave . . .").

10. Cannon, *Bishop Cannon's Own Story*, 116–17 and 170–71.

11. On petitions, see Appendix 2, Tables A2.1a and A2.1b. "Three Things to Be Done," *US* 40 (26 March 1914): 8; on lobbying efforts, see letters from Margaret Dye Ellis to Anna Gordon for this period, in Gordon Correspondence, FEWL.

12. *Amendment to the Constitution Prohibiting Intoxicating Liquors: Hearings*, 4.

13. Ibid., 18 ("double . . ."), 5 ("national . . .").

14. Ibid., 184–86.

15. Ibid., 20, 15, and 185.

16. H.J. Res. 168, *CR*, 63d Cong.; Ellis, "Our Washington Letter," *US* 40 (21 May 1914): 2; Ellis, "Our Washington Letter," *US* 40 (18 June 1914): 2; Ellis to Gordon, 1 July, 31 August, 14, 28, and 29 September 1914, Gordon Correspondence, FEWL; Exhibit B, "Minutes of the Regular Quarterly Meeting of the Executive Committee of the Anti-Saloon League of America, . . . January 28, 1915," folder 3, box 27, reel 82, Cherrington Papers, T&P.

17. Hobson to "Dear Colleague," 15 November 1914, Webb Papers, SHC; Hobson to Cora Stoddard, 7 December 1914, box 1 (AC6196), Hobson Papers, LC; *WCTU Minutes*, 1914, 61–63; Exhibit B, "Minutes of Executive Committee, January 28, 1915," Cherrington Papers, T&P.

18. H.J. Res. 168, *CR*, 63d Cong.; *CR*, 63d Cong., 3d sess., 594 ("proud boast . . .").

19. *CR*, 63d Cong., 3d sess., 530 ("we would . . .") and 526 ("declared . . ."). For other references to antislavery precedent, see ibid., 572 and 603.

20. Ibid., 526 ("us . . ."), 554 ("different . . ."), 507 ("right . . ."), 582 ("negro rule"), 499 ("bring . . .").

21. Ibid., 534–34 ("in our . . ."), 558 ("I do . . .").

22. Ibid., 555 ("limitation . . ."), 558 ("invade . . ."), 583 ("millions . . .").

23. Ibid., 502–3.

24. V238, House, 63d Cong., ICPSR.

25. "Report of the Legislative Committee," filed with "Adjourned Meeting of the Executive Committee of the Anti-Saloon League of America . . . July 5, 1915," folder 3, box 27, reel 82, Cherrington Papers, T&P; "Conference at Washington," *US* 41 (24 June 1915): 9; "Conference Approves 'Hobson Amendment,'" *US* 41 (29 July 1915): 9. On the composition of the committee, see "Conference Decides Hobson Resolution to Remain Unchanged," *AI* 22 (24 July 1915): 7. The NRA supported the campaign for prohibition, but it played no role in the lobbying effort for it.

26. "Committee Statement on History, Wording, and Scope . . . ," *AI* 22 (25 December 1915): 12–13; Morris L. Sheppard to "My Dear Senator," 5 February 1916, and unsigned, Attorney and General Counsellor for the ASL to Morris Sheppard, 2 February 1916, both in "Legislation—Prohibition" file, box 302, Walsh Papers, LC ("This wording . . .").

27. *WCTU Minutes*, 1915, 54–56; "Washington, D.C.," *AI* 22 (30 October 1915): 1; Dinwiddie to Webb, 9 August 1915, Webb Papers, SHC.

28. Ellis, "Our Washington Letter," *US* 42 (6 April 1916): 2; "Judiciary Committee Postpones Action on Prohibition Amendment," *AI* 23 (1 April 1916): 6; W. J. Bryan to Richmond P. Hobson, 12 August 1915, folder 53, box 29, reel 91, Cherrington Papers, T&P.

29. Cannon, "Report of Legislative Committee," in "Minutes of the . . . Executive Committee . . . March 30, 1916," folder 4, box 27, reel 82; Cannon, "Report of Legislative Committee," in "Minutes . . . January 11, 1917," folder 5, box 27, reel 82 ("leaders . . ." and "to secure . . ."), both in Cherrington Papers, T&P.

30. "Legislative Committee of the Anti-Saloon League Announces League's Program," *AI* 23 (18 November 1916): 12.

31. S.J. Res. 55, H.J. Res. 84, *CR*, 64th Cong.; 14 December 1916, Minutes, Committee on the Judiciary, RG 233, NA.

32. *CR*, 64th Cong., 1st sess., 4197; S. 1082, *CR*, 64th Cong., 2d sess.; "Smoot Dry Bill Is Beaten," clipping from *Washington Times*, 18 December 1916, 109, scrapbook 15, box 3L506, Sheppard Papers, CAH ("Most . . ."); V280, V305, and V306, Senate, 64th Cong., ICPSR.

33. Dinwiddie to Webb, 24 February 1917, Webb Papers, SHC; V160, House, 64th Cong., ICPSR.

34. "Liquor Ads Barred from Mail Sent to Prohibition States," *AI* 24 (24 February 1917): 1; *CR*, 64th Cong., 2d sess., 3330, 3335 ("shall . . ."); V348, Senate, 64th Cong., ICPSR.

35. Hobson to Cherrington, 17 February 1917, folder 21, box 2, Office Files, reel 5, Cherrington Papers, T&P; Hobson to Dinwiddie, 17 and 19 February 1917, box 3 (A6196), Hobson Papers, LC; Cannon, *Bishop Cannon's Own Story*, 182–83; Gordon to Mrs. Hungerford, 18 February 1917, Gordon Correspondence, FEWL; Ellis, "Our Washington Letter," *US* 43 (1 March 1917): 2.

36. Cannon and Wheeler to Tumulty, 2 March 1917; Dinwiddie to Wilson, 3 March 1917; and others letters in case file 144, reel 228, Wilson Papers, LC; "The Reed Amendment," *AI* 24 (21 July 1917): 8 ("Senator Reed's . . ."). The ASL also went to court in behalf of the Reed Amendment; see W. B. Wheeler, "Report of the Legal Department for Quarter Ending October 25, 1917," folder 5, box 27, reel 82, Cherrington Papers, T&P. For Wheeler's views in support, see Wheeler to Hobson, 2 March 1917, box 15 (AC6196), Hobson Papers, LC. The ASL Legislative Committee tried but failed to get an appointment to see Wilson in behalf of the Reed Amendment.

37. *Clark Distilling Company v. Western Maryland Railway Company and State of West Virginia*, 242 U.S. 311 (1917); "'Bone-Dry' Legislation," *AI* 24 (10 February 1917): 8; "Uncle Sam a 'Bone Dry' Advocate," *US* 43 (1 March 1917): 8. For state developments, see Hamm, *Shaping the Eighteenth Amendment*, 327 n. 18.

38. Levine, *Defender of the Faith*, 102–17; Cherny, *Righteous Cause*, 158; Dinwiddie to Bryan, 27 December 1916, and Morris Sheppard to Bryan, 10 January and 7 August 1917, all in box 31, Bryan Papers, LC. Crafts evaluates various factors behind the shift in "Reform Bureau up-to-date report, March, 1917," file 318, box 3 (A6146), Hobson Papers, LC.

39. "War Breaking Down the Barriers to Prohibition and Woman Suffrage," *Current Opinion* 64 (February 1918): 82–84; Clark, *Deliver Us from Evil*, 124; letters from the Shelby Shoe Company to Cherrington, folder 18, box 30, reel 92, Cherrington Papers, T&P; Timberlake, *Prohibition and the Progressive Movement*, 79 ("crystallized"). Although it argues for a longer role for big business, Rumbarger, *Profits, Power, and Prohibition*, 179–80, has evidence of increased financial help from big business between 1914 and 1916.

40. "Minutes of the Executive Committee . . . April 5th, 1917," 4–5, folder 5, box 27, reel 82, and Press Release, National Legislative Committee, ASL, 16 April 1917, folder 27, box 25, reel 77, both in Cherrington Papers, T&P; "Safeguard Our Soldier Boys!" *US* 43 (12 April 1917): 8; "Prohibition as a War Measure," *US* 43 (19 April 1917): 1; Gordon and Ellis to Althea G. Quinby, 21 April 1917, Gordon Correspondence, FEWL ("mothers' . . ."); copy of Cannon to Wilson from *Baltimore and Richmond Christian Advocate*, 26 April 1917, Cannon Papers, Duke ("The mothers . . ."); Ellis, "Our Washington Letter," *US* 43 (7 June 1917): 2 ("would rather . . .").

41. Cannon to Cherrington, 11 May 1917, folder 27, box 25, reel 77, Cherrington Papers, T&P; *CR*, 65th Cong., 1st sess., 1451 ("another . . .").

42. Circular by Irving Fisher, 23 April 1917, in Webb Papers, SHC; Irving Fisher, "Why War Prohibition Is a Necessity," *AI* 24 (26 May 1917): 3; Fisher to Wilson, 24 May 1917, case file 144, reel 228, Wilson Papers, LC.

43. H.R. 4961, *CR*, 65th Cong., 1st sess., 440; Wilson to Cannon, 29 June 1917, Cannon and others to Wilson, 30 June 1917, and Wilson to Cannon, 3 July 1917, all in Link, *Papers of Woodrow Wilson*, 43:42, 64–65, and 8; Baker, "Anti-Saloon League's Statement on Exemption of Wine and Beer," *AI* 24 (7 July 1917): 1.

44. Ellis, "Our Washington Letter," *US* 43 (12–19 July 1917): 2; Webb to W. J. Bryan, 26 July 1917, Webb Papers, SHC ("exempt . . .").

45. "Bone-Dry Prohibition the Ultimate Goal," *AI* 24 (21 July 1917): 8; Cannon to Cherrington, 6 March 1917, and letter and enclosure, Legislative Committee to State Su-

perintendents, 10 March 1917, folder 27, box 25, reel 77, Cherrington Papers, T&P; "Dr. Baker Announces New Notes in Prohibition Progress," *AI* 24 (31 March 1917): 1; "Approves Text of New Prohibition Resolution," *AI* 24 (14 April 1917): 1; "The Hour Has Struck," *AI* 24 (31 March 1917): 8 ("policy . . ."). That April, a National Temperance Council formed, representing a renewed challenge to the ASL, but it followed the same legislative policies.

46. S.J. Res. 17, *CR*, 65th Cong.

47. V131, Senate, 65th Cong., ICPSR. On Harding and Wheeler, see Wheeler's account in "The Inside Story of Prohibition's Adoption," *New York Times*, 31 March 1926, 25.

48. *CR*, 65th Cong., 1st sess., appendix, 669; *WCTU Minutes*, 1917, 207–12.

49. S.J. Res. 17, *CR*, 65th Cong.; Ellis, "Our Washington Letter," 43 (17 December 1917): 2.

50. V71, House, 65th Cong., ICPSR; Wheeler, "The Inside Story of Prohibition's Adoption," *New York Times*, 30 March 1926, 27; Anderson, interview, 86–88; "Where the Increased Vote Came From," *AI* 25 (19 January 1918): 2; "Side Lights on the Vote in the House," *AI* 24 (29 December 1917): 4.

51. *CR*, 65th Cong., 2d sess., 426.

52. "United Temperance Forces of America . . . ," *US* 44 (31 January 1918): 2; "It's Up to You," *AI* 25 (16 February 1918): 1. On wartime prohibition, see H.R. 11945, *CR*, 65th Cong., 2d sess.

53. "Mississippi and Virginia Ratify the Dry Amendment," *AI* 25 (19 January 1918): 1 and 4; "Make Forty-Eight White," *AI* (8 March 1919): 8; "South Carolina and North Dakota OK Amendment," *AI* 25 (2 February 1918): 1 ("Thus . . ."). Mississippi received the honor of being first, in part because its legislature met first.

54. *CR*, 65th Cong., 3d sess., 1502, 1505–6 ("greatest . . ."); Lenna Lowe Yost, "Our Washington Letter," *US* 45 (6 February 1919): 2.

55. Wayne B. Wheeler, "Report of the Legal Department for Quarter Ending February 27, 1919," folder 7, box 27, reel 87, Cherrington Papers, T&P ("distilled . . ."); "The One Half of One Per Cent Standard," folder 14, reel 2, Office of General Counsel and Legislative Superintendent, ASLAP, T&P; Lenna L. Yost, "Our Washington Letter," *US* 44 (26 December 1918): 2; Wayne Wheeler, "Definition of Intoxicating Liquor Should Be Made 'Near Beer' Tight," *AI* 26 (22 February 1919): 2.

56. H.R. 6810, *CR*, 66th Cong.

57. U.S. House Committee on the Judiciary, *Bill to Prohibit Intoxicating Beverages*; Webb to W. B. Wheeler, 13 February 1920, Webb Papers, SHC ("sovereigns . . .").

58. *CR*, 66th Cong., 1st sess., 2959 ("object . . ."), 2900 ("Throughout . . ."); "Dry Enforcement Code Wins in the House," *AI* 26 (2 August 1919): 1; "The Volstead Enforcement Code," *AI* 26 (2 August 1919): 8; "House Enforcement Code Not Drastic nor Unreasonable in Any Provision," *AI* 26 (9 August 1919): 3.

59. Hamm, *Shaping the Eighteen Amendment*, 266, stresses that the reliance on concurrent powers proved very important to the failure of Prohibition. For the Supreme Court's rule of "dual sovereignty" in concurrent enforcement, see the analysis of the Supreme Court's rulings on all issues related to prohibition in Murchison, *Federal Criminal Law Doctrines*.

60. "Constitutional Prohibition in Effect," *AI* 27 (17 January 1920): 1 ("the future . . ."); Timberlake, *Prohibition and the Progressive Movement*, 100–115.

61. Crafts to Cora F. Stoddard, 20 January 1916, box 4, STFP, NYPL.

CONCLUSION

1. Elizabeth P. Gordon, "Margaret Dye Ellis—In Memoriam," *US* 51 (30 July 1925): 7; *Newark Evening News*, 13 July 1925, 6.

2. On growing criticism of Comstock and attacks on various artists, see Broun and Leech, *Anthony Comstock*; Richard Johnson, "Anthony Comstock"; Bates, *Weeder in the Garden*; "Anthony Comstock—An Heroic Suppressor or an Unconscious Protector of Vice," *Current Opinion* 56 (April 1914): 288–89; and Beisel, *Imperiled Innocents*.

3. On WCTU's continuing efforts on censorship, see Parker, *Purifying America*.

4. Discussion here relies on Kerr, *Organized for Prohibition*, 211–83, and Dohn, "History of the Anti-Saloon League," on post-1920 developments. On Wheeler's role, see also Steuart, *Wayne Wheeler*, and Hogan, "Wayne B. Wheeler."

5. "Minutes of the Quarterly Meeting of the Executive Committee . . . May 8 and 9, 1919," 5 ("without . . ."), and letters in folder 27, box 25, reel 77, Cherrington Papers, T&P. See also "Mr. Dinwiddie's Betrayal of Prohibition—A Statement by William H. Anderson," filed in folder 2, box 25, reel 76, ibid. The two historians who have most closely studied Cannon's life differ on his guilt; compare Dabney, *Dry Messiah*, and Hohner, *Prohibition and Politics*.

6. On repeal, see Kyvig, *Repealing National Prohibition*. On success of Prohibition, see Burnham, "New Perspectives on the Prohibition 'Experiment.'"

7. On changing attitudes toward free labor, see Foner, *Reconstruction*, 512–13.

8. A similar pattern of denominational involvement emerged in the petitions sent to Congress. See Appendix 2, Tables A2.4 and A2.5.

9. Several historians have drawn a similar conclusion about women's attitudes toward government; for one of the earliest, see Baker, "Domestication of Politics."

10. In the statistical analysis cited in the notes to earlier chapters, a high percentage of Catholics in a district had not been inversely related to votes in favor of all forms of moral legislation, but on six of the seven bills examined in which the control of alcohol was involved, there was an inverse relationship between a representative's vote in favor and the percentage of Catholics in his district.

11. The statistical analysis of just southern representatives' votes on the Webb-Kenyon Act, after this southern shift had occurred, revealed that none of five social characteristics of House districts—population density, percentage of the population that was black, percentage that was foreign born, percentage that was Roman Catholic, and the total dollar value of manufactured goods produced—had a statistically significant influence on a vote for or against the bill. The difference in voting among southern representatives does not appear to reflect the social characteristics of their districts.

12. Foster, "Christian Nation," 128–29.

13. This point on the Mann Act is made well in Langum, *Crossing over the Line*.

14. Odem, *Delinquent Daughters*, does question the operation of age-of-consent laws.

BIBLIOGRAPHY OF WORKS CITED

MANUSCRIPTS

Ann Arbor, Mich.
  Bentley Historical Library, University of Michigan
    Wilbur F. Crafts Notebooks
    International Reform Federation Collection
Ann Arbor, Mich./Columbus, Ohio
  Temperance and Prohibition Papers, joint Ohio Historical Society–Michigan
      Historical Collections (microfilm edition)
    Anti-Saloon League of America Papers
    Anti-Saloon League of the District of Columbia Papers
    Ernest H. Cherrington Papers
    Historical File of the National Headquarters, Woman's Christian Temperance
      Union Papers
    Howard Hyde Russell Papers
    Scientific Temperance Federation Papers
Athens, Ga.
  Richard Russell Library, University of Georgia
    Dudley Hughes Papers
Austin, Tex.
  Research and Collections Division, Center for American History, University of
      Texas
    Lucile Sheppard Keyes Narrative
    Morris Sheppard Papers
Baton Rouge, La.
  Hill Memorial Library, Louisiana State University
    S. Homer Woodbridge, "Anti-Lottery Campaign: The Overthrow of the
      Louisiana Lottery"
Boston, Mass.
  Massachusetts Historical Society
    George Frisbie Hoar Papers
Cambridge, Mass.
  Schlesinger Library, Harvard University
    Papers of Mary Ware Dennett and the Voluntary Parenthood League. Part B,
      Series 3, Sexuality, Sex Education and Reproductive Rights. Women's Studies
      Manuscript Collections. University Publications of America, 1994.

Chapel Hill, N.C.
    Southern Historical Collection, University of North Carolina
        Tucker Family Papers
        Edwin Yates Webb Papers
Concord, N.H.
    New Hampshire Historical Society
        Henry W. Blair Papers
        Jacob H. Gallinger Papers
        Jonathan E. Pecker Papers
Durham, N.C.
    Rare Book, Manuscript, and Special Collections Library, Duke University
        James Cannon Jr. Papers
        Flavius Joseph Cook Papers
        Furnifold M. Simmons Papers
Evanston, Ill.
    Frances E. Willard Memorial Library
        Anna A. Gordon Correspondence
        Transcribed (by Carolyn De Swarte Gifford) journals of Frances Willard
Montgomery, Ala.
    Alabama Department of Archives and History
        John H. Bankhead Papers
        Oscar W. Underwood Papers
New York, N.Y.
    New York Public Library
        Records of the National Board of Review of Motion Pictures
        Scientific Temperance Federation Papers
Philadelphia, Pa.
    Department of Presbyterian History
        Fulton Mayhew Papers (Record Group 4)
        National Temperance Society and Publication House Records
            (Record Group 54)
        Charles Scanlon Papers
Pittsburgh, Pa.
    Reform Presbyterian Theological Seminary Library
        Minutes of the Synod of the Reformed Presbyterian Church
Richmond, Va.
    Virginia Historical Society
        John Randolph Tucker Papers
Ticonderoga, N.Y.
    Ticonderoga Historical Society
        Joseph Cook Papers
Washington, D.C.
    Manuscripts Division, Library of Congress
        William Jennings Bryan Papers

Grover Cleveland Papers (microfilm)
Samuel W. Dike Papers
Edwin C. Dinwiddie Papers
Walter Quinten Gresham Papers
Benjamin Harrison Papers (microfilm)
Richmond P. Hobson Papers
William McKinley Papers (microfilm)
Records of New York Society for the Suppression of Vice (microfilm)
William Howard Taft Papers (microfilm)
Thomas J. Walsh Papers
Woodrow Wilson Papers (microfilm)
National Archives and Record Service
Records of the U.S. House of the Representatives (Record Group 233)
Records of the U.S. Senate (Record Group 46)
Williamsburg, Va.
Swem Library, College of William and Mary
Virginia Anti-Saloon League Papers

INTERVIEWS

Anderson, William H. Interview. *New York Times* Oral History Program. Columbia
University Oral History Collection. Part 4 (1–219), No. 5. Sanford, N.C.: Microfilm
Corporation of America, 1979.
Boole, Ella Boole. Interview. *New York Times* Oral History Program. Columbia Uni-
versity Oral History Program Collection. Part 4 (1–129), No. 24. Sanford: N.C.:
Microfilm Corporation of America, 1979.

GOVERNMENT PUBLICATIONS

*The following hearings are reproduced in the Congressional Information Services, Inc.,
microform series (number in parenthesis is the CIS number). The following House and
Senate Reports and other documents are in the Serial Sets (number in parenthesis is the
Serial Set number).*

*Amendment to the Constitution Prohibiting Intoxicating Liquors: Hearings before a Sub-
committee of the Committee of the Judiciary, United States Senate, Sixty-third Con-
gress, Second Session, on S.J. Res. 88 and S.J. Res 50.* Revised ed. Washington: Govern-
ment Printing Office, 1914 (S52-3).
Congressional Globe
Congressional Record
*Federal Motion Picture Commission: Hearings before the Committee on Education,
House of Representatives, Sixty-fourth Congress, First Session on H.R. 456 . . . .* Wash-
ington: Government Printing Office, 1916 (H145-1).
Hearing before the Committee of the Judiciary, House of Representatives, March 11, 1896,

on H. Res. 28, Joint Resolution Proposing an Amendment to the Constitution of the United States. Washington: Government Printing Office, 1896 (HJ54-A).

Hearings before the Committee on Interstate and Foreign Commerce of the House of Representatives on the Bill H.R. 25825 . . . . Washington: Government Printing Office, 1911 (H36-1).

Motion Picture Commission: Hearings before the Committee on Education, House of Representatives, Sixty-third Congress, Second Session on Bills to Establish a Federal Motion Picture Commission No. 1. Washington: Government Printing Office, 1914 (H88-2 A&B).

Prevention of Transmission of Race-Gambling Bets, Hearings before Subcommittee on Interstate Commerce, April 3, 1916. Washington: Government Printing Office, 1916 (S82-3).

Prohibiting Shipment of Certain Motion-Picture Films: Hearing before the Committee on the Judiciary, House of Representatives, Sixty-fourth Congress, First Session, on H.R. 9521, Serial 34, Statement of Horace M. Towner, MC, March 17, 1916. Washington: Government Printing Office, 1916 (H152-8).

U.S. House. Ardent Spirits–Navy: To Accompany Bill H.R. 522, Letter from the Secretary of the Navy. 23d Cong., 1st sess., 1834. H. Doc. No. 486 (SS 259).

———. Economic Aspects of the Liquor Problem. 55th Cong., 2d sess., 1898. H. Doc. No. 564 (SS 3696).

———. Enforcement of the Anti-Polygamy Act, Letter from the Secretary of the Interior. 45th Cong., 3d sess., 1879. H. Ex. Doc. No. 58 (SS 1858).

———. Regulating Interstate Commerce in Certain Cases. 59th Cong., 2d sess., 1907. H. Doc. No. 522 (SS 5155).

U.S. House Committee on Alcoholic Liquor Traffic. Sale of Intoxicating Liquors on Reservations, etc.: Report to Accompany H.R. 7937. 55th Cong., 2d sess., 1898. H. Rept. No. 1629 (SS 3722).

U.S. House Committee on the District of Columbia. Age of Protection for Girls in the District of Columbia: Report to Accompany H.R. 1136. 55th Cong., 2d sess., 1898. H. Rept. No. 829 (SS 3719).

———. To Punish the Selling and Advertising of Lottery Tickets in the District of Columbia: Report to Accompany Bill H.R. 7880. 49th Cong., 1st sess., 1886. H. Rept. No. 1631 (SS 2440).

U.S. House Committee on Education. Federal Motion Picture Commission: Report to Accompany H.R. 14895. 63d Cong., 3d sess., 1915. H. Rept. No. 1411 (SS 6766).

———. Federal Motion Picture Commission: Report to Accompany H.R. 15462. 64th Cong., 1st sess., 1916. H. Rept. No. 697, parts 1 and 2 (SS 6904).

U.S. House Committee on Interstate and Foreign Commerce. Interstate Gambling: Report to Accompany H.R. 10355. 54th Cong., 2d sess., 1897. H. Rept. No. 3066 (SS 3556).

———. Interstate Transmission of Race-Gambling Bets: Report to Accompany H.R. 15949. 64th Cong., 1st sess., 1916. H. Rept. No. 773 (SS 6905).

———. Transmission by Mail or Interstate Commerce of Pictures or Any Description of

Prize Fights: Report to Accompany H.R. 10369. 54th Cong., 2d sess., 1897. H. Rept. No. 3046 (SS 3556).

U.S. House Committee on the Judiciary. *Acknowledgement of God and the Christian Religion in the Constitution.* 43d Cong., 1st sess., 1874. H. Rept. No. 143 (SS 1623).

———. *Bigamy: View of the Minority to Accompany Bill S. 10,* 49th Cong., 1st sess., 1886. H. Rept. No. 2735, part 2 (SS 2443).

———. *A Bill to Prohibit Intoxicating Beverages: Report to Accompany H.R. 6810.* 66th Cong., 1st sess., 1919. H. Rept. No. 91, part 2 (SS 7592).

———. *Marriage and Divorce: Adverse Report to Accompany H. Res 46.* 52d Cong., 1st sess., 1892. H. Rept. No. 1290 (SS 3045).

———. *Polygamy: Report to Accompany H. Res. 176.* 49th Cong., 1st sess., 1886. H. Rept. No. 2568 (SS 2442).

———. *Polygamy in the Territories of the United States: To Accompany Bill H.R. 7.* 36th Cong., 1st sess., 1860. H. Rept. No. 83 (SS 1067).

———. *Regulating Interstate Commerce in Certain Cases: Report to Accompany H.R. 4072.* 58th Cong., 2d sess., 1904. H. Rept. No. 2337 (SS 4583).

———. *Regulation of Commerce: Report to Accompany S. 398.* 51st Cong., 1st sess., 1890. H. Rept. No. 2604 (SS 2814).

———. *Sale of Alcoholic Beverages, Adverse Report to Accompany H. Res. 15.* 50th Cong., 1st sess., 1888. H. Rept. No. 249 (SS 2598).

———. *Sale of Cigarettes: Adverse Report to Accompany H.R. 4057.* 54th Cong., 2d sess., 1896. H. Rept. No. 2324 (SS 3554).

———. *Suppression of Polygamy in Utah: Report to Accompany Bill S. 10.* 49th Cong., 1st sess., 1886. H. Rept. No. 2735 (SS 2443).

U.S. House Committee on Military Affairs. *To Prevent the Sale of, or Dealing in, Beer, Wine or Any Intoxicating Drinks in Any Post Exchange, or Canteen, . . . View of the Minority to Accompany H.R. 8752.* 56th Cong., 1st sess., 1900. H. Rept. No. 1701, part 2 (SS 4026).

U.S. House Committee on Naval Affairs. *Spirit Ration in the Navy: To Accompany Bill H.R. 557.* 28th Cong., 2d sess., 1845. H. Rept. No. 73 (SS 468).

U.S. House Committee on Post Offices and Post Roads. *Certain Sections of the Revised Statutes Relating to Lotteries: Report to Accompany H.R. 11569.* 51st Cong., 1st sess., 1890. H. Rept. No. 2844 (SS 2815).

———. *Delivery of Registered Letters and Payment of Money Orders: Report to Accompany Bill H.R. 1911.* 48th Cong., 1st sess., 1884. H. Rept. No. 472, parts 1 and 2 (SS 2254).

———. *Lottery, Gift-Enterprise, or Other Circulars: Report to Accompany Bill H.R. 9121.* 49th Cong. 1st sess., 1886. H. Rept. No. 2678 (SS 2443).

———. *Selling and Advertising Lottery Tickets: Report to Accompany Bill H.R. 5933.* 50th Cong., 1st sess., 1888. H. Rept. No. 125 (SS 2598).

———. *Sunday Mail.* 21st Cong., 1st sess., 1830. H. Rept. No. 271 (SS 200).

U.S. House Committee on the Revision of the Laws. *Repeal of Certain Sections of the Revised Statutes.* 45th Cong., 2d sess., 1878. H. Rept. No. 888 (SS 1826).

U.S. House Committee on the Territories. *Marriages in the Territory of Utah: A Report to Accompany Bill H.R. 6765.* 48th Cong., 1st sess., 1884. H. Rept. No. 1351, parts 1 and 2 (SS 2257).

U.S. House Committee on Ways and Means. *Tariff Act of 1842: Letter from Secretary of Treasury, ...* 34th Cong., 1st sess, 1856. H. Ex. Doc. No. 126 (SS 859).

U.S. House Special Committee. *Case of Brigham H. Roberts of Utah: Report to Accompany H. Res. 107.* 56th Cong., 1st sess., 1900. H. Rept. No. 85, parts 1 and 2 (SS 4021).

U.S. Senate. *American Anti Saloon League.* 58th Cong., 2d sess., 1904. S. Doc. No. 159 (SS 4590).

———. *American Anti Saloon League: Report of the Legislative Department. . . .* 57th Cong., 1st sess., 1902. S. Doc. No. 133 (SS 4230).

———. *In the Senate of the United States: Memorial of Members of the Presbyterian Clergy of New Orleans Praying an Amendment to the Constitution to Prohibit Lotteries.* 51st Cong., 2d sess., 1891. S. Misc. Doc. No. 57 (SS 2821).

———. *In the Senate of the United States: Mr. Stewart Submitted the Following Memorial of the National Farmers' Alliance . . . .* 51st Cong., 2d sess., 1891. S. Misc. Doc. No. 59 (SS 2821).

———. *Journal of the Congress of the Confederate States of American, 1861–1865.* 7 vols. 58th Cong., 2d sess., S. Doc. No. 234 (SS 4610–16).

———. *Letter from the Secretary of the Interior . . . Report of the Governor of Alaska.* 54th Cong., 1st sess., 1896. S. Doc. No. 113 (SS 3350).

———. *Memorial of the General Assembly of the Presbyterian Church of the United Stats on the Subject of Polygamy.* 47th Cong., 1st sess., 1882. S. Misc. Doc. No. 30 (SS 1993).

———. *Memorial of the Pennsylvania State Temperance Society.* 25th Cong., 2d sess., 1838. S. Doc. No. 328 (SS 317).

———. *Moral Legislation in Congress . . . Report of the Work of the International Reform Bureau.* 58th Cong., 2d sess., 1904. S. Doc. No. 150 (SS 4589).

———. *Notes of a Hearing before the Committee on Education and Labor, United States Senate, Friday, April 6, 1888, on the Petitions Praying for the Passage of Legislation Prohibiting the Running of Mail Trains, Interstate Trains, and the Drilling of United States Troops on Sunday, and Other Violations of the Sabbath.* 50th Cong., 1st sess., 1888. S. Misc. Doc. No. 108 (SS 2517).

———. *Petitions Relative to Mails on the Sabbath.* 20th Cong., 2d sess., 1829. S. Misc. Doc. No. 46 (SS 181).

———. *State Control of Interstate Liquor Traffic.* 58th Cong., 2d sess., 1904. S. Doc. No. 168 (SS 4590).

———. *Sunday Rest Bill.* 50th Cong., 2d sess., 1889. S. Misc. Doc. No. 43 (SS 2615).

———. *To Regulate Interstate Commerce.* 61st Cong., 1st sess., 1908. S. Doc. No. 146 (SS 5566).

U.S. Senate Committee on the District of Columbia. *Memorial of the Officers of the Woman's Christian Temperance Union of the District of Columbia, Urging Legislation for the Prohibition of the Liquor Traffic in the District of Columbia.* 51st Cong., 1st sess., 1890. S. Misc. Doc. No. 114 (SS 2698).

U.S. Senate Committee on Education and Labor. *Report to Accompany Bill S. 1405.* 49th Cong., 1st sess., 1886. S. Rept. No. 85 (SS 2355).

———. *Report to Accompany S. Res. 12.* 50th Cong., 1st sess., 1888. S. Rept. No. 1727 (SS 2525).

U.S. Senate Committee on Epidemic Diseases. *Report to Accompany Petition of M. C. Dean and Others against the Sale, Manufacture, and Importation of Cigarettes in Any Form in the United States.* 52d Cong., 1st sess., 1892. S. Rept. No. 1001 (SS 2915).

U.S. Senate Committee on Immigration. *Foreign Immigration: Report to Accompany H.R. 12199.* 57th Cong., 1st sess., 1902. S. Rept. No. 2119 (SS 4264).

———. *White-Slave Traffic: Report to Accompany H.R. 12315.* 61st Cong., 2d sess., 1910. S. Rept. No. 886 (SS 5584).

U.S. Senate Committee on the Judiciary. *Regulation of Commerce between the States: Report to Accompany S. 4043.* 62d Cong., 2d sess., 1912. S. Rept. No. 956 (SS 6122).

U.S. Senate Committee on Post Offices and Post Roads. *Handling Money Orders and Registered Letters on Sunday: Adverse Report: To Accompany S. 165.* 59th Cong., 1st sess., 1906. S. Rept. No. 1426 (SS 4904).

———. *Post Office Appropriation Bill: Report to Accompany H.R. 21279.* 62d Cong., 2d sess., 1912. S. Rept. No. 955 (SS 6122).

———. *Report to Accompany S. 2834.* 52d Cong., 1st sess., 1892. S. Rept. No. 747 (SS 2914).

U.S. Senate Committee on Privileges and Elections. *Reed Smoot.* 59th Cong., 1st sess., 1906. S. Rept. No. 4253 (SS 4905-G).

U.S. Statutes at Large

SERIALS OF THE TIME

The American Issue
The Anti-Saloon League Year Book
The Christian Statesman
The Index
Minutes of the Annual Meeting of the Woman's Christian Temperance Union (a complete run is in the WCTU Papers, Temperance and Prohibition Papers)
Our Day
Proceedings of the Annual Convention of the Anti-Saloon League of America
The Union Signal

BOOKS, ARTICLES, THESES, AND DISSERTATIONS

Abbott, Lyman. *Reminiscences.* Boston, Mass.: Houghton Mifflin Company, 1915.

An Account of Memorials Presented to Congress during Its Last Session . . . Praying that the Mails May Not Be Transported, Nor Post-Offices Kept Open on the Sabbath. New York: Published at the Request of Many Petitioners, 1829.

Alexander, John. *History of the National Reform Movement.* Pittsburgh, Pa.: Shaw Brothers, 1893.

Alwes, Berthold C. "The History of the Louisiana State Lottery Company." *Louisiana Historical Quarterly* 27 (October 1944): 964–1118.

Badger, Reid. *The Great American Fair: The World's Columbian Exposition and American Culture*. Chicago: Nelson Hall, 1979.

Bailey, Richard R. "Morris Sheppard of Texas: Southern Progressive and Prohibitionist." Ph.D. diss., Texas Christian University, 1980.

Baker, Paula C. "The Domestication of Politics: Women and American Political Society, 1780–1920." *American Historical Review* 89 (June 1984): 620–47.

———. *The Moral Frameworks of Public Life: Gender, Politics, and the State in Rural New York, 1870–1930*. New York: Oxford University Press, 1991.

Bardaglio, Peter W. *Reconstructing the Household: Families, Sex, and the Law in the Nineteenth-Century South*. Chapel Hill: University of North Carolina Press, 1995.

Bascom, Frederick G., ed., *Letters of a Ticonderoga Farmer: Selections from the Correspondence of William H. Cook and His Wife with Their Son, Joseph Cook, 1851–1885*. Ithaca, N.Y.: Cornell University Press, 1946.

Basler, Roy P., ed. *The Collected Works of Abraham Lincoln*. 8 vols. New Brunswick, N.J.: Rutgers University Press, 1953.

Bates, Anna Louise. *Weeder in the Garden of the Lord: Anthony Comstock's Life and Career*. Lanham, Md.: University Press of America, 1995.

Beisel, Nicola. *Imperiled Innocents: Anthony Comstock and Family Reproduction in Victorian America*. Princeton, N.J.: Princeton University Press, 1997.

Bensel, Richard Franklin. *Yankee Leviathan: The Origins of Central State Authority in America, 1859–1877*. New York: Cambridge University Press, 1990.

Bittenbender, Ada M. *The National Prohibitory Amendment Guide*. Chicago: Woman's Temperance Publication Association, 1889.

Bitton, R. Davis. "The B. H. Roberts Case of 1898–1900." *Utah Historical Quarterly* 25 (January 1957): 27–46.

Blocker, Jack S., Jr. *American Temperance Movements: Cycles of Reform*. Boston, Mass.: Twayne Publishers, 1989.

———. *"Give to the Winds Thy Fears": The Woman's Temperance Crusade, 1873–1874*. Westport, Conn.: Greenwood Press, 1985.

———. *Retreat from Reform: The Prohibition Movement in the United States, 1890–1913*. Westport, Conn.: Greenwood Press, 1976.

Bochnowski, John F. "The Muckraker Crusade against White Slavery, 1907–1910." Master's thesis, University of Virginia, 1966.

Bordin, Ruth. *Frances Willard: A Biography*. Chapel Hill: University of North Carolina Press, 1986.

———. *Woman and Temperance: The Quest for Power and Liberty, 1870–1900*. Philadelphia, Pa.: Temple University Press, 1981.

Botein, Stephen. "Religious Dimensions of the Early American State." In *Beyond Confederation: Origins of the Constitution and American National Identity*, edited by Richard Beeman, Stephen Botein, and Edward C. Carter II, 315–30. Chapel Hill: University of North Carolina Press, 1987.

Boyer, Paul. *Urban Masses and Moral Order in America, 1820–1920.* Cambridge, Mass.: Harvard University Press, 1978.

Broun, Heywood, and Margaret Leech. *Anthony Comstock: Roundsman of the Lord.* New York: Albert and Charles Boni, 1927.

Burnham, John C. *Bad Habits: Drinking, Smoking, Taking Drugs, Gambling, Sexual Misbehavior, and Swearing in American History.* New York: New York University Press, 1993.

———. "New Perspectives on the Prohibition 'Experiment' of the 1920s." *Journal of Social History* 2 (1968): 51–68.

Bushnell, Horace. *Reverses Needed: A Discourse Delivered on the Sunday after the Disaster of Bull Run.* Hartford, Conn.: L. E. Hunt, 1861.

Cannon, Frank J., and Harvey J. O'Higgins. *Under the Prophet in Utah: The National Menace of a Political Priestcraft.* Boston, Mass.: C. M. Clark Publishing Co., 1911.

Cannon, James, Jr. *Bishop Cannon's Own Story: Life as I Have Seen It.* Edited by Richard L. Watson Jr. Durham, N.C.: Duke University Press, 1955.

Carradine, B. *The Louisiana State Lottery Company: Examined and Exposed.* New Orleans: D. L. Mitchell Publisher and Printer, 1889.

Carwardine, Richard J. *Evangelicals and Politics in Antebellum America.* New Haven, Conn.: Yale University Press, 1993.

Cetina, Judith G. "A History of Veterans' Homes in the United States, 1811–1930." Ph.D. diss., Case Western Reserve University, 1977.

Chamlee, Roy Z., Jr. "The Sabbath Crusade, 1810–1920." Ph.D. diss., George Washington University, 1968.

Cherny, Robert W. *A Righteous Cause: The Life of William Jennings Bryan.* Boston, Mass.: Little, Brown and Company, 1985.

Cherrington, Ernest H. *Standard Encyclopedia of the Alcohol Problem.* 6 vols. Westerville, Ohio: American Issue Publishing Co., 1926.

Chesebrough, David B. *"God Ordained This War": Sermons on the Sectional Crisis, 1830–1865.* Columbia: University of South Carolina Press, 1991.

Clark, Norman H. *Deliver Us from Evil: An Investigation of American Prohibition.* New York: W. W. Norton, 1976.

Clemens, Elisabeth S. *The People's Lobby: Organizational Innovation and the Rise of Interest Group Politics in the United States, 1890–1925.* Chicago: University of Chicago Press, 1997.

Colvin, D. Leigh. *Prohibition in the United States: A History of the Prohibition Party and of the Prohibition Movement.* New York: George H. Doran, Co., 1926.

Comstock, Anthony. *Frauds Exposed; or, How the People Are Deceived and Robbed, and Youth Corrupted.* New York: J. Howard Brown, 1880.

———. *Traps for the Young.* Edited by Robert Bremner. Cambridge, Mass.: The Belknap Press of Harvard University Press, 1967.

Connelly, Mark Thomas. *The Response to Prostitution in the Progressive Era.* Chapel Hill: University of North Carolina Press, 1980.

Constitution and Address of the National Association for the Amendment of the Consti-

tution of the United States. Philadelphia, Pa.: Jas. B. Rodgers, 1864.

Cook, Joseph. *The Relations of the Temperance Reform to the Future of Democracy in the United States.* Boston, Mass.: Nation Press, 1870.

—————. "Ultimate America." In *The World's Best Orations.* Vol. 4, edited by David J. Brewer, 1391–92. Chicago: Ferd P. Kaiser, 1899.

Cooper, William J., Jr. *The South and the Politics of Slavery, 1828–1856.* Baton Rouge: Louisiana State University Press, 1978.

Cornelison, Isaac A. *The Relation of Religion to Civil Government in the United States of America: A State without a Church, but Not without a Religion.* New York: G. P. Putnam's Sons, 1895.

Courtwright, David T. *Dark Paradise: Opiate Addiction in America before 1940.* Cambridge, Mass.: Harvard University Press, 1982.

Couvares, Francis G. "Hollywood, Mainstreet, and the Church: Trying to Censor the Movies before the Production Code." *American Quarterly* 44 (December 1992): 584–616.

Crafts, Wilbur F. *Before the Lost Arts and Other Lectures.* Washington: The Reform Bureau, 1896.

—————. *National Perils and Hopes: A Study Based on Current Statistics and the Observations of a Cheerful Reformer.* Cleveland, Ohio: F. M. Barton Company, 1910.

—————. *Patriotic Studies.* Washington: International Reform Bureau, 1905.

—————. *Patriotic Studies of a Quarter Century . . . .* Washington: International Reform Bureau, 1910.

—————. *Practical Christian Sociology: A Series of Special Lectures . . . .* New York: Funk and Wagnalls, 1895.

—————. *The Sabbath for Man . . . .* 6th ed. New York: Baker and Taylor Co., 1892.

Cresswell, Stephen. *Mormons, Cowboys, Moonshiners, and Klansmen: Federal Law Enforcement in the South and West, 1870–1893.* Tuscaloosa: University of Alabama Press, 1991.

Cumbler, John Taylor. *A Moral Response to Industrialism: The Lectures of Reverend Cook in Lynn, Massachusetts.* Albany: State University of New York Press, 1982.

Cushing, Marshall. *The Story of Our Post Office: The Greatest Government Department in All Its Phases.* Boston: A. M. Thayer and Co., 1893.

Dabney, Virginius. *Dry Messiah: The Life of Bishop Cannon.* New York: Alfred A. Knopf, 1949.

Davis, John W. "John Randolph Tucker: The Man and His Work." *The John Randolph Tucker Lectures Delivered before the School of Law of Washington and Lee University.* Lexington, Va.: School of Law, Washington and Lee University, 1952.

Davis, William C. *"A Government of Our Own": The Making of the Confederacy.* New York: The Free Press, 1994.

D'Emilio, John, and Estelle B. Freedman. *Intimate Matters: A History of Sexuality in America.* New York: Harper and Row, 1988.

Dohn, Norman H. "The History of the Anti-Saloon League." Ph.D. diss., Ohio State University, 1959.

Duke, Escal F. "The Political Career of Morris Sheppard, 1875–1941." Ph.D. diss., University of Texas, 1958.

Dwyer, Robert J. *The Gentile Comes to Utah: A Study in Religious and Social Conflict.* Washington, D.C.: The Catholic University of America Press, 1941.

Earhart, Mary. *Frances Willard: From Prayers to Politics.* Chicago: University of Chicago Press, 1944.

Ebersole, Luke E. *Church Lobbying in the Nation's Capital.* New York: The Macmillan Company, 1951.

Edwards, Rebecca. *Angels in the Machinery: Gender in American Party Politics from the Civil War to the Progressive Era.* New York: Oxford University Press, 1997.

Epstein, Barbara Leslie. *The Politics of Domesticity: Women, Evangelism, and Temperance in Nineteenth-Century America.* Middletown, Conn.: Wesleyan University Press, 1981.

Evans, Sara M. *Born for Liberty: A History of Women in America.* New York: The Free Press, 1989.

Ezell, John S. *Fortune's Merry Wheel: The Lottery in America.* Cambridge, Mass.: Harvard University Press, 1960.

Fabian, Ann. *Card Sharps, Dream Books, and Bucket Shops: Gambling in 19th-Century America.* Ithaca, N.Y.: Cornell University Press, 1990.

Farish, Hunter D. *The Circuit Rider Dismounts: A Social History of Southern Methodism, 1865–1900.* 1938. New York: DaCapo Press, 1969.

Farmer, James O., Jr. *The Metaphysical Confederacy: James Henley Thornwell and the Synthesis of Southern Values.* Macon, Ga.: Mercer University Press, 1986.

Faust, Drew Gilpin. *Confederate Nationalism: Ideology and Identity in the Civil War South.* Baton Rouge: Louisiana State University Press, 1988.

Feldman, Charles M. *The National Board of Censorship (Review) of Motion Pictures, 1909–1922.* New York: Arno Press, 1977.

Firmage, Edwin B., and Richard C. Mangrum. *Zion in the Courts: A Legal History of the Church of Jesus Christ of Latter-day Saints, 1830–1900.* Urbana: University of Illinois Press, 1988.

Foner, Eric. *Reconstruction: America's Unfinished Revolution, 1863–1877.* New York: Harper and Row, 1988.

Foster, Gaines M. "A Christian Nation: Signs of a Covenant." In *Bonds of Affection: Americans Define Their Patriotism,* edited by John Bodnar, 120–38. Princeton, N.J.: Princeton University Press, 1996.

Foster, J. M. *Reformation Principles Stated and Applied.* Chicago: Fleming H. Revell, 1890.

Franklin, Jimmie L. *Born Sober: Prohibition in Oklahoma, 1907–1959.* Norman: University of Oklahoma Press, 1971.

Fredrickson, George M. "The Coming of the Lord: The Northern Protestant Clergy and the Civil War Crisis." In *Religion and the American Civil War,* edited by Randall M. Miller, Harry S. Stout, and Charles Reagan Wilson, 110–30. New York: Oxford University Press, 1998.

————. *The Inner Civil War: Northern Intellectuals and the Crisis of the Union*. New York: Harper Torchbooks, 1965.

Gaustad, Edwin S. *Faith of Our Fathers: Religion and the New Nation*. San Francisco: Harper and Row, 1987.

————. "Religious Tests, Constitutions, and a 'Christian Nation.'" In *Religion in a Revolutionary Age*, edited by Ronald Hoffman and Peter J. Albert, 218–35. Charlottesville: University Press of Virginia, 1994.

Gerring, John. "Culture versus Economics: An American Dilemma." *Social Science History* 23 (Summer 1999): 143–49.

Ginzburg, Lori D. *Women and the Work of Benevolence: Morality, Politics, and Class in the Nineteenth-Century United States*. New Haven, Conn.: Yale University Press, 1990.

Gladden, Washington. "Moral Reconstruction." In *The Nation Still in Danger*. N.p.: Published by the American Missionary Association, 1875.

Glasgow, W. Melancthon. *History of the Reformed Presbyterian Church in America*. Baltimore, Md.: Hill and Harvey, 1888.

Goen, C. C. *Broken Churches, Broken Nation: Denominational Schisms and the Coming of the Civil War*. Macon, Ga.: Mercer University Press, 1985.

Goldsmith, Barbara. *Other Powers: The Age of Suffrage, Spiritualism, and the Scandalous Victoria Woodhull*. New York: Alfred A. Knopf, 1998.

Gordon, Elizabeth P. *Women Torch-Bearers: The Story of the Woman's Christian Temperance Union*. 2d ed. Evanston, Ill.: National Woman's Christian Temperance Union Publishing House, 1924.

Gorn, Elliot J. *The Manly Art: Bare-Knuckle Prize Fighting in America*. Ithaca, N.Y.: Cornell University Press, 1986.

Griffin, Clifford S. *Their Brothers' Keeper: Moral Stewardship in the United States, 1860–1865*. New Brunswick, N.J.: Rutger's University Press, 1960.

Grittner, Frederick K. *White Slavery: Myth, Ideology, and American Law*. New York: Garland Publishing, 1990.

Gusfield, Joseph R. *Symbolic Crusade: Status Politics and the American Temperance Movement*. Urbana: University of Illinois Press, 1963.

Hair, William I. *Bourbonism and Agrarian Protest: Louisiana Politics, 1877–1900*. Baton Rouge: Louisiana State University Press, 1969.

Hamm, Richard F. *Shaping the Eighteenth Amendment: Temperance Reform, Legal Culture, and the Polity, 1880–1920*. Chapel Hill: University of North Carolina Press, 1995.

Handy, Robert T. *Undermined Establishment: Church-State Relations in America, 1880–1920*. Princeton, N.J.: Princeton University Press, 1991.

Hardy, B. Carmon. *Solemn Covenant: The Mormon Polygamous Passage*. Urbana: University of Illinois Press, 1992.

Haven, Gilbert. *National Sermons: Sermons, Speeches, and Letters on Slavery and Its War*. Boston, Mass.: Lee and Shepard, 1869.

Hills, A. M. *The Life and Labors of Mrs. Mary A. Woodbridge*. Ravenna, Ohio: F. W. Woodbridge, 1895.

Hobson, Richmond P. *Alcohol and the Human Race.* New York: Fleming H. Revell Company, 1919.

Hogan, Charles M. "Wayne B. Wheeler: Single Issue Exponent." Ph.D. diss., University of Cincinnati, 1986.

Hohner, Robert A. *Prohibition and Politics: The Life of Bishop James Cannon, Jr.* Columbia: University of South Carolina Press, 1999.

Hood, Fred J. *Reformed America: The Middle and Southern States, 1783–1837.* University: University of Alabama Press, 1980.

Hoogenboom, Ari. *Rutherford B. Hayes: Warrior and President.* Lawrence: University Press of Kansas, 1995.

Hull, A. L. "The Making of the Confederate Constitution." *Publications of the Southern History Association* 9 (September 1905): 272–92.

Hunt, Alan. *Governing Morals: A Social History of Moral Regulation.* New York: Cambridge University Press, 1999.

Iversen, Joan S. "A Debate on the American Home: The Antipolygamy Controversy, 1880–1890." In *American Sexual Politics: Sex, Gender, and Race Since the Civil War,* edited by John C. Fout and Maura S. Tantillo, 123–40. Chicago: University of Chicago Press, 1993.

John, Richard R. *Spreading the News: The American Postal System from Franklin to Morse.* Cambridge, Mass.: Harvard University Press, 1995.

Johnson, Donald Bruce, comp. *National Party Platforms, 1840–1956.* Rev. ed. Urbana: University of Illinois Press, 1978.

Johnson, Richard C. "Anthony Comstock: Reform, Vice, and the American Way." Ph.D. diss., University of Wisconsin, 1973.

Johnson, Thomas C. *The Life and Letters of Benjamin Morgan Palmer.* Richmond, Va.: Presbyterian Committee of Publication, 1906.

Keller, Morton. *Affairs of State: Public Life in Late-Nineteenth-Century America.* Cambridge, Mass.: The Belknap Press of Harvard University Press, 1977.

———. *Regulating a New Society: Public Policy and Social Change in America, 1900–1933.* Cambridge, Mass.: Harvard University Press, 1994.

Kerr, K. Austin. *Organized for Prohibition: A New History of the Anti-Saloon League.* New Haven, Conn.: Yale University Press, 1985.

Kramnick, Isaac, and R. Laurence Moore. *The Godless Constitution: The Case against Religious Correctness.* New York: W. W. Norton, 1996.

Kyvig, David E. *Repealing National Prohibition.* Chicago: University of Chicago Press, 1979.

Lamar, Howard R. *The Far Southwest, 1846–1912: A Territorial History.* New Haven. Conn.: Yale University Press, 1966.

Langley, Harold D. *Social Reform in the United States Navy, 1798–1862.* Urbana: University of Illinois Press, 1967.

Langum, David J. *Crossing over the Line: Legislating Morality and the Mann Act.* Chicago: University of Chicago Press, 1994.

Larson, Gustive O. *The "Americanization" of Utah for Statehood.* San Marino, Calif.: The Huntington Library, 1971.

Leavitt, Emily W. *The Blair Family of New England.* Boston, Mass.: David Clapp and Son, 1900.

Leeman, Richard W. *"Do Everything" Reform: The Oratory of Frances E. Willard.* New York: Greenwood Press, 1992.

Lender, Mark E. *Dictionary of American Temperance Biography: From Temperance Reform to Alcohol Research, the 1600s to the 1980s.* Westport, Conn.: Greenwood Press, 1984.

Levine, Lawrence W. *Defender of the Faith: William Jennings Bryan: The Last Decade, 1915–1925.* New York: Oxford University Press, 1965.

Link, Arthur S., ed. *The Papers of Woodrow Wilson.* 69 vols. Princeton, N.J.: Princeton University Press, 1963–94.

Link, William A. *The Paradox of Southern Progressivism, 1880–1930.* Chapel Hill: University of North Carolina Press, 1992.

Litwack, Leon F. *Trouble in Mind: Black Southerners in the Age of Jim Crow.* New York: Alfred A. Knopf, 1998.

Livermore, Mary A. *The Story of My Life, or, The Sunshine and Shadow of Seventy Years.* Hartford, Conn.: A. D. Worthington and Co., 1899.

Loveland, Anne C. *Southern Evangelicals and the Social Order, 1800–1860.* Baton Rouge: Louisiana State University Press, 1980.

Lyman, Edward Leo. *Political Deliverance: The Mormon Quest for Utah Statehood.* Urbana: University of Illinois Press, 1986.

Lyon, T. Edgar. "Religious Activities and Development in Utah, 1847–1910." *Utah Historical Quarterly* 35 (Fall 1967): 292–306.

McAllister, David. *The National Reform Movement.* 1890. Allegheny, Pa.: Christian Statesman Co., 1898.

McCormick, Richard L. "Progressivism: A Contemporary Reassessment." In *The Party Period and Public Policy: American Politics from the Age of Jackson to the Progressive Era,* 263–88. New York: Oxford University Press, 1986.

McDaniel, Hilda M. "Frances Tillou Nicholls and the End of Reconstruction." *Louisiana Historical Quarterly* 32 (April 1949): 356–513.

May, Henry F. *Protestant Churches and Industrial America.* 1949. New York: Harper Torchbooks, 1967.

May, Lary. *Screening out the Past: The Birth of Mass Culture and the Motion Picture Industry.* Chicago, Ill.: University of Chicago Press, 1983.

Miller, Randall M., Harry S. Stout, and Charles Reagan Wilson, eds. *Religion and the American Civil War.* New York: Oxford University Press, 1998.

Morgan, H. Wayne. *From Hayes to McKinley: National Party Politics, 1877–1896.* Syracuse, N.Y.: Syracuse University Press, 1969.

Morison, Elting E., ed. *The Letters of Theodore Roosevelt.* 8 vols. Cambridge, Mass.: Harvard University Press, 1951–54.

Morris, Benjamin Franklin. *Christian Life and Character of the Civil Institutions of the United States, Developed in the Official and Historical Annals of the Republic.* Philadelphia, Pa.: George W. Childs, 1864.

Mulford, Elisha. *The Nation: The Foundations of Civil Order and Political Life in the United States.* New York: Hurd and Houghton, 1870.

Murchison, Kenneth M. *Federal Criminal Law Doctrines: The Forgotten Influence of National Prohibition.* Durham, N.C.: Duke University Press, 1994.

Murrin, John M. "Religion and Politics in America from the First Settlements to the Civil War." In *Religion and American Politics: From the Colonial Period to the 1980s,* edited by Mark A. Noll, 19–43. New York: Oxford University Press, 1990.

Musto, David F. *The American Disease: Origins of Narcotic Control.* New York: Oxford University Press, 1987.

Neely, Mark E., Jr. "Elisha Mulford and the Organic State." *American Quarterly* 29 (Fall 1977): 404–21.

Nevins, Allan, ed. *The Messages and Papers of Jefferson Davis and the Confederacy, Including Diplomatic Correspondence, 1861–1865.* Vol. 1. New York: Chelsea House-Robert Hector, 1966.

Novak, William J. *The People's Welfare: Law and Regulation in Nineteenth-Century America.* Chapel Hill: University of North Carolina Press, 1996.

Odegard, Peter H. *Pressure Politics: The Story of the Anti-Saloon League.* New York: Columbia University Press, 1928.

Odem, Mary E. *Delinquent Daughters: Protecting and Policing Adolescent Female Sexuality in the United States, 1885–1920.* Chapel Hill: University of North Carolina Press, 1995.

Owen, Thomas M. *History of Alabama and Dictionary of Alabama Biography.* Chicago: The S. J. Clarke Publishing Co., 1921.

Ownby, Ted. *Subduing Satan: Religion, Recreation, and Manhood in the Rural South, 1865–1920.* Chapel Hill: University of North Carolina Press, 1990.

Parker, Alison M. *Purifying America: Women, Cultural Reform, and Pro-Censorship Activism, 1873–1933.* Urbana: University of Illinois Press, 1997.

Parsons, Stanley B., William W. Beach, and Michael J. Dubin. *United States Congressional Districts and Data, 1843–1883.* New York: Greenwood Press, 1986.

Parsons, Stanley B., Michael J. Dubin, and Karen Toombs Parsons. *United States Congressional Districts, 1883–1913.* New York: Greenwood Press, 1990.

Pascoe, Peggy. *Relations of Rescue: The Search for Female Moral Authority in the American West, 1874–1939.* New York: Oxford University Press, 1990.

Pegram, Thomas R. *Battling Demon Rum: The Struggle for a Dry America, 1800–1933.* Chicago: Ivan R. Dee, 1998.

Pittman, Walter E., Jr. *Navalist and Progressive: The Life of Richmond P. Hobson.* Manhattan, Kans.: MA/AH Publishing, 1981.

Pivar, David J. *Purity Crusade: Sexual Morality and Social Control, 1868–1900.* Westport, Conn.: Greenwood Press, 1973.

Pointer, Steven R. *Joseph Cook, Boston Lecturer and Evangelical Apologist: A Bridge between Popular Culture and Academia in Late Nineteenth-Century America.* Lewiston, Maine: The Edwin Mellen Press, 1991.

"Proceedings of the First Confederate Congress." *Southern Historical Society Papers* 50 (1953).

Prucha, Francis Paul. *American Indian Policy in the Formative Years: The Indian Trade and Intercourse Acts, 1790–1834.* Cambridge, Mass.: Harvard University Press, 1962.

Quist, John W. *Restless Visionaries: The Social Roots of Antebellum Reform in Alabama and Michigan.* Baton Rouge: Louisiana State University Press, 1998.

Reed, Ralph. *Politically Incorrect: The Emerging Faith Factor in American Politics.* Dallas, Tex.: Word Publishing, 1994.

Ribuffo, Leo P. *The Old Christian Right: The Protestant Far Right from the Great Depression to the Cold War.* Philadelphia: Temple University Press, 1983.

Richardson, James D., ed. *A Compilation of the Messages and Papers of the Presidents, 1789–1902.* 10 vols. N.p.: Bureau of National Literature and Art, 1903.

Roberts, Randy. *Papa Jack: Jack Johnson and the Era of White Hopes.* New York: The Free Press, 1983.

Robinson, William M. J. "Prohibition in the Confederacy." *American Historical Review* 37 (October 1931): 50–58.

Rodgers, Daniel T. *Contested Truths: Keywords in American Politics Since Independence.* New York: Basic Books, 1987.

———. "In Search of Progressivism." *Reviews in American History* 10 (December 1982): 113–32.

Royster, Charles. *The Destructive War: William Tecumseh Sherman, Stonewall Jackson, and the Americans.* New York: Alfred A. Knopf, 1991.

Rumbarger, John J. *Profits, Power, and Prohibition: Alcohol Reform and the Industrializing of America, 1800–1930.* Albany: State University of New York Press, 1989.

Sammons, Jeffrey T. *Beyond the Ring: The Role of Boxing in American Society.* Urbana: University of Illinois Press, 1988.

Sanders, Elizabeth. *Roots of Reform: Farmers, Workers, and the American State, 1877–1917.* Chicago: University of Chicago Press, 1999.

Scomp, Henry A. *King Alcohol in the Realm of King Cotton.* N.p.: Press of the Blakely Printing Co, 1888.

Sechrist, Robert P. "A Comparative Analysis of Multi-Dimensional Diffusion Models: The Diffusion of the Prohibition Movement in the United States of America." Ph.D. diss., Louisiana State University, 1986.

Sheldon, Charles M. *In His Steps.* 1896. New York: Grosset and Dunlap, 1973.

Simpson, Craig M. *A Good Southerner: The Life of Henry A. Wise of Virginia.* Chapel Hill: University of North Carolina Press, 1985.

Skowronek, Stephen. *Building a New American State: The Expansion of National Administrative Capacities, 1877–1920.* New York: Cambridge University Press, 1982.

Slagell, Amy Rose. "A Good Woman Speaking Well: The Oratory of Frances E. Willard." Ph.D. diss., University of Wisconsin-Madison, 1992.

Sloane, J. R. W. *State Religion: A Discourse Delivered before the Reformed Presbyterian Synod in Rochester, N.Y. Sabbath Evening, May 27th, 1866.* New York: John A. Gray and Green Printers, 1866.

Snay, Mitchell. *Gospel of Disunion: Religion and Separatism in the Antebellum South.* New York: Cambridge University Press, 1993.

Sobel, Robert. *They Satisfy: The Cigarette in American Life.* Garden City, N.Y.: Anchor Press/Doubleday, 1978.

Spence, Floyd V. "Outstanding Policies Sponsored by James Cannon, Jr., as Editor of the Baltimore and Richmond *Christian Advocate*, 1904–1918." B.D. thesis, Duke University, 1935.

Steuart, Justin. *Wayne Wheeler: Dry Boss, An Uncensored Biography of Wayne B. Wheeler.* New York: Fleming H. Revell Company, 1928.

Strachey, Ray. *Frances Willard: Her Life and Work.* New York: Fleming H. Revell Company, 1913.

Strong, Josiah. *Our Country.* Edited by Jurgen Herbst. 1886. Cambridge, Mass.: The Belknap Press of Harvard University Press, 1963.

Tate, Cassandra. *Cigarette Wars: The Triumph of "The Little White Slaver."* New York: Oxford University Press, 1999.

Teaford, Jon C. "Toward a Christian Nation: Religion, Law and Justice Strong." *Journal of Presbyterian History* 54 (Winter 1976): 422–36.

Thomas, John L. *Law of Lotteries, Frauds and Obscenity in the Mails.* St. Louis, Mo.: F. H. Thomas Law Book Co., 1903.

Thompson, Margaret Sue. *The "Spider Web": Congress and Lobbying in the Age of Grant.* Ithaca, N.Y.: Cornell University Press, 1985.

Timberlake, James H. *Prohibition and the Progressive Movement, 1900–1920.* Cambridge, Mass.: Harvard University Press, 1963.

Tone, Andrea. "Black Market Birth Control: Contraceptive Entrepreneurship and Criminality in the Gilded Age." *Journal of American History* 87 (September 2000): 435–59.

Trumbull, Charles G. *Anthony Comstock, Fighter.* New York: Fleming H. Revell Company, 1913.

Tyrrell, Ian R. "Drink and Temperance in the Antebellum South: An Overview and Interpretation." *Journal of Southern History* 48 (November 1982): 485–510.

———. *Sobering Up: From Temperance to Prohibition in Antebellum America, 1800–1860.* Westport, Conn.: Greenwood Press, 1979.

———. *Woman's World/Woman's Empire: The Woman's Christian Temperance Union in International Perspective, 1800–1930.* Chapel Hill: University of North Carolina Press, 1991.

Unrau, William E. *White Man's Wicked Water: The Alcohol Trade and Prohibition in Indian Country, 1802–1892.* Lawrence, Kans.: University Press of Kansas, 1996.

Van Wagoner, Richard S. *Mormon Polygamy: A History.* 2d. ed. Salt Lake City, Utah: Signature Books, 1989.

Vos, Johannes G. *The Scottish Covenanters.* Pittsburgh, Pa.: Crown and Covenant Publications, 1940.

West, John G., Jr. *The Politics of Revelation and Reason: Religion and Civic Life in the New Nation.* Lawrence: University Press of Kansas, 1996.

Wiebe, Robert H. *The Search for Order, 1877–1920.* New York: Hill and Wang, 1967.

Willard, Frances E. *Glimpses of Fifty Years: The Autobiography of an American Woman.* Chicago: H. J. Smith and Co., 1889.

———. *Woman and Temperance; or, the Work and Workers of the Woman's Christian Temperance Union.* 1883. New York: Arno Press, 1972.

Willard, Frances E., and Mary E. Livermore. *Portraits and Biographies of Prominent American Women.* New York: The Crowell and Kirkpatrick Co., 1901.

Williamson, Joel R. *The Crucible of Race: Black-White Relations in the American South since Emancipation.* New York: Oxford University Press, 1984.

Wyatt-Brown, Bertam. "Prelude to Abolitionism: Sabbatarian Politics and the Rise of the Second Party System." *Journal of American History* 57 (September 1971): 316–41.

———. *Southern Honor: Ethics and Behavior in the Old South.* New York: Oxford University Press, 1982.

Zimmerman, Jonathan. *Distilling Democracy: Alcohol Education in America's Public Schools, 1800–1925.* Lawrence: University Press of Kansas, 1999.

INDEX